[UN]FRAMING THE "BAD WOMAN"

At the mouth of the serpent, Helen Escobedo's *Coatl*, 1980. Metal sculpture, 20 x 20 x 49 ft. UNAM Sculpture Garden, Ciudad Universitaria, Mexico City. Photo by Alma López.

[UN]FRAMING
THE "BAD WOMAN"

Sor Juana, Malinche, Coyolxauhqui
and Other Rebels with a Cause

ALICIA GASPAR DE ALBA

University of Texas Press   Austin

Requests for permission to reproduce material from this work should be sent to:
     Permissions
     University of Texas Press
     P.O. Box 7819
     Austin, TX 78713-7819
     http://utpress.utexas.edu/index.php/rp-form

♾ The paper used in this book meets the minimum requirements of ANSI/NISO
Z39.48-1992 (R1997) (Permanence of Paper).

LIBRARY OF CONGRESS CATALOGING-IN-PUBLICATION DATA

Gaspar de Alba, Alicia, 1958–
[Un]framing the "bad woman" : Sor Juana, Malinche, Coyolxauhqui, and other
rebels with a cause / by Alicia Gaspar de Alba. — First edition.
     pages cm
  Includes bibliographical references and index.
  ISBN 978-0-292-75761-5 (cloth : alk. paper) — ISBN 978-0-292-75850-6
(pbk. : alk. paper)
     1. Hispanic American women—History.   2. Mexicans—History.   3. Women—
  Identity.   4. Women—Conduct of life.   I. Title.
  HQ1166.G37   2014
  305.4—dc23

                                                                    2013038465

doi:10.7560/757615

For my darling wife, Alma,
whose rebellious heart beats with my own

CONTENTS

Figure f.1. Alma Gómez-Frith, *Santa Gloria de la Frontera*, © 2009. Oil on panel, 8 x 10 in. Used by permission of the artist.

Letter to Gloria Anzaldúa, in Gratitude for Your Tongues of Fire[1]

Dear Gloria,

When I left El Paso in 1985 to embark on my adventure in doctoral studies at the University of Iowa, I wasn't motivated by the idea of getting a PhD and becoming an academic. I was just pulling a geographic, trying to put many miles between my ex-girlfriend and me. I had chosen a field called "American Studies," which I had never heard of, but which intrigued me with its focus on "the study of American life and thought." I had been sneaking in assignments on folklore and family rituals in my Freshman Composition classes at the University of Texas in El Paso (UTEP), where I had worked as a part-time lecturer since receiving my MA degree (1983), and I surmised that "the study of American life and thought" would probably be a good fit for someone interested in studying cultural traditions and legends.

Within a few weeks of starting the program at Iowa, and reading endless articles about "how to *do* American Studies," I quickly realized that no one seemed to know what that methodology actually entailed. Even worse, I saw that "American life and thought" did not include *mi América*, the bilingual/bicultural America that you and I were born into on the Texas-Mexico border.

Dazed with culture shock, I kept asking myself, what is a Chicana from the El Paso–Ciudad Juárez border doing in the Midwest? Little did I know how many other Chicana/os inhabited that cold landscape. It wasn't the long winter that scared me, or the way the sixty-degree-below-zero wind chill bit into my earlobes and turned my feet blue on the walk home. What really terrified me was sitting in those classrooms listening to white men lecture about what it meant to "do" American Studies, and whether the frontier or the garden were better ways to conceptualize "the West" from the point of view of the pioneers. From what I could gather, "doing" American Studies meant reading white male historians and white male literary critics and white male literature, trying to find the immanent "American" mind and character. There was some wiggle room in the curriculum to take Black Studies or Women's Studies classes, but mainly we were supposed to study "American life and thought," and "American" clearly meant white, male, and middle class. At least, that's how it was being done at Iowa and other places, despite the challenges of the Radical Caucus and Betty Chmaj's 1979 critique of the "Golden Years" of consensus scholarship and the monolithic myth-symbol-image approach to the discipline.[2]

I can't tell you the intellectual malaise I wallowed in that first semester, feeling for the first time in my life like a cultural alien in a white wilderness. Little did I know I was in the throes of what you called the *nepantla* state, "that uncertain terrain one crosses when moving from one place to another . . . To be disoriented in space is to experience bouts of disassociation of identity, identity breakdowns and buildups."[3] I had definitely disassociated from my identity, at least the identity I had brought with me after twenty-seven years of living on the El Paso–Juárez border. By the end of the fall semester, I convinced myself that if I could just make it to the end of the academic year, I would leave Iowa City, leave academia altogether, and buy a one-way ticket to some warm beach in Mexico.

Then, you came to town, Gloria. I couldn't believe it, a *tejana fronteriza* dyke like me who could speak the same three tongues as me. *Lenguas de fuego*, you named them, tongues of fire—the lesbian tongue, the poetic tongue, and the forked tongue of the Texas-Mexico border. You were working on the essays that would become *Borderlands/La Frontera: The New Mestiza* and were trying out some of your theories—*la facultad*, the Shadow-Beast, the Coatlicue State, mestiza consciousness—on a college audience of white dykes, queer Cubans, Puerto Ricans, South Americans, Chicanas/os, as well as African American and Anglo professors in Iowa City.

Even among all those *maricones* and *tortilleras* (who knew I would find such queer Latinidad in Iowa?), your lecture settled over us like cosmic dust from another planet. The whites in the room, even the liberal ones wearing Guatemalan shirts under their parkas, shifted uncomfortably in their seats whenever you called out white privilege or said something in Spanish and chose not to translate it; the more honest ones stared at you as though you'd just dropped a crop circle in their cornfield.

I saw how the queers, the rape survivors, and the people of color responded with recognition to your idea about a certain faculty of mind that people who live in the margins develop early in life, a "survival tactic," you called it, that teaches us to become aware of the racist, the rapist, or the homophobe in the room before that person even approaches.[4]

The African American and white women faculty, whatever their sexuality, saw themselves reflected in that beastly mirror of self-doubt and self-hate that you explained was a consequence of internalized racism and sexism.

I completely identified with your discussion on linguistic terrorism and the way those of us who are bred in the borderlands develop an ability to negotiate two languages and two cultures as a way of surviving cultural schizophrenia.

But when you got to the part about the shedding of skins, the way identity must be fluid like the river, the immersion into crisis when an old self dies and a new self awakens with a tolerance for contradictions and ambiguity and a talent for seeing through "serpent and eagle eyes"[5]—you lost us. More accurately, you plunged us into that in-between "*nepantla*" state that nobody knew how to navigate.

I remember standing in line with my brand-new copy of *This Bridge Called My Back* for you to sign, and my knees and voice were shaky. I introduced myself as your *paisana* from the border, said I was a writer working on my PhD in American Studies, and you wrote "Contigo en la lucha, Gloria" in my book. Your visit and later Olga Broumas's poetry reading in the spring semester were clearly the highlight of that whole year at the University of Iowa.[6]

After nine months of reading about the Puritans, the pioneers, the simple white folk that populated the Great Plains (wait, I wondered, weren't there some Native Americans there, too?), the Gold Rush, Coney Island, and the White City of that big fair in Chicago in 1893 that apparently was so very important to our doctoral exams, I understood one thing about my chosen field: it had nothing to do with me, or my interests, or the kind of teaching and research I could see myself doing for the rest of my life. It had nothing to do with the kind of "*lucha*" that you were alluding to in your dedication, the antiracist, antisexist, antihomophobic struggle that you were already fighting with your work. I left Iowa that summer, never thinking I'd return to the ivory tower.

Because the only thing I really cared about was writing that served some greater good, I followed your advice to "throw away abstraction and the academic learning, the rules, the map and compass,"[7] and dropped out of PhD school. I moved to Boston to "live the writer's life" and try to get a job in publishing. I figured the closer I was to New York, the better were my chances of getting a book published. I was working on a novel about a Mexican wise woman/*bruja* named Estrella González, set in a remote Mexican make-believe coastal village in Oaxaca, but was also researching the Salem witch trials for another novel I was envisioning that would connect the story of Sor Juana Inés de la Cruz with that of a mestiza accused of witchcraft in seventeenth-century Boston.

I wrote in the mornings, taught English as a Second Language (ESL) classes part-time at UMass Boston, and worked part-time at a Braille press transcribing children's books into Braille (that was as close as I ever got to working in the publishing industry). It was fun to learn Braille, ride the T for transportation, take daily strolls through the Public Garden, and read the microfilmed transcripts of the Salem witch trials in the Boston Library, but I was getting really tired of teaching my ESL students how to punctuate sentences and write paragraphs. I had ideas for all kinds of exciting, culturally germane courses (not the least of which was a course on Sor Juana, but also, a course on border literature) that I wasn't allowed to teach because I lacked the credentials. Like you, I lacked those three magic letters after my name: PhD.

Meanwhile, back at the ivory tower, the diversity debates (at times mired in "politically correct" rhetoric) had struck the American Studies frontier. In October 1988, Linda Kerber's keynote address to the American Studies Association, "Diversity and the Transformation of American Studies," reflected upon the "cultural explosions" she had witnessed in the discipline since the days of the myth-symbol giants.[8] To use your language, Gloria, she was describing the process of institutional molting, the shedding of the consensus skin and the emergence of a new disciplinary identity founded upon a new "paradigm drama"—diversity.

The following year, Allen F. Davis, in his presidential address to the association, warned the new breed of diversity scholars not to be seduced by deconstructionism, new historicism, or poststructuralism. "Our main task should not be to write about theory, but to write a narrative, to tell a story and to explain American culture to as wide an audience as possible . . . In telling the story of the American people, we must describe the diversity, the conflict, the racism, the despair."[9] That speech resonated with what you (and other radical *mujeres*) were saying in *Making Face, Making Soul/Haciendo Caras* (1990) about the need for new theories. You were calling on scholars and writers of color to create "*teorías* that will rewrite history using race, class, gender and ethnicity as categories of analysis, theories that cross borders, that blur boundaries . . ."[10] All of this motivated me to return to school and finish that PhD I had started in Iowa City. I was also homesick for the desert, and I knew that it was time to return to the Southwest.

I applied and was accepted to the American Studies program at the University of New Mexico (UNM) and moved to Albuquerque. Luckily, the program at New Mexico had learned how to "build a square tomato,"[11] and had instituted regional Southwest studies as well as race and gender studies into the American Studies curriculum. Happily, it was a more diverse program than the one in Iowa, with a core faculty of five women, most of whom identified as feminists. Alas, however, the mandatory reading list for all PhD's to master at the time of our qualifying exams contained no books or essays by Chicana or Chicano scholars, no work by Native American scholars, and only one book by an African American woman. In fact, that ream of essays on American Studies methodology, all of those books about the Puritans and the pioneers and the simple folk of the plains that I had slogged through in Iowa were on the required reading list at New Mexico. Because a few of us complained about the reading list, the faculty asked us to suggest alternative titles, and from our suggestions they composed another *supplemental* list of readings that we could incorporate into our exam preparation, if we wanted to. However, this would be an optional list, and would not be required of all PhD students. Rather than changing the required reading list to incorporate the work of scholars of color and thereby diversify the degree requirements, we had simply added to our workload. Now, we would have to master the required list as well as the optional one. There was no escape, I realized. No matter where I went in my academic career, I was doomed to doing irrelevant work.

In the spring 1991 semester, however, just as I was debating yet another PhD dropout *movida*, three life-changing events happened. First, I took a seminar titled Theories and Methods of Popular Culture Studies with a young white professor named Jane Caputi, who showed me that it was possible to do the kind of teaching I wanted to do in higher education: deconstructive radical feminist pedagogy. The Gulf War had started in January, and Jane guided us through a keen critique of the way the war was being represented on television, via jingoism of the highest order, and the complete opposite of how the Vietnam War had been televised. I was especially focused on the media and military manipulations of language such as the term "collateral damage," a euphemism for the murder of innocent civilians, which clearly belonged to what George Orwell called "the catalogue of swindles and perversions" in political speech and writing.[12] I couldn't stop videotaping the constant barrage of footage shown on all the news broadcasts and news channels, held in thrall by the blatant brainwashing that was taking place and that Jane was helping us deconstruct.

I remember thinking that this professor spoke my language. Unlike the lectures of all the white men I had listened to in Iowa, her lectures were lucid; I understood the critiques, the jokes, the textual analysis, the breakdown of images. That was the kind of teacher I wanted to be: incisive, passionate, focused on everyday life, critical of the patriarchal status quo, and above all, clear. She could handle jargon like any theorist, but it was not the language she spoke in her classes. I think Jane was modeling activist scholarship for me—I just didn't know what to call it at the time. That she was a white woman and I wasn't did not deter my admiration of her, for she assumed an entitlement to her place in the academy that I also needed to assume.

Second, I was awarded a special teaching assistantship that allowed me to teach a class on any topic I wanted (for which I conceptualized and developed the very first Border Consciousness in Film, Literature, and Music syllabus). It was such a joy to teach something other than paragraph-writing techniques in English. I was "doing" Border Studies before I'd even heard of Border Studies, and I was doing Chicana and Chicano Studies by emulating what I had learned in the one and only course that appeared on my college transcripts that focused on anything Chicana/o: the Chicano Literature course I had taken with Professor Theresa Meléndez-Hayes back in the late 1970s at UTEP, the same class where I first claimed my Chicana identity.[13] In other words, I found my *lucha* in the academy, not only in Chicana/o representation in the academy, but also in the study of the border. It would not be American life and thought for me, but Border Life and Thought and Chicana/o Studies. I also discovered the organic joy of the interdisciplinary approach; integrating Chicana/o literature, film, music, art, popular culture, and mass media to study the culture of the border came very naturally to me. It was this first Border Consciousness class that brought me back to you, Gloria, and led me to *Borderlands/La Frontera: The New Mestiza*, which I have been using, reading and rereading, in my classes for the last two decades to help my students discover their own border identities, a location that, as we both know, encompasses much more than geography.

The third life-changing event for me at the University of New Mexico was that the *CARA*[14] exhibit came to town. What can I tell you about the huge border that I crossed that April day of 1991 when I walked into the Albuquerque Museum of Art to see the *Chicano Art: Resistance and Affirmation, 1965–1985* exhibition, which had already traveled to four other mainstream museums in the United States. It wasn't that I was a big fan of Chicano art; the truth is, I didn't know much about it. Originally, I went to the *CARA* show to see if it might make a good field trip for my Border Consciousness class. What dawned on me as I walked through room after room of Chicano and Chicana paintings, silk screens, photographs, sculptures, murals, mixed-media installations, and cases of ephemera, surrounded by Mexican music and bright banners of *papel picado*, was how utterly ignorant I was about Chicano art, the Chicano art movement, the Chicano civil rights movement, and the field of Chicana/o Studies in general. How could I be getting a PhD and not know anything about my own Chicano/a culture?

I stood there staring at my reflection in Judith Baca's *Tres Marías* installation, and realized *CARA* was bringing me face-to-face with my own identity as a first-generation Chicana from El Paso, Texas, and showing me the activist scholar I would have to become in order to fill in all the gaps in my education, and all the lacunae in the education of my students.

In the fall of 1991, the newly minted Stanford PhD and assistant professor Chon Noriega arrived at UNM, the first Chicano faculty member to be hired in the American Studies Department. I left a note in his box, told him I was working on the *CARA* exhibit for my dissertation, and asked him to be my advisor. As a film scholar, he was already immersed in the Chicano/a visual art world, and his own mentor had been Tomás Ybarra-Frausto, one of the handful of Chicano art historians at the time, who also happened to be on the *CARA* Advisory Committee and therefore became a very important source for my dissertation research. Chon's feedback on my *CARA* paper helped me conceptualize a culture-specific structure for the model I was constructing to envision "*la casa*" of Chicana/o popular culture in contradistinction to the "all-American" bungalow style of the mainstream house of popular culture studies.[15] Sadly for UNM, Chon lasted only one year before being recruited away to the School of Film and Television at the University of California, Los Angeles (UCLA), but he continued to serve as the coadvisor for my dissertation, along with Jane Caputi.

Serendipitously, when I advanced to candidacy in 1992, I received a Chicana Dissertation Fellowship at U.C., Santa Barbara, and this brought me to Southern California. Not only was it now possible for me to meet regularly with Chon at UCLA, but also, the evolving *CARA* archives were being housed partly at the Wight Art Gallery at UCLA and partly at the Armand Hammer Museum in Westwood.[16] On a personal level, my partner at the time taught at Pomona College and lived in Claremont. Clearly, life had plans for me to stay in Los Angeles.

A big year for "Hispanics" in the art world and the mainstream cultural industry was 1992. It was the year of the Columbus Quincentennial, and Hispanics were *It*. The multicultural debates had given way to a new frontier. Suddenly everyone was running for the border, as the Taco Bell commercials in those days advised. From border art to border epistemology, everything was coming up borders. No longer imagined as either a wilderness or a garden whose protagonist was the rugged white male pioneer, the frontier became *la frontera*, and it moved from the margins to the center of our academic discourse as well as to the commercial center of American society.[17]

That's when American Studies, not just the lesbians and the feminists of color who had already tapped into the Anzaldúan universe, turned to your work for direction and guidance for how to navigate that land in the middle.[18] Women's Studies, Chicano/a Studies, Ethnic Studies, Sexuality Studies, Diaspora Studies, Postcolonial Studies, Cultural Studies—all intertextualized your methods for studying hybridity in all of its forms. Some of us even adopted your personal/political approach to teaching and writing. In fact, the Radical Caucus in the American Studies Association had called for just such an integration back in the 1970s, the praxis of "fusing our personal experience and world view with the social reality we live in, with our inner life, our history, our economics, and our vision."[19]

In 1994, my dissertation defense earned me the designation "with distinction" on my diploma, and, thanks to that same white woman— Jane Caputi—who nominated "Mi Casa [No] Es Su Casa: The Cultural Politics of the Chicano Art: Resistance and Affirmation Exhibit" to the American Studies Association Dissertation Prize Committee, my dissertation won the Ralph Henry Gabriel Award for Best Dissertation in American Studies (the first Chicana or Chicano to receive this award in the history of the association). Later that year, the job talk I gave based on my dissertation research helped me land a tenure-track position in Chicana/o Studies at UCLA, and the dissertation morphed into a book on Chicano/a art and popular culture that was published in 1998 and helped me get early tenure in 1999.[20] One paper, one course, one professor, and one exhibition of Chicano and Chicana art all came together for me in the spring of 1991 and started me off on my own yellow brick road through the enchanted forests and poisonous poppy fields of academia.

Making the transition from graduate student to professor is like moving from a black-and-white to a Technicolor universe, a universe you thought to be safely "over the rainbow." Suddenly, you are the one sur-rounded by munchkins; you are the slayer of wicked witches, the libera-tor of helpless colleagues, the whippersnapper with the big mouth always getting into trouble. You try to get home, but your new red shoes hurt your feet, someone casts a spell on your friends or absconds with your research into the dark castle, and there is always one more ghost or flying monkey to wrestle. The most disconcerting part is this: the "wonderful Wiz that was," the miracle worker you thought was going to solve all your problems, turns out to be nothing more than a neighbor from your own hometown. He knows as much about working miracles as you do. Emerald City, the ivory tower—whatever you call the academy—is both your own invention and the make-believe reality of many generations of others who came before you, other "little [men and women] behind the curtain." That doesn't mean it isn't real, or that lives are not at stake. It's just that nobody prepares you for the changes you're going to undergo on the trip. Nobody tells you about the way you'll be tested along the way.

In my case, for example, none of my professors at UNM told me that as a brand-new assistant professor at a major research institution I could ask for senior faculty mentorship or a reduced teaching load in the first year to protect my research time, neither of which I got. Nobody pointed out that I would have to design new courses and redesign old ones that were core requirements of the major at the same time that I would be writing new lectures every week; teaching hundreds of students every year; grading thousands of papers; advising a line of students that stretched down the hall during every office hour; reworking the dissertation into a book; revising the curriculum; helping build a new academic major from the ashes of its previous incarnations; dueling with heterosexist and homophobic administrators, colleagues, and students; serving on committees; and commuting 60 miles across several Los Angeles freeways to get to work every day.

Because creative writing was the only way for me to stay sane through all of this, somewhere in my copious free time, I continued working on my Sor Juana novel and writing poetry. Nobody said it would be easy, I know that. But nobody said I would be passing through the nine inner circles of hell, either.

Like Dorothy and her three companions in *The Wizard of Oz*, I grew to understand that everything I needed to survive my academic journey, to feel whole and capable of making a difference, was already within me. As the Scarecrow learned, the diploma gave him confidence in his own innate abilities, just as the ticking testimonial convinced the Tin

Man that he really did have a heart after all, though he had always felt empty on the inside. All the Lion needed was the recognition of a medal to feel courageous, and Dorothy just had to believe that she did indeed have the power to return herself back to her own side of the rainbow.

But I also know that without your insights, Gloria, I could not have theorized about how cultural schizophrenia is the disempowered form of border consciousness, or about the "alter-Nativity" of Chicana/o identity, the way in which we are simultaneously Other and native to the land base of the Southwest, nor could I have contributed to the radical "mirror of Malinchismo," wherein Chicana feminists alter the reflection of the traitor into the face of the warrior against sexism and homophobia.[21] And clearly, I'm not the only one who has benefited from your *lenguas de fuego*.

The way I see it, your border theories have not only changed Chicana/o Studies, Feminist Studies, and Queer Studies; they have also provided a model for Americanist scholarship of the twenty-first century and a foundation for thinking and writing about the multiple histories, languages, genders, and racial realities that are converging in that great big cornfield of "American" life and culture. For me personally, your words and metaphors crafted a new way of writing "*teorías*," and of making my own face as a Chicana lesbian feminist academic who "does" American Studies and Chicana/o Studies in the borderlands, building bridges as I go.

One February evening in 1993 on the UCLA campus, as I walked to Lot 3 from what is now Broad Plaza after a full day of research in the *CARA* archives at the then Wight Gallery, I remember staring at the full moon shining down over the sculpture garden and saying to myself, with absolute clarity and certainty: *I am going to teach here one day*. I could not have foreseen the hunger strike that was to take place a few months later,[22] or the career that I would develop at UCLA, as a founding faculty member of the new César E. Chávez Center for Interdisciplinary Instruction in Chicana and Chicano Studies, which would become a full-fledged Department of Chicana and Chicano Studies in 2005, of which I would serve as department chair from 2007 to 2010, and where we would welcome our first cohort of PhD students into our new graduate program in 2012.

I could not have known that my advisor would become the director of the Chicano Studies Research Center, or that I'd still be walking to Lot 3 twenty years later. All I knew that February evening was that the *CARA* exhibition anchored me to Chicana/o Studies scholarship and made it possible for me to do meaningful, relevant work in the academy. That's why I always say the *CARA* exhibit saved my academic career.

When students ask my advice about how to survive in higher education, I say this: Take a deep breath and roll up your sleeves, especially if you're a woman, a woman of color, a lesbian, a gay man, bisexual, transgendered, or physically challenged. Here and there, you'll catch a glimpse of Glinda in a gleaming bubble just outside your peripheral vision. That's a good sign. The Universe has sent help. More than likely, you'll find yourself alone, cleaning up after tornadoes. More than likely, you'll be calling out to your equivalent of Auntie Em, thinking "there's no place like home."

I think the trick is to make the academy your home. And that's especially hard if you come from a community that has not typically found the academy a hospitable place. That old saying, "*mi casa es su casa*" doesn't always apply to Others in academia. If the house doesn't fall on us first, we have two choices. We either move out and build our own house, or stay and renovate, fully understanding that renovation is costly, and rebuilding is no guarantee against earthquakes or wicked witches on broomsticks. We never give up, we endure, we survive. Indeed, this is the *mystery of survival* in the *master's house*; that, and never losing sight of our first or *second dream*, which for me has always been writing.

In "Speaking in Tongues: Letter to Third World Women Writers," whose form I have been emulating with this preface, you told us, Gloria, that the most important thing we could do to resist the erasure of our lives was to write down our stories. "Forget the room of one's own," you said, "write in the kitchen . . . in the welfare line . . . sitting on the john." You told us to forget the self-sabotaging distractions, forget the paralyzing fear, and forget the hunger and the self-destructive habits. "Don't let the ink coagulate in your pens . . . Put your shit on paper." This raw kind of writing, born of the "innards, in the gut, and out of living tissue—*organic* writing," you called it, that's where the power is.[23]

It was to thank you for your legacy of words and poetry that I visited your tomb in Hargill, Texas, on your birthday in September 2004, four months after your death. I remember the sudden rainstorm that drenched my blue guayabera and fogged my view of the large headstone in the cemetery that read simply, ANZALDUA. Chavela Vargas's "La Llorona" blared from the speakers of my car as I left my offerings on your grave.[24]

I could feel your presence as much in the whiptail lizards that darted across my path as in that sudden Texas storm. At your memorial in

Santa Cruz later that year, I was enraged to the point of weeping when representatives from the University of California at Santa Cruz bestowed on you a posthumous PhD in literature, in recognition of the contributions your work had made to literary discourse.

We learned that you had been working on your dissertation for years and had been close to finishing it when you went into a diabetic coma and died. But wait, I thought, wasn't *Borderlands*/La Frontera already a dissertation? Weren't all of those anthologies you edited and coedited that brought together so many important voices (and *lenguas de fuego*) already critical contributions to the academy? Would your life have been saved if that recognition had come much earlier, through a tenure-track job that offered security and health benefits so that you wouldn't have had to die from untreated complications due to diabetes? It made my throat fill up with thorns that they were offering you that posthumous PhD now that you were lying in the ground, no longer a living threat to the gatekeepers. That part of the ceremony seemed profoundly ironic, not to mention unfair and hypocritical, and I made a commitment to you then and there that in every class I ever taught, I would make sure my students knew your work; in every piece I ever wrote, I would credit you for all of the ways your ideas expanded my awareness and contributed to my own epistemology.

Later, as the storytelling started, and I sat there listening to all of the *testimonios* of your friends, loved ones, and writing *comadres*, I kept staring at Annie Valva's photograph on the altar, the by-now-famous picture of you walking into the Pacific Ocean fully dressed, playing in the water like a mermaid or a siren. You seem to be in your element, completely happy and at home surrounded by all that water. I kept asking you, in my mind, "Why were you so happy that day, Gloria? What was it about being in the water that made you so happy?" I imagined it had something to do with growing up thirsty in Texas. With connecting to the wide, salty body of the goddess. Yes, you said, answering me in the lines of a poem that wrote itself in my journal that afternoon. They may not have been your exact words, Gloria, but they are the words I heard as I watched you frolic in the white waves of the divine Feminine.

I offered you my poem at your grave eight years ago, and now, I choose to open this collection of work from my first twenty years along the yellow brick road of the academy with this letter to you because I want you to see how much I have heeded your advice about not letting "the ink coagulate in [my] pen." At times, my pen has generated poetry, at others, stories, novels, or academic essays like the ones in this volume. No matter what the form is, I have learned how to tap into the healing, transformative power of the written word. "The act of writing is the act of making soul, alchemy,"[25] you called it.

The alchemy you speak of is my daily bread. You remain with me *en la lucha, tu paisana* from the border,

Alicia

May 1, 2013

ACKNOWLEDGMENTS

Since the early 1990s, I have received research support from various sources, at UCLA and beyond, without which I could not have completed much of the work collected in this book. I gratefully acknowledge the following research support:

- The Chicana Dissertation Fellowship in the Department of Chicana/o Studies at U.C., Santa Barbara, 1992–1993, which brought me to Southern California.
- The PEW Foundation/Tomás Rivera Center Dissertation Completion residencies that hijacked several of us into a remote Radisson in San Antonio, Texas, and sat us next to a computer and a faculty mentor for two hot weeks in July to hammer out drafts of dissertation chapters.
- The Ford Foundation/National Research Council Fellowship Dissertation Completion Fellowship, 1993–1994, which introduced me to the power of networking.
- The Postdoctoral Minority-Scholar-in-Residence Fellowship at Pomona College, 1994–1995, which gave me time to develop new courses in Chicana/o Studies and prepared me for life in the fast lane at UCLA.
- The several faculty research grants I received from the UCLA Academic Senate over the years, which have allowed me to employ undergraduate and graduate research assistants, especially during the pretenure years as I worked at transforming my dissertation into a book.
- The two Institute of American Cultures grants administered through the Chicano Studies Research Center at UCLA, which allowed me to complete my popular culture anthology.
- The generous Shirley Collier Literary Prize I received from the UCLA English Department for my Sor Juana novel, and my then colleague Greg Sarris, who nominated the book.
- The Rockefeller Fellowship for Latino/a Study at the Smithsonian Institution, which took me to Washington, DC, in spring 1999 to begin my project on place and identity in Chicana art.

- The Roderick Endowed Chair in English I received from the University of Texas at El Paso, which took me back to my alma mater in fall 1999, where I began my research into the Juárez femicides.
- The UCLA Gold Shield Alumnae Award for Faculty Excellence that the kind ladies of that prestigious organization bestowed on me in 2008, which came with a $30,000 monetary award that helped fund two years of research and resulted in two new research articles and two new anthologies—one on the Juárez femicides and the other on a controversial art piece by Alma López.

I would also like to acknowledge the influence, example, and *comadrazgo* of my academic *familia*, Emma Pérez, Deena González, Ellie Hernández, Antonia Castañeda, and Arturo Madrid. A special shout-out to Jane Caputi and Chela Sandoval for their supportive and constructive remarks on this manuscript, and their brilliant work that has so impacted my own scholarship. And to Theresa May, editor-in-chief at UT Press, with whom I have had the great fortune of working over the last twenty years, since that first meeting of Ford Fellows in 1993.

To the different students I've mentored over these two decades, and who worked closely with me on research projects, conference organizing, index building, and administrative tasks, I express my deepest gratitude: Elena, Angélica, Mike, Heather, Georgina, Allison, Rachel, Kendy, and the rest of you whose names aren't listed here but who know who you are.

Finally, I would also like to acknowledge the hunger strikers who in 1993 put their lives at risk for the establishment of a Chicana/o Studies department at UCLA, and my colleagues at the César Chávez Department, especially my fellow founding faculty members, who together kept the program grounded in the face of musical chairpersons, student mutiny, and collegial boycotts in those early years. We lived through some interesting times, but most of us are still here, and collectively, day by day, year by year, we have created a permanent academic home for Chicana/Chicano Studies at UCLA.

To Olivia Díaz, Elena Mohseni, and Ellie Hernández—the staff at the Chávez Department—without whose rock-solid support, *buen humor*, and expertise I could not have endured my three-year chairship.

To Vice Chancellor Scott Waugh, for all of his support of my research, my teaching, and my leadership over these past twenty years.

To my allies on campus, among whom I would especially like to recognize Rosina Becerra, Christine Littleton, Abel Valenzuela, Charlene

Villaseñor Black, María Cristina Pons, Vilma Ortiz, Chon Noriega, Rafael Pérez-Torres, Arthur Little, and Jim Schultz.

More than anything, I am blessed by the stabilizing presence, support, and TLC of my wife, Alma López, who has held my hand, fed my hunger, and massaged my back through the completion of this and several other books, pulling all-nighters with me in solidarity. For your artistic magic, your skills as a visual professional, and your activist spirit, darling, I am so very grateful. This book is for you.

[UN]FRAMING THE "BAD WOMAN"

Figure i.1. *Woman with Frames*, © 2010. UNAM Sculpture Garden, Ciudad Universitaria, Mexico City. Photograph by Raymond Meier. Photo credit: Trunk Archive.

Activist Scholarship and the Historical Vortex of the "Bad Woman"

A Meta-Hermeneutics

At a San Francisco book signing for my novel *Desert Blood* in spring 2005, my friend Elizabeth "Betita" Martínez (hardcore *veterana* of several social justice movements and author of *De Colores Means All of Us: Latina Views for a Multi-Colored Century*) asked me a very intriguing question. "How," she asked, "does the same mind that produced such a lyrical historical novel about Sor Juana Inés de la Cruz for a first novel create such a gritty, contemporary mystery about the murdered women of Juárez for a second book?" It was a compliment, to be sure, but it also got me to thinking about the underlying Ariadne's thread that connects not only *Sor Juana's Second Dream* (1999) and *Desert Blood: The Juárez Murders* (2005), but also the latest one, *Calligraphy of the Witch* (2012),[1] set in seventeenth-century Boston at the time of the witchcraft trials. What do these seemingly diverse stories about a defiant nun, the Ciudad Juárez femicides, and the victims of the New England witch hunts have in common that transcends both time and place? Furthermore, I pondered, how does that common denominator find expression in my academic work as well—my book on the *CARA* exhibition, my anthologies on popular culture and Chicana/o sexualities, on femicides and Free Trade, and on the controversial *Our Lady* by Alma López,[2] and my essays on La Malinche, Sor Juana, Las Maqui-Locas, and Chicana artists? What was this common denominator, anyway?

Seen from a retrospective angle (which is one of the privileges of being a baby boomer), the answer to Betita's question and to my subsequent inquiries and cogitations now seems obvious, but perhaps, at the time, I couldn't see it because I was focusing too much on each subject individually without attaching it to a continuum or an architecture of what Michel Foucault calls similitude, or one of the four ways by which things resemble each other: by proximity, by imitation, by analogy, and by affinity.[3] "Is not any resemblance, after all, both the most obvious and the most hidden of things?" asks Foucault in *The Order of Things*. Indeed, finding resemblances is perhaps the most fundamental way to organize knowledge. Before I could name the resemblances in my own novels, I had to uncover the common purpose that connects all of my work—from my novels to my research to my teaching at UCLA. In part, Betita was asking me the dreaded question of methodology. By what method do I connect all of these diverse subjects and approaches, and for what purpose?

When I was a graduate student, preparing to take my orals and advance to PhD candidacy, the word *methodology* used to send very non-sexy shivers down my spine. The dreaded question for me in the interdisciplinary field of American Studies studying Chicana/o art was not "what's your theoretical framework," but "what's your methodology?" But the problem was bigger than that, because American Studies itself seemed to be asking the same thing: what does it mean to *do* American Studies? What *are* American Studies methodologies? Are we interdisciplinary, cross-disciplinary, transdisciplinary, postdisciplinary? Talk about linguistic terrorism. I didn't know that language. That was academic language, the master's language, and I had refused to learn that language on the grounds that it didn't speak to my reality nor, apparently, to that of the professors who couldn't seem to explain the concept of methodology very well.

Like Malcolm X, I turned to the dictionary for help and found that, all along, I knew what the word meant; it was simple; methodology was nothing more than a way of doing something, a set of procedures and techniques for conducting, organizing, and writing an academic study. In the case of my dissertation, then, "what's your methodology," translated into "how are you going to look at the *Chicano Art: Resistance and Affirmation* exhibition, specifically, and at the Chicano art movement more broadly within an American Studies context, that is, within a field that purports to study "American life and thought?"

Maybe because I was working on a visual subject—an art exhibition—I immediately associated the question of methodology, of procedures and techniques, not just with the idea of *looking at* something analytically but with the physical act of *seeing* itself. I grew to understand methodology, then, as a way of both doing and seeing my academic praxis, and to see implied the *eye*, as well as the *I*, of the seer and the seen. One of the reasons methodology is so hard to understand is that it isn't taught through the body, as body practice. We do not see irrespective of our bodies, nor can we see the subjects of our study (Sor Juana or Chicano/a art, for example) outside of the bodies that have produced them or of the historical, political, or cultural context in which they have been produced. Methodology, then, perforce involves the material experiences of the body, both of our own bodies as scholars as well as of the bodies we are studying. To know the body means primarily to know that bodies come packaged with signifiers that determine how we see and how others see us; some of those signifiers are biological: race, phenotype, sex; others are social: class, gender, culture, ethnicity, language, religion; and still others pertain to nation, vocation, generation, and desire.

Stuart Hall argues that "all discourse is placed, positioned, situated, and all knowledge is contextual,"[4] the context understood as ethnicity. "That is to say, a recognition that we all speak from a particular place, out of a particular history, out of a particular experience, a particular culture, without being contained by that position . . . We are all, in that sense, *ethnically* located and our ethnic identities are crucial to our subjective sense of who we are."[5] To decolonize the concept of ethnicity from a totalizing singularity (such as "the Black experience" or the "American mind"), Hall believes new ethnicities must be retheorized and disarticulated from the dominant "equivalence with nationalism, imperialism, racism, and the state."[6] For Hall, ethnicity implies "the extraordinary diversity of subjective positions, social experiences, and cultural identities which compose the category"[7] of any ethnicity; therefore, knowledge and discourse about any ethnicity must represent multiple identities grounded in difference.

If, then, methodology is tied to identity politics, and identity politics is tied to a complex understanding of ethnicity, as Hall argues, then methodology, or what we do and how we see academically, is filtered through the diverse particulars of our ethnicity, which include history, culture, language, and place. My Chicanidad is grounded in the post–Chamizal Treaty[8] El Paso–Juárez border, which is quite different from the post-NAFTA border, or the non-border-patrolled Paso del Norte of the Mexican Revolution. Ethnically, I am a first-generation bilingual and bicultural Mexican American, but generationally, I am a baby boomer. Politically, I am a Chicana radical lesbian feminist, with light-skin privilege, and socially, I straddle a working-class sensibility with a middle-class, tenure-track position. It is from these particulars that I perform my own brand of Chicana theory, pedagogy, and research methodology; these are the different worlds that I intersect and represent in my writing.

The academic praxis that engages me is one that centers experience, and extrapolates from that experience the theories, ideas, and concepts by which I can give back to the world, develop a user-friendly paradigm of analysis rooted in my own language and location, what Chicana historian Emma Pérez calls a "*sitio y lengua*,"[9] that is, a discursive site from which to see, write about, and represent the world, and thus, from which to construct a method of study. As a Chicana radical lesbian feminist from the border, what I do in terms of methodology is going to reflect those *sitios* of my identity from which I see and recognize the resemblances and differences of the subjects that I'm studying: Chicana/o art, a seventeenth-century Mexican nun, the Salem witchcraft trials, the murdered women of the U.S.-Mexico border, the imaginary homeland of Aztlán, or Chicana lesbian artistic renditions of La Virgen de Guadalupe.

This is an *activist methodology*, engaged in for a specific political purpose: to raise awareness, to effect social change, to represent, to give voice, to make visible, to expose, to problem-solve, to bridge community needs with academic resources. Paraphrasing Ruth Wilson Gilmore's notion of "organic praxis"[10] in academia as "political bargaining," or rather, how a scholar engages with "oppositional action beyond that of writing for academic audiences,"[11] Laura Pulido offers a few examples of her experience as a scholar activist and advises young scholars to think carefully about the ethical implications, responsibilities, and diffi-cult choices that this level of engaged scholarship entails. Indeed, as Charles Hale, one of the editors of *Engaging Contradictions: Theory, Politics, and Methods of Activist Scholarship*, notes in his introduction to the volume: "Activist scholars work in dialogue, collaboration, alliance with people who are struggling to better their lives; activist scholarship embodies a responsibility that these 'allies' can recognize as their own, value in their own terms, and use as they see fit."[12]

I agree completely with Gayatri Spivak's point that "one way or another academics are in the business of ideological production; even academics in the pure sciences are involved in that process."[13] Empiricism and the scientific method notwithstanding, objectivity is a myth, a colonial imposition, a prerogative of the privileged. Hale also sees objectivity as the opposite of the goals of the activist scholar:

> For people who feel directly and personally connected to broader experi-ences of oppression and to struggles for empowerment, claims of objectiv-ity are more apt to sound like self-serving maneuvers to preserve hierarchy and privilege; and the idea of putting scholarship to the service of their own communities' empowerment and well-being is more apt to sound like a sensible, if not inevitable, way to practice their profession.[14]

After all of this self-analysis, I could see how activist scholarship was my methodology, the "sensible and inevitable way to practice [my] profession" as a Chicana/o Studies, Gender and Sexuality Studies, Border Studies cultural critic and writer. But I had not yet fully answered Betita's question. I still needed to discern and articulate the common denominator shared by my different subjects. Foucault explains that "to search for a meaning is to bring to light a resemblance. To search for the law governing signs is to discover the things that are alike."[15] Thus, if I stripped away the differences of each woman's life—such as historical time (seventeenth century vs. twentieth century), geographic location (New England vs. New Spain), language (English vs. Spanish), ethnicity, vocation, and sexuality (a cloistered nun vs. a New England goodwife vs. a Mexican maquiladora worker vs. a Chicana lesbian artist, for example)—and looked only at their affinities, at the ways they could be seen as analogous to each other, as emulating each other, as identical, I would be able to decipher the overall meaning of my work. I had to engage "the totality of [my] learning and skills that enable [me] to make the signs speak . . . to discover their meaning,"[16] which Foucault defines as hermeneutics.

From this meta-hermeneutics, I found that what the women I write about have in common, and the reason they interest me in the first place, is that they are all rebels with a cause, and I see myself represented in their mirror. I recognize my own rebellion against heteronormative gendered behaviors as the struggle of my early life. At school, I didn't want to sit "like a lady," with my ankles crossed and my knees closed; I wanted to wear shorts under my uniform so that I could run and wrestle and climb trees. Nor did I care to learn how to knit, no matter how often I was struck on the knuckles with the knitting needles. I was a bad girl who talked back to my authority figures, especially female ones like my grandmother at home and the nuns at school.

My grandmother often called me *rebelde sin causa*, a rebel without a cause, believing, as she did, that I had nothing at all to protest, no cause to defy, disobey, and disrespect. To give me something to really cry about or really object to, my grandmother always punished me for my bad behavior with either a slap or a pinch (or, if I was really bad, a belt whack) or by taking something away: television, a visit with a friend, phone privileges, or a few hours with Nancy Drew. I had to be useful, stop wasting time, stop being a good-for-nothing. She wanted me to grow up to be the kind of woman a man would want to marry; I had to learn how to cook and clean and sew and garden and fold laundry and serve my grandfather at the table. She pretended not to see that my grandfather never imposed this gendered behavior on me. I was his oldest and favorite grandchild, his *consentida*. He was the one who bought me my Nancy Drew books at Kmart, who let me watch *Dark Shadows* every day after school, who vetoed my grandmother's decision not to let me join the Girl Scouts; he's the one who gave permission for me to go on camping trips with my troop and allowed me to join the volleyball and basketball teams, even if that meant he would have to sit in his car in 100-degree El Paso heat, waiting for me to get out of practice to drive me home from school. For as indulgent as my grandfather was with me, he expected strict obedience from my grandmother and his own daughters. My gendered life was as bifurcated as my language, part of the cultural schizophrenia that I discuss at length in my personal essay "Literary Wetback."[17]

I lapse into this personal reverie to illustrate the kind of activist scholarship that I'm about. The struggle I identify with and seek to contribute to through my writing, research, teaching, and organizing is the one that begins at home, the gendered socialization process that children are saturated with by the time they get to kindergarten. My struggle was the continuous resistance of a first-generation Chicana granddaughter against the heteronormative gender codes of a "good girl" dictated by Mexican patriarchy and Roman Catholicism and enforced by a feisty immigrant grandmother with a second-grade education who was married off at fourteen and gave birth to eight children; a grandmother who ran the family with despotic efficiency, who taught me how to be an autonomous human being with a fully bilingual tongue, while she herself never learned to drive or speak English.

At the time, the historical materialist facts of my grandmother's life did not mean anything to me, certainly they did not explain the way that mothers and grandmothers are prime collaborators with their own oppression, not of their own choice, but because of a lack of knowledge and agency that are the very consequence of patriarchal proscriptions of the female body.

Because gender was a very early site of resistance for me, the stories of other bad girls, or strong girls, as I preferred to see myself, were always my favorite. But gender wasn't the only context in which I understood that life was unfair. Getting publicly humiliated for not being able to pronounce the words to the "Pledge of Allegiance" in the first grade, getting fined or smacked for mixing English and Spanish, and seeing my friend Edna cry because Sister Rose Clair said people with kinky hair and dark skin didn't go to heaven brought two other forms of injustice to my awareness: linguistic terrorism and racism.

I wrote my first play in the fourth grade about Edna, and published my first piece in the eighth grade, about my grandfather's sudden heart attack (the loss of my champion for equal rights). Since then, I think, I have been writing about death and discrimination. I have been questioning social discourses of gender, race, and language, which implicated class, citizenship, nationality, and sexuality. I had to learn how to navigate the crossroads between what Gloria Anzaldúa calls *"lo heredado, lo adquirido, lo impuesto,"*[18] or that which is inherited, acquired, and imposed—colonialism, racism, sexism, heterosexism, misogyny, homophobia, xenophobia. As a Chicana lesbian body, I share the isms and phobias that oppress raced, gendered, and sexed bodies that are like mine and unlike mine, but I also share the collective memory of struggle, resistance, and rebirth inherent in all of these bodies.

The historically situated women whom I write about—La Malinche, Sor Juana, Chicana lesbian feminists and artists, the so-called Salem witches, and even the murdered girls and women of Juárez—as well as the characters of myth and legend— Coyolxauhqui, the warrior goddess; La Llorona, the "bad mother"; or Lupe, the Boxing Glove Virgin Dressed in Roses—all refused to comply with those social discourses by which "good girls" and "good women" are constructed; hence, they fall into the category of "bad women," as defined by their place, culture, and time, and are held responsible for the consequences of their bad behavior.

What links these historically and socially diverse figures that I've been studying and writing about throughout my academic career is the stereotype of the "bad woman," by which women since the legendary Eve have been measured, judged, compared, and censured. Variations of the "bad woman" include "unfaithful wives," "negligent mothers," "rebellious daughters," "insubordinate nuns," "loose women," "treacherous sisters," "manly women," and "lesbians"—all of them confrontational to a patriarchal worldview, from the pre-Columbian past to the transnational present.

In Mexican and Chicano/a culture, the "bad woman" stereotype is part of a typology of the feminine gender that I call the Tres Marías Syndrome,[19] which gives women only three roles to play in the narrative of Chicana identity politics: virgins, mothers, or whores. In *The Labyrinth of Solitude*, Octavio Paz calls the Mexican version of this bad woman "la Chingada":

> What is the Chingada? The Chingada is the Mother forcibly opened, vi-
> olated, or deceived . . . To the Spaniard, dishonor consists in being the
> son of a woman who voluntarily surrenders herself: a prostitute. To the
> Mexican, it consists in being the fruit of violation . . . In effect, every
> woman—even when she gives herself willingly—is torn open by the man,
> is the Chingada. In a certain sense all of us, by the simple fact of being
> born of woman, are *hijos de la* Chingada, sons of Eve . . . [20]

Simply put, "La Chingada," or "the Fucked One," whether or not she allowed herself to be fucked, is Everywoman. The biological fact of a woman's openness, says Paz, which puts her on the receiving end of that fucking, grants her the ignominious reputation of a whore, and because all women (at least all heterosexual women who engage in sexual relations with men) get fucked, Paz's logic goes, not only are they all "*chingadas*" but also, we are all sons and daughters of La Chingada. For all of the ways in which this abject identity of openness and penetrability has been naturalized as the normal condition of the female species—which, according to Octavio Paz, attends all females, but especially Mexican ones—and which it is incumbent upon men to redeem (primarily through marriage), paradoxically, motherhood remains the highest expression of the "good woman's" socialization, for a good woman redeems the constitutional ignominy of her sex only by giving birth to and raising legitimate sons of the father.

A "bad woman" defies these limited/limiting roles—virgin, mother, whore—and spurns the duty of her sex to provide pleasure for the husband, solace for the son, and heirs for the father. A "bad woman" is dangerous, contagious, viral. A "bad woman" is a snake, the proverbial "snake in the grass" that got Adam's first wife, Lilith, evicted from the Bible (not to mention Paradise), that tempted Eve to transgress against God's Law not to eat of the forbidden tree of knowledge, that poisoned the mind of Adam, and caused *man*kind's fall from grace and expulsion from the Garden of Eden.

Because of the innate weakness and wickedness of the female, the Bible tells us, the serpent tempted Eve first, knowing that Eve would surrender to her constitutional sin of disobedience and would then use her inchoate powers of seduction over Adam, who became the victim of both the serpent and the woman. In reaping the wrath of God for her insubordination, Eve was punished with the pain of childbirth and the abject condition of enslavement to her husband's will,[21] a legacy that every female in Christendom has inherited from her primordial mother, for we must all bear the penance for the mother's original transgression against the Father. The serpent, we are told, was also punished, and instead of walking upright, it was sentenced to slither over the earth on its belly, to be perpetually crushed by the epitome of good women: the immaculate Virgin Mary and perfect Mother of God.

This image of the crushed serpent constitutes another similitude between the different subjects I write about. Perhaps the most signifying element of their "badness" is the social punishment meted out to "bad women" as a consequence of their noncompliance with patriarchy, some form of physical, verbal, or psychological abuse, persecution, harassment, incarceration, torture, or murder for their defiance/disobedience/rebelliousness/insubordination. "Well-behaved women seldom make history," goes the famous adage by Laurel Thatcher Ulrich, but sometimes "bad women" become persecuted women and they die an early, gruesome, or unjust death.

Tracking the "Bad Woman"

Certainly, the brilliant Sor Juana Inés de la Cruz, one of the most popular and prolific writers of the seventeenth-century Spanish Golden Age (although she was actually a product of New Spain and now graces the two-hundred-nuevo-peso note in Mexico), was persecuted relentlessly for her intelligence, her defiance of Church and convent traditions, and her dedication to learning. She talked back to her superiors in the convent, penned love poems to other women, and dared to rebut the arguments of the Church fathers, for which she was persecuted relentlessly and died an unjust death.

"World, why do you persist in persecuting me?" she asked in a poem, "How do I offend, when all I seek / is to place beauty in my mind / rather than my mind on beauty?"[22] How did seeking knowledge and the enlightenment of books offend her superiors in the Church, both the bishops and archbishops who sought to punish and control her genius and also her sisters in the convent who were jealous of her worldly reputation and the favoritism bestowed on her by the viceregal court? How could a woman, and a nun at that, challenge the double standards of patriarchy in her poem about "stubborn men who accuse / women for no reason / not seeing yourselves as the cause / for that which you malign?"[23]

What secret was she alluding to in her naughty poem to her "divina Lysi" that she tore to pieces and swallowed to protect the confidence entrusted in her? Was this a consummation of erotic desires, or a transubstantiation of flesh into words? With what flagrant disobedience and aberrant lack of modesty, her Church fathers wondered indignantly, did this woman think she had a right to have her "scribblings" published, read, and endorsed by some of the most renowned theologians in the mother country?

Suffice it to say—because, of course, I want you to read *Sor Juana's Second Dream* as well as my Sor Juana essays in this volume, and Sor Juana's own work—that she was "bludgeoned into submission,"[24] as the scholar Luis Harss puts it. Perhaps she was not physically bludgeoned (although the Catholic Church is certainly no stranger to employing extreme physical violence to coerce a desired result), but certainly, she was persistently attacked, bullied, harassed, and punished.

In the last two of her twenty-seven years of cloistered life, after she had renounced reading and writing and stopped engaging in any form of intellectual discourse with the world outside the convent, Sor Juana renewed her vows in her own blood, calling herself "la peor del mundo" and "la peor que ha habido," the worst of all women who have ever lived (perhaps, the "baddest" girl of New Spain), because she refused to be the passive, silent, and obedient kind of woman/nun that colonial patriarchy demanded her to be.

Defiant to the bitter end, however, at least in my interpretation, Sor Juana chose death by contagion rather than an abject life. Some argue that she capitulated to the demands of her superiors, or that she finally saw the light of the Holy Spirit, and succumbed to her vocation, but most Sor Juana scholars agree that our Latin American "Tenth Muse" battled between reason and passion all of her life (which is the subject of her ode to the Enlightenment, *Primero sueño*), neither of which the Church wanted her to exercise freely. I feel honored to have been chosen by Sor Juana as the twentieth- or twenty-first-century Chicana lesbian poet-academic from the border who gets to bring our Tenth Muse out of the epistemology of the closet.

Sor Juana's "crimes," those four thick volumes of her collected works, outlived her and created a legacy that women writers all over the Americas (and Europe, too) have been trying to emulate for three centuries, and which contemporary playwrights and opera composers are rediscovering in their quest for the quintessential Sor Juana. But what about those thousands of young Mexican women who have been

Figure i.2. Cover of Alicia Gaspar de Alba's *Sor Juana's Second Dream*. Image by Francisco Benítez, © 1999 (University of New Mexico Press).

viciously slaughtered on the El Paso–Juárez border since 1993, and who have gone down in history as Maqui-Locas, that is, maquiladora workers living *la vida loca* of a double life on the border? What is their legacy? What were their crimes?

As Ivon Villa, the amateur sleuth in *Desert Blood* (2005) discovers, their only "crime" is being poor, young, Mexican, and fertile female bodies living too close to the chain-link fence and the shallow waters of the Promised Land. In what is sure to become one of the longest gendered crime waves in modern history, there are many perpetrators, many theories about "whodunit" and who "asked for it." Many actions are taken by groups ranging from grassroots NGOs to international organizations for human rights and social justice, but there are no solutions, no punishments; there is no evidence beyond the raped, mutilated, dismembered remains in the desert that these persecuted young Mexican women even lived. Ironically, the only signifier of their lives is a corpse half buried in a sand dune. Why are the young, brown, female, and completely disenfranchised victims of the Juárez femicides blamed for their own deaths and accused of luring their perpetrators to commit unimaginable crimes upon their allegedly transgressive female bodies? What underlying social message about a woman's place in patriarchy, and a brown woman's place in a transnational border economy, do their tortured remains communicate?

Figure i.3. Cover of Alicia Gaspar de Alba's *Desert Blood: The Juárez Murders*. Image by Segundo Pérez, © 2005 (Arte Público Press).

The official line from the very beginning has been that the victims "asked for it," that they were "bad girls" who chose to hang out with "bad people" and did "bad things" and ended up getting what was coming to them, or, that they ran off with their boyfriends. The more industrialized the border between the United States and Mexico becomes, the more immersed both sides get in what Jane Caputi calls "the age of sex crime,"[25] when the serial rapist, mutilator, and killer of allegedly "bad girls" and "bad women," rather than being brought to justice, instead gets hailed as a cultural hero.

In this climate, not only do the victims get blamed for their own deaths, but also the perpetrators, like modern-day Jack the Rippers, get memorialized by the media, the Internet, the informal tourist industry that capitalizes on the murders with T-shirts that read "I Killed 40 Prostitutes in Juárez and All I Got Was This Bloody T-Shirt," websites that cater to the callous and the morbid, and makeup and fashion trends that capitalize on the "sleepwalking girl" aesthetic.[26]

In writing a novel about the femicides, my objective was not to "solve" the crimes, as they seem to have no apparent solution, for to this day, twenty years after the first bodies started cropping up in the Juárez desert, the femicides continue, as all those black on pink crosses painted on telephone poles all over the city attest, one cross for every found victim, at least eight hundred and counting. Instead, I had a twofold purpose in writing *Desert Blood*: to break the silence that shrouded these crimes and protected the perpetrators, and to raise questions about accountability that did not point the finger only at the Mexican government, as these are not just Mexican crimes, but binational crimes that implicate the governments of both sides of the Rio Grande and sacrifice future generations of brown daughters on the border. Using the mystery genre, I wanted to explore the issue of whose interests were being protected and served by these misogynistic crimes, and especially, to ponder the interesting synchronicity between the increased militarization of the border, the implementation of the North American Free Trade Agreement that lures hundreds of young women a day into the ground zero of gendered and economic exploitation known as the maquiladora, or twin plant, industry, and the burgeoning worldwide market for the sexual trafficking of poor immigrant women and girls.

Migrants to the border, lured there with the promise of a job at a twin plant, or maquiladora, the eventual femicide victims don't realize they've come to an alien land where they and their reproductive systems will become the target of social control. Concepción Benavídez, on the other hand, the mestiza protagonist of my third novel, *Calligraphy of the Witch* (2007, 2012), knows very well that she's been brought to an alien land by the pirate ship she boarded in Veracruz, after having escaped from the convent of San Jerónimo in Mexico City, where she served as scribe and apprentice to Sor Juana Inés de la Cruz.

The merchant who buys Concepción Benavídez's bill of sale from Laurens-Cornille de Graaf, the pirate who captures her in Veracruz and rapes her repeatedly on the journey to New England, is outraged to have to pay fifty pounds for a half-breed Indian with two-color eyes. But her unusually accomplished calligraphy shows she has an education and will probably prove useful to his business. Her fancy calligraphy in the Romish, or Spanish, tongue also bespeaks her papist Catholic upbringing. The merchant changes her name to Thankful Seagraves because she should

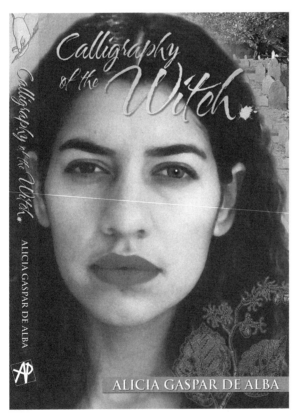

Figure i.4. Cover of Alicia Gaspar de Alba's *Calligraphy of the Witch*. Image by Alma López, © 2012 (Arte Público Press). Special thanks to Lysa Flores.

be thankful, he tells her in a language she can't understand, that she was delivered to the "chosen children of God" in New England, people of the true faith whose idea of religious tolerance meant tolerance only for their own religion. Seeing that she's being sold as chattel, Concepción chooses to drown herself rather than live as a slave; however, she survives the icy waters of the Atlantic just as she survived her Middle Passage across the Spanish Main, and several months later gives birth to a baby girl, product of the pirate's violation. The baby looks white, though she is a mixture of Spanish/mestiza and Dutch/mulatto blood.

The members of the Puritan society in which Concepción awakens to her new life as a slave call themselves the "Visible Saints," but she soon learns that there is nothing saintly about the way they treat anybody who's different from them. They don't tolerate Spanish; they fear Indians and Catholics like the plague; there's not one single church where she can light a candle to the Virgin of Guadalupe; and they shun the papist profanities that they think spout from Concepción's mouth whenever she speaks Spanish to her daughter (the English-only movement has long been a tenet of mainstream American culture).

For eight years, Concepción struggles to adapt to the English language and Puritan culture in Boston. By 1692, she has learned the skills of chicken farming, peddling, and haggling with midwives, and her tongue is finally able to communicate in the master's language, even if she speaks it with a strong accent. Everyone knows her in town as the foreigner and the pirate's wench. The daughter she delivered, whom she has named Juana Jerónima (in honor of Sor Juana and the convent of San Jerónimo) but whose name was Anglicized to Hannah Jeremiah, hates Concepción as much as she hates the Spanish that her mother teaches her in secret. Coveted by Rebecca, the merchant's wife, the girl prefers the white mother to the brown, English to Spanish, Puritan to Catholic. In March 1692, three women get accused of witchcraft, all brought to Boston from Salem in a witch's cart. One of them is Concepción's only friend, Tituba Indian, whose skin is even darker than Concepción's, and who shares a past in New Spain. The other two are white but old, considered no more than hags, and though one is rich and the other a beggar with a four-year-old child, both have problems with their neighbors.

Soon all manner of "bad women" get accused as witches by a group of perhaps hysterical, perhaps theatrical young girls: single women, widowed women, slave women, beggar women, and old women. An occasional man is accused as well, particularly if his views conflict with the merchants, magistrates, and ministers who run the colony, but it is mostly women who populate the jail cells of Essex County. It is only a matter of time before Concepción gets thrown in the dungeon, arrested for the attempted murder of her merchant master (the rape he perpetrated on her, which unleashed her murderous fury, is never mentioned at her trial) and named for a witch by her own child. She is tried for the crimes of papacy and witchcraft, the evidence of which are her uncanny calligraphy in the Romish tongue and the "devil's verse" that she has embroidered on a sampler with which she was bewitching her child by teaching her to memorize the evil words.

Little do her Puritan inquisitors know that the verse Concepción is using to teach her daughter Spanish is Sor Juana's illustrious poem about those "hombres necios" who doggedly pursue and pay for women while at the same time accusing them of temptation. "Philosophical Satire" was the last poem of Sor Juana's that Concepción copied before her escape from the convent of St. Jerome, and over the course of her eight years in the white wilderness, the poem comes to symbolize Concepción's inscrutable and suspicious Mexican past as well as her lost self at the hands of stubborn men. Like her diasporic longing to return to Mexico, the poem is permanently stitched to her memory. Sor Juana's wisdom, embroidered in Concepción's uncanny calligraphy on the sampler, is the evidence that condemns her to a witch's fate on the gallows. In the mind of the terrified child being socialized to hate everything that her brown mother represents—her alien language, culture, and religion—the poem becomes "the devil's verse."[27]

What happens to Concepción? Does she swing from the gallows like the nineteen victims who were hung for witchcraft in 1692 New England? Does she rot away in the Boston dungeon, like her friend Tituba Indian, waiting for her jail fees to be paid? Does she escape the fate of her difference? And what becomes of her bilingual, half-breed assimilated daughter? Does she lose her mother tongue along with her mother?

There it is again: a story about a woman persecuted, not for being a woman, as is the case of the Juárez femicides, or for her genius, as was Sor Juana's case, but for being *different* in color, language, religion, and place of origin. And isn't the deadly violence against Mexicans in Arizona since 2010 and against all those Mexican women on the border since 1993 a little too reminiscent of modern-day witch hunts? And wasn't Sor Juana herself hunted down, her intellect sacrificed to the Church fathers? And weren't all of them persecuted for being *queer*—gender-queer, color-queer, language-queer, social-queer, body-queer—that is, different from the norm? For all of the ways in which they differ from each other historically and otherwise, these characters resemble each other in at least three of the four ways Foucault discusses in *The Order of Things*: by imitation, by analogy, and by affinity.

> There is something in emulation of the reflection in the mirror: it is the means whereby things scattered through the universe can answer one another. . . . The relation of emulation enables things to imitate one another from one end of the universe to the other without connection or proximity. . . . [The] power of analogy is immense, for the similitudes of which it treats are not the visible, substantial ones between things themselves; they need only be the more subtle resemblances of relations. . . . [S]ympathy is an instance of the *Same* so strong and so insistent that it will not rest content to be merely one of the forms of likeness; it has the dangerous power of *assimilating*, of rendering things identical to one another."[28]

In the raced, classed, and gendered hierarchy that we call hegemony, all women who refuse to abide by patriarchal dictates and a social pecking order based on the rule of the white Father are reflected in the social mirror as "bad women," no matter how "scattered through the universe" or through time they may be; their similitudes may not be immediately apparent, but they are related to each other by virtue of this "bad woman" analogy and by the same punishments and persecutions they suffer for their transgressions. Jack Holland, author of *Misogyny: The World's Oldest Prejudice*, puts it best when he says, "What we call history is merely the tale that patriarchy wants to tell, and misogyny is its ideology, a system of beliefs the aim of which is to explain the domination of men over women."[29] The "bad girls" and "bad women" who interest me, as a writer and a scholar, are the transgressive bodies who queer/alter the male-centric history, politics, and consciousness of Chicana/o culture.

Framing My "Body of Work"

For some time, I have wanted to put together a coherent collection of my previously published academic essays, some written as far back as 1991, while completing my doctoral coursework, and which are scattered about in different journals and anthologies. The epiphany I had thanks to Betita Martínez's question helped me see that rebellious and persecuted "bad girls" were the chosen subjects for my activist scholarship, but I couldn't see the connective theoretical tissue that would help hold together a book. When I commented to my artist wife, Alma López, that the different subjects I've been writing about since the 1990s are all bordered by this "bad woman" ideology, she said (ever the visual artist), "That sounds like a frame." Of course! Sor Juana, La Malinche, Coyolxauhqui, the dead women of Juárez, the Salem witches, Chicana lesbian feminists— these are all *framed bodies*, that is, bodies framed within a particular discourse and patriarchal imperatives, which are capitalist, racist, and imperialist imperatives.

It occurred to me that gender ideologies themselves are framed by time and place, by culture and class, by race and religion. Alma pointed out that framing a piece of art means putting a border or a box around it, so a stereotyped body, a body that is framed by the gender ideologies such as the "bad woman" stereotype, is, in fact, bordered and boxed, contained and fixed. In *Webster's New World College Dictionary* (4th ed.), there are a total of sixteen denotations for the noun form and nine denotations for the verb form of the word *frame*. Framing can be defined as "the way that anything is constructed or put together; a set of circum-stances that serve as background to an event; a condition or state; an established order or system."[30] In photography, a frame is the rectangular image composed of whatever objects, scenery, or people the camera has focused on; in cinematography, a frame is the action and imagery isolated in a second of time; a frame can be the skeletal structure of a house or a body, or one of the ten divisions in a game of bowling, or the armature around a pair of eyeglasses. "To frame" can mean to design, to con-struct, to conceive, to fashion; to put into words; to adapt for a particular fit. But the notion of "framing" is also (and here's where the light bulb really started to blaze in my head) about *blaming* or incriminating some-one for something they didn't do and conspiring to set them up to appear like the guilty parties.

Suddenly, each of the subjects in my essays was standing inside her own time/place/culture/class/race/religion framework, some of which intersected, and all of which were further framed/boxed/blamed by the overarching and all-encompassing social structure of capitalist, imperialist patriarchy.

To be framed, then, is to be

• Bordered/demarcated
• Conceived/imagined
• Isolated/focused
• Constructed/interpreted
• Stereotyped/fixed

- Structured/fastened
- Blamed/accused
- Persecuted/punished

Like a Rubik's cube, all the squares fell into place. I had finally found both the coherent theory (the "bad woman" ideology) and the cogent method (framing, or rather, [un]framing) by which to organize the essays in this book and structure the narrative of my entire research agenda. Because all of the pieces that I wanted to include in the book were about women who had rebelled against the race/class/gender frames imposed by capitalist patriarchy, and because this rebellion was integral to my own development as an activist scholar, I decided to title the book *[Un] Framing the "Bad Woman": Sor Juana, Malinche, Coyolxauhqui, and Other Rebels with a Cause*. I also wanted to play off the 1970s slogan and bumper sticker that signified the beginning of my own feminist consciousness at age thirteen: "Eve Was Framed," pictured on the cover of the August 13, 1971, issue of *Life* magazine next to a drawing of the naked Eve, genitals covered by a fig leaf, holding a red apple.

Although written at different times and for different purposes, the essays collected in *[Un]Framing the "Bad Woman"* look at how specific brown female bodies have been framed by racial, social, cultural, sexual, national/regional, historical, and religious discourses of identity. To anchor their intersecting and sometimes contradictory identities, I focus on the frame of the "bad woman," not as a universalizing gesture that puts all women in this category, but to show that within their specific chronological and societal contexts, Sor Juana, Malinche, Coyolxauhqui, the murdered women of Juárez, the Salem witches, and Chicana lesbian feminists have all been perceived as "bad women," and as such, they have been persecuted and blamed for their own persecution.

Thus, the "bad woman"—the uppity *marisabia*, or know-it-all woman, who exceeded her place, the *chingada* who sold herself, the traitor to her nation, the weeping woman who killed/aborted/abandoned her child, the witchy dark woman, the illegal foreign woman, the girl who "asked for it," the sister who betrayed her brother and killed her mother, the wannabe white woman, the woman who shamed her community/ family by loving another woman—is "framed" for her own failure to succeed or survive. My work, then, is dedicated to *unframing* these "bad women" and rewriting their stories within a revolutionary frame.

Signs from the Universe

A few months after I had the framing conversation with my wife, I received a sign from the Universe that confirmed I was on the right track. It was a Sunday in late September 2010, and I was reading an article in the *Style Magazine* of the Sunday *New York Times* called "Generation Mex" by Randy Kennedy about the new art—visual, cinematic, performance, and culinary—that is being produced in Mexico City, which the author says has "become a kind of Disneyland for a wave of travelers who have been seeking it out recently . . . for its art."[31] Because it's a travel piece, the author writes more about the different restaurants he's experiencing and less about the art or artists pictured in the magazine (among whom are the celebrated Mexican photographer Graciela Iturbide and the actor Diego Luna). I'm enjoying reading about how the creative spirit in Mexico City seems to alchemize from the good conversation and good food served up at restaurant tables, "art bubbling up out of good food and drink and the seemingly endless spool of talk that ties together many of [Mexico City's] creative communities."[32] This resonates with my own experience; many of my own best ideas for a story or a poem have originated at kitchen tables over good meals and especially during the *sobremesa*, or the after-meal conviviality, that can sometimes last for hours.

I don't realize it yet, but the image reproduced as Figure i.1 is putting a spell on me, working its magic into my unconscious. At first glance, it just looks like an abstract sculpture consisting of huge multicolored empty frames, stacked spatially like the vortex of an angular tornado in a landscape of trees and scrub brush. The photographer's name is Raymond Meier, and to the right of the sculpture in the picture, he has positioned a statuesque woman in a flowing yellow and green Versace dress that repeats the colors and geometric shape of the frames. The model is looking beyond the frame of the photograph, away from the center of the vortex, which only draws me deeper into that center. The caption reads: "The singer Mayumi Toyoda of the group Sweetsuite in front of Helen Escobedo's work at the UNAM sculpture garden."

I have never heard of the singer or the sculptor, and I ask Alma to look at the picture. She recognizes the sculpture, says she's seen it at the Universidad Nacional Autónoma de México (UNAM), she's actually stepped inside it. It's only then that it dawns on me why that image snagged my attention. Leaping out at me from the *New York Times Style Magazine* is the visual representation of the *unframed woman* of my title for this book. Here was the connective tissue I had been looking for, the sign of a coherent structure and method for this book. Foucault clarifies what a sign is:

> In its simple state as an idea, or an image, or a perception, associated with or substituted for another, the signifying element is not a sign. It can become a sign only on condition that it manifests, in addition, the relation that links it to what it signifies. It must represent; but that representation, in turn, must also be represented within it.[33]

Not only did that photo in the magazine represent my title, it actually embodied my whole idea of how the "bad woman" stereotype is a recurrent frame of reference for transgressive women in patriarchy, part of a hegemonic discourse of identification, valuation, and domination that frames women's bodies across time, place, and culture. The composition of this picture of Mayumi Toyoda standing beside Escobedo's structure of frames represents the relation between the woman's body and this notion of being framed in both a figurative and a literal way. First, the colors of the dress and the right angles created by the model's stance make her appear to be of a piece with the sculpture, as though a frame had come loose from the structure and become animated into this body of a woman, unframed. The second and more literal representation is that, as a mestiza product of that landscape, part Mexican, part Japanese, Mayumi Toyoda's identity politics are constructed by the intersection of multiple frames—racial, sexual, cultural, geographical, historical—all of which demarcate different aspects of her subjectivity.

Subjectivity is composed of two opposing processes, identification and perception—the many ways we see or identify ourselves, and the ways we are perceived by others. Because our subjectivity is composed of these multiple identities, and because each identity functions like a frame that we claim or inhabit, we can envision a stack of frames stretching out behind us, the way Escobedo's frames stretch behind me in the frontispiece, creating a vortex of selves, meanings, and identity politics, what Gloria Anzaldúa called "a geography of selves," which she defined as "a kind of stacking or layering of selves, horizontal and vertical layers, the geography of selves made up of the different communities you inhabit."[34]

Some of the frames in the vortex are interior frames, that is, they come from within, where we have selected how we want to define ourselves and how we want to structure our reality; but other frames in the vortex (sometimes the biggest and the heaviest) are imposed upon us from the outside, and these exterior frames are often incompatible with our interior frames in the way they contain us by interpretations of our lives and identities that diametrically oppose how we construct and imagine ourselves. Escobedo's structure of frames, then, represents an overarching social frame of reference, as well as a progression of individual frames or identities we inhabit within this social frame; moreover, the sculpture contains the representation of framing within it.

A Brief Detour into Framing Theory

For Erving Goffman in the 1970s, "framing" was a methodology for perceiving, identifying, and interpreting everyday life, as much within the local as within the global registers of experience.[35] In Goffman's view, frames were socially imposed and adopted by individuals to make sense of their experience. Todd Gitlin in the early 1980s applied this notion of framing to analyze how negative media representations of social protest movements created a negative frame that influenced how people thought of those movements. In the same decade, William Gamson et al. took Gitlin's ideas about media framing to the political field to show how "breaking the frame" of an imposed interpretation of social justice events led to reframing those events within alternative interpretations. What they called "reframing acts," then, became the precursors to social justice frames, and led to the use of framing to study collective action. "In its simplest of terms, framing functions in much the same way as a frame around a picture: attention gets focused on what is relevant and important and away from extraneous items in the field of view."[36]

In their 1992 publication, "Master Frames and Cycles of Protest," David Snow and Robert Benford further adapted framing theory to discuss and analyze the interpretive frames of social movements, what they called "collective action frames" that both identified injustices and also motivated social action in protest of those injustices. These collective action, or protest, frames are manufactured by the agents of those movements through a process they call "frame amplification," or the increased focus on one prominent issue, significant event, or important belief relevant to a particular community. Protest frames, in turn, also generate collective identities, as those who participate in these social actions see themselves framed by the politics, ideologies, and meanings that are being produced by their social justice work and that of their predecessors.[37] They see themselves identifying with others who share the same political goals and ideological perspectives, and in so doing, they claim new identities, which become new ways of seeing themselves and organizing their experience within the frame of their collective actions.

Eight years later Benford and Snow clarify the meaning of framing even further as "the conscious strategic efforts by groups of people to fashion shared understandings of the world and of themselves that legitimate and motivate social action."[38] Although Erving Goffman, Todd Gitlin, William Gamson, and Benford and Snow were taken to task for their supposed substitution of the word "framing" for the more politically charged "ideology," and criticized for oversimplifying social movement theory,[39] the frame theory they developed remains at the forefront of social movement research.

In *Beyond the Frame: Women of Color and Visual Representation*, editors Neferti X. M. Tadiar and Angela Y. Davis—both professors in the (alas, now defunct) History of Consciousness program at University of California, Santa Cruz—collaborated with their graduate students in the Research Cluster for the Study of Women of Color to produce a collection of essays that analyze the cultural construction of women of color by looking closely at the photographic frame. Advertisements, album covers, activist periodicals, family albums, and self-portraits all offer different audiences and occasions for the representation of women of color. Looking specifically at the intersection between photography as not just a medium but also an ideological field and the concept of "women of color" as a political not just racial category, the essays in *Beyond the Frame* aim their critical gaze outside of what is actually pictured within the four corners of a photograph to examine the meanings and assumptions about "women of color" that are embedded in each image. Ultimately, the purpose of this analytical approach is, as the editors tell us in their introduction, to

> foreground the processes of production of racial, gender, and sexual differences, and the ways that these historical differences have been deployed both by state and civil apparatuses to secure various cultural logics of domination and by marginalized social groups struggling against those cultural logics to bring about social transformation.[40]

Frames, then, can work with or against social movements, with or against cultural logics of domination or transformation.

"Framing is the process by which sense is made of events," states the sociologist Diana Kendall in her study of the way media representations frame wealth and poverty in the United States.[41] Kendall explains that it is through media representations that we make "sense" of what class means in this country, in other words, how we understand class and how class fits into the logic of capitalism by which we shape our perceptions and judgments about wealth and poverty. Kendall frames her discussion of media framing within value-ridden chapter titles, such as "twenty-four-karat gold frames," to represent the rich and famous; "tarnished metal frames" to represent the working class and the working poor, and "splintered wooden frames" to represent the weakening middle class. Thus, she embodies the very methodology of her study on the framing of class with actual frames, underscoring that, in its most obvious application, framing also means to put a border around a piece of art for purposes of display.

In analyzing the persistence of gender inequalities in contemporary U.S. society, Cecilia Ridgeway, in *Framed by Gender*, argues that the "staying power" of gender inequality

> derives from people's use of *sex* (that is, the physical status of being male or female) and *gender* (shared cultural expectations associated with being male or female) together as a primary frame for organizing the most fundamental of activities: relating to another person . . . the use of gender as a framing device spreads gendered meanings, including assumptions about inequality embedded in those meanings, to all spheres of social life that are carried out through social relationships.[42]

But gender inequalities are not the only inequalities that persist in the twenty-first century. Ridgeway must not forget that gender is also circumscribed by race, class, religion, and nationality in contemporary America. These are other primary social categories by which we who are not white women or men, or U.S. citizens, or middle class, or Christian might classify others, and ourselves, and which include embedded assumptions about superiority, privilege, and power. This is what Kimberle Crenshaw meant by the "intersectionality" of oppressions, or how the particular gendered, raced, and classed bodies of women of color are constructed, represented, and oppressed by hegemonic and intersecting social hierarchies. Intersectionality also explores how the brown female body resists that "matrix of domination," as Patricia Hill Collins named the intersecting "systems of race, social class, gender, sexuality, ethnicity, nation, and age that form mutually constructing features of social organization, which shape our experiences and, in turn, are shaped by us."[43] The "bad woman" stereotype functions like this matrix of domination; it links different systems of oppression that enclose the female body within rigid gender binaries that are also raced, classed, sexed, and otherwise socially constructed, and which prescribe how that bad woman is to be punished, persecuted, arrested, tortured, imprisoned, or killed. As Ridgeway asserts, the persistence of gender framing, and thus domination by gender inequalities, is based on

> two mutually reinforcing social processes. First, we learn from early childhood to automatically sex-categorize any person we attempt to relate to in any concrete way. Second, we also learn early on to associate the categories of male and female with widely shared gender stereotypes that define how the sexes are expected to behave."[44]

We also learn early on to race-categorize, language-categorize, and stereotype by nationality and sexuality. The "bad woman" stereotype is an intrinsic part of the patriarchal gender framing system, which is also intrinsic to a complex network of other oppressive frames.

As we can see by studying ancient legendary women such as Eve, Lilith, Mary Magdalene, Coyolxauhqui, and Medea and their more modern Mexican and Chicana contemporaries La Llorona, La Malinche, and La Maqui-Loca, the frame of the "bad woman" is replicated not only transnationally, transculturally, and transhistorically, but also intra-categorically, within discourses of antiracist resistance and gender/sexual liberation, that is, the sexism and homophobia in the Chicano movement or the classism and racism of the women's movement. The women I write about have all been framed by this matrix of domination, have all rebelled against the imposition of this framework over their lives and bodies, and have all been punished as well as remembered for their rebellion.

Following the Serpent

I can't stop staring at that image of Helen Escobedo's sculpture, marveling at how perfectly it represents my idea for this book, but I realize I know nothing about the artist. On her website, I learn that Helen Escobedo's given name is Elena Escobedo, that she was Mexican on her dad's side and British on her mom's, and, sadly, that she passed away on September 16, 2010, after a two-year battle with cancer. I can't find an image of "the frames piece" anywhere on her website, so I Google her name again with the word "frames" and click on "Images," and finally, after a few false leads, I see pictures of the work taken by other Mexican photographers with other female models standing in front of it, and I learn that the title of the piece is *Coatl*, the Nahuatl word for serpent.

How perfect is that, I say aloud to the ghost of Gloria Anzaldúa, who has suddenly materialized before me, happily swinging her legs off the edge of my desk. I don't believe in coincidences, but serendipity continues to be a galvanizing force for this book. Who could have imagined that by following that image into the cyber collective unconscious of the Internet, I would find such a strong resonance between an abstract sculpture in Mexico City created by a Mexican/British artist in 1980 and the border mestiza theories of Gloria Anzaldúa (also produced in the 1980s), which are anchored in ancient Mexican epistemology?[45] Indeed, the serpent is one of Anzaldúa's primordial symbols for identity and transformation.[46]

Anzaldúa reminds me that "in pre-Columbian America the most notable symbol was the serpent,"[47] which, for the Olmecs and their descendants in Mesoamerica, symbolized creativity; femaleness; and the never-ending cycle of life, death, and rebirth. "The Olmecs associated womanhood with the Serpent's mouth, which was guarded by dangerous teeth, a sort of *vagina dentata*. They considered it the most sacred place

Figure i.5. Side view of Helen Escobedo's *Coatl*, 1980. Metal sculpture. UNAM Sculpture Garden, Ciudad Universitaria, Mexico City. Photo by Alicia Gaspar de Alba.

on earth, a place of refuge, the creative womb from which all things were born and to which all things returned.[48]

Coatl brings to mind Quetzalcoatl, the Plumed Serpent, one of the primary deities of the Mesoamerican peoples, including the Mixtec, the Toltec, and the Maya. The Aztecs venerated Quetzalcoatl as creator of the people of the Fifth Sun, the god of knowledge, civilization, and the priesthood. His legend has many similarities with the legend of Jesus Christ, including his association with a star (Venus), his sacrifice for the redemption of humanity, and his return from the land of the dead. Coatl was the name of the fifth day on the Count of Days and protected by the goddess Chalchiuhtlicue, "She of the Jade Skirt." But it's "She of the Serpent Skirt," Coatlicue, that I see represented in Escobedo's *Coatl*. As the great mother of the Aztec gods, Coatlicue was the goddess of birth and death.

> [Coatlicue] represents duality in life, a synthesis of duality, and a third perspective—something more than mere duality or a synthesis of duality . . . *Coatlicue depicts the contradictory*. In her figure, all the symbols [the serpent, the heart, the hands, the skulls, the eagle talons, the feathers, the breasts] important to the religion and philosophy of the Aztecs are integrated. Like Medusa, the Gorgon, she is a symbol of *the fusion of opposites*: the eagle and the serpent, heaven and the underworld, life and death, mobility and immobility, beauty and horror.[49] (emphasis added)

To be swallowed by Coatlicue, Anzaldúa explains—which is a crucial first step on the journey toward mestiza consciousness[50]—is to be plunged into the state of physical and psychic immobility that she terms the Coatlicue State. The Coatlicue State is usually brought on by illness or depression or crisis, when all of the contradictory parts of the self must face each other in a psychic showdown culminating in the death of one part and the birth of another, a metaphoric shedding of skins, a transformation that leads to increased consciousness of the self. For Anzaldúa, in her incarnation as Cihuacoatl, or Snake Woman, the Serpent also symbolized something else, "the dark sexual drive, the chthonic (underworld), the feminine, the serpentine movement of sexuality, of creativity, the basis of all energy and life."[51]

Just as the snake sheds skins as it matures, so do humans shed identities, so do queer and mestiza bodies, through a process of self-awareness and ideological border crossing that Anzaldúa calls "mestiza consciousness," shed those systems of domination that have kept them rooted to an abject sense of self. Now, Escobedo's piece itself is framed not only by the pre-Columbian history associated with the word *coatl*, but also, by an Anzaldúan theory of consciousness that is predicated by releasing the power of the feminine—the creative and destructive power of Coatlicue—through the body; for Anzaldúa, that power was released through her writing, but it manifests in all forms of creativity, as well as in activism and spiritual practice.

Someone not familiar with this Mexican history or this Chicana theory would not experience Escobedo's work in the same way and might see it just as an abstract pile of multicolored frames or a good background for a photograph in a travel article. However, the fact that the piece, along with six other large abstract metal sculptures, is installed on the grounds of the main campus of the National Autonomous University of Mexico,[52] which is known for its mosaic murals of pre-Columbian icons and motifs by Juan O'Gorman, as well as the murals of David Alfaro Siqueiros, presupposes an educated Mexican audience, one that at the very least has seen and studied Aztec glyphs, knows the revolutionary content of Mexican muralism, and recognizes the Aztec referent (if not the Chicana take on that referent) and the indigenous/nationalistic past that it all represents.

Presenting the Absent

In "The Frame of Representation and Some of Its Figures," Louis Marin explains the double work involved in the process of artistic representation:

> To represent first means to substitute something present for something absent . . . This substitution is clearly ruled by a mimetic economy; the postulated similarity of the present and the absent authorize this substitution. Yet to represent can also mean to display, to exhibit something that is present. Here it is the very act of presenting that constructs the identity of that which is represented, that identifies it as such . . . in other words, to represent signifies to present oneself representing something. Every representation, every representational sign, every process of signification thus comprises two dimensions . . . first, reflexive—to present oneself—and second, transitive—to represent something.[53]

Coatl is a presentation of Helen Escobedo representing a pre-Columbian serpent, symbol of life, death, and rebirth. It is presented by a structure composed of twenty square metal frames, approximately 20 feet high by 20 feet wide, mounted on cement bases and arranged spatially to suggest, or imitate, the cylindrical body of a 15-meter-long (49-foot-long) snake.

The title plaque of the piece (Figure i.6) is a few feet away, heavily tagged and barely visible now, but it is the only clue that tells the viewer about the transitive meaning of the work: the Nahuatl word, *coatl*, representing the absence of the indigenous past that the piece is making present. Without knowing the title, we see only the frames and the twisting tunnel they create, isolated in a natural landscape that is populated by other abstract metal sculptures with Aztec-sounding names or allusions like *Ocho Conejo* (1980) by Federico Silva, and *Colotl* (1978) by Sebastián.[54] Like something out of *Alice in Wonderland*, a square rabbit hole pulling us relentlessly into its slanting depths, we are drawn into Escobedo's piece almost as if through a vertiginous time tunnel or a carnivalesque hall of brightly colored mirrors where the mirrors are absent, and we see not distorted reflections of ourselves but our bodies framed within a hollow field of representation. We become subject and viewer simultaneously, and the playfulness of the colors, the warm reds, oranges, and yellows of the spectrum, as well as the dynamic movement in the spatial arrangement of the frames, invites us like the rides in a playground: the spinning merry-go-round, the swing, the slide, the jungle gym. We are momentarily transformed as we experience the piece from end to end, so that even without knowing the title or the Aztec symbolism for transformation that it represents, we enact the "mimetic economy" of a snake shedding its skin. Like its hollow field of representation, the pre-Columbian history embedded in the piece is transparent, invisible, nonexistent except in the collective unconscious of the Mexican psyche, buried under the signs of an urban, industrialized life like the title under the graffiti.

For Helen Escobedo, a favorite theme of her sculptures was an "emphasis on transparency," whether her materials were solid steel or bronze or fiberglass. In her obituary in *The Guardian*, we learn of her philosophy of sculpture: "I did not want to stand out, I wanted to merge with nature. I did not need background, I wanted to be background. I did not want to interfere with but wanted to enhance what was already there."[55] Thus, the "very act of presenting" the absent pre-Columbian past in a series of empty frames "constructs the identity" of *Coatl* as a hollow shell or shed skin, the remnants of the Aztec past still clinging to the landscape on the outskirts of Mexico City.

Figure i.6. Title panel of Helen Escobedo's *Coatl*, 1980. UNAM Sculpture Garden, Ciudad Universitaria, Mexico City. Photo by Alicia Gaspar de Alba.

The Frame Speaks

In *The Rhetoric of the Frame*, editor Paul Duro argues that a frame around a painting or a photograph, or a pedestal under a statue, has a function beyond simply enclosing, protecting, or embellishing the art. Instead, he believes, "the frame serves to create a space for the artwork that the work in itself is incapable of furnishing,"[56] and thus, the frame and the art piece together constitute the rhetoric of the work, the way the work speaks to us, and what it says. Building on Jacques Derrida's concept of the "parergon," or limits of the frame, and on Immanuel Kant's notion of the frame as a complement to the art, Duro's collection aims to bring the space of the frame—as background, context, border, or "ideological signifier of value"—out of invisibility.[57]

Whatever may seem abstruse to the reader in the theories outlined above becomes perfectly clear when embodied in the example of a painting by Leonardo da Vinci that I saw at an exhibition of his sketches at the Getty Center in West Los Angeles. Most of the drawings on display were small pages from da Vinci's notebooks, showing different sketches of his most iconic work. The Getty had installed the Maestro's unfinished painting of *St. Jerome* (ca. 1480) in a deep niche painted a dark chocolate color, set apart from the rest of the exhibition, where it occupied the entire back wall of the niche. The 29" x 41" piece was framed in a thick, gold, ornate frame that extended the dimensions of the piece by at least 10 inches all around. The frame had a ledge or cornice at the bottom, making it seem more like an altar than an unfinished painting of the loin-clothed, half-starved hermit saint, patron of librarians and archivists and translator of the Old Testament from Hebrew into Latin.

What intensified the sense of "holiness" exuded by the piece was its placement, or framing, not only within the lavish, gilded border but also within this dark niche, separate from the rest of the show, commanding all of the light in the space and drawing the viewer's attention to the

Figure i.7. Leonardo Da Vinci, *St. Jerome*, circa 1480. Oil on wood, 103 x 75 cm. Pinacoteca, Vatican Museums, Vatican State. Photo credit: Scala/Art Resource, NY.

penitent holy man, the virile lion at his feet, the golden aura around the saint's bald head, the jagged lines of his rapturous face etched to perfection but unpainted. Although we are supposed to marvel at the realism and precision of da Vinci's drawing skill and the rarity of the item on display, which hails from the Vatican Museums, the framing and staging of the piece practically demanded that the viewer get on her knees to venerate the permanence of the saint, the artist, and the Catholic faith. Suddenly, Derrida and Kant made perfect sense, and I understood what Duro meant by "the rhetoric of the frame."

With these ideas in mind, I concluded that the rhetoric of Escobedo's *Coatl* was an inversion of da Vinci's *St. Jerome*; rather than valuing a single, elite subject fixed within its golden frame for eternity, Escobedo's piece makes the viewer the subject, which changes as often as new viewers/subjects literally step into the frame. Thus, *Coatl* has multiple subjects, human and wildlife alike. On any given day, the piece can be visited/inhabited by students, teachers, tourists, taggers, drunks, aerosol artists, children, homeless people, dogs, cats, birds, and literal snakes—all held within that invisible body signifying life, death, and rebirth. Rather than isolated within a dark, enclosed space inside an elite museum, Escobedo's piece is installed in an outdoor landscape of trees and scrub brush, sunlight and shadow, flora and fauna, a more natural habitat, if you will, for the eponymous snake referenced in the title. Indeed, *Coatl*, like the other six massive sculptures installed in the outdoor Espacio Escultórico of the UNAM,[58] was made to invite movement within:

> The sculptures are geometric forms developed in various meters and in all directions, made for movement within them, and in some cases, to be penetrated by the viewer, as by the very air of the place, because the formal and spatial continuity is part of the very environment conditioned by each piece, which means that the sculptures do not end in the limits of the materials that construct them, but rather, that each one suggests its proper prolongation, the air passes through them, and continues across them.[59]

Instead of the background appearing within the field of representation inside the frame, the work is framed by the background and merged with the background. More than attracting the viewer's sustained gaze, it awakens a desire to participate in the piece, to climb inside it, to take pictures and frame ourselves being framed by the frames. Instead of evoking stillness in the viewer to facilitate veneration of a single image, the piece invites the irreverent practice of tagging a work of art in the same way one would tag a bathroom wall.[60] The graffiti marking the girders as well as the cement bases suggests a confluence of high art and popular art, and so the piece is imbued with both an institutional and a tribal past.

In fact, the graffiti completes the cyclical process implied by the title, embodying the contradictory essence of *coatl* as a creative and a destructive force. Its placement in the Espacio Escultórico of the UNAM campus provides another frame for the piece—not just a university setting, but the oldest university in the Americas marking its quincentenary with the creation of this outdoor sculptural space, but also an urban context, one of the largest metropolises in the world representing "the vanguard of modernization in Mexico."[61]

When I actually visited the piece and stood within its representational space, I felt caught in a quantum time zone where I was simultaneously one of three different twenty-first-century mestiza lesbian bodies standing in her own set of frames, and part of a collective experience rooted in Aztec, Toltec, and Mayan myth as well as colonial history. I was connected to the other bodies in the photo by virtue of that shared past that embraced us like that vortex of frames.

By connecting the frames to the concept of snakeskins, as well as to the theories of intersectionality, the matrix of domination, and mestiza consciousness, *Coatl* the art piece by Helen Escobedo and *coatl* the "bad woman" stereotype that slithers across time periods, cultures, and nations serve as the mythic links between not only colonial and postcolonial Mexico, but also between Mexico and Aztlán. This "bad woman" framework stretches back in Chicana/o chronographic memory and links La Malinche to Sor Juana Inés de la Cruz to the Chicana "gender nationalists"[62] of the Chicano movement to the so-called Maqui-Locas of the U.S.-Mexico border, and even to the accused witches of Salem.

Revenge of the "Bad Girls"

The "bad woman" stereotype is not an objet d'art created by an artist, but an artifice of patriarchy created to oppress women and at the same time promote the interests of men. The women who are the subjects of the essays collected here have all struggled against the cultural logic of capitalist, racist, heterosexist, phallocentric domination, wittingly or by necessity. Some, such as the femicide victims on the border and the condemned witches in Salem, paid a deadly price. Others, like Sor Juana, who was persecuted relentlessly by the Church fathers for her refusal to fit within the mold of a good, submissive, and, most of all, silent bride of Christ, were "bludgeoned into submission." Others continue to struggle, in the academy, in their communities, in their homes. In the process, they have created new and indelible frames by which to perceive, interpret, and understand our daily lives; they have, as Gloria Anzaldúa advised, made theory out of flesh and flesh into theory. Because of how they represent and implement change, which is also encoded in the body of the snake with each molting, these subjects, these "bad women," I argue, must be reframed as revolutionaries/*revolucionarias*, in the way that Alma López reframes the image of the Virgin of Guadalupe with her 1999 photo collage, the very controversial *Our Lady* (see Figure 6.2), as "the poster image for the first successful act of mass nonviolent civil resistance/disobedience on this continent."[63] As Clara Pinkola Estes argues, seeing La Virgen de Guadalupe as the minimized "*virgencita*," or docile little virgin, bound to one race, one tradition, one interpretation, is a view that "diminishes her: she is made into the quiescent 'good girl' in phony opposition to . . . the less quiescent 'bad girl.'"[64]

To answer Betita's question with which I began this introduction, I guess you could say that not only my novels but also my entire academic enterprise, from research to publishing to teaching, is a celebration of rebellious, revolutionary women in Chicana/o and Mexicano history, and a reinvention of their lives from a radical politics of recognition and a social justice perspective. I employ an interdisciplinary methodology of the body that encompasses both sides of the brain to include fiction, poetry, feminist and cultural theory, and critical analysis with the avenging spirit of the Furies. But mine is a fury fueled by what Chela Sandoval calls "oppositional consciousness," a methodology of the oppressed that "engages the technologies of semiotics, deconstruction, meta-ideologizing, democratics, and differential movement . . . [to] comprise a hermeneutic for defining and enacting oppositional social action as a mode of 'love' in the postmodern world."[65] This love—a painful awareness or psychic rupture or puncture that Sandoval calls a "punctum," borrowing from Roland Barthes, or a "Coatlicue State," borrowing from Anzaldúa[66]— is rooted in a deep love for my culture, for the women of my culture, and for the queer, those who dare to be different, and dare to preach and practice the rebellious politics of equality and social justice. I agree with Sandoval, invoking Che Guevara and Paulo Freire,[67] that "it is love that can access and guide our theoretical and political '*movidas*'— revolutionary maneuvers toward decolonized being."

The work of women-loving artists like Alma López will live on in perpetuity, whether on our walls, on our bookshelves, or in cyberspace. Sor Juana left a legacy of early feminist thought that challenged the double standards of "stubborn men" and asserted a woman's right to share her mind and her work with the world and with posterity. Malinche, the Salem "witches," and the Juárez Maqui-Locas have all left their own indelible marks in cultural memory, and their lives and tragic deaths will continue to be written about, scripted, painted, filmed, sung, and studied across the world. Our Chicana-feminist-centered art, literature, and scholarship, indeed all of what we make, write, and leave to the world as evidence of our revolutionary love is what I call "revenge of the bad girls."

Chapter Summaries

I have organized the book chronologically to show the development of my activist scholarship and interdisciplinary methodology as a cultural critic. Chapter 1, "The Politics of Location of La Décima Musa: Prelude to an Interview," based on a paper that I wrote in 1991, while a graduate student at the University of New Mexico, in which I "interviewed" Sor Juana Inés de la Cruz with questions framed within twentieth-century feminist theory, to which Sor Juana "responded" with excerpts of her published poetry and prose, was published originally in 1998 in the collection *Living Chicana Theory*, edited by Carla Trujillo. The piece had a slightly different title, and frames what would become for me a lifelong, ongoing dialogue and intervention into the mind, body, and heart of this foremother of Chicana feminism.

Chapter 2, "Malinche's Revenge," a shorter version of which I wrote in 1999 for a talk I presented at the conference "U.S. Latino/a Perspectives on La Malinche," held at the University of Illinois at Urbana-Champaign, was published six years later (2005) in the proceedings of that conference, *Feminism, Nation and Myth: La Malinche* (edited by Rolando Romero and Amanda Nolacea Harris). In this piece, I look at the commonalities between the white male symbolic order and the racist politics of the Mexican caste system as well as the misogynistic politics of Mexican and Chicano patriarchy to show how Chicana lesbian feminists "have begun to transform the story of [the treacherous] Malinche into a mirror of Chicana resistance against female slavery to [the laws of the penis]."

Chapter 3, "There's No Place Like Aztlán: Homeland Myths and Embodied Aesthetics," is a substantially expanded version of "There's No Place Like Aztlán: Embodied Aesthetics in Chicana Art," published originally in 2004 in *The New Centennial Review*. In this piece, I explore the connections between identity and place as nutrient sources for aesthetic practice in the artistic creations of exiled or displaced people. By looking at several place-based aesthetic systems such as the diasporic aesthetics of some Cuban, Filipino, and Latin American artists; the indigenous aesthetics of Native American artists; and the Aztlán aesthetics of the Chicano art movement, I investigate to what degree identity goes beyond questions of national origin or geographical location to incorporate other signifiers of the homeland such as religion, community, or the body—other ways of framing the representation of place—in the work of four Chicana artists. I also provide a graph by which to track the intersecting meanings of the land base known simultaneously as the West and el Norte, the virgin land and the homeland, the frontier and Aztlán.

Chapter 4, "Coyolxauhqui and Las 'Maqui-Locas': Re-Membering the Sacrificed Daughters of Ciudad Juárez," is an expanded version of "Poor Brown Female: The Miller's Compensation for 'Free Trade,'" which I published in an anthology on the murdered women of Juárez titled *Making a Killing: Femicide, Free Trade and La Frontera* (2010) that I coedited with my then graduate student Georgina Guzmán. Beginning with the myth of the dismembered sister of the Aztec war god as an example of what happens to women in patriarchal cultures who dare to challenge the brother's or the father's authority, the piece looks more deeply into the working conditions of the maquiladoras, the social discourse of the "bad woman" that blames the victims for their own deaths, the different meanings of and punishment for rape in the Mexican penal codes, and the possible link between the inordinate number of registered sex offenders who are sent by the Texas Parole Board to live out their conditional release in El Paso and the increasing numbers of sex crimes in Juárez.

Chapter 5, "Mapping the Labyrinth: The Anti–Detective Novel and the Mysterious Missing Brother" (unpublished, but written in 2011), looks at my process of writing *Desert Blood: The Juárez Murders*. Although I intended to use the popular genre of detective fiction to raise consciousness about this epidemic of murdered young Mexican women on the border, with the hope of informing the widest possible English-speaking audience, I was caught in the significant conundrum of both employing the trappings of the detective novel genre and subverting the genre's quest for resolution and symbolic restoration of social order. Because there was no resolution to the Juárez femicides, my detective's quest would be a fruitless one, but the purpose of the book, I was to discover later, was to lead my detective into a labyrinth of clues and conspiracies, and expose the different theories that I had unraveled in the course of my research into the post-NAFTA political economy of the U.S.-Mexico border, which to me explained the silence and the impunity of the crimes. Without knowing it, I had been writing an "anti–detective novel," which I found to be a very apt methodology for social protest, a form that I will continue to use in my activist scholarship and social justice pedagogy.

Chapter 6, "Devil in a Rose Bikini: The Inquisition Continues," is an updated version of "Devil in a Rose Bikini: The Second Coming of Our Lady in Santa Fe" that I published originally in *Our Lady of Controversy: Alma López's "Irreverent Apparition"* (2011), a text I coedited with my wife, Alma López. In this chapter, I look at social responses to both *Our Lady*, the art piece, and the controversy that ensued in turn-of-the-twenty-first-century Santa Fe for Alma López's supposed sacrilege against the Virgin of Guadalupe by representing her as a Chicana Everywoman showing bare abs and legs, arms akimbo, and framed by roses.

Perhaps the most galling aspect of López's representation for the protestors was not only the bare female flesh visible outside of her rose bikini (although for some, this was enough reason to censor the piece from the exhibition and lynch the artist with the rope of social stigma), but also the defiant stance and gaze of the model, whose expression is not one of subservience or forgiveness but rather an assertion of pride in her womanhood, an attitude that commands the same respect for the female body as that given to La Virgen. I provide an in-depth analysis of the protest by comparing the different audience responses to the work, as seen in the comment book of the museum, the media coverage, and especially the public spectacles and performance art of the protest, the staged processions and pilgrimages that simultaneously decried and created an irreverent apparition. In this updated version, I include a new conclusion that looks at two recent manifestations of the controversy spawned by the America Needs Fatima Inquisition against *Our Lady* and *Our Lady of Controversy* in Oakland, California, and Cork, Ireland.

Chapter 7, "The Sor Juana Chronicles" (also unpublished, and finished in 2013) compares four fictional chronicles of the life of Sor Juana Inés de la Cruz—Dorothy Schons's unpublished novel manuscript, "Sor Juana: A Chronicle of Old Mexico" (circa 1930s), archived in the Benson

38   [Un]Framing the "Bad Woman"

Library at the University of Texas at Austin; Estela Portillo Trambley's three-act play, "Sor Juana" (1983); my own *Sor Juana's Second Dream* (1999); and Paul Anderson's *Hunger's Brides* (2005)—to examine the diverse Sor Juanas that Sor Juana herself understood she would be constructed as. In the lines to an unfinished poem that was among the last pieces she was writing before she died in 1695, Sor Juana wrote, "diverse from myself / I exist between your plumes / not as I am, but as you / have wanted to imagine me." The "you" she is addressing are in fact her readers and critics; thus, I argue, she gives us license to imagine her any way our heart desires—as a conquered Sor Juana, a penitent Sor Juana, a hungry Sor Juana, or, in my case, a lesbian Sor Juana. To construct my woman-loving Tenth Muse, I employ the "radical politics of *re-conocimiento*," which extends Anzaldúa's epistemology of the self that she calls "*conocimiento*" into a praxis of recognizing the self in the Other in the narrative mirroring and reframing of Sor Juana's life.

In all, this book reflects the academic productivity of my first twenty years at UCLA, interspersed with three novels, three anthologies, a monograph on Chicano art, and other scribblings.

Figure 1.1. Teyali Falcón, *Athena among Calla Lilies*, © 1999. Oil on canvas, 14 x 18 in. In the collection of Alicia Gaspar de Alba.

Chapter 1

THE POLITICS OF LOCATION OF LA DÉCIMA MUSA

Prelude to an Interview

For the past five years, I have been living with Sor Juana in my head, my heart, and my dreams. I have been researching her life, listening to the underside of her words, letting her entrap and guide me through the webs of logic, pun, and metaphor that she so meticulously spun in her writing. She converses with me constantly, but ours has not been just a scholarly or critical relationship. She wants me to narrate her story, to write a novel about her through both her eyes and mine. Her vision—that of an intellectual, intrepid seventeenth-century Mexican nun, scholar, and poet struggling against the subjection of her female body—appears in her poetry, her prose, and her plays, and is filtered through my vision, that of a twentieth-century Chicana lesbian writer who can claim the choices and identities not available to Sor Juana, even though she constructed them quite lyrically in her "scribblings." It is through our combined visions that I introduce you to Sor Juana Inés de la Cruz.

Biographical Overview

She was born in 1648, in the small Mexican town of San Miguel de Nepantla. The third "natural" daughter of Doña Isabel Ramírez, she was baptized as Juana Inés Ramírez, "daughter of the Church," a euphemism for daughter born out of wedlock, the patriarchal institution of legitimacy. From her earliest years, she was attracted to learning, and at the age of three, she managed to convince her sisters' teacher to give her reading lessons. At six or seven, as she relates in her famous intellectual autobiography, *Respuesta a Sor Filotea de la Cruz*, "having learned how to read and write, along with all the other skills of needlework and household arts that girls learn,"[1] she was ready to attend the University of Mexico; all her mother had to do, she said, was dress her in boy's clothing and send her to live with relatives in Mexico City. Because her mother refused to grant her bold request, Juana Inés dedicated herself to reading all of the books in her grandfather's library, despite continuous scoldings and punishments.

Doña Isabel and her three daughters lived in Panoayan, on the outskirts of Mexico City, at the foot of the volcanoes Popocatépetl and Ixtaccíhuatl. The hacienda belonged to Doña Isabel's father, Don Pedro Ramírez. It is known that Juana Inés felt a strong attachment to her grandfather; not only was he her surrogate father, but she was his *consentida* (favorite), and they shared a love of letters and books that clearly fostered her scholarly nature.

When Juana Inés was eight, her grandfather died and her mother gave birth to her first half sibling, a brother named Diego. For reasons that critics can't explain with any certainty, Juana Inés was sent to live in Mexico City with Doña Isabel's wealthy sister and brother-in-law. Critics have wondered what motivated Doña Isabel to dispose of her eight-year-old daughter under what must have been very emotionally abusive circumstances for the child. Some critics have suggested that economic duress was the cause of Doña Isabel's decision; others believe that Doña Isabel's new consort did not like Juana Inés and wanted her out of his way. Yet others surmise that the girl's recalcitrant "oddness," her attachment to books, her curious and hermetic nature, made her mother deeply uncomfortable. One thing is certain: Doña Isabel was not sending her daughter away to school.

Nonetheless, Juana Inés persisted in her pursuit of knowledge. During the eight years that she lived with her aunt and uncle in Mexico City, Juana Inés, with the help of her books and her inkwell, taught herself. She enjoyed visiting bookstores on her own and participant-observing the metropolis around her, renouncing certain foods (such as cheese) that she thought contributed to a slow mind. She learned Latin grammar in twenty lessons, denying herself the pleasure of long hair until she had learned what she had set out to learn, for, in her young but disciplined mind, she saw "no cause for a head to be adorned with hair and naked of learning."[2] In lyrical vignettes, Margarita López-Portillo's *Estampas de Sor Juana Inés de la Cruz* tells that Juana Inés had a male tutor for these lessons, one Don Martín de Olivas, an undergraduate at the university, who also introduced her to the texts of Homer, Ovid, and the like.[3] Perhaps it was he who helped shape Sor Juana's opinion of male teachers, which she relates in the interview.

In 1664, during Juana Inés's sixteenth year, a new viceroy and vicereine arrived from Spain and moved into the palace in Mexico City. By this time, the rumors of Juana Inés's erudition had already spread throughout the city, and the vicereine, La Marquesa Leonor Carreto de Mancera, devoted patroness of the arts, lost no time in extending an invitation to Juana Inés's uncle to present the girl scholar of New Spain at court. Sor Juana does not record what the interview was like, but she must have greatly impressed the viceroy and vicereine because from her sixteenth year to her twentieth year, she lived at the palace as a lady-in-waiting to the vicereine. One of the most popular stories about her stay at the viceregal court recounts the time the viceroy sponsored a tournament between nineteen-year-old Juana Inés and approximately forty scholars, including historians, mathematicians, theologians, philosophers, and poets. For the outcome of the tournament, I turn to the words of the viceroy: "In the manner that a royal galleon might fend off the attacks of a few canoes, so did Juana extricate herself from the questions, arguments and objections these many men, each in his specialty, directed to her."[4]

We must remember, however, that those were dangerous times for an intelligent and independent female; the spies of the Holy Inquisition lurked in every household. Literacy for criolla[5] girls was tolerable, even desirable in some circles; genius was another story. Fortunately for Juana Inés, the Inquisitors of Mexico did not take her as seriously as the French Inquisitors took Joan of Arc; and, later, when her fame was as vast as her knowledge, she had very powerful protectors in the Mexican viceroys, at least until 1688.

It is believed that shortly after the tournament, Juana Inés experienced three months at a Carmelite convent. Her reasons for entering the severely ascetic order of Barefoot Carmelites is unknown, but three months later, she had returned to the palace. In his 658-page biography of Sor Juana, Octavio Paz discounts the theory that illness brought her back to the palace; instead, he believes that Juana Inés was not cut out for the ascetic life. Within a year and a half, however, she was signing her testament of faith to the Order of Saint Jerome, which was, Paz informs us, "an order known for the mildness of its discipline."[6] The order was so mild, in fact, that the nuns were permitted to own slaves, jewels, and property. The nuns' cells were two-story apartments, complete with kitchens and parlors. Sor Juana, it is known, had a substantial library, a collection of musical and scientific instruments, and an assortment of souvenirs given to her by the nobles who often visited her in the convent. She also had investments in convent property and owned a slave, a mulatto woman named Juana de San José, given to her by her mother when she signed her temporal vows.

Convent life consisted of a number of rituals, most of which were "repugnant" to Sor Juana, as she confesses in her autobiographical *Respuesta a Sor Filotea de la Cruz*. Anything that might disturb her studies—be that the seven canonical hours during which the sisters congregated to pray, or quibbling maids in the courtyard, or visits from other sisters during the siesta and recreation hours—interrupted the solitude she needed to concentrate on her research and her writing. Obviously, she had not joined the convent to marry Christ, although it was because marriage was her only other alternative and because she felt, as she says, "total antipathy for marriage" that she donned the veil. She also deemed the convent the most fitting place to "insure [her] salvation."[7]

A radical feminist analysis of a few of Sor Juana's poems, particularly the requiems she wrote for La Marquesa de Mancera, the vicereine who took her under her wing, and all of the poems she wrote for another vicereine, María Luisa Manrique de Lara y Gonzaga, or La Condesa de Paredes, will explain not only why Sor Juana chose to live a separatist life by joining the convent but also why she was concerned for her salvation. Both during and before her bride-of-Christ days, Sor Juana was often criticized for being too "masculine," that is, for indulging her mind too much, for speaking out, for reading and writing, for not being submissive to her superiors. Such crimes were punishable by the Inquisition, no small threat to seventeenth-century New Spain, let alone to a woman with an inclination for knowledge and a disinclination for men.

Of course, Nobel laureate Octavio Paz, who is considered (and no doubt considers himself) the foremost authority on Sor Juana, would radically disagree with such a radical feminist analysis. Octavio Paz is not the only one of Sor Juana's critics and biographers to declare that there was nothing "abnormal" (to use their word) about Sor Juana; still, Paz is unique because instead of simply dismissing the possibility, he tries to prove that any traces of "masculinity" that may have surfaced in Sor Juana's character derive from a combination of psychic traumas: melancholia, subjection to the Church, compensation for the absent father, menopause, and, perhaps, even a courtly love affair (with a man, of course) gone awry. Paz draws a complex analysis of Sor Juana's intense friendship with La Condesa, arriving at the conclusion, by way of some very Freudian and, need I add, homophobic logic, that both women were suffering from "an excess of libido," which, moreover, did not have an outlet in the opposite sex. "A different object," says Paz, "—a female friend—had to take its place." Thus evolved what Paz calls the "platonic love-friendship" between Sor Juana and the countess.[8]

We are indebted to La Condesa for having the first anthology of Sor Juana's poetry published when she and her husband returned to Spain. The volume was released in 1689, bearing as one of its subtitles: *La décima musa de América*, the Tenth Muse of America. She was not the first "tenth muse," however. The Greek lesbian poet Sappho was baptized with that epithet by Plato seventeen hundred years earlier. It is doubtful that Sor Juana did not know this bit of literary trivia, but Paz would twist his tongue around in his mouth to make us believe that La Condesa's allusion to Sappho (it was La Condesa, after all, who titled the book) was but a baroque compliment to the sublimity of Sor Juana's verse.

In the last five years of her life, Sor Juana experienced, first, international recognition as a writer and then, her fall from grace. Despite the fact that La Condesa and her husband left Mexico in 1688, Sor Juana and La Condesa engaged in a prolific correspondence, which, unfortunately, has been lost to us. Between 1689 and 1691, two volumes of her writings were published in Spain. In 1690, she wrote what she calls "a little trifle"[9] she titled *Primero sueño* [First dream] the most difficult, the most tangled, the most arcane of Sor Juana's "scribblings," as she called her writing. Thanks to Luis Harss, we have an English translation of the work in which he not only translates from Spanish to English, but also annotates Sor Juana's imagery, symbolism, and allusions in the context of the scholarly traditions and esoteric mysteries upon which they draw. The gist of *Primero sueño* is also the gist of Sor Juana's life: in the darkness, she seeks knowledge and freedom, a solitary journey guided by a spirit that is enemy to daylight, a quest for the dark truths within the universe and within herself that ends in failure, in waking up to the light of reason. For me, *Primero sueño* is a prophetic work, predicting what would happen to Sor Juana within the next five years.

In 1691, she wrote the autobiographical *Respuesta a Sor Filotea de la Cruz*, which, although published posthumously, created concentric circles of scandal within the clerical community in which it circulated. *Respuesta* is perhaps Sor Juana's most important work for those interested in the details of her life as well as in her intellectual discourse and writer's craft, but it is also the source of Sor Juana's downfall. It was in *Respuesta* that Sor Juana revealed the depth and scope of her intelligence and powers of logic. Here it was that she expressed her negative feelings about marriage, her "natural impulse" for learning, her rebelliousness as a child, her displeasure with the other nuns who envied and persecuted her for her studies, her indulgence in melancholia, and finally, what we could call her feminism, her defense of a woman's right to learn and develop her mind for the purpose of exalting her soul.

Respuesta was Sor Juana's last manuscript. In 1692, (the same year that the witch craze hit New England), Luis Harss tells us,

Sor Juana gave away her books and instruments . . . and signed gloomy Church documents renouncing the world and renewing her vows as a nun . . . At least one of these papers—a Profession of Faith signed "the worst of women"—was written in her blood . . . So Sor Juana may have gone through a spiritual crisis, or allowed herself to be finally bludgeoned into submission.[10]

Once, Sor Juana had called herself both martyr and executioner, and now, the very instrument that she had relied on for liberation was signing her own bill of sale to the Church. What happened? Why did she give up? It is my theory that she was a victim of an ultimatum. As powerful as her protectors had once been, she now faced not just her confessor, her Mother Superior, and the rest of the convent, but the archbishop of Mexico and the Holy Office as well. Their ultimatum must have been quite simple: either prostrate yourself to the Church or be publicly humiliated in the Quemadero (the place set aside for burning heretics). After renouncing her books and her studies, Sor Juana devoted herself to nursing the nuns who had fallen prey to an unidentified plague that scourged New Spain.

Almost 320 years ago, on April 17, 1695, at four o'clock in the morning, the woman who is today hailed as the "Tenth Muse of America" died of plague in a convent in Mexico City. She was not yet forty-seven years old and had spent twenty-seven of those years cloistered in the convent, separated from the world, writing, reading, learning, fighting for her rights, and hiding (though not very effectively at times) the spade that her critics and biographers have called everything but a spade: her lesbianism.

Colonial Feminism

The life of Sor Juana Inés de la Cruz offers fertile opportunities for feminist scholarship, particularly for that branch concerned with the theories and questions that constitute a woman's politics of identity specifically because of her "location in a female body."[11] In "Relating to Privilege," Aida Hurtado points out that white women have a privileged relationship to white men and are, therefore, guilty of perpetrating a similar domination over women of color as that practiced by white men over white women. While the white women who were canonized as pioneers for women's rights were *married* to [rich] white men, Hurtado explains, black women who were fighting against the multiple oppressions of race, class, and gender were *owned* by white men. "Relating to privilege," then, breaks down to two primary subordinations: seduction and rejection. White men seduce white women into being their lovers and wives so that they may bear racially "pure" offspring who will inherit and perpetuate the status quo; women of color, on the other hand, are rejected by white men because they would reproduce racially mixed offspring who would threaten the white male privilege.[12] Interestingly, Sor Juana both seduced and rejected white men. Certainly, her beauty, wit, and rhetoric seduced the nobles and aristocrats (not to mention their wives) who sought her company as much in the "galanteos de palacios"[13] as in the *tertulias* she held in the convent; however, she also rejected white men for the same reasons that white men reject women of color: reproduction. Her rejection of what Adrienne Rich calls "compulsory heterosexuality"[14] meant that she would be nobody's mother, wife, or mistress.

One of the more popular epithets attached to the name of Sor Juana Inés de la Cruz is "first feminist of the Americas." That Sor Juana was considered the "first" feminist implies a class privilege, for if she had not been of the educated class, if she had not had the protection and support of the viceregal court and the ecclesiastical council of seventeenth-century New Spain, if she had not entered one of the wealthiest and most prestigious convents, she would not have had the political connections necessary for getting her work published and distributed, solicited and reviewed.

Criollo academics like Paz "validate" Sor Juana's scholarly inclinations as either divine inspiration or masculine identification, both privileges that ultimately subjugate Sor Juana to the clergy and the state, and that define for her the role of Hispanic bourgeois intellectual. I propose to reconfigure Sor Juana, not as a Hispanic, but as a Chicana lesbian feminist. There is no sense in denying Sor Juana's membership in the educated class, nor in denying that Chicana lesbian feminists also share that privilege (regardless of our individual class backgrounds).[15] But we must also keep in mind that, as gendered bodies within patriarchy, we share Sor Juana's subjugated condition, her struggles for autonomy, and her search for meaning and transcendence through education and cultivation of a personal/political voice.

The "of America" part of the epithet signifies a nationalist consciousness. Through a literary analysis of Sor Juana's lyrical, comical, and theatrical verses, particularly those using Nahuatl and Afro-Latino idioms, María González argues that Sor Juana should not be classified as a writer of the Golden Age, that is, as a peninsular *gachupina*, but as a Mexican writer with an evolving nationalist consciousness. González believes that in Sor Juana's work we can find a sketch of the mestizo/a, "[el] nuevo ciudadano que se bullía entre dos patrias: una lejana y desconocida; y la otra muy cerca a los ojos y al corazón."[16] In this new citizen can be perceived the spirit of Mexican independence that would manifest itself a century later. In Sor Juana, then, we see a model of the *nueva ciudadana*, a woman of the Americas, product of colonization, employing her agency and her tongue to create an autonomous identity within the confines, and, indeed, through a methodology, of male sovereignty. Moreover, because her experience is rooted in the soil of the so-called New World (despite her liaisons with the Spanish aristocracy), and because the bulk of her education takes place within the musty covers of European books, she is a product of cultural *mestizaje*. She is, in fact, a mestiza in Gloria Anzaldúa's sense of the word, a crosser of cultural and (as we shall soon see) sexual borders, a woman deeply immersed in the mirror of her writing and in the Coatlicue State of crisis and restoration.[17]

What remains of the epithet, the "feminist" label, is what intrigues me most. Given Sor Juana's class and cultural affiliations, her keen awareness of and resistance to gender-specific oppression, her empirical career in the camp of what we now know as women's liberation, her continual struggle for survival, her evolving nationalist consciousness, her separatist strategy, and her very postmodern sense of multiple identities, can it be argued that not only was Sor Juana a feminist but, in fact, a symbolic foremother of Chicana lesbian feminism?

My main purpose in this interview is to dig beneath Sor Juana's identity as a criolla and as a nun, and thus reveal what kind of "sister" she really was. The school of Sorjuanistas, of which Octavio Paz is the self-appointed leader, finds it too threatening to entertain the notion that the "first feminist of the Americas," the female Mexican cultural symbol second only to the Virgin of Guadalupe, was, in fact, of the lesbian persuasion. Insists Paz:

> To think that she felt a clear aversion to men and an equally clear attraction to women is absurd. In the first place, because even if that supposition were true, it is not likely that while she was still so young she knew her true inclinations; in the second, because only by attributing to her an intellectual and sexual license more appropriate to a Diderot heroine than to a girl of Juana Inés's age and social class in New Spain could she cold-bloodedly have chosen as refuge an institution inhabited exclusively by persons of

the sex that supposedly attracted her . . . it is futile to try to learn what her true sexual feelings were. She herself did not know.[18]

I am convinced, however, that Sor Juana *did* know the contours of her own desire, and I identify her as a lesbian separatist feminist who cross-dressed as a nun to hide, even from herself, what in seventeenth-century Spanish America would have been interpreted as heresy. Despite Octavio Paz's admonition that there are no "documents" to prove her "Sapphic tendencies,"[19] through both her writings and her strategic silence, Sor Juana offers us ample evidence of her true inclinations. She certainly would not be the first lesbian nun in the history of the Catholic Church.[20]

In Sor Juana's perpetual conflict between reason and passion, we see the enactment of Anzaldúa's Coatlicue State, a particular faculty of the mind characterized by "psychic unrest," in which the multiple layers of a mestiza consciousness interface either consciously or unconsciously, leading from crisis to restoration.[21] It is this repressed identity, this hidden Other within herself, that constitutes the politics of location that Sor Juana and I will construct through our interview. The two Coatlicue States that I try to illuminate in the interview are Sor Juana the mestiza offspring of white male discourse (imperialism) and female subjugation (América), and Sor Juana the lesbian, crosser of spiritual and sexual borders.

I should explain that the theoretical questions put to Sor Juana in the interview are framed within the discourse of white feminism, not because I choose to privilege white feminist discourse over Third World and Chicana feminisms, but because, in the colony of New Spain, founded upon the binary oppositions of the European "fatherland" and the "virgin" New World, gender oppression was a way of acting out not just male privilege but imperialist dogma. Norma Alarcón describes the "gender standpoint epistemology"[22] in relation to women of color as a theory that posits women's subjectivity primarily in relation and opposition to men while ignoring or subsuming the impact of race and class upon that subjectivity. Being of the same race and class as her opponents in the Church and the convent, then, the gender standpoint was the cause for which Sor Juana lived and died: colonial feminism.

Although there was no First World–Third World dichotomy in the fifteenth through eighteenth centuries, it can be argued that New Spain, because of its condition as a colony of a European superpower, consti-tuted the equivalent of a Third World country (a legacy that continues under a different master). The hierarchical structure of colonialism applied both vertically and horizontally to the women of New Spain. Horizontally, because for every criollo and mestizo there was at least one criolla and mestiza, each one living out the prescriptive codes of her class and caste. Vertically, of course, because the criolla was considered superior to the mestiza. There was, however, a common ground between the classes that applied only to the female gender. Whether criolla or mestiza, women in colonial Mexico were subalterns. Like the land and the indigenous people, women were taken, claimed, owned, exchanged, pillaged, conquered, silenced, dispossessed of their own destinies. As Alan Trueblood says in his introduction to *A Sor Juana Anthology*:

> Woman's subordination was absolute in colonial Spanish America. In the secular sphere she was to be a homemaker, assuring males at all social levels a dependable domesticity that would free them for the careers or labors to which tradition or chance assigned them. If instead of marrying she became a nun, as bride of Christ she had a duty to be completely submissive to His living body, the Church.[23]

Hence, although the hierarchical structure of colonialism created class divisions among women as much as among men, gender oppression intersected those class divisions and made all women members of the subaltern, disenfranchised class. It is true that Sor Juana exercised even the rights she did not have during her lifetime, despite her being cloistered in the convent; for all her popularity, however, and probably because of it, she was silenced by the Church, and lived in that silence for two and a half centuries after her death. Being silenced, however, is not the same as being silent, and before the final muffling came, Sor Juana left what later became four volumes of *Obras completas*, from which I have drawn for her responses to my questions in the interview.

Lesbian Drag: Sor Juana's Separatist Habit

Aside from its deconstruction of gender oppression, white feminism's radical branch (which Chicana lesbian feminists have adapted to our own ends) offers separatism as a strategy for resisting and rejecting that oppression. Although entering the convent was ultimately a form of subordination to the patriarchal Church, nunhood was essentially a separatist condition for Sor Juana, the cloister a woman-only space. In *Respuesta* she tells us that she joined the convent to escape the fate of marriage. In so doing, she refused to "become," in Simone de Beauvoir's sense, a woman,[24] that is, to participate in the social construction of her body. She also rejected her essential femaleness, the biological destiny attached to womanhood, which would involve sexual intercourse with men, childbearing, and motherhood. In choosing to become a nun, Sor Juana was, in effect, as Monique Wittig says, refusing "to become (or to remain) heterosexual."[25] Hiding her body under the habit and the veil was the equivalent of cross-dressing as a lesbian.[26] Since "lesbians" did not "exist" in the seventeenth-century Americas, however, it follows that Sor Juana also did not "exist." She had renounced her gender and her sex; she did not live "in the world," but rather in a community of other degendered and (supposedly) asexual beings; moreover, her body was reduced to a *condition*: of servitude, obedience, abnegation.

But Sor Juana also refused to conform to these three requisites of her chosen condition. Habits and vows notwithstanding, the nun's condition was still located in and circumscribed by a body with mammary glands and ovaries. Cinctured, bound, shorn, and veiled as this body was, it was still the kind of body that became a "bride" of Christ, and lived either as a "sister" of all of the other "brides," or as a "Mother" Superior. As the holiest of holies, her "Husband" was not of the flesh, but His corporeal substitute was the pope, and His emissaries were the good "Fathers" of the Church, all of whom started out as "brothers" and became surrogate "husbands," invested with the power to tell His "wives" what to do. A mainstay of this power was the ritual of confession, which, as Michel Foucault explains,

> unfolds within a power relationship . . . [in which] the agency of domination does not reside in the one who speaks . . . but in the one who listens and says nothing; not in the one who knows and answers, but in the one who questions and is not supposed to know.[27]

The vows of chastity, poverty, and obedience functioned as Church laws, and any infringement of the laws had to be confessed to the "Fathers," who, alone, had the power to mediate and punish, eavesdrop and absolve.

All of the "Fathers," "Mothers," "sisters," and "brothers" of the (again) Mother Church were, in fact, a family. According to Chris Weedon in *Feminist Practice and Poststructuralist Theory*, the family is "the instrument *par excellence* of the oppression of women through male control of female sexuality and procreative powers and [also men's] control of economic power."[28] Hence, heterosexual relationships as defined by the institution of the family were implicit in the nun's condition; moreover, it was a polygamous heterosexuality, on behalf of the "Husband" and "Fathers" (naturally), not always sublimated to spiritual terms (read: rape). The nun, then, was woman and female, a wife, after all.

In the first part of *Plotting Women: Gender and Representation in Mexico*, Jean Franco deconstructs what she calls the "religious narrative" of colonial Mexico, as expressed by the "holy" women of the age, equating the visionary confessions of mystical nuns to fantasy literature, wherein the repressed feelings and desires of the nuns had room to transform themselves into ecstatic visions, not of little sublimated sexual content, which was then disclosed to a father confessor. Another function of mystical literature was its transmission of sacred knowledge; even illiterate nuns could "know" and, thereby, become empowered. In her second chapter, which focuses on Sor Juana, Franco discusses the two domains of discourse that framed Sor Juana's life and choices: the palace was one domain, the convent the other. Franco argues that at court, women were allowed some measure of choice, if only in courtly games and rituals, and were thus slightly superior to women in convents. In the religious domain, women's only recourse to discourse was through the hysteria of mysticism; knowledge was transmitted by the Holy Spirit and recorded by the nuns, who were only seen as channels. As a bridge between the palace and the convent, however, Sor Juana exercised the privilege of a courtly lady and suffered the physical/sexual constraints of the hysteric.[29]

Why did Sor Juana choose this paradoxical existence? True, she escaped cohabitation with a man, sexual intercourse, and childbearing, but was she not still oppressed, owned, and socially constructed? Yes and no. I argue that, apart from being a nonexistent lesbian, Sor Juana was also a separatist feminist to the extent that she was aware of her spiritual and intellectual rights, which, for a criolla woman in colonial Mexico, could only be fulfilled through separation from the social restraints placed upon her class and gender. The only road to autonomy and fulfillment, narrow as that road was for a woman, came through separation from society, and this meant joining a convent. Although the convent was subject to the patriarchal mandates of the Church, it was closed to men and governed, for the most part, by the women living within its walls. As Asunción Lavrin points out, "Reading [in convents] must have been almost universal since nuns were supposed to use part of their leisure time in the reading of exemplary books."[30] And, although an education, per se, was not the goal of convent life, Sor Juana's reputation as a "scholar"; her connections to the viceregal court, the aristocracy, and the ecclesiastical council; her prolific pen; and her indefatigable pursuit of knowledge (arcane, sacred, and secular) all helped Sor Juana cultivate—though not without persistent persecution—an impressive literary and scholarly career within the convent.

In Mirta Aguirre's *Del encausto a la sangre*, published in Cuba in 1975,[31] I find interesting resonances between Aguirre's title and the title of one of Anzaldúa's chapters in *Borderlands*/La Frontera. *Encausto* refers to the red ink used by the Aztec emperor to write and sign his royal documents. Aguirre's title implies that Sor Juana's pen once flowed with the prestige of an Aztec emperor, but later, when she renounced all traces of that prestige, the red ink became the blood with which she renewed her vows and called herself "la peor," the worst of nuns. Anzaldúa's chapter, "*Tlilli, Tlapalli*/The Path of the Red and Black Ink," discusses the trials and tribulations of a writer's life. "Escribo con la tinta de mi sangre,"[32] says Gloria, which is both literally and metaphorically how Sor Juana lived and outlived her own life.

What happened to Sor Juana's body during her twenty-seven-year deluge of intellectual activity? Or rather, what happened to her sexuality, to her desire, to her politics of identity? Let's find out. Let's ask *her*.[33]

Figure 1.2. Mexican 200-peso note, series D-1.

Interview with Sor Juana Inés de la Cruz

AGA: Sor Juana, three hundred years after your life span, you are hailed across the Western world as the "first feminist" and "Tenth Muse of America" because you were one of the earliest advocates on this continent for a woman's right to an education. What argument did you use to try to convince the patriarchy that women owned this right?

SJ: "Like men, do [women] not have a rational soul? Why then shall they not enjoy the privilege of the enlightenment of letters? Is a woman's soul not as receptive to God's grace and glory as a man's? Then why is she not able to receive learning and knowledge, which are the lesser gifts? What divine revelation, what regulation of the Church, what rule of reason framed for us such a severe law?"[34]

AGA: Your major premise, indicated by the previous set of questions, is that, yes, a woman's soul is rational and yes, a woman's soul is just as receptive to God's grace as a man's, that, in other words, men and women are equal in the eyes of God and should, therefore, be equal in the eyes of society. This is a revolutionary theory for your time, a dangerous theory that could lead to an inquisition, a trial, perhaps even a visit to the stake in the Quemadero.

SJ: "Reason, just like a sword
can be wielded at either end:
the blade, to wound to the death;
the hilt, to provide defense.

       "If, well aware of the danger,
you insist on using the blade,
how can you blame the sword
for a choice you yourself have made?"[35]

AGA: Indeed, this conviction of yours that women had as much right to knowledge and self-expression as men, and your long and unabashed practice of that right, convicted *you* to the persecution of everyone around you. What was the root of this persecution?

SJ: "A head that is a storehouse of wisdom can expect nothing but a crown of thorns . . . [but] I do not wish to say. . . that I have been persecuted for my love of wisdom and letters, having achieved neither one or the other."[36]

AGA: But you *were* attacked as well as envied for your achievements in the field of reason.

SJ: "Whatever eminence, whether that of dignity, nobility, riches, beauty, or science, must suffer [the burden of envy and persecution]; but the eminence that undergoes the most severe attack is that of reason . . . For no other cause except that the angel is superior in reason is the angel above man; for no other cause does man stand above the beast but by his reason; and thus, as no one wishes to be lower than another, neither does he confess that another is superior in reason, as reason is a consequence of being superior."[37]

AGA: Let me try to deconstruct what you've just said. It's not that you consider yourself eminent in reason and therefore superior to those who have not developed their reason; you seem to be saying that human nature is rational and therefore superior to animal nature; and that, as a woman, you should not be persecuted for being rational nor considered inferior in reason because women are human and reason is a consequence of human nature. In fact, it is this rational essence that you use as your primary line of reasoning in your defense of women's rights. Nonetheless, weren't you the target of incredibly irrational attacks?

SJ: "The most noxious, those who most deeply wounded me, have not been those who persecuted me with open loathing and malice, but rather those who in loving me and desiring my well-being . . . have mortified and tormented me more than those others with their abhorrence. 'Such studies are not in conformity with sacred innocence; surely she will be lost; surely she will, by cause of her very perspicacity and acuity, grow heady at such exalted heights.' How was I to endure? An uncommon sort of martyrdom in which I was both martyr and executioner."[38]

AGA: And the arrows did not stop there.

SJ: "Even having a reasonably good handwriting has caused me worrisome and lengthy persecution, for no reason other than they said it looked like a man's writing, and that it was not proper, whereupon they forced me to deform it purposely."[39]

AGA: Your father confessor and your sisters in the convent weren't the only ones who accused you of masculinity. I'm thinking, of course, of that Peruvian man who sent you some clay vessels and a letter saying that you should have been born a man. In your reply to the Peruvian, you say something about womanhood that ties directly into what both Simone de Beauvoir and Monique Wittig say about the myth of woman. They say that woman is a creation of the patriarchy, that the institution of heterosexuality turns females into women, that gender is a by-product of heterosexuality. Would you recite those lines in your response to the Peruvian that begin with your allusion to Salmacis, the magical spring in Greek mythology that supposedly could change someone's sex?

SJ: "Here [in the convent] we have no Salmacis,

whose crystal waters, so they tell,

to nurture masculinity

possesses powers unexcelled.

"I have no knowledge of these things,

except that I came to this place

so that, if true that I am female,

none substantiate that state."[40]

AGA: One of the fundamental concerns of feminist theory is what is known as "subjectivity." Chris Weedon defines subjectivity as "the conscious and unconscious thoughts and emotions of the individual, her sense of herself and her ways of understanding her relation to the world."[41] Sor Juana, what is your sense of yourself, specifically of your body?

SJ: "I know only that my body,

not to either state inclined,

is neuter, abstract, guardian

of only what my Soul consigns."[42]

AGA: If you are not inclined toward the masculine or the feminine state, and you feel, as you say, "a total antipathy for marriage,"[43] then it seems to me that you are rejecting two of the basic tenets of the patriarchal system: a strictly dichotomized gender order and heterosexuality. If your subjectivity is not constructed by these two very powerful socializing forces, what is it constructed by?

SJ: "My dark inclination has been so great

that it has conquered all else!"[44]

AGA: And what exactly is this "dark inclination?"

SJ: "From the moment I was first illuminated by the light of reason, my inclination toward letters has been so vehement, so overpowering, that not even the admonitions of others—and I have suffered many—nor my own meditations—and they have not been few—have been sufficient to cause me to forswear this natural impulse that God placed in me."[45]

AGA: How did living in the convent affect this "natural impulse," this "negra inclinación,"[46] as you called it?

SJ: "Once dimmed and encumbered by the many activities common to Religion, that inclination exploded in me like gunpowder proving how *privatio est causa appetitus* [privation is the source of appetite]."[47]

AGA: By "privation" you don't just mean that convent life provided little time for learning and writing. Weren't you also forbidden to study at one point?

SJ: "At one time this was achieved through the offices of a very saintly and ingenuous Abbess who believed that study was a thing of the Inquisition, who commanded me not to study."[48]

AGA: But you studied anyway, not in books, but through observation of things around you, particularly in the kitchen.

SJ: "Lupercio Leonardo spoke well when he said: how well one may philosophize when preparing dinner . . . Had Aristotle prepared victuals, he would have written more."[49]

AGA: Yes, so you told the bishop of Puebla in your *Respuesta*. What kinds of discoveries did you make during this period of abstention from your books?

SJ: "Once in my presence two young girls were spinning a top and scarcely had I seen the motion and figure described, when I began, out of this madness of mine, to meditate on the effortless modus of the spherical form . . . I had flour brought and sprinkled about, so that as the top danced one might learn whether these were perfect circles it described with its movement, and I found that they were not, but, rather, spiral lines that lost their circularity as the impetus declined . . . And what shall I tell you . . . of the natural secrets I have discovered while cooking? I see that an egg holds together and fries in butter or in oil, but, on the contrary, in syrup shrivels into shreds; observe that to keep sugar in a liquid state one need only add a drop or two of water in which a quince or other bitter fruit has been soaked; observe that the yolk and the white of one egg are so dissimilar that each with sugar produces a result not obtainable with both together. I do not wish to weary you with such inconsequential matters, and make mention of them only to give you full notice of my nature, for I believe they will be occasion for laughter."[50]

AGA: Padre Antonio, your father confessor, did not intend for you to for-swear learning altogether, did he? I thought he was mainly perturbed by the fact that you wrote poetry, scandalous secular poetry that was either commissioned or encouraged by the viceregal court or by the nobles and poets who often visited you in the convent. Didn't Padre Antonio tell your Mother Superior that, had he known you would write verses, he would have married you off to a man rather than placed you in the convent?[51]

SJ: "But, most beloved Father," I said to him, "whence your direct author-ity . . . to dispose of my person and the free will God granted me? . . . Vexing me is not a good way to assure my submission, nor do I have so servile a nature that I do under threat what reason does not persuade me, nor out of respect for man what I do not do for God; and to deprive myself of all that can give me pleasure, though it be entirely licit, it is best that I do as self-mortification, when I wish to do penance, and not because Y[our] R[everence] hopes to achieve it by means of censure."[52]

AGA: How bold of you to use the word "pleasure" to a censor of the Holy Office, a scout of the Inquisition. Again, Sor Juana, you are preceding feminist theory by three centuries.

SJ: "What we need is a seminar
with no other aim than showing
not the ways of human learning
but the comforts of not knowing.

"Exempt from need for caution,
taking pleasure in all things,
we'd scoff at whatever threats
the stars' influence brings.

"Thought, let's learn not to know
since so plainly it appears
that whatever we add to our minds
we take away from our years."[53]

AGA: It is well known that you are autodidactic, that after being taught to read and write at the age of three, you were responsible for the breadth and depth of your own education with, as you say, "no other than a mute book" for a teacher and "an insentient inkwell" for a colleague.[54] What is not so commonly known is your opinion of male teachers.

SJ: "I do not find that the custom of men teaching women is without its peril, lest it be in the severe tribunal of the confessional, or from the remote decency of the pulpit, or in the distant learning of books—never in the personal contact of immediacy."[55]

AGA: You believe that there would have been more educated women in your time had there not been a dearth of older women teachers. Can you elaborate on that?

SJ: "If a father desires to provide his daughters with more than ordinary learning, he is forced by necessity, and by the absence of wise elder women, to bring men to teach the skills of reading, writing, count-ing, the playing of musical instruments, and other accomplishments, from which no little harm results, as is experienced every day in dole-ful examples of perilous association, because through the immediacy of contact and the intimacy borne from the passage of time, what one may never have thought possible is easily accomplished. For which rea-son many prefer to leave their daughters unpolished and uncultured rather than to expose them to such notorious peril as that of familiar-ity with men . . . for what objection can there be that an older woman learned in letters and in sacred conversation and customs, have in her charge the education of young girls? This would prevent these girls being lost either for lack of instruction or for hesitating to offer instruc-tion through such dangerous means as male teachers."[56]

AGA: One of your most famous poems is the "Philosophical Satire" in which you explore the myth that women are responsible for men's sins. Would you please recite just the first two quatrains of this *redondilla*?

SJ: "Hombres necios que acusáis
a la mujer sin razón,
sin ver que sois la ocasión
de lo mismo que culpáis:

   "si con ansia sin igual
solicitáis su desdén,
¿por qué queréis que obren bien
si las incitáis al mal?" [57]

AGA: In this poem, you're revealing the "occasion" for sexual transgression, which is men, and thus you contradict the patriarchal ideology that says women are inherently sinful. If women are sinful, you say, it is because men provide the occasion for sin to flourish. By soliciting and inciting women to sin, and then turning around and accusing women of having sinned, men behave the way Satan behaved in tempting Christ. Hence, men are the tempters and women the victims of temptation—another twist on the traditional idea. The seductress becomes the one who is being seduced, solicited, objectified; the seduced, because he occupies the power position as male and as client, is actually the seducer, the cause of women's fall from grace.

SJ: "Who is more to blame,
although both are guilty of wrongdoing,
she who sins for pay,
or he who pays for sin?

     "Why act so surprised [, señores,]
at what is your own fault?
Love what you have created
or create what you can love."[58]

AGA: You say you joined the convent of your own free will, but some of your modern-day critics, and I'm thinking primarily of Octavio Paz, believe that because you were born out of wedlock in a patriarchal society and were thus an illegitimate child, no honorable man would marry you, and so your only choice was the convent.

SJ: "I entered the religious order, knowing that life there entailed certain conditions (I refer to superficial, and not fundamental regards) most repugnant to my nature; but given the total antipathy I felt for marriage, I deemed convent life the least unsuitable and the most honorable I could elect if I were to insure my salvation."[59]

AGA: In other words, becoming a nun was the logical alternative for your life; not only would you not have to live with a man and bear his children, but you would also not be out in the street; rather than lose prestige and find yourself on the road populated by "hombres necios," you would still be protected by an honorable institution of the patriarchy. By joining the convent, you tried to resist being created in the patriarchal image of woman.

SJ: "I know . . . that they were wont
to call wife, or woman, in the Latin
uxor, only those who wed,
though wife or woman might be virgin.

     "So in my case, it is not seemly
that I be viewed as feminine,
as I will never be a woman
who may as woman serve a man."[60]

AGA: Meaning you will never have sexual intercourse with a man, which is what the etymology of "woman" signifies; thus, you should not be considered a woman. Here is another outright rejection of heterosexuality; but the question is, did you reject sexuality? Although you say that your body was "neuter" and "abstract," you painted the bodily proportions of your most excellent friend, La Condesa de Paredes, in a most sensual and highly erotic way. I'm thinking of that poem you sent to María Luisa after she left Mexico. Would you recite that middle section in which you describe La Condesa's throat, arms, and fingers?

SJ: "A passageway to Venus' gardens,
your throat is as an ivory organ
whose music melodiously ensnares
the very wind in bonds of ecstasy.

"Tendrils of crystal and snow
your two white arms incite desires doomed
to barrenness, like those of Tantalus:
thirst unslaked by water, fruitless hunger.

"Your fingers are alabaster dates
springing in abundance from your palms,
frigid if the eye beholds them,
torrid if the soul should touch them."[61]

AGA: And what about the poem you wrote to commemorate a secret that La Condesa confided to you, a secret that you literally swallowed?

SJ: "The page, discreetly, will relate
how, the moment it was read,
I tore your secret into shreds
that shreds be not the secret's fate.
And something more, inviolate,
I swallowed what you had confessed,
the tiny fragments of your note,
to guard the secret that you wrote
and honor thus your confidence, lest
even one scrap escape my breast."[62]

AGA: Forgive me if I press the point, Sor Juana, but those lines are charged with erotic feeling, and I have a difficult time accepting that the mind that produced those images lived inside an "abstract" body. I think what you mean by "abstract" is the concept of a body that is doomed, like Tantalus, to perpetual temptation and unfulfilled desire.

SJ: "Let us renounce this argument,
let others, if they will, debate;
some matters better left unknown
no reason can illuminate."[63]

AGA: From which I interpret that being a woman-identified woman was not rational to you or your society, but also such things were "unknown," the choice did not logically exist; hence entering the convent would be

the only rational way of hiding an irrational inclination and of exercising an unknown choice.

SJ: "Este amoroso tormento
que en mi corazón se ve,
sé que lo siento, y no sé
la causa por qué lo siento."[64]

AGA: Is it that you still find it difficult to talk about your desire, even after
three hundred years, or that you don't have the words to name that
desire?

SJ: "Of things one cannot say, it is needful to say at least that they cannot
be said, so that it may be understood that not speaking is not the same
as having nothing to say, but rather being unable to express the many
things there are to say."[65]

AGA: That reminds me of Foucault, who says in *The History of Sexuality*,
Vol. 1: "Silence itself—the things one declines to say, or is forbidden
to name, the discretion that is required between different speakers—is
less the absolute limit of discourse . . . than an element that functions
alongside the things said."[66] In one of your poems to La Condesa, you
play with this notion of silence, and yet your passion for La Condesa
comes out quite lyrically. Would you mind quoting some lines from that
work?

SJ: "I love you with so much passion
neither rudeness nor neglect
can explain why I tied my tongue,
yet left my heart unchecked . . .

"And, although loving your beauty
is a crime beyond repair,
rather the crime be chastised
than my fervor cease to dare . . .

"Let my love be ever doomed
if guilty in its intent,
for loving you is a crime
of which I will never repent.

"This much I find in my feelings—
and more that I cannot explain;
but you, from what I have said,
may infer what words won't contain."[67]

AGA: I understand now why you gave yourself the epithet, *la peor*, implying that you were the worst of nuns,[68] when you renewed your vows
in blood after capitulating at last, to your father confessor's and the

archbishop's persecution. Not only was that a common way for nuns to debase themselves (as was expected of them) in documents such as testaments of faith, but you were also telling the truth: you were the worst of women because you refused to be the kind of woman your society and your superiors expected you to be. You rejected their creation of you.

SJ: "If this is a sin, I confess it,
if a crime, I must avow it;
the one thing I cannot do
is repent and disallow it.

      "The one who has power to probe
the secrets of my breast,
has seen that I am the cause
of my suffering and distress.

      "Well he knows that I myself
have put my desires to death—
my worries smother them,
their tomb is my own breast.

      "I die (who would believe it?)
at the hands of what I love best.
What is it puts me to death?
The very love I profess."[69]

Figure 2.1. Delilah Montoya, Detail from *La Llorona in Lilith's Garden*, © 2004. Photographic mural on canvas. Used by permission of the artist.

Chapter 2

MALINCHE'S REVENGE

In Chicano/a popular culture, La Malinche is as much an iconic figure as the Pachuco or the *vato loco*, even though they embody diametrically opposite identity politics. Whereas the Pachuco in his stylized drapes, bilingual patois, and street-wise attitude came to signify Chicano pride and *carnalismo*, as well as resistance to assimilation and stereotyping, La Malinche, or people who are labeled Malinches or Malinchistas, signifies betrayal to everything that the *vato*, the Pachuco, the *carnal*, and the "homey" represent. In short, she is a traitor to Chicanismo.

Chicanos did not invent this treacherous view of La Malinche. That was inherited from Mexican patriarchy and its "colonial imaginary,"[1] to use the term coined by Chicana historian Emma Pérez. Nowhere is there a better example of the colonial imaginary than Octavio Paz's interpretation of La Malinche. For Paz, the self-proclaimed guru on the Mexican mind, Malinche is "*la Chingada*," the violated mother, the seed of shame that every Mexican, but especially every Mexican male, carries inside him and that is, to a large degree, responsible for his Mexican fatalism and continued colonization. In her analysis of Paz's essay "Sons of La Malinche,"[2] Emma Pérez refers to Paz as "el Chingón" (the great fucker) with a major castration complex, and reinterprets his interpretation of La Malinche (the primordial "*chingada*," or fuckee) from a Chicana working-class lesbian vantage point.

> To Paz, the Aztec princess Malinche "gave" herself to Hernán Cortés, the symbol of the Spanish Conquest, therefore, Paz charges her with the downfall of Mexico. In Paz, we have the symbolic son, the mestizo, repudiating the symbolic father, Cortés. The Oedipal triangle is completed by *la india* that they both raped and tamed, literally and metaphorically. . . . For Paz, *la india* personifies the passive whore who acquiesced to the Spaniard, the conqueror, his symbolic father—the father he despises for choosing an inferior woman who begat an inferior race, and the father he fears for his powerful phallus.[3]

Thus, the Mexican mestizo son is as reviled by the European father as the Pachuco is reviled by the Mexican father; the former because of his Indian (i.e., inferior, uncivilized, licentious) mother, the latter because of the loss of language and culture that results from life in the belly of beast. In this case, the Pachuco "becomes" in an existential way, like La Malinche, selling herself/himself to the white conqueror and thereby betraying his Mexican patrimony. Despite the mestizo son's fear of the all-powerful white father, however, he is born with the father's gender privilege and the mother's racial stigma.

Let me attempt, here and in the triangulated figure below, to deconstruct the Oedipal-conquest triangle that Pérez places as a template over Octavio Paz's rendition of Malinche's history. At the pinnacle of the triangle, of course, sits the white father, the colonizer, the political and ideological power of the State symbolically represented in Mexico by the conquistador Hernán Cortés. At the bottom left and right sit, respectively, the Indian mother—La Chingada, the Mexican Eve, the conquered land that is the foundation of Mexican nationalism—and the fruit of the union between the white father and the Indian mother—the bastard mestizo son. The son is the crossroads not only of two races, but also of two mutually contradictory qualities: machismo, the power of the phallus, and nationalism, the veneration of the mother, which churn inside him like cultural schizophrenia. The etymology of *nation*, the root word of *nationalism*, is the Latin word *natio*, which signifies birth. We could say, then, that while machismo is an overt manifestation of the father's supremacy, that is, patriarchy, nationalism pledges allegiance to the womb (the land) that birthed the mestizo son. But the mestizo son loves and hates his white father; loves and hates his Indian mother; is loyal to both of them at the same time that he rejects their imposition on his character: the father's rape that gave birth to him, the mother's passivity and weakness in which he sees himself reflected. By choosing patriarchal privilege over racial roots, by promoting the white father's disavowal of that which is indigenous and female or in any way open and penetrable, the mestizo son attempts to become *like* the father at the same time that he is spurned by the father because of the marker of his inferiority, the color of his skin, the intractable and irreducible trace of La Chingada. Hence, his phallus, though strong in the service of patriarchy and in the domination of women, can never compare to the father's, can never achieve the same level of power and privilege. As Emma Pérez explains:

Within a racist society, the mestizo male is a castrated man in relation to the white-male colonizer father. His anxiety is not only reduced to the fear of losing [the phallus], but also to the fear that his will never match the supreme power of the white man's. While the white son has the promise of becoming the father, the mestizo, even when he becomes the father, is set apart by his skin color and by a lack of language, the dominant language of the colonizer. Moreover, he must repudiate *la india y la mestiza* for fear that he could be like her, a weak, castrated betrayer of his people. Hence, he colludes with the white-colonizer-father as they both condemn la Chicana.

The conquest triangle dictates the sexual politics of miscegenation in the twentieth century.[4]

The Mexican Caste System

The Mexican colonial imaginary constructs betrayal to the culture as betrayal to the race, original sin *a lo mexicano*. In the popular 1997

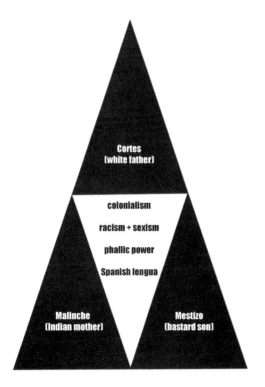

Figure 2.2. The colonial "conquest triangle." Digital graph. Courtesy of Alma López.

telenovela María Isabel, for example, we find the story of a supposed Indian woman who falls in love with her "white" employer.[5] The Malinche, in this case, is not the Indian woman, who is, after all, just looking to move up in the racial hierarchy and thus to improve the lot of her children by whitewashing the race; the real Malinche, or traitor, is the rich *patrón* who betrays his culture, his class, and especially his race by marrying someone lower on the totem pole of the racial caste system: a Huichol Indian woman.

We need not dwell on the fact that the actress chosen to portray the Huichol protagonist (Adela Noriega) has more of a European than an indigenous phenotype (the producers probably couldn't find any "real" Indian actresses to audition for the part). What is significant here is the way this late twentieth-century popular narrative illustrates the long-term legacy of the infamous "sistema de castas" by which racial relations were determined in colonial New Spain. As defined by R. Douglas Cope in his book, *The Limits of Racial Domination*, the "sistema de castas" was "a hierarchical ordering of racial groups according to their propor-tion of Spanish blood."[6] The taxonomy was based on seven general racial categories (which included skin color, facial features, body types, and hair textures): thus, *criollo* was a Spaniard born in New Spain; an *indio* was a native of Mexico; a *negro* was an African; a *mestizo* was a product of Spanish and Indian miscegenation; a *mulatto* was a product of Span-ish and African miscegenation; a *castizo* was a product of Spaniard and mestizo mixing; a *morisco* was a product of Spaniard and mulatto mix-ing. From these seven general categories, more than forty different types of racial mixtures were traced, each one indicative of a different shading, or color, and given, as above, a separate name. The most removed from Spanish blood were, of course, at the bottom of the hierarchy, and this meant that blacks were at the bottom of the scale, for it was believed that eventually the Indian castes would "whiten" up after enough genera-tions of intermarriage, whereas the same was ostensibly not true of the black castes. Even blacks intermarrying with Spaniards (mulattos) would not "whiten" in the same way that Indians intermarrying with Spaniards would; as blacks were the most cohesive of the castes, they tended to intermarry within their own category or with mulattos, mestizos, and Indians—none of which really improved or "whitened" their status.

New Spain, upon which the Mexican nation was founded, operated under this caste system until Mexico's independence from Spain in the early nineteenth century, but even after Mexican independence, the caste system was in effect, that is to say, those in power were still the white-skinned, landowning criollos, and their servants were still the dark-skinned *indios*, mestizos, mulattos, and they continued to "own" black slaves until 1829. The fact that they were all "Mexican," that is, part of the sovereign nation of Mexico, did not liberate anybody from the racial ideology of the "sistema de castas." This ideology is still in effect, as we see amply represented in Mexico's cultural production, be it the writings of its Nobel laureate Octavio Paz or the mass culture narrative of a *telenovela*.

In the Chicano colonial imaginary, on the other hand, betrayal to the culture is tracked along the axis of gender rather than race. As representatives of the new *mestizaje*, Chicanos inherited the colonial father's racial stigma against the Indian inside them; at the same time, claiming their Indianness was the very source of Chicano pride, a pride and a politics that were encoded into the Chicano label itself. Because the Indianness is associated with the feminine gender, however, and because Chicanos, too, are "*hijos de la chingada*," it became necessary to transgender the Indian inside them, to transform the root of their pride from something passive and feminine, like Malinche, into something aggressive and masculine, like an Aztec emperor, Moctezuma; or the Aztec god of war, Huitzilopochtli; or the prototypical Chicano calendar image of an Aztec warrior named Popocatépetl carrying his fallen maiden, Ixtaccíhuatl.[7] To this day, this iconography, overdetermined as it became in the imagery of the Chicano art movement, continues to represent Chicano political beliefs and values. Embedded in that iconography is not only the repudiation of Malinche and her daughters but also the reenactment of the colonial father's rape and the mestizo son's disdain for his Indian mother. Elizabeth "Betita" Martínez calls this "chingón politics" in *De Colores Means All of Us*.

> The concept of Aztlán has always been set forth in super-macho imagery. The Chicano activist today rarely sees taking Aztlán as a concrete goal but might like to imagine himself garbed in an Aztec warrior outfit, looking ferociously brave next to some red-lipped princess with naked breasts. If you note the whiff of sexual possession there, it's no accident. As often applied, the concept of Aztlán encourages the association of machismo with domination.[8]

What we need to remember, however, is that the image here is a Chicano version of Michelangelo's *Pietà*, which depicts the virginal blessed Mother holding her fallen, sacrificial son. By changing the image of the son for that of a bare-breasted Aztec princess, by reinscribing the bereaved mother into a brave Nahua warrior, supermacho Chicano activists who find themselves represented by the image are, in reality, identifying with the mother rather than with the son of the original image. The implicit and ironic message here: Chicanos/as survive because the mother survives, not the other way around. *Chingón* politics are really the mother's politics, *la primera madre*, La Malinche.

Chingona Politics

Mujeres of the Chicano movement had three roles to play, "the three f's," as Cherríe Moraga has put it: "feeding, fighting, and fucking."[9] Their job was to struggle beside, behind, and beneath their men in *la lucha* for race and class consciousness in white "Amerikkka." The other job, of course, was procreation, to breed more Raza for the struggle. "It reminds us painfully of how, within the movement, Juana usually stayed home with the kids or typed the minutes or nursed a domestic black eye while her *mero cabrón* played Aztec chieftain," writes Betita Martínez.[10] Thus, *feministas* in the early days of El Movimiento—that is, women who believed they should have more of a role in La Causa than typing up the minutes or making the food for the meetings, or having the future Emilianos and Panchitos of the movement—those *mujeres* were said to be dividing the movement and spouting Anglo middle-class beliefs that had no place in the life of La Raza. They were called men-haters and *"agringadas"* and sellouts because, in seeking equality with men and personal liberation for themselves as women, they were accused of putting the individual before the culture. Rather than working toward cultural nationalism and the empowerment of the Raza brotherhood, they were said to be polluting the movement from within and splitting up the Chicano Holy (not to mention heterosexual) Familia. For this opposition they were ridiculed, humiliated, and consistently harassed by the men and their female loyalists. To make matters even more interesting, it was rumored among the more paranoid of the Chicano leadership that *feministas* were actually FBI infiltrators seeking to undermine the revolution.[11]

Traitors, infiltrators, wannabe *gabachas* (or white women), and reactionaries against the true goals of Chicano liberation—all Malinche traits ascribed to women who wanted their *hermanos* and *hermanas* of La Raza to practice the politics of liberation they were preaching to apply to all Raza. Did this make them *chingonas*? Possibly, but not in the "common" sense in which that term is understood when it applies to women; not in the sense that they had penis envy and wanted to strap on a visible manifestation of male power.

The Laws of the Penis

Defined broadly, feminism is fundamentally a politics of resistance against patriarchy, and in a patriarchy, men are in power and women are their subordinates. If we break the word down, we get *patri*, or father, and *archy*, or supremacy; thus patriarchy is a social organization based on the supremacy of the father. In a patriarchal social order, those who are like the father—that is, male, but especially, white, rich, heterosexual males—are privileged over those who are unlike the father—that is female, nonwhite, nonrich, nonheterosexual. What gives the father his power is the phallus, the penis, which he passes on to his sons, and they to their sons, and so on across the centuries. The mother figures into the transaction, of course, but only as the carrier of the father's seed, as the vessel through which the son (and future father) comes into being. Because the mother has no penis, she is not allowed a leadership role in patriarchy, nor does she get to participate in the making of the laws that perpetuate that order, the laws of the father.

Although the laws of the father are inclusive and do not just pertain to family relations, it is the male-dominated family, in which the father is superior to the mother, the son to the daughter, the brother to the sister, the uncle to the aunt, the nephew to the niece, and so on, that composes the primary unit through which the laws of the father become established as normative and natural. But because they are fundamentally about domination, the laws of the father apply to every facet of the social system—from governance to education, from religion to popular culture, from foreign policy to fashion, from sex to gender, from class to race. Everywhere we look, in any page of Western history, we see the laws of the father enacted.

Conquest of the so-called New World was the enactment of the laws of the father, in this case, the European, capitalist-driven, Christian fathers of Western civilization. Colonization is also based on the laws of the rich white father. So is Manifest Destiny. So is the Treaty of Guadalupe Hidalgo. So is Operation Wetback. So is NAFTA. All of these are ways in which the white male penis perpetuates and enforces its power to rule over its subjects—be they women, or people of color, or indigenous inhabitants of the lands he wants to conquer, or the poor, or those whose sexual practices fail to conform to the symbolic order of reproduction. The importance of reproduction, we must remember, is not only to propagate the human race but also to breed clones of the father and thus assure that his laws are also proliferated. This is what feminism resists: the continued dominion of the father and the rule of the white male penis.

Iconically, the white male penis is represented all around us. We see it in the shape of nuclear projectiles and spacecrafts. In cigarette ads and army recruitment posters. In church steeples and skyscrapers. The airplanes that plowed into the twin towers of the World Trade Center on September 11, 2001, showed us what happens when the white male penis gets hijacked and its power pointed back at itself by enemies intent on giving the world a demonstration of "Fuck You Back" politics. Look on the original cover of the *Little Mermaid* video and tell me that isn't a penis back there disguised as a tower of the prince's castle. Disney's big hit *The Lion King* is nothing but an ode to the laws of the white father, epitomized by the big blond feline king who rules over the lowly animals of the jungle, including the dancing, drum-beating Africans. And what about the Wicked Witch in all those fairy tales we grew up on? Who is she, but the aging stepmother narcissistically obsessed with her own image, jealous of the young and beautiful stepdaughter who threatens to take away the father's attention. In league with powers beyond her domain as a woman, the Wicked Witch can never be a surrogate for the sweet and submissive Snow White. And Snow White herself, even though she is taller and whiter than the seven dwarfs, nonetheless knows her place as the maid of the household until she reenacts Eve's original sin and bites into a bad apple. The only cure that can restore her back to the symbolic order is a heterosexual kiss from the manly prince. Appropriately married off to a good son of the father (as opposed to living in sin among the seven deadly vices), she can now fulfill her role as a woman and begin the cycle of reproduction.

This is what is meant by the social construction of gender. "One is not born, but rather becomes, a woman," said the early French feminist Simone de Beauvoir in *The Second Sex*.[12] Originally published in 1949, *The Second Sex* is considered the first manifesto of the liberated woman (although actually our Latina feminist foremother, Sor Juana Inés de la Cruz, produced her feminist "scribblings" two hundred and fifty years earlier).[13] What Beauvoir's famous premise means is that woman and female are two different things; woman is a gender, while female is a sex. One is born male or female, says Beauvoir, that is, with a specific set of sexual genitalia, but one becomes constructed as a man or a woman by society and culture, by civilization as a whole—all of which have been dominated by the laws of the father for over two millennia. In such a world, the sexes are conditioned socially to serve patriarchal interests and safeguard patriarchal power. "The child is persuaded that more is demanded of boys because they are superior," says Beauvoir. "To give him courage for the difficult path he must follow, pride in his manhood is instilled into him; this abstract notion takes on for him a concrete aspect: it is incarnated in his penis."[14] Thus, the male child's gender is constructed: superiority, courage, competitiveness, pride, and reverence for the penis help him become a man. A female child's gender, on the other hand, is constructed as opposite a male's, as Other. She is inferior, weak, submissive; she lacks the organ that gives her brother, her father, the special privileges they enjoy. Like her genitals, the girl exists inside. Outside, where the penis is, is where the boys are. A boy's plaything and alter ego is his penis; a girl's is a doll. One is alive, autonomous, and active; the other is inert, dependent, and passive.

Such is the stuff that genders and inequalities are made of.

Still, there is more to patriarchy than sexual inequalities, and subordinates come in all sizes and colors. The laws of the father upon which all other laws are based are primarily the laws of the white, heterosexual, landowning father. The father, in other words, is inscribed with a sex, a race, a class, and a sexuality—all of which converge in the meaning of patriarchy. To fully resist patriarchy, then, one must go beyond gender inequalities—this is the message of Third World, black, Latina, and Chicana feminists. Our genders, like our struggles, are colored, sexed, and classed. We cannot and must not rank any of our oppressions: race above gender, gender above race, class above sex. Yet we continue to see that tug-of-war, and meanwhile, the stereotypes that define and degrade us get more and more entrenched in our collective unconscious.

We know that Mexican/Chicano patriarchy assigns three attributes to the feminine gender: *la madre, la virgen y la puta,* iconographed by the image of the Virgin of Guadalupe (who is both virgin and mother) and La Malinche (the prototypical fucked one). Chicana feminists label this the Tres Marías Syndrome, from the three Marys in the life of Jesus: the Virgin Mary, who is, paradoxically, both virgin and mother, and Mary Magdalene, the reformed whore. For the mestizo son, the difference between the virgin/mother aspect and the whore aspect explains his own ambivalence toward the female sex, how he can venerate and denigrate women at the same time, a trait of Mexican machismo that Chicano culture has internalized and adapted to its own social construction of gender. Octavio Paz, in "Sons of La Malinche," explains the roots of this dichotomy thus:

> Guadalupe is pure receptivity, and the benefits she bestows are of the same order: she consoles, quiets, dries tears, calms passions. The Chingada is even more passive. Her passivity is abject: she does not resist violence, but is an inert heap of bones, blood, and dust. Her taint is constitutional and resides, as we said earlier, in her sex. This passivity, open to the outside world, causes her to lose her identity: she is the Chingada. She loses her name; she is no one; she disappears into nothingness; she *is* Nothingness. And yet she is the cruel incarnation of the feminine condition.[15]

Woman as nurturer, forgiver, and carrier of the race must be idolized and protected; woman as instigator of "original sin" (whether that sin is disobedience or miscegenation), as willing or unwilling portal to enemies and conquerors, cannot be forgiven. In patriarchy, a woman's sex is the site of her deepest power (creation, which must be controlled and monitored at all times) and her deepest weakness (penetration, which must be punished). In between the mother and the whore that is La Malinche, there is the virginal condition, that ethereal state of womanhood, which can be owned, traded, and renamed to signify the transfer of property from father to son/husband.

The Dirty Name

One of the accusations launched at the *feministas*, apart from calling them *agringadas*, Malinches, and FBI spies, was the term *lesbian*. Because they were believed to be anti-*familia*, they could be nothing but lesbians, according to the *machista* logic, and the term *lesbians*, of course, was a bad word, a dirty name. Those of us who study the subject know that *feminist* and *lesbian* are not synonymous terms. We know that in the early days of the women's movement, lesbians were either ostracized or thrown out of organizations like NOW, the National Organization for Women. It wasn't until the lesbian feminists started to organize on their own and devise agendas that directly critiqued the mainstream feminist movement for its heterosexism and homophobia that the lesbian voice started to be integrated into mainstream feminism. Similarly, not all of the early feministas of the Chicano movement were lesbians, despite being called that by the men who were suddenly forced to look at, if not own up to, their own sexist politics. In fact, the main reason these feminist-oriented Chicanas denied the term *feminist*, apart from the fact that they didn't want to be seen as wannabe white women, is that they did not want to be associated with lesbianism, for they, too, believed that the women's movement was not only white and middle class but also a lesbian movement. Homophobia and heterosexism, in other words, did not just infect *los hijos de Cuauhtémoc*; the straight women, too, were guilty of fearing homosexuality and assuming that real Chicanas were straight Chicanas.

Chicana lesbians, seen as polluted by the sexual license of the white feminist movement to believe we can do what we want with our bodies, including using them to pleasure or be pleasured by other women, are the most treacherous of all. As Cherríe Moraga tells us in her classic essay "A Long Line of Vendidas,"[16] a Chicana lesbian was considered the most extreme Malinche of all because she rejected heterosexuality, male domination, and the biological destiny imposed by patriarchy that ensures the perpetuation of the laws of the almighty Apá.[17] "The Chicana lesbian," says Moraga, "is the most visible manifestation of a woman taking control of her own sexual identity and destiny."[18]

In an article entitled "Chicana Lesbians: Fear and Loathing in the Chicano Community," Carla Trujillo discusses four reasons that lesbians threaten the Chicano community: sexuality, identification, motherhood, and religion. All of these reasons are, of course, linked to patriarchy. Lesbians reverse the religious and cultural doctrine that sexuality—for women, anyway—is meant for reproduction, not for pleasure or self-fulfillment, and they reverse the assumption that lesbians are just wannabe men rather than women-loving women. To be a woman-loving woman means that men are not the object of desire, and this means that women cannot be controlled by what they are conditioned to desire: a good man or a heterosexual family. Lesbians show that there is another way to identify women that is not dependent on relations with men, that women can have autonomous lives without needing to be seen as attachments to men, and thus, can become the owners and creators of their own destinies. Lesbians either fail to propagate the race, and thus fail their calling as good Catholic women if they choose not to bear children, or they subvert the sanctified male-female paradigm of "*la sagrada familia*" if they do choose to raise children, as indeed, more and more lesbians are doing.[19]

Patriarchy controls women primarily by controlling our bodies, by dictating what we can and cannot do with our bodies. Because reproduction is one of the primary mandates of patriarchy—both to produce sons and heirs for the father and to perpetuate the laws and interests of the father—the heterosexual imperative is one way of assuring reproduction. Dictating who and how women can love and what legitimate forms our desire can take are ways in which the established social hierarchy gets perpetuated. Because lesbians refuse to participate in the heterosexual imperative, they threaten the patriarchal order. Cherríe Moraga says that our sexuality is "both a source of oppression and a means of liberation."[20] Lesbians are oppressed by practicing a sexuality that contradicts the patriarchal social order, and yet we are liberated from the restrictive and prescriptive roles that patriarchy imposes.

In describing one of the main reasons that Malinche is called the betrayer, Sandra Messinger Cypess tells of an Amerindian male that Malintzin Tenepal is said to have rejected. "[This] is perhaps the most serious of the charges that cling to her image; it becomes a metaphoric act signifying the repudiation of the native in favor of the foreign."[21] Ultimately, the Chicana lesbian is charged with the same act: the repudiation of *el chingón* in favor of *la chingada*. For a mind that is socialized and conditioned to venerate *el chingón* and denigrate *la chingada*, what could be more insulting than this?

Malinchismo

Chicana historian Deena González argues that "Malinche was truly at the crossroads of all that the Spanish conquest had come to symbolize, mistress of conquerors, mother of their sons, and initiator as well of a new role for women."[22] It is that new role as intermediary, diplomat, and translator that eludes male interpretations of Malinche. In Nahuatl, the term *malinche* applied generically to outsiders (thus, Cortés was as much a *malinche* as Malintzin Tenepal, the Maya noblewoman who belonged to Moctezuma's harem of slaves); in any culture, outsiders or strangers have always been seen as potential traitors, and the Aztecs were no different in that regard. Malintzin Tenepal, having been sold into slavery by her mother at a young age, owed no loyalty to the Aztecs. They were her conquerors, as well as the conquerors of all of the other native tribes who inhabited the Valley of Anahuac, and who eventually teamed up with the foreigners on horseback in a bloody insurrection. Little did they know, of course, that the new empire would mean their own genocide as well as the Aztecs'. The Aztecs knew; in fact, it was predicted in their prophecy of the Quinto Sol. And still, Moctezuma refused to see the writing on the pyramid. Malintzin Tenepal had already learned several Indian languages before she was given to Cortés as part of Moctezuma's tribute to the conquistador whom he believed to be the god Quetzalcoatl. She became Doña Marina to the Spaniards, and because of her facility with languages, because of her translation and diplomacy skills in mediating between the Aztec emperor and the Spanish conquistador, because she became Cortés's lover and bore him children, she was said to have become, like Cortés, a *malinche*, or La Malinche.

Ironically, five hundred years of internalized racism and misogyny have transformed La Malinche from the great Chingada to the great Chingona, the woman with all the power to bring down the Aztec civilization. As my poem says, "Centuries she has been blamed for the murder of her / child, the loss of her people, as if Tenochtitlan would not have fallen without her sin." Curiously, no one ever accuses Moctezuma of betraying his people, of reaping the hatred of the subordinate tribes, of receiving the conqueror with open arms (or legs), of ignoring the prophecy that foretold of the collapse of the Aztec Empire, of buying a *malinche*'s favors with gifts and tributes worthy of a god. More than anything La Malinche could have done, it was Moctezuma's actions and inactions that facilitated the fall of Tenochtitlan. As Ana Castillo notes in *Massacre of the Dreamers*:

> [Moctezuma] called upon the thousands of dreamers who were sharing the same premonition: the prophesied arrival of Cortés and the subsequent annihilation of the Empire. Moctezuma's order to have the dreamers murdered en masse did not stop the landing of those alien ships that were already on their way with those whose intentions were to take whatever riches found at any cost.[23]

And yet, Chicano patriarchy has adopted Moctezuma's image as the symbol of indigenous pride, while La Malinche is reviled as the eternal and unforgivable traitor.

Chicano patriarchy continues to evoke La Malinche's name to malign Chicanas who refuse to conform to their prescribed biological functions. In *Sister/Outsider*, Audre Lorde warned that "the master's tools will never dismantle the master's house."[24] For all of its dissent against the domination of the white father, the Chicano movement used some of the father's tools, including gender politics that not only privileged the men, but also perpetuated the *madre/virgen/puta* stereotypes of its women, which only served to fulfill the sexist fantasies of the Chicano penis. But Chicana feminists and particularly Chicana lesbian feminists have begun to transform the story of Malinche into a mirror of Chicana resistance against female slavery to patriarchy—be it the brown patriarchy of La Raza or the overarching patriarchy of the white father. Malinche also represents affirmation: of a woman's freedom to use her mind, her tongue, and her body in the way that she chooses and to cultivate her intellectual skills for her own survival and empowerment. From this mirror arises the vision of Malinchismo, a new theory of Chicana identity politics that takes the pejorative term "Malinchista" and turns all of its negatives into positives (just as Chicanos did in the 1960s and as queers did in the 1990s). "Our challenge," says Emma Pérez, "is to rebel against the symbol of the white father and affirm our separation from his destructive ideology to create a life-affirming *sitio*."[25]

If the best revenge, as they say, is living well—and I interpret that to mean not just economic wellness but, more important, the wellness of spirit that comes from loving ourselves and living true to our natures rather than embodying that "inert heap of bones, blood and dust" that Octavio Paz labeled "the cruel incarnation of the feminine gender"—then Malinche's revenge is upon us, and there is no turning back. Slouching toward the new Aztlán of the twenty-first century, Malinche's rebellious Shadow-Beast[26] dares us to look in the mirror and experience what Gloria Anzaldúa called "the knowing," the inner power that results from our underworld journeys into consciousness. "Suddenly the repressed energy rises, makes decisions, connects with conscious energy and a new life begins."[27]

Figure 3.1. John Gast, *American Progress*, 1872. Oil on canvas, 11 1/2 x 15 3/4 in. (29.2 x 40 cm). Autry National Center, Los Angeles; 92.126.1.

Chapter 3

THERE'S NO PLACE LIKE AZTLÁN

Homeland Myths and Embodied Aesthetics

I don't know [where Kansas is], but it *is* my home, and I'm sure it's somewhere.[1]

—**L. Frank Baum,** *The Wonderful Wizard of Oz*

When Dorothy of the film version of *The Wizard of Oz* pronounced the magic phrase "There's no place like home," and was consequently able to return herself to Kansas, she was learning the quintessential lesson of all displaced, misplaced, and replaced people: home, or place, is a fundamental aspect of identity. If, as Dorothy discovered, there is "no place like home," then home is in a sense a utopia, a place that is not a place, an imaginary space occupied by memory and desire.[2] As a "place where one's domestic affections are centered,"[3] home is different from any other place; it is not the same as any other place. For as magical, colorful, and marvelous as the Land of Oz was, Dorothy admitted to the Great and Terrible Wizard that "I don't like your country, although it is so beautiful";[4] instead, she articulated her preference for the familiar, albeit humble and not-so-beautiful, place she called home.

Exiled from her land, however, she must navigate the challenges of displacement in an "uncivilized"[5] and exotic country, guided only by the singular quest to return home to a specific place, Kansas, and a specific person, Aunt Em. Like all exiles, Dorothy yearns for reunification with the maternal body that signifies home. The problem is, she doesn't know how to get back, or even where in the topography of Oz it might be located. Somewhere on the monochromatic side of the rainbow is a land called Kansas, but the only place where it exists in Oz is in Dorothy's domestic affections.

In differentiating herself as not belonging to the Land of Oz, Dorothy enacts the diasporic condition as a body out of place and out of self. Through this recognition of her difference, through her process of dis-location and the challenging of her mind, heart, and courage, Dorothy finds her identity. With that comes her ability to return herself back to

the homely prairies of the Midwest, a power she has unknowingly carried with her all along in her silver shoes (or ruby slippers, as they are
changed in the film) but had not been able to use until she reached the
end of the yellow brick road, her journey of self-discovery.

Dorothy's story is of interest to me because it illustrates issues that
I have been thinking about for a number of years—about how artists
living in exile, diasporic artists, as well as artists who are indigenous
but dispossessed exiles in their own homeland, represent their journeys
toward wholeness in the absence of place, where place signifies a home,
a nation, a community, a landscape, or even a body. A mythology of
place evolves, and the mythos is translated into what I call *place-based
aesthetics*, a system of homeland representation that immigrants and
natives alike develop to fill in the gaps of the self.

For nearly forty years, the myth of Aztlán,[6] or the lost land, has been
at the core of a Chicano male identity and has had a formative influence
not only on Chicano psychology but on Chicano cultural production as
well. Based on racial pride, historical awareness, brotherhood, cultural
unity, and the claim to nativity in the land base of the Southwest, the
myth of Aztlán calls for the reclamation of "the land of our birth," a lost
or stolen *mother*land that was taken involuntarily and that the Chicano
"hijos de Cuauhtémoc" were destined to redeem through the political
as well as the cultural manifestations of el Movimiento, or the Chicano
movement of the 1960s and 1970s.

In this gendered relationship to land (or homeland), sexual politics is
clearly articulated into the ideology of Aztlán and its representation in
the arts. This chapter explores the concept of Aztlán as both an aesthetic
category and a cultural myth of origin, looking specifically at how the
gendered politics of the myth shape and signify an aesthetic tradition
that is deeply rooted in a place of contradiction, a place that is both
the "free" American West and the "conquered" Mexican North. What
cultural negotiations are necessary to mitigate these opposite locations
and contradictory interpretations of land and history? How do we claim
space in the territory of the oppressor and demand the rights and privileges
of citizenship, and at the same time stake out a private sanctuary for the
disenfranchised and the oppressed? If Aztlán is the dominant conceptual
framework for interpreting Chicano identity, activism, and cultural
production, then what are the perceptible differences between the visual
art produced by male nationalists and the work produced by feminists
within the Chicano nation of Aztlán? How do Chicana artists represent
the homeland? Have they gone "beyond" Aztlán?

Beyond Identity

Back in the multicultural heyday of the 1990s, I attended a symposium on Latin American art sponsored by the Art History Department at the University of Texas; the symposium purported to find a new rubric under which to study the art of the Americas south of the border, including the art created by Chicanos and Latinos in the United States—all lumped together under the politically correct/incorrect label of Latin Americans. This new critical framework by which to study the art of the Americas would go, according to the title of the symposium, "Beyond Identity," that is, beyond an essentialist interpretation rooted in the artist's country of origin, both because national identity was a reductive view of the art, and also because the assumption of a unified cultural character known as "Latin America," supposedly evoked and represented by the art made by Latin Americans, was as false as the assumption of a culturally unified and therefore indivisible United States. "Scholars of Latin American art," wrote the organizers of the symposium in the event's brochure, "no longer submit Latin American art to the demoralizing and generalizing question of how a certain piece of art represents its country of origin. Rather, contemporary scholars are now concerned with *post-identity* issues in Latin America: how Latin American art is a complex and distinct expression, which reflects the diversity between and within the countries that comprise Latin America."

I agree with critics of the "identity" paradigm that nationality is not the only way to understand Latin American art; but then, nationality is not the only way to configure identity, either. In seeking to move forward, to advance "beyond" identity as a paradigm within which to contextualize the art of Latin Americans, the organizers of the symposium were operating under the assumption that nationality itself is synonymous with "country of origin." Though willing to acknowledge and, indeed, seeking to account for "diversity between and within the countries that comprise Latin America," the organizers never got the point that in a world of globalization and transnational capitalism, a world created by markets as much as by movements of people, place of origin does not explain or define identity.

"It is the trope of our times to locate the question of culture in the realm of the *beyond*,"[7] says Homi K. Bhabha in "Beyond the Pale: Art in the Age of Multicultural Translation." Bhabha deconstructs the notion of "beyond" as both a modernist term that presupposes the existence of a future and the notion of progress (as in, there is something out there, beyond here and now, toward which we are inevitably moving), and as a postmodernist term that exists between moments of the present. Those moments of "presence" are characterized by contradiction and negotiation between the differences that frame any given identity. As Bhabha says, it is "theoretically innovative and politically crucial . . . to think beyond narratives of origin and initiatory, initial subjects and to focus on those moments or processes that are produced in the articulation of 'differences.'"[8] Paradoxically, what is produced in this articulation of differences is identity, and the paradox lies in the fact that *identity* literally signifies the opposite of difference.

Rather than visualizing the "beyond" in terms of a future, Bhabha sees the "beyond" occurring simultaneously in the present, in that moment of identity in which a subject negotiates her/his differences. By asking "How are subjects formed 'in between' or in excess of the sum of the 'parts' of difference?"[9] Bhabha suggests a new way of interpreting identity based on an analysis not only of the several "parts" that make up the whole of one's identity but also of the interstices between those parts where the idea of excess or beyond is located.

If we translate this idea into an equation of signifiers, it could look something like an elongated, if superficially simplistic, problem in addition. Identity = race + gender + class + sexuality + language + generation + nationality (and/or place of origin) + religion + political identity + vocation + education + anything else that might signify the self. For Homi Bhabha, the "beyond" lies not outside of any of these terms or identities, but in the spaces in between them, which he calls moments of presence. Thus, to go "beyond identity," in Bhabha's universe, anyway, is to "think beyond narratives of origin" and to focus, instead, on the several interstices that exist between our individual and collective differences. In the friction created by the interaction of these signifiers lives the spark that we call identity.

In a sense, we could say that Dorothy was "beyond identity" in the Land of Oz, for she was beyond the place in which she was the same as others, and found herself negotiating differences between this place and that place "over the rainbow." It was the articulation of her desire—"I want to go home"—and her resistance to hegemony—"I don't like your country"—that gave her the agency she needed to claim her full self, and with that came her ability (her *poder*, or power) to re-place herself in Kansas and return to the familiar safety of Aunt Em's arms.

As the Emmy-award-winning PBS documentary on the U.S.-Mexico War showed, Chicano/as (like other dispossessed people) cannot go "beyond identity" in the same way that either Dorothy or Latin Americans can go beyond identity—that is, beyond the preoccupation with and (in the case of artists) representation of nationality—because of a very real problem of geography, of contested terrain, territorial loss, and a conceptual homeland that, as Guillermo Gómez Peña says in his performance poem "Border Brujo," "float[s] on the ether of the present tense of California and the past tense of Mexico."[10] He is, of course, alluding to Aztlán, which, rather than a "no-man's-land," is more accurately a "no-place-land," a utopia.

If identity in the arts has for some time now been configured through place of origin, and if that place of origin is no place except in the utopian imaginary construct of Aztlán, then identity for Chicano artists must be rooted in nonexistence, in the subjunctive netherlands of desire and imagination—if only I had a homeland—rather than in the lament for a lost wholeness—there's no place like home. Clearly, to fully deconstruct the paradoxes of identity in the visual arts, identity must be problematized beyond place of origin, but also, place must be seen as more than a physical location or landscape.

Place-Based Aesthetics

In the early part of my research, as I worked at constructing a theoretical paradigm for understanding the relationship between place, identity, and gender in aesthetic development and production, I studied the historiography and exhibition books of African American, Latin American, Cuban, Filipino, Native American, and Chicano/a art.[11] I also looked at the artistic production of the women's art movement in the 1970s, particularly art that depicted what Judy Chicago and Miriam Shapiro referred to as a "'cunt positive' attitude,"[12] as well as the work of gay and lesbian artists whose images of overt sexual practices catapulted the National Endowment of the Arts into a paranoiac reactionary frenzy in the early 1990s.

From this exploration, I discovered seven separate aesthetic systems that substantiated my theory of *place-based aesthetics*:

1. Race-based aesthetics (African American artists)
2. Diasporic aesthetics (Asian American, Filipino, Cuban, Central American, Latin American artists)
3. Santería aesthetics (Caribbean and Brazilian artists, called "Candomblé" in Brazil)

4. Indigenous aesthetics (Native American artists)
5. Aztlán aesthetics (Chicano artists)
6. Feminist aesthetics (women artists subscribing to a "feminist" agenda)
7. Queer aesthetics (gay, lesbian, and queer artists)

All of these aesthetic practices, I found, were rooted in specific constructs of place, but they also problematized the subject *beyond* "place of origin" to include race, religion, community, and the body as sites of identity. The purpose of this chapter is not to explore each of these systems in more depth, but rather, to give a general description of the first four systems before moving on to a more detailed analysis of Aztlán aesthetics, which must be understood in the context of both the homeland myth of Aztlán and the nation-building myth of Manifest Destiny. I will conclude by looking at how four Chicana artists disidentify (i.e., reject the disempowering aspects) from Aztlán aesthetics, and instead practice the politics of feminist embodiment, or "embodied aesthetics" in their work.

Race-based aesthetics is a name given to a movement of American art that stirred to life approximately thirty years after the modernist "avant-garde" began appropriating the images and styles of Africa, Native America, the Pacific Islands, and pre-Columbian countries, which eventually resulted in mainstream movements such as cubism, surrealism, and primitivism. As early as the 1920s, African American art historians Alain Leroy Locke (1885–1954), James Vernon Herring (1887–1969), and James Amos Porter (1905–1970) began to postulate theories about a "racially based" aesthetic system that would help galvanize the political spirit of African American artists, and at the same time counter the racist appropriations of the avant-garde.

> Early African American scholars noted that what was most needed in critical circles was a scholarly compendium that began not with the enslavement of the African in the New World, but with the history of the ancient empires of the African past where art played a central role in birth, life, and death.[13]

This new modern aesthetic system looked to Africa, the motherland, and to the ancestral arts of Africa for inspiration and content and gave rise to an artistic production that was known, in the twenties, as the New Negro Movement, which later became the "Harlem Renaissance," a rebirth, not of Harlem, per se, but of the African soul that resided in Harlem.

Melding modernist styles and techniques such as abstraction, minimalism, cubism, collage, and assemblage with Egyptian-style figures painted in profile, images of slavery and bondage, African masks, Yoruba gods and goddesses, Egyptian pyramids, colors and designs reminiscent of African fabrics, and other signifying iconography of the African past, African American artists were able to represent a cultural ideology rooted in the African homeland but transplanted to the formal environment of the Euro-American art world. The purpose of this art was to stir the historical memory and cultural pride of African-descended people in the United States, and in so doing, to produce political empowerment and social commentary about racism, poverty, and the color line.

> A major difference between African American and Euro-American artists is that the former know their politics is racial, while the latter claim that their politics is economical. Although the two propositions are not mutually exclusive, the African American one gets specifically to the heart of the downtrodden, who believe that poverty is not the cause of racial bias but the result. African American art proponents establish their case by the evidence of their relationship between their color and their disenfranchisement.[14]

Although called *race-based* aesthetics, it should be noted that race operated as a signifier for place, and place signified both the African homeland and the social location of a slave-descended population in the United States. Thus, African American artists in the early part of the twentieth century, particularly those who were part of the Harlem Renaissance, found a way of politicizing their identity through representations of a place most would only see in exhibitions of black artists from Africa, a place that had no claim of nativity for them but that nonetheless had roots in their racial memory.

In the 1960s, African American race-based aesthetics gave way to Pan-Africanism, which, "more than a concept of race," according to Keith Morrison,

> is the collective celebration of African culture the world over by black people especially, but also by others who are dedicated to the African experience . . . The bond of these people of color seems to be Africa, not only because many share this legacy, but because African Americans

have paved a path for universal cultural redemption through their telling of the African story.[15]

Pan-Africanism is one form of *diasporic aesthetics*. Rather than focusing on roots, *diasporic aesthetics* explores the reality of being uprooted, the act of cultural migration from a native homeland to a foreign country, and the perpetual desire of returning.

Filipino American artist Carlos Villa believes that one of the primary questions artists of the diaspora interrogate is: "What's the difference between staying and leaving?"[16] Home, then, becomes a shifting signifier; it can mean motherland, adopted country, or alien nation. In the existential process of simultaneously staying and leaving, are the implied negotiations of coming and going, of taking and abandoning, of borrowing and inventing that Filipinos, Cubanos, Salvadoreños, Chilenos, Argentinos—and other artists of immigrant origins—must engage in on a daily basis. The key word here is, of course, *immigrant*.

Unlike the forced migration of Africans in the seventeenth century (read: slavery), or the repeated invasions of Euro-Americans endured by the indigenous populations of the New World (read: conquest), Third World immigration—whether for political or economic reasons, as an act of will or of survival—is, like the emigration of Jews out of Europe from the sixteenth century to the twentieth, a diasporic experience, an exile from home and nation.

"Diaspora is a culture without a country," say Elazar Barkin and Marie-Denise Shelton in their volume, *Borders, Exiles, Diasporas*. "Diaspora is about choice."[17] Though I disagree with them that diasporic peoples always have a choice about whether or not to leave their homeland (how much choice is implied by a Holocaust or a military coup, for example?), there *is*, eventually, the choice, or at least the possibility, of returning. Filipina writer Jessica Hagedorn speaks to this notion of return very eloquently:

> I who had been away [from the Philippines] so long that I almost qualified for the title of foreigner was gripped by the conviction that I too had a city and a history to reclaim, and it may be that writers in my position, exiles or immigrants, expatriates are haunted by a sense of loss, some urge to reclaim, to look back, even at the risk of being mutated into pillars of salt. But if we do look back, we must do so in a knowledge that gives rise to profound uncertainties—that our physical alienation from [our countries of origin] almost inevitably means that we will not be capable of

reclaiming precisely the thing that was lost. Then we will create, in short, fictions, not actual cities or villages, but invisible ones, imaginary homelands, Philippines of the mind.[18]

Those imaginary representations of "home," like the nostalgic contemplations of "returning," are as much a part of the diasporic aesthetic as representations of the leaving.

I see *Santería aesthetics* as a combination of diasporic and race-based aesthetics, for it uses as its nutrient source the rituals, forms, and symbols of the Afro-Cuban religion known as Santería. Originating in the Yoruba religion of Africa, and transplanted to Brazil, the east coast of Mexico, and the islands of the Caribbean by the slave trade in the sixteenth and seventeenth centuries, Santería harks back to the racial and spiritual homeland of Africa, at the same time that it also signifies the Latin American landscapes, colonial histories, and Catholic syncretism of its diaspora living in exile. One could say that while race signifies place in race-based aesthetics, in Santería aesthetics, place is signified by religion; indeed, as a nature-based religion, Santería is always tied to the natural landscape from which it is born and wherein it is practiced. Thus, Santería makes the homeland more mobile, for it can be rooted to any latitude and longitude that the orishas (the gods and goddesses of Santería) find hospitable.

Nowadays, "the orishas inhabit Manhattan and Miami, Los Angeles and Kansas City, [and] the Hudson is as much La Sirene's and Yemaya's as the Caribbean is."[19] Hiding in the guises of Catholic saints,[20] the Afro-Cuban orishas have their own names, character traits, and personal preferences, and each one requires representation and worship through his/her own colors, clothing, foods, natural elements, and other symbolic objects, which the orisha must find aesthetically pleasing.[21] The aesthetic, then, has a sacred function, and the practice of making and assembling these ritual objects in an altar or a throne is akin to the practice of making art. Contemporary Latino and Latin American artists who work in the Santería tradition and represent this Afro-Cuban spiritual belief system employ the styles and forms of the art world, namely installation, sculpture, performance, conceptual art, and earth-body art, to create a place-based aesthetic system that transcends continents, landscapes, and geopolitical boundaries.[22]

Unlike in Santería aesthetics, where art functions in the service of the sacred, some subject matters for indigenous artists, particularly if they pertain to sacred rituals meant only for insider eyes, are off-limits to artistic representation. Only those "images associated with nature and landscape and [public] ritual life [are] found in mural painting, pottery, and textile design, and, of course, rock art."[23] In *Indigenous Aesthetics*, Steven Leuthold defines indigenous aesthetics as aesthetic practices of "people who are minorities in their own homeland, [and] who have suffered oppression in the context of colonial conquest."[24] As native self-representation, indigenous aesthetics "express place attachment." Place attachment is not landscape art; it is a sustained affective tie to the land and the community that has occupied, used, and cared for the land since time immemorial. Thus, place attachment is attachment to land, to community, to culture, and to memory.

In contrast to race-based aesthetics, which looks outward from the colonial experience to a collective memory of a homeland that will most likely never be seen, indigenous aesthetics is born from within the colonial context and looks inward into a collective experience of the homeland's colonization. "The question of indigenous self-representation can only arise in the context of neocolonialism,"[25] argues Leuthold. In that context, indigenous aesthetics is concerned with portraying a native community's process of self-determination, cultural survival and continuity, preservation of traditions, negotiation of inside-outside dynamics, political empowerment, and economic sovereignty. In this aesthetic system, community becomes the signifier for place or homeland, for dispossessed people, particularly Native Americans, are also deterritorialized people, relocated by government edict to reservations that lie far beyond their place of origin or that occupy token space on the map of their own homeland.

Within this colonial (and neocolonial) context, then, that which cannot be claimed by a flag or a homestead—in other words the Native community more than the land base—becomes that place of attachment, that common ground in which indigenous identity is rooted. Although some Native American critics may think I am privileging people/community and disregarding the importance of land base to Native identity, as, indeed, Nancy Marie Mithlo argues in *Our Indian Princess: Subverting the Stereotype* when she states that my "representational construct fails to capture the unique status of Native Americans as sovereign nations,"[26] I am, in fact, arguing that for artists from relocated, and therefore deterritorialized, sovereign nations, their relationship to their original land base is more akin to diaspora aesthetics.

Aztlán Aesthetics

What the different aesthetic systems discussed in the previous section have in common with Aztlán aesthetics is that they are all, to quote Leuthold again, "aesthetic practices that express attachment to place." But place means more than geographical location. For Third World people in the United States, place means race, religion, community, and (as we shall see later) body, as well. Central to all of these practices is the concept of *homeland*, the idea that the land of the artist's birth or the place of origin of the artist's people/group/race, as well as the history and cultural beliefs and practices of that land, all inform the content and theme of the art.

Like race-based aesthetics (which to a large degree includes both diasporic and Santería aesthetic systems), Aztlán aesthetics depicts a strong spiritual, physical, and symbolic connection to the artist's place of origin. That place of origin, however, is not Mexico, for as many Chicana and Chicano writers who have made that journey have discovered, when natives to Aztlán, that is, Mexican Americans, go "home" to Mexico, they find that Mexico is not the homeland after all but a foreign land in which they are perceived as "gringo wannabes" and "sellouts" to their Mexican culture. Nor is the United States the homeland, for within that territory, natives and descendants of Aztlán are viewed as foreigners, outsiders, interlopers, wetbacks, and illegal aliens.

Like indigenous aesthetics, Aztlán aesthetics is a representation of both territorial dispossession and cultural reclamation. The dispossession aspect of this aesthetic can be extrapolated from the many visual and literary allusions to war and its tropes and "heroes": the Mexican War of Independence in 1810, when the native criollos and mestizos of Mexico, led by an insurgent priest, Father Miguel Hidalgo, held their ground against the Spanish colonials and brandished the image of the Virgin of Guadalupe like a nationalist banner for a sovereign nation; the U.S.-Mexico War, which took place between 1846 and 1848, but really started ten years earlier with the Alamo and the illegal Anglo invasion of Texas; the Mexican Revolution, 1910–1921, that made heroes of civilian guerrillas Emiliano Zapata, Pancho Villa, and their female followers, epitomized by the image of *la soldadera*, or La Adelita; and, finally, the war in Vietnam, which claimed a disproportionate number of Chicano lives on the front lines and gave rise to martyrs back home like Rubén Salazar, the Chicano journalist killed during an antiwar demonstration in downtown Los Angeles. Another Chicano resonance with Vietnam was the notion of foreign occupation of a sovereign territory, an issue that would be duplicated in U.S. invasions of the Panama Canal, Nicaragua, and El Salvador. In the same vein, gang-related wars, turf wars, economic wars, social wars—all fought in the streets and homes of the large urban centers of colonized Aztlán—gave another face to the meaning of community loss.

The dispossession aspect of the Aztlán aesthetic also connotes land itself by depicting campesinos, braceros, and farmworkers laboring in a land that no longer belongs to them under the most inhumane of working conditions that included the short-handled hoe, pesticide poisoning, and lack of stability in wages due to no union representation. Advocates for the farmworkers such as César Chávez and Dolores Huerta, who cofounded the United Farm Workers union, thus form part of the heroic iconography of the Aztlán aesthetic, and images of hands and arms, of furrows and crops, bespeak both the dignity of the workers and the indignities visited upon their bodies and working lives. One of those continuing indignities, particularly in the wake of California's blatantly racist Proposition 187,[27] is the issue of deportations from Aztlán, as well as border crossings into that contested terrain between the lost and the promised land.

The other side of the coin, the reclamation aspect of the Aztlán myth, becomes visually manifest in the proliferation of Aztec and Native American iconography that gets reproduced in Chicano murals, particularly that of Indian heroes like Moctezuma and Geronimo,[28] and indigenous symbols, like the Aztec calendar. We find multiple representations of indigenous practices engaged in by both male and female nationalists, such as ritual dancing and *curanderismo*, or faith healing.

But the concept of reclamation is perhaps most aptly expressed in the varied and constant depictions of "home" and "*familia*" that we find breeding quite prolifically in the work of both Chicano and Chicana (heterosexual) artists, particularly in the first decade of the Chicano art movement. In Aztlán aesthetics, then, we could say that *familia* becomes the primary signifier for place of origin, and place of origin amalgamates mother's womb, barrio or neighborhood, and regional landscape—all of which constitute the lost and living homeland in the Chicano imagination.

By regional landscape, I mean more than "the West" or "the Southwest," although they, of course, must come into play against the mainstream imaginary of what those places and directions really signify.

Within the West and the Southwest, there are many regions, many different landscapes: the arid desert of the El Paso–Ciudad Juárez border is not the same high desert of Northern New Mexico, with its forests and mesas. The rain-soaked beaches of the Pacific Northwest coast offer vastly different vistas from the congested cement beaches of the Los Angeles freeways. The fertile fields of California's Central Valley do not produce the same crops or images as the scorching furrows of South Texas or the stream-fed acreage of the Rocky Mountain states. Regional differences, I argue, are as crucial to shaping an artist's aesthetic vision as gender or political identity, as we will see later when we take a quick look at the place-based art of Patssi Valdez, Delilah Montoya, Carmen Lomas Garza, and Laura Aguilar.

Chicana/o culture is not a diasporic culture but, instead, what I have called elsewhere an *alter-Native* culture, that is, an Other indigenous culture to the land base now known as the West and the Southwest.[29] The historical fact that Chicanos/as constitute a legacy of nativity to this land base gets submerged under the "immigrant" rhetoric typically applied to people of Mexican descent since the Treaty of Guadalupe Hidalgo. Like indigenous aesthetics, Aztlán aesthetics pertains to a people who are colonized in their own land, and portrays the cultural hybridity that occurs because of that colonization. Generation by generation, Chicanos lose their connection to the Mexican past and become ever more melted into the American present. Thus, we have non-Spanish-speaking Chicanos, for example, for whom the language of their grandparents is as remote from their experience as walking on the moon. We have assimilated Mexican Americans who forgot, rejected, or simply never learned their cultural history. Memory, then, the missing link between the past and the future, is what must be restored. Knowledge of Aztlán must replace historical amnesia. Aztlán becomes the memory, and the aesthetics of Aztlán portrays not only the social environment in which Chicanos live their daily lives but also multifaceted images of the mythologies, histories, ideologies, and conquests that have shaped the collective memory of "*la raza cósmica*"[30] *de Aztlán.*

MapQuest to Aztlán

Who knows the way to Aztlán? Shall we consult MapQuest? Shall we tap our heels three times and repeat Dorothy's magic phrase, "There's no place like home"? Most of us who identify as Chicanos and Chicanas probably think we know all about Aztlán. We know that Aztlán is a cultural myth of Chicanismo, the myth of the lost homeland that galvanized the Chicano movement. John Chávez argues in *The Lost Land: The Chicano Image of the Southwest* that Aztlán is the central organizing belief that forged the radical Chicano consciousness of the 1960s.[31] According to this cultural myth, Aztlán is the conceptual homeland of Chicanos/as, said to be the Aztecs' place of origin prior to their migration and settlement in the southern Valley of Anahuac, which is present-day Mexico. Believed to be located in what was once the Mexican North and is now the American Southwest, and currently home to over thirty million Mexican-descended peoples,[32] Aztlán represents the Chicano homeland. Chávez argues that this myth is a fundamental component of the politicized Chicano consciousness. Indeed, Aztlán is the foundation of the most basic precept of Chicanismo—cultural nationalism—and its attendant themes of *carnalismo* (brotherhood), *familia*, and community pride, upon which the Chicano ideology of "El" Movimiento was built.

In the discourse of framing as it applies to social movements, Aztlán is a protest frame. It has a motivational function that builds a critical mass by a process known as frame amplification, which focuses on one issue, event, or belief significant to that community, and provides a social justice lexicon and a vocabulary of protest. As Sean Chabot illustrates in his work with African American "itinerant intellectuals," *motivational framing* is one of the interpretive tasks of framing within social movements; the other two are *diagnostic framing*, used to diagnose a social problem, and *prognostic framing*, for communicating solutions to the problem. Chabot also identifies different processes by which social movements are aligned "with potential constituents or resource providers."[33] Social movements and their publics are aligned not only by frame amplification but also by *frame bridging*, connecting two unrelated frames via a particular issue; by *frame extensions*, extending a protest frame's political reach beyond its original interests; and by *frame transformations*, creating new ways of interpreting reality.[34]

Social movements, however, are not agents in and of themselves. It is activists who denounce injustices, who diagnose social problems, who make demands for the rectification of those problems, who motivate others to join their causes, who devise strategies by which to interpret their experiences; in other words, it is activists who make movements. The essays in Supplement 12 of the *International Review of Social History,* titled *Popular Intellectuals and Social Movements: Framing Protest in Asia, Africa, and Latin America* and edited by Michiel Baud and Rosanne Rutten, analyze Third World protest frames, or "contentious politics," by examining the relationship between the activists themselves and the social movements in which they're involved.

> We have tentatively called these individuals "popular intellectuals." We refer here to persons who—formally educated or not—aim to understand society in order to change it, with the interests of the popular classes in mind. They seek to define the problems of subaltern groups, articulate their grievances, and frame their social and political demands.[35]

It is popular intellectuals who generate the "collective action frames" that spawn social movements and social change. Chicano activists in the 1960s, for example, used the imaginary homeland of Aztlán as a way of reinterpreting the history of the Anglo colonization and conquest of the Mexican North by amplifying the frame of indigeneity to a land base that in the last one hundred and fifty years has been mapped as the American Southwest, but that was the Mexican North for three hundred years before that, and indigenous land centuries before maps or treaties divided the land between the white male conqueror and the conquered Indian and Mexican, of whom the latter-day Chicano/a is the progeny. Aztlán, as we have seen, is the conquered Mexican homeland, unjustly occupied, colonized, and stolen in the nineteenth century by rapacious pioneers and their government who came, saw, and conquered under the aegis of Manifest Destiny. As a conquered homeland for all people of Mexican or mestizo/a heritage, Aztlán must be reclaimed by Mexican Americans, and those who believe in this reclamation, those who protest the illegal occupation of Aztlán by the white man, those who see themselves as native to this land base, name themselves and their movement: Chicano.

Those political activists and poets who came up with the concept of "Aztlán" in the 1960s were not only popular intellectuals in the Gramscian sense of the word but also "innovators," that is, they produced "new interpretive frames and new languages for articulating collective interests, identities, and claims."[36] The identity articulated by the concept of a Chicano homeland named Aztlán is not Mexican, Hispanic, Latino, or Mexican American, but Chicano (and Chicana), which itself has now become the "master frame" for organizing and interpreting the experience, history, and culture of mestizos and mestizas in the United States. This master frame has spawned a social movement, an academic field, a cultural category, a political ideology of resistance and affirmation, and a separate but equal, albeit imaginary, homeland.

In Chicano nationalism, the Indian-Hispanic culture of Mexico, along with its Columbian and pre-Columbian history, becomes the abstract Chicano "nation" of Aztlán, championed by the primary symbol of maternity and cultural hybridity, the Virgin of Guadalupe. By pledging allegiance to the culture of Aztlán, Chicanos demonstrated pride in both the indigenous and mestizo aspects of their Mexican heritage, including Catholicism, Aztec and Toltec theology, the Spanish language, and native cultural practices and beliefs. This pride forged a sense of nationalistic loyalty to this imaginary homeland and gave rise to a mestizo identity rooted, quite literally, in the land base of the American Southwest. Thus, says Chávez, "the belief that the Southwest (especially the areas long settled by Mexicans) is the Chicano homeland and the belief that Mexicans are indigenous to and dispossessed of the region are beliefs that have had a formative and continuing influence on the collective Chicano mind."[37]

Paradoxically, Aztlán was conceptualized as a nation autonomous and separate from the United States, but "La Causa Chicana" that this homeland myth inspired was as much about achieving equality of education and opportunity as American citizens as it was about affirming the separatist spirit of Chicano identity and resisting assimilation, racism, and historical amnesia. While separating themselves politically from the dominant culture and value system of the Anglo colonizer, Chicanos also considered themselves exiles in their own land, and protested their social and political marginalization within what Rodolfo Acuña calls "occupied America."

The contradictory and paradoxical nature of the Aztlán struggle was further reproduced in the gender dynamics of La Causa, which dictated the proud liberation of the "macho" and the willful subordination of women in the movement. "Chicanos are an occupied nation within a nation," writes Cherríe Moraga in "Queer Aztlán: The Re-Formation of Chicano Tribe," "and women and women's sexuality are occupied within Chicano nation."[38] Moraga spells out the danger she sees in the strategy of separatism, which "can run dangerously close to biological determinism and a kind of fascism."[39] But the other inherent danger to Chicano nationalism, which Moraga names "its institutionalized heterosexism, its inbred machismo,"[40] is directly related to a male perception of land that is not constrained to Aztlán or limited to Chicanos.

Myths of Origin

As a cultural myth, or myth of origin, Aztlán has much in common with the Judeo-Christian genesis story, for example, or the Anglo-American myth of Manifest Destiny. According to the myth-symbol-image school of cultural analysis espoused in the field of American Studies in its "golden" early years, cultural myths are typically expressed in symbols or images that resonate with a culture's deeply held beliefs, values, and goals, out of which a national or cultural identity can be extrapolated or defined. Thus, cultural myths function as both creation stories and political ideology.

Manifest Destiny, particularly as enacted by the nineteenth-century Anglo-American pioneers that migrated from the Atlantic to the Pacific seaboard in manifestation of their God-given right and destiny to rule the continent, is an American creation story, the prime nation-making narrative, or cultural myth, of the United States. In the language of frame analysis, it would be considered a "master frame" in the ideological formation and nationalist construction of what we call "the American mind."

Of course, we know that Manifest Destiny was more than a myth. The dictionary definition of Manifest Destiny—"an ostensibly benevolent or necessary policy of imperialistic expansion"—transmutes myth into policy: a strategy, a guiding principle, and a course of action. This policy, moreover, is not only "necessary" but also presupposes the pre-ordainment of the United States as an empire that requires expansion. Founded by intrepid pilgrims and rebels who were fleeing religious persecution in England, the story goes, the empire was built by English-speaking Europeans, or Anglo-Saxons, who considered themselves the chosen people of God, and who came to the shores of the New World to build a "city upon a hill," that is, a society above all others.

From Plymouth Rock to the Thirteen Colonies to the national anthem evolved the concept of Manifest Destiny, which gave Euro-Americans the legitimate right and spiritual obligation to spread Christianity and Western civilization from "sea to shining sea," from the Eastern Seaboard to the West Coast. Thus, it has been the collective inevitable destiny of Anglo-Americans to migrate west toward an open land on the edge of civilization and manifest the "ostensibly benevolent" practices of raping, pillaging, plundering, and claiming ownership of the land; saving the heathens; and rewarding themselves with as much "free" land as they could get. Not only was it their moral duty to conquer and civilize the heathen inhabitants, Catholic and Indian alike, but it was also their divine mission to flourish and prosper on that land, with a little help from their friends—the Native Americans and Mexicans whom they displaced, and the enslaved Africans who built their fortunes. The discovery of gold in California a few weeks before the signing of the Treaty of Guadalupe Hidalgo only reinforced the idea of the West as a golden land of promise and plenty.

As the myth-symbol-image school of American Studies taught us,[41] cultural myths are embodied by symbols, and symbols are images or signs of a universal experience. The symbol for Manifest Destiny in the nineteenth century was the frontier, and the frontier brought to mind two conflicting images: that of a bountiful garden just waiting to be plucked, or that of a wilderness on the edge of civilization populated by wild animals and savage Indians. Contradictory though these images of the frontier were, they both symbolized the "universal" experience of American exceptionalism and entitlement, to which, in 1839, the journalist John L. O'Sullivan, in an article titled "The Great Nation of Futurity," attached the expansionist vision that we now know as Manifest Destiny.

> The far-reaching, the boundless future will be the era of American greatness. In its magnificent domain of space and time, the nation of many nations is destined to manifest to mankind the excellence of divine principles; to establish on earth the noblest temple ever dedicated to the worship of the Most High—the Sacred and the True. Its floor shall be a hemisphere—its roof the firmament of the star-studded heavens, and its congregation an Union of many Republics, comprising hundreds of happy millions, calling, owning no man master, but governed by God's natural and moral law of equality, the law of brotherhood—"of peace and good will amongst men." . . . Yes, we are the nation of progress, of individual freedom, of universal enfranchisement.[42]

Since that article was written nearly a quarter of a century before Emancipation, we must assume that O'Sullivan was referring to a brotherhood "of peace and good will amongst [white] men" and that the "great nation of futurity" he invoked would be a nation of white male supremacy.

As a garden, the frontier represented a land of untold opportunities for free men recently liberated from the yoke of European colonialism and anxious to sow their independent seeds across the West. But the garden was also a wilderness, a "meeting point between savagery and civilization,"[43] as Frederick Jackson Turner described it in 1893 in his seminal (I use the word on purpose) paper "The Significance of the Frontier in American History." For Turner, the frontier signified the place in which the transplanted Europeans actually became Americans; thus, he saw the frontier as the place of origin for the American mind and character (which, naturally, was also inscribed with a specific race, color, and gender).

At first the frontier was the Atlantic Coast. It was the frontier of Europe in a very real sense. Moving westward, the frontier became more and more American . . . Thus the advance of the frontier has meant a steady movement away from the influence of Europe, a steady growth of independence on American lines. And to study this advance, the men who grew up under these conditions, and the political, economic, and social results of it, is to study the *really American* [emphasis added] part of our history.[44]

Betita Martínez, in *De Colores Means All of Us*, offers another view of this "really American" narrative, particularly in the late twentieth-century reality of a multicultural, multiracial America:

The [Manifest Destiny] myth's omissions are grotesque. It ignores three major pillars of our nationhood: genocide, enslavement, and imperialistic expansion. . . . Manifest destiny saw Yankee conquest as the inevitable result of a confrontation between enterprise and progress (white) versus passivity and backwardness (Indian, Mexican). . . . Given its obsession with race and the supremacy attached to whiteness, the U.S. national identity inevitably reserved a special disdain for "half-breed" peoples—above all, Mexicans.[45]

Certainly, the landscape movement of the nineteenth century pictured precisely what that significant frontier held in store for pioneering, enterprising white male citizens of the New World seeking to escape the crowded cities of the Eastern Seaboard: a boundless horizon of uncharted and unclaimed real estate rife with natural resources, led by the enlightened and enterprising white spirit of Columbia as she spreads her imperial light over the uncivilized darkness ahead, as we see in John Gast's iconic *American Progress*, 1872 (see Figure 3.1).

Indeed, the description of *American Progress* in the Smithsonian Institution's Art Inventories Catalog reveals all of the work's imperialist trappings:

A woman with long blond hair, dressed in classical style in a flowing white gown that is off one shoulder, floats westward through the air. She is the figure of "Progress," and on her forehead is a gold star, the "Star of Empire." In her proper right arm, she holds a book, and telegraph wire is looped around her elbow. In her proper left hand, she is trailing the telegraph wire westward. On the ground below her, three trains travel westward, as do a stagecoach, a covered wagon, farmers with cattle, and men on horseback, including a Pony Express rider. In the left side of the painting, Indians and buffalo are retreating westward from Progress, leaving behind buffalo skeletons.[46]

In *The Lure of the Local*, Lucy Lippard explains that the controversial 1991 exhibition *The West as America* showed "how nineteenth-century landscape and genre paintings reflected this dichotomy [of the East as metropolis and the West as wilderness] and lured settlers westward where farmers were pictured in vast fields as their Eastern counterparts went about their tasks in cramped farmyards."[47]

The "Chicano mind," or rather, the frame of mind that coalesced out of the identity struggles, political demands, and self-determination rhetoric of the Chicano civil rights movement, had its own master frame, which operated in direct contradiction to Manifest Destiny: the myth of Aztlán, spawned by the revolutionary poetics of the Chicano civil rights movement as the story of the lost or stolen "homeland" of the Mexican North that was conquered by "the irresistible army of Anglo-Saxon emigration"[48] during the U.S.-Mexico War from 1846 to 1848 and ceded to the United States as spoils of war.

The Aztlán myth evolved in the late 1960s out of a selective interpretation of *La raza cósmica*,[49] or *The Cosmic Race*, the treatise by Mexican Secretary of Education José Vasconcelos about the new and ultimate race that was evolving in the Americas as a result of European and Indian *mestizaje*. Seeing themselves as representatives of this "cosmic race," Chicano activists embraced Vasconcelos's ideology wholeheartedly, ignoring the eugenic underpinnings and patent racism of the work as well as the celebration of Anglo-American racial "vigor and solid social virtues,"[50] and focusing only on the idealistic aspects of racial fusion and brotherly love, expressed for example in this sentence:

The future race will not be a fifth, or a sixth race, destined to prevail over its ancestors. What is going to emerge out there is the *definitive* race, the *integral* race, made up of the genius and the blood of all peoples, and, for that reason, more capable of true brotherhood and of a *truly universal* vision.[51] (emphasis added)

At the 1969 Denver Youth Crusade, three Chicano poets, Alurista, Corky Gonzales, and Ricardo Sánchez, penned the first manifesto of the movement, *El Plan Espiritual de Aztlán*. Naming the conquered Southwest the native soil of their Aztec forefathers, by virtue of the Chicanos' genealogy and ancestral roots in that land base, they declared it to be the lost homeland of *la raza cósmica* of Aztlán.

> In the spirit of a new people that is conscious not only of its proud historical heritage but also of the brutal "gringo" invasion of our territories, we, the Chicano inhabitants and civilizers of the northern land of Aztlán from whence came our forefathers, reclaiming the land of their birth and consecrating the determination of our people of the sun, declare that the call of our blood is our power, our responsibility, and our inevitable destiny.[52]

It would be misguided, I think, to imagine that *El Plan de Aztlán* was not written, in part, as both rebuttal and response to the ideology of Manifest Destiny. As opposed to the latter's "chosen children of God," whose destiny and divine right it was to move toward the frontier, to conquer and civilize "the West," we have in the former "the people of the sun" (a reference to the Aztec sun god, Huitzilopochtli, by the way) whose destiny it is to move into the streets, the fields, and the classrooms to reclaim and civilize the Mexican North. Both are driven by their male desire to control the land and by the "call of [their] blood"—be it white or brown, race is still the driving force, the power, behind their movement.

> With our heart in our hands and our hands in the soil, we declare the independence of our mestizo nation. We are a bronze people with a bronze culture. Before the world, before all of North America, before all our brothers in the bronze continent, we are a nation, we are a union of free pueblos, we are *Aztlán*.[53]

These young Chicano poets borrowed from Vasconcelos only the overarching concept of *"mestizaje"* as the racial hybridity of the four major races of humankind—African, Asian, Indian, and Caucasian—that was forced by the Spanish Conquest of the Americas and that resulted in a "cosmic race," which Vasconcelos named "*la raza de bronce*," or the Bronze Race. When the Mexican descendants of that original Spanish-Indian *mestizaje* were conquered and colonized by the Anglo-Americans in 1848 ("the brutal 'gringo' invasions of our territories"), a new racial, cultural, and linguistic hybridity developed, resulting in "a new [Chicano] people"; thus, Chicanos constitute a new race and culture on the American continent ("the bronze people with a bronze culture"), La Raza de Aztlán, the mestizo natives of a lost homeland located in the conquered Mexican North, aka the American Southwest.

Utopic though the idea was, the myth of Aztlán took hold in the Mexican American revolutionary imagination across the Southwest and became a central tenet of Chicanismo, the ideology of a politicized *indigenista* identity of empowerment and resistance to discrimination, colonization, and racism. I interpret Chicano/a indigenism as an "alter-Native" identity,[54] an identity that is both Other (alter) and indigenous (native) to a specific geography. Ancestrally, Mexicans and their indigenous forebears occupied the land base of the American Southwest for centuries prior to the founding of the American colonies on the Eastern Seaboard. Millennia before Anglo-American pioneers and soldiers claimed the territory as a possession of the United States by right of conquest, the territory belonged to the sovereign nation of Mexico. Close to three hundred years before that, it was a colony of Spain, though technically it "belonged" to the indigenous inhabitants of the area. As descendants of those original inhabitants, and of the conquered Mexicans who lost their country and their citizenship overnight with the signing of the Treaty of Guadalupe Hidalgo at the close of the U.S.-Mexico War, Chicanos and Chicanas share the sense of ancient nativity in that land base, reclaimed as the conceptual homeland of Aztlán, as well as the racial, ethnic, and linguistic marginalization and alienation of a colonized culture. Indeed, this conceptual homeland can be said to have galvanized the Chicano civil rights movement as a struggle for community awakening that was manifesting itself in the streets, the fields, the classrooms, and the sweatshops of this twice-"occupied America."

The overarching ideal of a homeland, whether framed as the homeland of the pre-American Southwest, the mythic Aztlán, or barrio of the "homey," remains a deeply embedded—if metaphorically fluid—unifying symbol for a community that in its various manifestations and regional developments remains recalcitrant in the face of social domination since 1848.[55]

The myth of Aztlán represents the lost homeland of the Mexican American descendants of the Treaty of Guadalupe Hidalgo, but what universal experience does Aztlán signify? *El Plan* makes it clear:

> Aztlán belongs to those who plant the seeds, water the fields, and gather the crops and not to the foreign Europeans. We do not recognize capricious frontiers on the bronze continent . . . Brotherhood unites us, and love for our brothers makes us a people whose time has come and who struggle against the foreigner gabacho who exploits our riches and destroys our culture.[56]

In other words, Aztlán signifies a brotherhood of native-born, working-class Chicanos, a proletariat consciousness signified by all of those images of laboring in the land, "plant[ing] the seeds, water[ing] the fields, and gather[ing] the crops," that is united by the motivational image of a giant bronze race waking up to fight against Anglo exploitation. The brotherhood signifies a nation, and the nation signifies a family of like-minded activists, workers, and organic intellectuals inspired by the civil rights movements of the day and stirred to action by the cultural myth of Aztlán. Thus, the United Farm Workers movement, led by César E. Chávez and Dolores Huerta, is said to have been the catalyzing struggle for the Chicano civil rights movement in 1966, as represented in the multiple posters generated during the movement era and beyond.

The Third Myth

I see another cultural myth coming into play here, one that precedes either Manifest Destiny or Aztlán, a myth that both bisects and connects the other two, but which has been ignored in the genealogy of Aztlán. I call it the "myth of the Holy Familia." Back when the Southwest was neither American nor Mexican but flew instead the Spanish flag, the territory was colonized by priests and conquistadores whose mission it was to extend the power of the Holy Roman Empire, which was both Catholic and Spanish. More land and subjects for the Roman Empire meant more wealth for the royal families of Castilla and Aragón and more souls for the pope and the Mother Church. The Reformation that split Western Europe into Catholics and Protestants and the defeat of the Spanish Armada in 1588 had weakened the ramparts of Spanish dominance. Not only was Spain losing its economic advantage, but also the Catholic Church was losing its spiritual control over Europe. Thus,

Spain needed to bolster its political, territorial, and spiritual assets, but it could only do so by expanding its colonial holdings. In order to mitigate the losses suffered to Protestantism in the religious revolt created by the Reformation, the king and queen of Spain needed more subjects and more lands to recuperate the power of the Roman Empire. In the spiritual realm, the Holy Father, the pope; and his wife, the Mother Church; and their prolific extended Familia of saints and martyrs needed more souls in the heavenly Family to reinvigorate the power of Catholicism, which had been dealt a heavy blow when Henry VIII of England divorced Catherine of Aragón, the daughter of Spain, and thus launched England's split from the Roman Catholic Church. La Conquista, then, financed by the Spanish Crown (the symbolic patriarch) and the Church (the spiritual matriarch) was about growing the empire of the Holy Family of Spain and the Catholic Church, and thus restoring them both to their dominant position in Europe.

Traditional American history books tell us that what motivated the Puritans to come to the New World was the religious intolerance of England that expected them to conform their beliefs to the official Church of England. The national character of the United States is encoded with the idea that religious freedom was the primary motive that brought the English settlers across the Atlantic and that the Puritan founding fathers believed in this idyllic vision of a land where people were free to worship as they pleased. In fact, this was not the case, for the Puritans were as religiously intolerant as their compatriots back in the Old World; the only difference was they wanted everyone to conform to the Puritan version of Christianity and to Puritan morals and Puritan practices. Those who didn't were either exiled to another colony or put in jail or accused of witchcraft and put to death.

The Puritans saw themselves as the chosen children of God, and New England was their great experiment upon a hill, an experiment of what they called godliness that would not tolerate any other religion in its midst, especially not Catholicism, which they felt represented the anti-Christ. Even the Indian religions were more tolerated than Catholicism because it was believed that the "simple-minded" Indians didn't know any better and just had to be educated in the true way in order to become civilized human beings rather than ignorant heathens. Catholics, in the Protestant mind, were beyond redemption; they were evil itself.

Indeed, the English notion of the "Black Legend," popularized during the Reformation in the sixteenth century, portrayed the Spaniards as cruel, destructive idol worshippers who burned people at the stake and gave more credence to a man called the pope than to the word of God as recorded in the Bible. This belief in the Black Legend was as active in England as it was in the English colonies, and it informed much of the animosity between the English diaspora and the Spanish diaspora in the Americas that Vasconcelos himself discusses in *La raza cósmica* as "the old conflict of the two stocks [the Spanish and the English],"[57] a hostility that came to a head at the intersection of the myths of Manifest Destiny and the Holy Familia, in a place called el Norte or the West, the Frontier or La Frontera, the Southwest or Aztlán.

That place is the border, not the border as the periphery of empire, which is the dominant interpretation of Manifest Destiny's "frontier," nor the border as the militarized zone between two supposedly friendly nations, but the border as a bridge and a crossroads. The border as a *nepantla* space, or space in-between, created by the confluence of three (not two) cultural myths. A contested, utopic terrain that is an integral component of the Chicano/Chicana political mind.

The Crux of the Matter: Re-framing the Borderlands[58]

Where exactly is the border? How do we map the borderlands? Is the border located horizontally on the map, as the American pioneers positioned it? Or is it a vertical point, as immigrants from the south see it? Is it the front door to the Promised Land or the back portal to the Third World? We need to go back five centuries to answer this question.

From the southern perspective of the Spanish missionaries and conquistadores of the sixteenth century and their colonial descendants, the borderlands was located in the North; from the Eastern Seaboard perspective of the Anglo-Americans, the area was positioned in the West. Oriented at different points on the compass, these locations suggest radically different points of departure for narrating or visualizing the history of the same territory, a history that is intersected by conflicting cultural myths and their divergent symbolic meanings and representations. To help me better visualize these different interpretations of and relationships to this same land base, I have constructed the graph in Figure 3.2, composed of two intersecting lines that form four quadrants, within which we find eight opposing frames of reference for the same territory.

In this graph, the East => West axis represents the cultural myth of Manifest Destiny, and the slightly longer South => North axis, the cultural myth of the Holy Familia. Already the graph takes on a particular

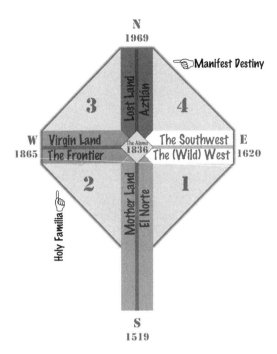

Figure 3.2. The four quadrants of Aztlán. Digital graph.
Courtesy of Alma López.

shape, more cruciform than square, the closed quadrants reminiscent of a Native American "ojo de Dios," or eye of God, structure. In my mind, the northern half of the chart represents the United States, and the southern half, Mexico. To signify the standards of the two nations, imagine the horizontal cross arms on the graph in red and white, the northern section of the vertical arm in blue, and the southern section in green. The crossroads between them show the conflicts, contradictions, and convergences that actually created the U.S.-Mexico border where these two Eurocentric cultural myths—Manifest Destiny and the Holy Familia—collide, intersect, and reproduce in the myth of Aztlán.

The horizontal Manifest Destiny line tracks 245 years between two foundational nation-making moments of the United States: the Pilgrims' landing at Plymouth Rock (1620) and the end of the Civil War (1865), a trajectory that includes numerous local wars with the Native nations; the Revolutionary War (1763–1783); the War of 1812; the U.S.-Mexico War (1846–1848); the Civil War (1861–1865); and naval engagements with France, Spain, Canada, China, Japan, Algiers, Sumatra, Samoa,

Fiji, Africa, and almost all of Latin America. This horizontal perspective shows how the land between the Atlantic and the Pacific Oceans was perceived in the colonial imaginary of Anglo-American pioneers in those intervening centuries. Seen as either a wilderness in need of saving or a garden in need of planting, the land "west" of the Mississippi represented a wide-open frontier of opportunities and possibilities, a virgin land ripe for plowing, taming, and civilizing, a golden promised land; hence, the horizontal line on the graph tracks the development of the American mind, or rather, the imperialistic national character of the United States that was born at the contact point between the European colonizer and the Native colonized.

The vertical line tracks four and a half centuries between the arrival of the Spanish conquistadores in Mexico (1519) and the 1969 drafting of *El Plan Espiritual de Aztlán*, considered by activists to be the Chicano Declaration of Independence. This trajectory covers three major wars in Mexico—the War for Independence from Spain (1810–1821), the U.S.-Mexico War (1846–1848) against Anglo occupation, and the Franco-Mexican War after French occupation of Mexico (1862–1867)—and two colonial takeovers, from the first conquest of Mexico by Hernán Cortés in the sixteenth century, when a land once cultivated by Toltecs, Aztecs, Mayas, Mixtecs, Huicholes, Zapotecs, Chichimecs, Comanches, Apaches, and Pueblos (to name a few of the native peoples that populated that huge land base) was claimed and occupied in the name of the Holy Roman Empire, to the second conquest in the nineteenth century by the westward-bound Anglo-Americans. Sovereignty for Mexico did not come quickly or easily, as it took close to three hundred years for the mestizo and other mixed-race descendants of those conquistadores and missionaries (and the native women they raped) to come into their own consciousness as a people and a nation.

Little did the Mexicans know that fifteen years after winning their independence from their Spanish conquerors, they would be fighting a greedier colonizer in their good neighbor to the north, who invaded Texas in droves, extorted it away from Mexico, and later instigated the U.S.-Mexico War, which annexed the provinces of California and New Mexico and areas that later became the states of Utah, Nevada, and parts of Arizona and Wyoming—more than half of Mexico's territorial integrity—through the Treaty of Guadalupe Hidalgo. The treaty sold the northern half of Mexico's land base to the United States for 15 million dollars (one of the best real estate swindles in the history of the Americas) and transformed the Mexican citizens who "chose"[59] to remain in the occupied north into second-class residents of annexed territory. Literally overnight, then, they lost their country, their citizenship, and eventually their land and their language.

As Laura Gómez reveals in her book *Manifest Destinies: The Making of the Mexican American Race*, the province of New Mexico at the time of the Anglo conquest of the Mexican North exceeded the size of Texas and California combined. In this vast territory lived the majority of northern Mexicans and Indian tribes, including "15,000 Pueblo Indians and perhaps 60,000 other Indians."[60] Relations between the Mexicans and the Pueblos were often hostile, as Mexicans represented the genocide wreaked upon the native peoples by the Spaniards. Mexicans and Indians shared an uneasy inhabitation in New Mexico and far outnumbered the Anglo-American settlers and carpetbaggers. "When Euro-American colonizers arrived in New Mexico, one of their goals was to cement the divide between Mexicans and Pueblo Indians. One way to do this was to allow Mexican Americans to designate themselves as legally white while preventing Pueblo Indians from doing so."[61] Through culture, religion, and language, then, "whiteness" for the Mexicans in New Mexico was inculcated as meaning Spanish. Thus was born what Carey McWilliams in *North from Mexico* calls "the fantasy heritage,"[62] a colonized imaginary that remains popular in New Mexico and California, to describe those Mexican Americans who insist on calling themselves Spanish American and to perpetuate the fantasy that their lineage can be traced directly to the loins of Hernán Cortés, Juan de Oñate, or Diego de Vargas with no native women in the mix.

The four quadrants created by the juncture of Manifest Destiny and the Holy Familia in Figure 3.2 reveal the different ideological perspectives that evolved in the contact points between the Anglo-American and the Mexican American/Chicano/Hispano orientations of history. We've already established that the Anglo-American conquerors were moving west while the Spanish conquistadores had been moving north in their respective quests for and conquests of the promised land, their different migrations creating an imaginary cartography of this territory that was laden with their colonial nation-state ideologies. If we analyze these four quadrants and eight frames created by the juncture of these two cultural myths, we come away with distinct and contradictory relationships between place and identity, all located on the same land base.

1. El Norte/The (Wild) West
2. The (Mexican) Mother Land/The Frontier
3. The Lost Land/The Virgin Land
4. Aztlán/The Southwest

The historical and political underpinnings of the first quadrant form the foundation for the place-identity constructs of the other quadrants and must be unpacked in some detail. The first quadrant establishes the view of the borderlands as a place of both unknown dangers and limitless wealth for both the northbound conquistador and the westbound pilgrim. "If myth set [the Spaniards] in motion," writes Carey McWilliams, "it was the Indians who lured them still further from their bases with tales of gold and silver, always seeking to draw them out of the Southwest. Where they had expected to find cities of gold, they found mud villages and uninhabited desert wastes."[63] In other words, what drove the Spaniards northward in their conquest of the borderlands was not the quest to redeem the "Indian savage" but the Legend of Cíbola, or rather the search for the "seven cities of gold," said to be located somewhere in the north. For the Spanish explorers and missionaries who embarked on the quest, "el Norte" signified a dream of fabulous wealth and promise, the same significance it holds today for the Mexican, Central American, and other Latino immigrants who come here seeking "the American Dream."

The Anglo-American pioneers heading west three hundred years after the Spanish Conquest, guided by their conviction in their manifest right to conquer the hemisphere, believed they were going into an uncharted wilderness that they wanted to tame into a bountiful and civilized garden (hence the "wild west" designation that became so popular in Hollywood and penny westerns); a land of progress and prosperity for a recently liberated race of men who, according to John O'Sullivan, represented "the nation of human progress" that "no earthly power" could stop or "set limits to [their] onward march" because "Providence [was] with [them]."[64]

By 1821, Mexico had already won its independence from Spain, and for fifteen years, the mestizos and criollos that populated the land base that had once been the colony of New Spain saw it as the independent Mexican nation, or Mexican motherland; they had their own government, their own militia, and their own map of the country, including the vast territories of the northern provinces of Texas, New Mexico, and California, which were in trouble with the Indians (who had their own way of conceptualizing that same land base). Unaware of the ideology of American exceptionalism that was driving the Anglos west of the Mississippi, and in the same year that the United States issued the Monroe Doctrine (1823), basically barring any more European colonies in the Americas, the Mexican government offered a land grant to Anglo-American Moses Austin to help settle the province of Texas and provide some protection against Indian raids on the missions and settlements of the north. The only conditions for the land grant were for Moses Austin and those who came with him to convert to Catholicism and pledge allegiance to Mexico. Agreeing to the terms (but never actually following through on the promise), Austin settled into his new land, bringing his family, his friends, and his slaves with him. Essentially, Mexico had established what amounted to an open-door policy to Anglo immigration into Texas and other parts of the northern frontier. In 1829, Mexico abolished slavery, but by then, Austin and his Anglo neighbors had already rooted themselves and their cotton fields in Texas, which they could not cultivate without slave labor. The first stirrings of Anglo rebellion against the central government in Mexico were felt as early as 1830, when Mexico closed the border to Anglo immigration into Texas. By 1835, however, the number of now "illegal" Anglo immigrants in Texas had more than tripled since the closing of the border. Far outnumbering the native Mexican inhabitants of the province, the new Anglo majority declared Texas a new, independent republic, in effect launching a war for independence from Mexico, which was construed as a backward nation ruled by a tyrannical president, Antonio López de Santa Anna, who presided over Mexico on and off between 1833 and 1855. In 1836, seeing that he had no choice but to pick up the gauntlet thrown down by the Anglo dissenters in Texas, Santa Anna brought the full power of the Mexican army to bear on the Alamo mission, which the so-called Texas Freedom Fighters had occupied as the headquarters of the rebellion. Outmanning and outgunning the Freedom Fighters holed up inside the Alamo, the Mexican army, led by Santa Anna himself, massacred the Anglo brigade in 1836, giving rise to the Anglo clarion call "Remember the Alamo!"[65]

For the Anglo-Americans fighting for the liberation of Texas, "Remember the Alamo" actually signified remember the treachery and savagery of the Mexicans, remember you can't trust Mexicans, and remember Mexicans will slaughter you if you're not careful, even if you're doing something for their own good, such as liberating them from tyranny and oppression. "Remember the Alamo," in fact, harked back to "remember the Inquisition," "remember the Black Legend," "remember the cruelty of the Spaniards and the Catholics."

In the end, however, due to a tactical mistake of Santa Anna's, Sam Houston's renegade army launched a surprise attack on the Mexican army along the San Jacinto River, captured Santa Anna, and won the war; thus, Mexico lost the enormous territory of Texas, which became the Lone Star Republic until 1845, when it was admitted to the United States.

The second quadrant shows the historical clash between the Anglo-American pioneers migrating to the Frontier in the nineteenth century and the citizens of a new nation-state who felt their recently liberated "Mother Land" was being invaded by so many illegal Anglo settlers, ultimately culminating in a war between the two nations and a treaty that dispossessed, displaced, and disenfranchised the native Mexican inhabitants of the region.

The third quadrant depicts the different post-Anglo conquest views of the area, after the Treaty of Guadalupe Hidalgo ceded half of Mexico's northern territory to the United States at the close of the U.S.-Mexico War in 1848, transforming it into a "Lost Land" in the consciousness of the losing country and its conquered descendants indigenous to the area. For the conquerors, the West was now a "Virgin Land," ready to be seeded, husbanded, and made productive by the industrious pioneer.

Finally, the fourth quadrant politicizes the area now geographically mapped as the American Southwest as the Chicano cultural homeland of Aztlán. The crux of the matter is that Aztlán is a product of the cultural conjoining of mutually antagonistic nations, histories, languages, locations, and myths of origin: English and Spanish, Mexican and American, the West and el Norte, the homeland and the frontier. As John Chávez tells us, "Throughout the Southwest, Mexicans saw [their] struggle for racial and cultural survival within the United States as part of the larger conflict between the Latin and Anglo-Saxon civilizations, a conflict that dated at least as far back as the defeat of the Spanish Armada in 1588."[66] This historical conflict, I argue, lies at the heart of Aztlán and at the heart, as well, of the Anglo-Mexican marriage connoted by the Treaty of Guadalupe Hidalgo.

In the four quadrants of the Aztlán graph above, I depict the Battle of the Alamo as the contact point between the myth of Manifest Destiny and the myth of the Holy Familia, the moment of conception for the myth of Aztlán, for it was here that the forces of the Anglo Empire first crossed paths and rifles with the descendants of the Spanish Empire. Ten years later, the crossroads between Manifest Destiny and the myth of Aztlán would be the U.S.-Mexico War, at the culmination of which the Mexican North was seized as spoils of war in the name of freedom and democracy. It was here that the English and the Spanish stocks went head to head once again, as Vasconcelos would say, and that the English stock established its dominance over the Spanish stock in the New World.

For all of the Edenic possibilities of the frontier, the Battle of the Alamo and the U.S.-Mexico War proved to the Anglo-American mind that "the West" was still a wilderness, a land at the edge of civilized society populated by "wild Indians" and "bloodthirsty" Mexican descendants of the cruel Spaniards who were not willing to acknowledge the superiority of the Anglo-Saxons and their divine mandate to civilize the natives.

What Manifest Destiny and the myth of Aztlán have in common, despite the racial, ideological, and religious differences of the cultures that spawned them, is that they are both colonial discourses. The "American" narrative of the conquest of the West and the "Mexican" narrative of the conquest of the North both reified the male colonizer and gendered land as female—mother or virgin—to be taken, protected, returned to, or exchanged by men.

Framing the Nation: Virgins, Mothers, and Whores, Oh My!

The myth of the frontier (expressed as either garden or wilderness) saw the agents of Manifest Destiny as male—industrious, progressive, dominating—and the land (as well as its native inhabitants) as female—abject, stagnant, passive. "Pushed aside by the course of empire," writes Erika Doss in "'I *Must* Paint': Women Artists of the Rocky Mountain Region," "the Rocky Mountain landscape and its indigenous population were central to the construction of the mythical American frontier but essentially disposable when it came to the business of conquering, and settling, *that place*"[67] (emphasis added). Rather than a *mother* land to which they wanted to return, or with which they were seeking reunification, these Anglo-American trailblazers imagined the "West" as a *virgin*, just waiting to get hitched to the wagon of Western civilization. Rather than displaced sons in a constant state of separation anxiety, these Anglo pioneers imagined themselves hardy, rugged husbands and future fathers. We can read westward migration, then, in two ways: as an act of raping the virgin, metaphorized, for example, by the image of the plow, the covered wagon, and the church steeple, all cutting steadily into and across the landscape; but also, in the symbolic imaginary that interpreted the "West" as the new garden of Eden to be *husbanded* by the intrepid pioneer, as an act of marrying the land to build an empire.[68]

"In the gendered dyads that structure the Western imaginary," says Amy Kaminsky in *After Exile: Writing the Latin American Diaspora*, "the exile occupies the male position—or at least one of them—of child in the process of separation, while the feminine position is the maternal place left behind."[69] As a lost land, Aztlán is a metaphor for the vanquished Indian mother, the raped, abject mother symbolized by La Malinche as well as the sacred, all-powerful mother represented by La Virgen de Guadalupe. Chicana historian Emma Pérez argues that Aztlán is not actually an internal colony of the United States, but rather a "maternal imaginary" of the dispossessed Chicano psyche. In *The Decolonial Imaginary: Writing Chicanas into History*, Pérez describes the Chicano version of what Kaminsky sees as a prevalent leitmotif in the literature of South American men living in exile: the image of nation as maternal body. Says Pérez:

> The nationalist imperative is to move back in time, a regression, a return to the mother, but the mother cannot be Malinche. She must be La Virgen de Guadalupe; she cannot be sexual. She must be pure for the nationalist dream. In this way, Aztlán is not an empirical, internal colony, but an imaginary, a maternal imaginary . . . And the land is maternal; it is pure, virginal; it is where the family will all be safe in the womb. Hence, nationalism becomes a return to the mother—Aztlán—where woman can be only metaphor and object.[70]

Like one of the mythic lost tribes of Israel, Aztlán is a lost nation, and Chicano nationalism, that is, allegiance to the nation of Aztlán, is a sense of devotion and loyalty to a land that is as much a sacred place of origin as the site of original sin—miscegenation—connoted by the rape of conquest (both Spanish and Anglo). Somewhere between shame and veneration is where Chicano nationalism is located.

But what, exactly, is nationalism? Etymologically, the word springs from *nation*, which itself springs from the Latin word *natio*, which means birth, nation, and people. In Spanish, the connection is more obvious: *nación/nacer* and *nacionalismo/nacimiento*. The word *native* is also connected to birth, and hence, to mother. Nationalism, then, is a claim to nativity, a fierce allegiance to the womb (the land) that gave birth to the people that constitute the family (the nation) of Aztlán. Although we could see nationalism as a form of mother worship, where mother represents homeland, and where nation represents *familia*, the mother's worth is purely symbolic, a vehicle for nationalist redemption from the shame of conquest.

There are several ironies to Aztlán. To say "I am native to Aztlán" is to say, I was born of an imaginary mother, conceived in the immaculate devotion of a dispossessed progeny in search of a symbol to galvanize their mythic "return" to their place of origin. Thus, while the offspring of Aztlán are very much a material and historical reality, the *mother*land is an imaginary construct that came into being through the political imagination and literary representations of the Chicano poets who conceptualized *El Plan Espiritual de Aztlán*. We could say, then, that Aztlán (the concept of motherland, not the land base) was born of the son, not the other way around. Another irony is that, in Chicano nationalism, the object of devotion and loyalty is female (land) or female-centric (*familia*), but the objective of the revolution is male control of both terrains. It is, in other words, a *reconquista*, a reconquest of the land (and, by extension, of the female body) that will assure the liberation and survival of the race via the male line.

Both the Chicano ideology of a conquered *mother*land and the Anglo-American ideology of a free and primitive *virgin* land look to Aztlán/ the West as the place of opportunity and rebirth, and both gender land as female. How does the juncture of these two cultural myths that have had a formative influence on the cultural character of their respective nations, by virtue of occupying the same land base, intersect in the Chicano psyche (whether Chicanos like to admit it or not)? How does the common denominator of gendered dynamics that connects these two myths create an aesthetics of place, a representational politics of homeland, that depicts the same place of origin as both vanquished mother and potential, if primitive, virgin?

The emphasis on "forefathers" in the first passage quoted above from *El Plan Espiritual de Aztlán*, just like the reification of male unity we see in phrases like "Brotherhood unites us, and love for our brothers makes us a people whose time has come" and "Our cultural values of life, family, and home will serve as a powerful weapon to defeat the gringo dollar value system and encourage the process of love and brotherhood"—all indicate the sexual hierarchy that will prevail in the nation of Aztlán and the heroic role that the brothers are going to play in the struggle, aided and supported, of course, by their "Adelitas," or female revolutionaries.

"The problem is the *gabacho*, not the macho" was a popular slogan of the female loyalists (read: antifeminists) of the Chicano movement, implying to the *hocicona* (loudmouthed) women who were protesting too much about Chicano sexism that, first, their loyalty was to their race, not to their gender, and second, that as long as *las hermanas* were working to liberate the macho, they were also working to liberate *la familia de Aztlán*.[71]

As a metaphor for the brown-skinned cosmic race forcefully forged during the Spanish Conquest of the so-called New World, the trope of *familia* functions as both figurative and literal reminder of conquest, hybridity, and cultural survival. Thus, *familia* (from the Latin word *famulus*, which means a gathering of slaves) encompasses each Chicano's own immediate and extended relations as well as all Mexican-descended peoples who are engaged in the struggle for liberty, continuity, and dignity in the face of colonization.

For all of its connotative function, however, this aspect of the Aztlán aesthetic is the most problematic for me as a feminist critic, because, as we well know, both "home" and "family" are heavily gendered areas, that is, they set the mold for gender identity and political interactions between the genders. Home and family are, moreover, considered part of the domestic domain, and as such, are believed to be under the control of women. Chicano patriarchy, however, always asserts its own preeminent control of women's lives and bodies, and for as much "power" as women may be said to wield within the home and family, they are nevertheless subservient to the almighty 'Apá. *Famulus* indeed. Only the laws of the Father govern Aztlán, though it is the Mother who is pictured over and over again as holding together the family, the house, and thus the culture. This imbues the mother figure with a biological mystique and a symbolic role as the beating heart of Aztlán. Any divergence from that role, be it through a political engagement with the ideology of women's liberation, as in the case of Chicana feminists, or through rejection of the heterosexual imperative, as in the case of Chicana lesbians, immediately casts Chicanas who subscribe to either or both of these choices in a suspect light.

Viewed as "wannabe" white women, Chicana feminists are still accused in some inner circles of betraying the Chicano revolution and subscribing to a divisive politics that breaks up the *familia*—both symbolically by criticizing the "brothers" and "*jefes*" of the movement and calling them on their sexism and heterosexism, and literally, by not using their sexuality in the service of breeding new revolutionaries for La Causa, or simply by "refusing the favor"[72] of male domination. To represent this betrayal of La Raza, the Malinche label is branded on all who would put gender or sexuality on par with race or class as sites of oppression and struggle within the Chicano movement.

> In this postmodern age of shifting signifiers and signifieds, and in the same way that early feminist artists reclaimed the word "cunt" and that gay and lesbian discourses have reappropriated the word "queer" and invested it with the power of self-naming, Chicana lesbians [and feminists] can take "Malinchista" away from the oppressive and degrading signification of patriarchy . . . To be a Malinche *is* to be a traitor: to the essentializing, stereotypical, male-privileged gender codes of the race; thus, Malinche is a new mirror for Chicana posterity to look upon and in which to be reflected. From this mirror arises the mirror of Malinchismo, a new theory of Chicana resistance.[73]

Witness Yolanda López's famous triptych, which casts the Virgin of Guadalupe as an Everywoman committed to empowering her own life— by working at a job outside the home for thirty years, for example, or running a marathon—rather than waiting around on a pedestal of womanly perfection.[74] How about Ester Hernández's vision of the Virgin as a tattoo on a woman's back, being offered a symbol of female sexuality by another woman's hand, or Guadalupe as a karate expert kicking at the face of both patriarchy and racism, or Hernández's reinscription of the Statue of Liberty as a pre-Columbian Libertad, welcoming her "poor" and "oppressed" *gente* south of the border into the free land of Aztlán.[75] In the mixed-media triptych *Las Tres Marías*, Judy Baca critically interrogates the virgin/mother/whore stereotypes that Chicano patriarchy has fixed on women's lives.[76] Flanked by the representation of a 1940s Pachuca on one side and a 1970s Chola on the other, the middle panel is a mirror in which the viewer has no choice but to see him/herself reflected. By positioning the viewer in the paradigm, the piece ridicules the stereotypical representation of Chicanas that we see repeatedly in Chicano patriarchy: a refrain of mothers, daughters/virgins, and whores, with, actually, one of those Marys receiving most of the limelight.

Among Chicana feminists, this paradigm has come to be known as the Tres Marías Syndrome, in honor of the three Marys who were present at the Crucifixion of Jesus: The *Virgin* Mary; Mary, the *Mother* of James; and Mary Magdalene, sister of Lazarus and reformed *Whore*. "Implicit in the virgin/mother/whore trilogy of oppressions represented by the three Marys of the Crucifixion are the images of La Virgen de Guadalupe, La Llorona, and La Malinche—the female trinity of

Chicana identification that [Chicana artists, writers, and theorists] have reappropriated to their own ends."[77] Employing the politics of "disidentification" that José Muñoz discusses in his book by the same title, these "gender nationalists"[78] (as Chicana feminists have been termed by macho and male-identified compatriots in Chicano/a Studies) choose not to separate completely from the dominant ideology of Chicanismo, but to "transform its cultural logic [of sexism and homophobia] from within, always laboring to enact permanent structural change while at the same time valuing the importance of local or everyday struggles of [Raza] resistance."[79]

Actually, this investigation into place, identity, gender, and aesthetics emerged out of my dis-ease with the rigid patriarchy and entrenched sexism of Chicanismo and led me to question whether Aztlán, as both concept and aesthetic, signified the same thing to women as it does to men. Land as mother/womb/virgin is the dominant construction in Chicano cultural nationalism. To what extent do Chicana artists and writers apply or oppose this patriarchal ideology in their own aesthetic constructions? If Aztlán is populated by machos, misogynists, and homophobes, as well as by more middle-of-the-road types who nonetheless subscribe (consciously or not) to the Tres Marías as the appropriate role models for women, then to what degree does the male nationalist construction of Aztlán inform the political identity of Chicana artists?

My hypothesis is that, rather than expressing their attachment to place as either dispossessed of or exiled from their native land, Chicana artists have a more intimate and embodied connection to place. Whereas Anglo and Chicano men have already laid claim to the land as either their virgin or their mother, Chicanas are actively deconstructing and reconstructing the Malinche face of the Tres Marías, the ideological aspect that represents the traded, penetrated, and bifurcated body of the land. It is, in other words, a politics of the body and of self-creation; rather than "they took my place of origin" or "I was forced to leave my place of origin," Chicana artists seem to be saying "I *am* my place of origin."

Transmuted into art, this politics of the body produces an *embodied aesthetic*, one that frees the Chicana artist from the shackles of a relational identity as some man's wife, mother, daughter, or mistress. Instead of dispossession, ownership, or reclamation of a place outside the self, embodied aesthetics uses the body as the signifier for place. As such, the body functions as site of origin, bridge between worlds, and locus of liberation.

In this chapter I have employed a Chicana feminist praxis that Emma Pérez calls "sexing the colonial imaginary," that is, using sexuality as a methodology by which to reveal the trappings of sexual power that are embedded in colonial acts such as the conquest and occupation of a foreign territory.

> Where women are conceptualized as merely a backdrop to men's social and political activities, they are in fact intervening interstitially while sexing the colonial imaginary. In other words, women's activities are unseen, unthought, merely a shadow in the background of the colonial mind. Yet Chicana, Mexicana, India, mestiza actions, words spoken and unspoken, survive and persist whether acknowledged or not. Women's voices and actions intervene to do what I call sexing the colonial imaginary, historically tracking women's agency on the colonial landscape.[80]

Let us see now how four Chicana artists from completely different regions and landscapes in Aztlán—Southern California, Northern New Mexico, and South Texas—engage in the task of "tracking women's agency on the colonial landscape" of their respective homelands.

The Body as Place

The art of Patssi Valdez and Laura Aguilar from Los Angeles; Carmen Lomas Garza from Kingsville, Texas; and Delilah Montoya, born in Texas and raised in Nebraska but with ancestral roots in Northern New Mexico, is located squarely in the landscapes, histories, and politics of their respective locations. By looking at and comparing the impact of regional differences between Southern California, rural South Texas, and Northern New Mexico,[81] and exploring how those differences are represented in the art and politics of these diverse Chicana artists, I suggest that it is possible to analyze the hidden role that *place*, not just as homeland or motherland but as body and self, when intersected with gender, plays in the construction of a politicized aesthetic vision.

In so many of Patssi Valdez's acrylic paintings, Aztlán has been condensed into one room, such as the one depicted in *The Magic Room* (1994), a room of shadows and vertiginous angles, of bright chromatic tones and inanimate objects swirling with life. Hallucinations of identity, stability, and home haunt the perimeters of the room. This is the inner-city Aztlán, the Aztlán of drive-by shootings and high school blowouts, the schizophrenic, multigenerational, ultramestizoized and technologized

Aztlán of Los Angeles that, according to the 2010 Census, accounted for more than four million "Hispanics" in Los Angeles County alone. In the early days of her artistic career, Valdez's motto was "I'm going to paint my way out of this place." "This place" referred specifically to the East L.A. barrio where she grew up, a place riddled with violence, racism, and the perpetual sense of entrapment.

We find the same sense of entrapment in *LA/TJ* (1987), her earliest silkscreen print, now in the collection of the Los Angeles Museum of Art (as well as in the author's private collection), which Josh Kun describes as "drive-by snapshots of a fluid urban geography on a collision course with the national edge,"[82] in other words, the border. For Kun, the piece interrogates the artist's discomfort with her own bordered identity as a Mexican American, the divisiveness in the image representing "a personal equator, a dividing line of Valdez's subjectivity that also becomes a defining feature of her aesthetic lexicon."[83] Embodying an aesthetics of claustrophobia, her landscapes are in the main interior ones, where the outside is either completely shut out of view or poses a more serene perspective than what's on the inside, and the chaotic images of

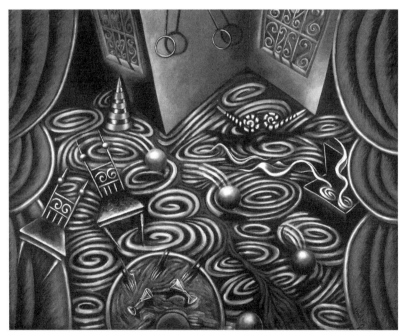

Figure 3.3. Patssi Valdez, *The Magic Room*, © 1994. Acrylic on canvas, 96 x 119 5/8 in. Smithsonian American Art Museum, through the Smithsonian Institution Collections Acquisitions Program.

home she paints with such vigor symbolize the artist's displacement and confusion in that milieu of contradictions and cultural brouhaha that is Southern California.[84] These images suggest that the only way out of the claustrophobia is through leaving the house and embodying her own power as both a woman and an artist, seeking her own retribution for racial exclusion from the mainstream art world and the pervasive stereotyping of her gender. Rather than weeping women and suffering mothers, Valdez's female iconography depicts queens and goddesses, not at the mercy of their social environment, but in control of their respective emotional and topographical realms.[85]

Delilah Montoya, biologically half-Anglo and half-Hispana and politically a full-blooded Chicana, trains her camera on the spiritual practices of her mother's native land, Northern New Mexico, and therein finds the link that ties her to the landscape of her chosen homeland. For

Figure 3.4. Patssi Valdez, *LA/TJ*, © 1987. Serigraph, 20 x 26 in., edition of 59. Used by permission of the artist.

Montoya, spiritualism is the binding force of Aztlán. From her sepia collotypes of the Sacred Heart, a symbol that connects the baroque world of European Catholicism with the religious practices of Aztec worship, to her *Saints and Sinners* installation, which integrates landscapes of Northern New Mexico with materials and iconography used by the Penitente Brotherhood[86] as a type of visual alchemy that distills sins and purifies transgressions, Montoya's photographs return again and again to the themes of life, death, and salvation. The most telling of these images are what she calls her "glass jar series," which

> refers to the alchemist's method of transmutation. The alchemist places a material together with a catalyst in order to change it into a superior material. The jar symbolizes the corporeal and the materials placed inside symbolize the soul. The exterior environment in which the jars float represents the land as altar space. The exterior landscape echoes the interior ambiance of the jar.[87]

Thus, the human body and soul, as represented by the jar and its contents, are made sacred by the land. Often, however, there is dissonance in Montoya's work, such as the severe beauty of a Northern New

Figure 3.5. Delilah Montoya, *Jesus Is Stripped, Station #10*, from *Saints and Sinners Installation*, © 1992. Cibachrome, 8 x 10 in. Private collection. Used by permission of the artist.

Mexico landscape whose resources—natural or human—have all been tapped and contained by either a monolithic theology or a corporate power plant mining uranium out of a still radioactive ground. Or the memory of the newlyweds killed in a car accident by the side of the road. Or the body sacrificed to drugs, the soul hovering inside a crack house that itself is cracking to reveal the dry earth that the body will become. Or the beating, living heart of Aztlán, densely textured and layered with religious and political meaning, as imagined by Chicano gang members and spray-can artists from the barrios in Albuquerque.

With her background in forensic photography, Delilah Montoya perhaps sees through the body, like an X-ray that brings the bones and organs into focus, that reads the internal hope and suffering of all who cross her camera's lens, from the Penitent Brotherhood clinging desperately to its secret rituals to the tourists leaving imprints of themselves on the New Mexican landscape. We could call Montoya's aesthetic an embodiment of spirit.[88]

Carmen Lomas Garza's domestic vignettes of rural life in South Texas in the 1950s contrast sharply to both Montoya's and Valdez's work. Gone is Montoya's almost anachronistic quest for the spiritual syncretism that resides in the heart of Aztlán; absent is Valdez's claustrophobic imaginings of inner-city survival; instead, Lomas Garza offers us a

Figure 3.6. Delilah Montoya, *Jesus Falls a Third Time, Station #7*, from *Saints and Sinners Installation*, © 1992. Cibachrome, 8 x 10 in. Private collection. Used by permission of the artist.

pastoral tranquility that, on the surface, at least, reads almost like a eulogy to innocence. In her inimitable "monitos" style, often equated with folk art, primitive art, and children's art, Lomas Garza offers us a child's view of daily life in her neck of Aztlán. The rituals that define the community's social and familial life—the Christmas Posada, the making of tamales, the visit to the local healing woman, the church bazaar with its inevitable cakewalk, the telling of Llorona stories on the front porch, the birthday piñata party—all of these get rendered in the most minute and meticulous detail. The child's eye takes it all in, remembers these tiny details that spell "home" and those community gatherings in which the child was safe from the racism and linguistic terrorism of the South Texas schools that she had no choice but to attend; and the adult, the artist, fashions the child's memories and her own politicized conscious-ness as a Chicana into an aesthetics of healing.[89]

"Children's art," Lomas Garza said in an interview, "is very simple and direct. If you want to see a message, it's right there. That's what I wanted—to be direct, simple, easy to read. I wanted to make the point that the aspects of Chicano culture that we take so much for granted are beautiful and worthy of depiction in fine art."[90] Not surprisingly, those cultural aspects that are taken for granted all relate to the environment of the home, the domestic space ruled by women. It is because she focuses on women's lives, and because she employs a method some find to be infantilizing or "cute," that Lomas Garza has always been considered a "safe" artist, both by her own Chicano counterparts in the Chicano art movement and by art critics like Paul Richards of the *Washington Post*, whose review of her show at the Hirshhorn in 1995 lamented the fact that there were no "cockroaches to be seen" in her pristine kitchens. Yet they miss the point, for *safety* is precisely what the child growing up in the midst of rampant racism and virulent hatred against "greasers" most craved. Operation Wetback was in full force; McCarthy was hell-bent on persecuting anybody believed to be an outsider and potential enemy of the state. Restaurants were still allowed to post their "No Dogs or Mexicans Allowed" signs in the window. To be home was to be safe, even if violence or danger always lurked around the corner or even in your own backyard. To paint safety was to heal from the wounds caused by the social circumstances and political history of Mexicans in occupied Texas.

As an embodiment of healing, Lomas Garza's work resonates not just with other Tejanas and border women who share her history but also with every new generation of Chicanitas and Chicanitos who find themselves *present* in a mainstream museum, their culture eulogized and valued, a subject of aesthetic representation rather than ridicule or marginalization. For all of the ways in which Lomas Garza has been attacked by her own Chicano compatriots for her lack of an overtly political (read: male-inscribed) message, nothing could be more political, nothing could say "Viva la Raza!" more lyrically or loudly, nothing could assert the power of physical presence on the landscape of colonized Aztlán more than the portrayal and celebration of cultural memory and survival in the face of conquest, dispossession, and violence.

In direct juxtaposition to the deceptively innocent quality of children's art as a response to racism and xenophobia that we find in Lomas Garza, yet playing on the same sense of personal isolation and out-of-body experiences that we see in Valdez and Montoya, the work of Laura Aguilar is an ode to the naked self, the untouched body that feels caressed

Figure 3.7. Laura Aguilar, *Stillness #23*, © 1999. Gelatin silver print, edition of 10, 16 x 20 in. Courtesy of Susanne Vielmetter Los Angeles Projects. Used by permission of the artist.

by wind and rock and water, at home in monumental landscapes and stark desert light. By baring her own non-normative Chicana lesbian body to the camera's incessant gaze, as she does in her silver gelatin photographs and again in her short film, *Untouched Landscapes* (2007), Aguilar exposes her vulnerabilities, her despair and depression, her lack of physical contact with other human beings, confronting the discomfort she knows her large, naked brown body provokes in the viewer and transforming it into an attitude of defiant self-acceptance. Aguilar's placement of her naked body in natural landscapes underscores that she is not only a lover and a child of nature, but also, another natural (read: normal) element of that landscape.

Aguilar's embodied aesthetic is the diametrical opposite of the thin white body idealized by the place she calls home, not Rosemead, per se, but Los Angeles, and its Hollywood imaginary of movie stars, beach bunnies, rock stars, and surfers. In "Laying It Bare: The Queer/Colored Body in Photography by Laura Aguilar," Yvonne Yarbro-Bejarano discusses Aguilar's manipulation of the artistic traditions of the nude and the self-portrait to interrogate not just body image but also Chicana/o identity politics, lesbian desire, and the male gaze. "Aguilar's lesbian

Figure 3.8. Laura Aguilar, *Nature: Self Portrait,* © 1996. Gelatin silver print, 16 x 20 in. Used by permission of the artist.

portraiture," says Yarbro-Bejarano, "runs parallel to writing by Chicana lesbians that addresses internalized oppression and the need to foster self-love as lesbians and mestizas."[91] There is no self-pity or resentment in Aguilar's work, just the clear-cut need to "lay it bare," to use her art to manifest her own body's presence in the world.

Beyond Presence?

Several years ago, I was invited to comment on a panel on "Latinos in Museums" for the annual meeting of the American Anthropological Association. The scholars and museum professionals on that panel were interrogating how Chicano/a and Latino/a identity is placed, dis-placed, mis-placed, and re-placed in museum representations. Although "identity" was the object of scrutiny, the true subject of the panel was the difference between *space* and *place*, which the panelists were con-figuring as the museum, be it an anthropological institution or a com-munity center.

In her paper, Constance Cortez of Santa Clara University examined the interplay of place and identity by positioning her *Imágenes e Historias/Images and Histories—Chicana Altar-Inspired Art* exhibition in three different places, their differences marked not only by regional location (East Coast, West Coast, and North Texas), but by each venue's historical relationship to and understanding of Chicano/a identity.[92] Indeed, as each venue proved, not only does location shift identity, it also shifts the meaning of an exhibition, and Chicana identity can be interpreted as Hispanic in one place, Mexican in another, and what I call Born-Again-Aztec in a third, depending on the place in which that identity is being represented. "As things turned out because of the distinct geographic loci of the institutions, a different aspect of Chicano identity was privileged over others at each of the venues. The show was Hispanicized at Tufts, indigenized at Santa Clara, and Mexicanized at Texas Tech."[93] Despite curatorial intention, ultimately place determined how Cortez's exhibition was to be installed, displayed, and received. Does this mean identity, like beauty, exists in the eye of the beholder? Or that identity, as representation, as art, as substitute for bodily presence—whether the white museum administrator, the tourist, or the "authentic" Mexican interprets it—becomes a kind of cultural currency that reduces race, ethnicity, and gender to the equivalent of a donkey cart?

At the Smithsonian Institution, the subject of another of the papers on the panel, the matter of presence versus representation of Latino/a identity, has been a critical issue since the release of the 1994 study "Willful Neglect: The Smithsonian Institution and U.S. Latinos," conducted by the Smithsonian Institution Task Force on Latino Issues. What Magdalena Mieri's subsequent paper revealed was that at the Smithsonian, Latino/a identity remains willfully neglected and marginalized at nearly every level of representation: collections, publications, employment, exhibitions. Programming, at least since 1992, was the one area in which more Latino/a presence could be measured in the form of theater, music, film, and educational lectures and seminars; however, Mieri concluded, true institutional transformation could only occur if the Smithsonian goes "beyond presence and achieves full representation."[94] Again, we are back to that question of "beyond" that we saw at the beginning of this chapter, and that the organizers of the 1995 University of Texas conference saw as a critical new way of interpreting Latino/a art, "beyond identity."

To go "beyond presence" at the Smithsonian, Mieri proposed a project of online/virtual exhibitions that she called the Latino Virtual Gallery as a space in which "full representation" was possible. On a purely personal basis, I love the idea of the Latino Virtual Gallery, particularly as a teaching and research tool. Cyberspace is, after all, the new frontier, and Latinos/as have always been represented as "new world" citizens. Virtual exhibitions would certainly be cost effective, and would offer unprecedented opportunities for all sorts of inter- and intracultural collaboration.

Nevertheless, I keep worrying about this point: How can we go "beyond presence"? To be present means to be there, to exist or occur in a place. If we can say that presence is measured in terms of how many bodies are standing in one place—sort of like angels dancing on the head of a pin—and if, as Magdalena Mieri suggests, virtual reality is the only space at the Smithsonian Institution where Latino/a identity can be fully represented, then wouldn't it be logical to say that rather than improve Latino/a representation at the Smithsonian, the Latino Virtual Gallery would actually make the situation worse, would not only enable the continued marginalization of Latinos/as at the Smithsonian, but would actually contribute to our virtual nonexistence, that is, our nonpresence?

If Latinos/as can be virtually every place, they can also be actually no place at the Smithsonian, as occupying bandwidth in cyberspace is not the equivalent of standing in place. I worry that by providing cyberspace representation as an option to "willful neglect," we might, in effect, dislodge that single foot wedged in the door of the master's house in 1992.

If we stop existing as bodies in a place and rely on the representation of our bodies in virtual reality, then what institutional transformation have we really achieved? Through a virtual gallery, will Latinas and Latinos be fully embodied or merely imagined at the Smithsonian?

Similarly, through the Aztlán aesthetic, will Chicanos and Chicanas be fully present or merely represented in the art world? An imaginary homeland, I argue, like a virtual gallery, is not a place but a conceptual *space* that only perpetuates our "nonexistence." It is a technology of memory, a device meant to help us remember and represent our history as colonized subjects in the Americas, as internal exiles in an occupied homeland, but rather than locate us bodily in the land base that we claim as our place of origin, it dis-locates our identity from that place and leaves our bodies out of the equation of signifiers that connects our multiple and diverse "moments of presence," as Homi Bhabha calls them.

To remember Aztlán is as much a ceremonial act as a political endeavor, yes; but remembering is not returning. Aztlán, the homeland, is a purely mythic place. Tapping our heels three times and invoking Dorothy's exilic lament will not get you back where you belong (assuming you ever left). Despite the title of a 2001 traveling exhibition I saw at LACMA (the Los Angeles County Museum of Art), there is no "road to Aztlán." Despite any markings on the mountain, you can't really drive to Aztlán.[95] You can fly to Cuba or Africa, you can follow a road map to one of the Indian pueblos in New Mexico, you can get caught on the border, but to get to Aztlán you have to suspend your disbelief and go into an *X-Files*-like dimension, where the past and the present converge in one place, and where the more you learn of the aliens, the more they sound like yourself. Really, Auntie Em, there's no place like Aztlán.

Figure 4.1. Alma López, *La Llorona Desperately Seeking Coyolxauhqui*, © 2003. Serigraph, 16 x 22 in. Special thanks to Coral López. Used by permission of the artist.

Chapter 4

COYOLXAUHQUI AND LAS "MAQUI-LOCAS"

Re-Membering the Sacrificed Daughters of Ciudad Juárez

The story begins with Coatlicue's miraculous impregnation. One day while sweeping at the top of Coatepec (Serpent Mountain), Coatlicue placed a stray ball of [feathers] in her bosom. Later that day she realized she was pregnant. Upon learning of Coatlicue's pregnancy, her children, Coyolxauhqui (Painted With Bells) and the Centzon Huitznahua (Four Hundred Southerners), were furious at their mother's sexual transgression and decided to kill her. Still in the womb, Huitzilopochtli learned of the plot and spoke to his mother, reassuring her that all would be well. When the battle began, Coyolxauhqui beheaded her mother, Coatlicue. However, at the moment of Coatlicue's death, Huitzilopochtli emerged from the womb fully armed [with Xiuhcoatl, the fiery serpent], decapitated his half-sister Coyolxauhqui, and routed his half brothers. He then threw Coyolxauhqui's body down the mountain, resulting in her dismemberment.[1]

I have read many versions of the Coyolxauhqui myth, such as Debra Blake's summary above, and most of them contain the same elements of the tale as the one recorded pictographically, and bilingually in Nahuatl and Spanish, in *The Florentine Codex* (1561–1565), credited to Bernardino de Sahagún.[2] This is the legend of the immaculate conception of a god, the enraged eldest daughter and her army of four hundred brothers, the attack on the mother, the birth of the full-grown armored god of war, and the decapitation and dismemberment of the malevolent sister and destruction of her rebel army.

Some anthropologists have interpreted the story of Coyolxauhqui's dismemberment as an allegory for the different phases of the moon, "losing body parts as it moves closer to the sun."[3] Others say the cosmic struggle between the sun god, the moon goddess, and the four hundred siblings is but a mythical depiction of the sun rising from the earth on a daily basis and chasing away the moon and the stars. Susan Milbrath argues that the story was used to explain solar and lunar eclipses in "seasonal cycles of the [Aztec ceremonial and] festival calendar."[4] But, as Debra Blake points out, "the solar-lunar explanation . . . overlooks the historical, social, and political underpinnings of the Mexica narratives and fails to acknowledge the militarism of the Mexica toward their neighboring city-states."[5]

Looking precisely at those political underpinnings, Gloria Anzaldúa interpreted Coyolxauhqui as "the first sacrificial victim"[6] of the Aztec patriarchal military state that developed under Huitzilopochtli's reign as the patron god of the Mexica. For me, Coyolxauhqui is the first femicide victim in Mexico, her ritual beheading and dismembering reenacted on the tortured female bodies on the U.S.-Mexico border, such as the victim found in a public place in Ciudad Juárez in October 2009, with her head inside a plastic bag beside the torso.[7]

Femicide is "the killing of females by males because they are females,"[8] Diana E. H. Russell explains, "often condoned, if not sponsored, by the state and/or by religious institutions."[9] We will see in the course of this chapter how the state—the binational state that we call the border and the systems that govern and regulate the border in everything from homeland security to free trade agreements—not only condones these crimes but also permits them to flourish.

Since May 1993, over eight hundred[10] women and girls have been found brutally murdered on the El Paso–Juárez border, and thousands more have been reported missing and remain unaccounted for, making this the longest epidemic of femicidal violence in modern history. The victims are known colloquially as "*las inditas del sur*," the little Indian girls from the south of Mexico—poor, dark skinned, and indigenous

Figure 4.2. Birth of Huitzilopochtli and Dismemberment of Coyol-xauhqui, original drawing from *General History of the Things of New Spain by Fray Bernardo de Sahagún: The Florentine Codex. Book III, The Origin of the Gods.* 1577 CE. Volume 1, Folio 420. World Digital Library (accessed April 28, 2013, http://www.wdl.org/en/item/10614/).

looking—who have arrived alone and disenfranchised in Juárez to work at a twin plant maquiladora and earn dollars to send back home. Not all of the victims are rural; not all of them are outsiders to the border metropolis; not all of them worked at a maquiladora, lived alone, or had indigenous features, but most of them were Mexican, impoverished, and young. And all of the victims of this particular crime wave were female.[11]

There was a time when no one knew about the Juárez femicides, or *feminicidios*, as these crimes have come to be called to differentiate them from generic "homicides" or gender-neutral murders, and to signify the misogyny of the perpetrators and the race- and class-based nature of the crimes. There was a time when little coverage could be found in newspapers or television shows or on the Internet about what was happening in Juárez to poor, young Mexican women. Nowadays, we know too much, and yet we continue to know nothing. In the process of learning; reading; researching; raising consciousness; signing petitions; writing stories, poetry, music; making art; organizing conferences; and editing anthologies, only two things have changed. The number of victims continues to grow. And now the Juárez femicides have become a legend, the "black legend" of the border.

The Mexican government's new line, after years of inept investigations and covert maneuvers to derail progress on any of the cases, is that the femicides are nothing but an invention of some crazy feminists and the attention-grubbing mothers of a few dead prostitutes, a way of making Juárez look like a modern-day reincarnation of the Spanish Inquisition out to hunt down, torture, and sacrifice young women—an image that city officials and merchants say is spoiling tourism to the city.

Despite these negations of history, by now you have probably heard of the gendered death toll in Ciudad Juárez. You already know that between 1993 and 2010, upward of seven hundred[12] poor Mexican women and girls, some as young as five years old, some in their sixties and seventies, have been violently slain in Juárez, across the border from El Paso, Texas. That their bodies were found strangled; mutilated; dismembered; raped; stabbed; torched; or so badly beaten, disfigured, or decomposed that the remains have never been identified. That many bore the signature of serial killings: the bodies half clothed, hands tied behind their backs, showing evidence of rape and genital mutilations. You know that a majority of the victims shared the same physical profile—they were predominantly between the ages of eleven and twenty, young, slim, petite, dark haired, and dark skinned—and their brutalized bodies were dumped in deserted lots around Juárez as well as in landfills, motels, downtown plazas, and busy city intersections. You may even know that bodies were found inside trash dumpsters, brick ovens, vats of acid, and abandoned cars, as well as on train tracks, under beds in hotel rooms, and across the street from a police station or the headquarters of the Maquiladora Association (AMAC). You know, perhaps, that the victims are also called Maqui-Locas, assumed to be maquiladora workers living *la vida loca*, or *vida doble*, of a border metropolis, coded language for prostitution.

In fact, you may know quite a bit about these dead women because, first of all, the bodies have been accruing for twenty years, and second, we now have a plethora of cultural products about the femicides. Since 1999, for example, a repertoire of songs has emerged from artists as diverse as Tori Amos, At the Drive-In, Lila Downs, Los Tigres del Norte, and Jaguares.[13] For online video fans, countless short films are available on YouTube alone, including one by Amnesty International.[14] Beyond the early documentaries such as *Maquila: A Tale of Two Mexicos* (2000) and Lourdes Portillo's *Señorita Extraviada* (2001), which alone helped raise consciousness about the crimes all over the world, we now also have two Hollywood films,[15] one pulp Mexican film,[16] one mainstream Mexican film,[17] at least three new documentaries, and a *telenovela*.[18]

In print so far, other than my mystery novel and a collection of poetry about the murdered women of Juárez by Marjorie Agosín, we have another detective story published originally in French and translated to Spanish, a fictionalized first-person account of life for a maquiladora worker in the "capital city of murdered women," a novel about a gringo boxer that somehow becomes embroiled in the femicides, and a section in the massive *2666* by Roberto Bolaño focusing on similar misogynist crimes in a fictional border city.[19] We also have three book-length journalistic accounts;[20] several monographs;[21] numerous articles published in journals and as book chapters; and at least three anthologies,[22] not to mention Charles Bowden's virtual library of Juárez-related books, stories, and pictures.[23]

In the academic world, numerous panels have been presented at conferences for organizations such as the American Studies Association, the Modern Language Association, the National Association for Chicana and Chicano Studies, and MALCS (Mujeres Activas en Letras y Cambio Social). New Mexico State University, UCLA, Ohio State University, the University of Texas at El Paso, the University of Nebraska, and Stanford University (to name only a few institutions in the United States alone) have all hosted conferences and symposia dedicated specifically to the

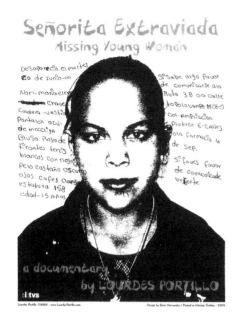

Figure 4.3. Ester Hernández, *Missing Young Woman*, © 2002. Promotional poster for the film *Señorita Extraviada* by Lourdes Portillo. Screenprint, 17 x 22 in. Used by permission of the artist.

Juárez femicides. Additionally, numerous writers, visual artists, and performance artists on both sides of the border have lent their talents to a massive binational outrage over these crimes and their continued impunity.[24] Coupled with the investigative reports of major newspapers and television news shows across the country as well as across the world, and the denunciations of international human rights and women's rights organizations—all of these cultural and political efforts have contributed to what you've learned about the femicides over the last twenty years.

But there's another reason you know something about the dead daughters of Juárez. You know about them because they *are* dead, because they *are* part of this sensational unresolved twenty-year heinous crime wave that has taken the public by storm and has suddenly put this border on the radar of every human rights organization in the known universe. Ironically, the main signifier of their lives is a corpse half buried in a sand dune. As Marjorie Agosín says in a poem from her collection about the murdered women of Juárez, *Secrets in the Sand*, "All we know about them / is their death."[25]

We didn't know anything about these "*muchachas del sur*," or girls from the south, when they were alive, didn't even realize they existed just a stone's throw from downtown El Paso, Texas, or understand the degree to which their deaths on the border began long before their bodies were ever found in a sand dune. For those victims of the femicides who were employed by the maquiladoras, the twin plant factories that burgeoned after the North American Free Trade Agreement (NAFTA) was signed into law by President Clinton in 1993, their deaths began as soon as they set foot on the factory floor to apply for a job.

Maquilando Mujeres

Those young women piecing together our microwaves and televisions and tennis shoes and computers, many of whom are actually below the legal working age in Mexico, are economically exploited and sexually harassed. We don't see them walking through the dark, deserted lots to catch the *transporte de personal* bus to work, where all day they will stand at their mind-numbing, carpal-tunnel-warping factory jobs, struggling to support themselves and their families. But we don't know that because we can afford not to know that. We choose not to know that their slave wages afford them nothing but squalid and inhumane living conditions in a squatter colony with no electric lights, no running water, no sewage system, no paved streets, no city services whatsoever. And we care little about the fact that those employed at these predominantly American-owned maquiladoras are earning less than $5 a day, making it impossible to make even the most basic ends meet.

According to the 1990 Mexican census, 50 percent of the economically viable population was working at a maquiladora, and most of these workers were female. After the implementation of NAFTA in 1994, the number of female workers in the twin plant industry increased dramatically. According to the website Maquiladora FAQ, managed by the El Paso Regional Economic Development Corporation (REDCO), as of April 2012, over 330 maquiladoras employ close to 180,000 workers in Juárez alone,[26] of whom "approximately 60% are women."[27] Not all of them are sixteen, the legal working age; the only documents needed to apply for a factory job are a grade-school diploma and a birth certificate—both of which can be and are falsified by girls as young as twelve and thirteen who are desperate for work. Indeed, hundreds of young women arrive daily from remote areas in Mexico and Central America, unprepared for the dangers of border life or the tragic exploitation that awaits them at work: slave wages; ten- to twelve-hour work shifts on their feet; working conditions that include dangerous levels of noise pollution, toxic fumes, and sexual harassment by management; manic production schedules and the constant threat of dismissal for not meeting quotas, for being late, for getting pregnant; demeaning beauty pageants disguised as work incentives and morale boosters; pregnancy testing at the time of hiring; enforced birth control through pill, injection, or Norplant implants; and the strict monitoring of their reproductive cycles through monthly menstruation checks. I wonder if it is general protocol for women factory workers in the United States to have to show bloody tampons or menstrual pads to the factory nurse each month to prove they are not pregnant, or to submit to urine tests when they apply for a job.[28] Maybe it happens, and it's one of those untold stories of the manufacturing industry, but I don't think so. I doubt this kind of sexual surveillance is legal north of the border.

In a January 13, 1998, article in the *New York Times*, Sam Dillon wrote that "the United States Labor Department reported today that thousands of border assembly plants administer medical tests to weed out pregnant applicants and harass pregnant workers to coerce their resignation."[29] The Labor Department's report was issued in response to a complaint from Human Rights Watch "that managers of Mexico's tax-free assembly plants, known as maquiladoras, routinely require female applicants to take urine tests and question them about their menstrual cycles and sexual activity to screen out pregnant women." While the Labor Department stated that this was a form of sexual harassment and violated Mexican labor laws, the Mexican Labor Ministry argued that "administering pregnancy tests to job applicants was not illegal because Mexico's labor laws protect workers only after they have been hired." This is the kind of doublespeak that NAFTA enables.

Of the victims whose occupation was known, Julia Monárrez Fragoso tells us in "Serial Sexual Femicide in Ciudad Juárez, 1993–2001," that nearly one in six were students and at least a third were employed by or seeking employment from a maquiladora.[30] And yet, the maquiladoras themselves, or rather the American and other multinational corporations behind them, have seemed little interested in pursuing the investigation of these murders affecting the lives of their personnel, or in seeing justice prevail. To leave from or return to their *colonias*, the desert shantytowns where they live in cardboard and plywood shacks, the women employed at the maquiladoras must walk in the early morning or late night through the pitch-black desert to reach paved roads and city buses or personnel shuttles. More often than not, the drivers of these shuttles are not licensed bus drivers nor do the factories that employ them screen them for police records or evidence of drug addiction. Anything can and does happen in these *transportes de personal* that carry the mostly female personnel back and forth between the industrial parks and the squatter colonies on the outskirts of town where the majority of the workers live. Safety is a commodity the workers can't afford. Nor, it seems, can their employers, despite the huge profits they make on products assembled with cheap *mano de obra* (labor). They can't afford to screen bus drivers to make sure they're not drug addicts or sex offenders or ex-convicts. They can't provide monies to the city to incorporate the *colonias* so workers can have the most basic of services, such as running water and electricity. Employers can't even afford to provide some measure of economic assistance to the orphans of victims who were their own employees.

In 1998, the daily wage paid to female maquiladora workers was $3.40. What could they buy or pay for on $3.40 a day? Even working six days a week, which is a common workweek in Juárez, their weekly wage was $20.40. That amount did not even pay for bare subsistence, let alone rent, utilities, and transportation. According to the statistics compiled at Maquilaportal.com, in 2005, while twin plant corporations in Mexico raked in a gross production profit of $186 billion, they reported an average direct labor wage of $1.87 per hour to 1,169 employees. If you do the math and multiply that hourly wage times an eight-hour workday times six days a week times four weeks a month times twelve months a year times the total number of employees who earn that wage (1.87 x 8 x 6 x 4 x 12 x 1,169), the price of labor cost these companies approximately $503,661 in comparison to the $186 billion that this cheap labor made for them in profit. More than 75 percent of these factories are owned by American corporations like Nike, Acer, RCA, Delphi, and General Motors.

Nothing about *las hijas de Juárez* was of any interest to us, until they died, and even then, it took over three hundred bodies piling up over ten years and the noisy interventions of First World celebrities like Eve Ensler, Jane Fonda, Sally Field, and Christine Lahti (who in 2004 led us through the V-Day march in Juárez that drew a crowd of thousands from both sides of the border) for us to really pay attention to the presence of these women in our midst. I myself—native of that very border, with family living on both sides of the Córdoba Bridge—didn't find out about the crimes until 1998, five years after the bodies began piling up in the desert, when I read a story called "The Maquiladora Murders" by Sam Quiñones in the May/June issue of *Ms.* magazine.[31]

Reading the story enraged me, not only because these crimes were happening right across the border from my own hometown of El Paso, Texas, and because very little about them had been reported in any major U.S. newspaper or even the local papers of El Paso and Las Cruces; but also because, as a scholar of Border Studies and Gender Studies, as a native of that very place on the map in which the femicides were unfolding at a rate of two per month, I, too, had been caught in the web of silence that surrounds these crimes. As a personal mission, I set about researching as well as writing and teaching about the crimes as an integral part of my activist scholarly endeavors.

In 1999, my search for media coverage on the femicides resulted in only a handful of stories. Other than the Sam Quiñones article in *Ms.*, I found an earlier piece by Debbie Nathan in *The Nation*, a piece in the *Los Angeles Times*, one in the *New York Times*, and a two-part, multiple-page spread in the *Washington Post*. On television, only two news shows, *20/20* and *60 Minutes,* had broadcast exposés. After those eight ravaged bodies were discovered in a cotton field directly across from the Maquiladora Association offices in November 2001, the U.S. media swarmed over the story, and suddenly we were reading about the Juárez femicides not only in the newspapers but also in periodicals that ranged from left to right of the political spectrum: the *Utne Reader*, *Mother Jones*, *People*, and the *Texas Observer*.

These were all signs of interest, finally, in a tragedy that has been accruing bones since 1993. Nowadays, of course, the Internet and You-Tube provide access to stories about the femicides worldwide, but when I first started my own research after reading Quiñones's exposé, the World Wide Web had precious little; I found a link to a story done by the BBC in London, another link to the *Frontera NorteSur* digest from Las Cruces, and finally, a link to the now defunct Sagrario Consortium, named after one of the victims, Sagrario González Flores.[32]

In my research, the main question I wanted to answer was not "Who is killing the women of Juárez?" I was more interested in the why and the what. Why were these young women and girls being killed in such vicious ways? Aside from the crimes themselves, it was the silence that most perplexed and disturbed me. What was at the root of the silence? In other words, whom was the silence protecting? Surely such a crime spree would sell newspapers, if nothing else. And where were the academics,

I wondered? Where were the Mexican, Chicana/o, and Latino/a academics, particularly those working on labor issues, immigration policy, NAFTA, or the abuse and exploitation of women workers on the border? Why weren't they, especially my U.S. colleagues, bringing their time, energy, and academic resources to this issue? Why was there such little scholarship on the crimes?[33] Was it fear or apathy that defined the silence? It was partly to help break that silence and inform the broadest possible English-speaking public about the femicides, as well as to convey my theories about the crimes and the cultural, economic infrastructure in which those crimes were multiplying, that I chose to write a mystery novel about the femicides, *Desert Blood: The Juárez Murders*.[34]

Breaking the Silence

In 2002, while completing the manuscript for *Desert Blood*, I decided to organize a conference titled "The Maquiladora Murders, Or, Who is Killing the Women of Juárez?"[35] I had just been appointed associate director of the UCLA Chicano Studies Research Center, and I was leading a yearlong undergraduate research internship, Death, Gender and the Border, in which we were trying to develop an interdisciplinary methodology for studying the Juárez femicides. With the devoted assistance of a handful of those students and the cosponsorship of several departments, administrators, and student organizations on campus, as well as with the support of colleagues and community members who helped us with fundraising efforts, in-kind donations, and website development, we were able to raise the close to $180,000 necessary to make that conference a success.

Our conference logo, designed by Chicana digital artist Alma López, was called *Coyolxauhqui's Tree of Life*, both to commemorate the primordial dismembered daughter of Aztec mythology, who was slashed to pieces by her brother, the war god Huitzilopochtli, and to reconstitute her many pieces into a whole self. My intention as the organizer of the conference was not only to raise consciousness about the crimes, at UCLA specifically and in Los Angeles more broadly, and to provide a forum for discussing, analyzing, and taking action against the binational silence that has protected the perpetrators for so long, but also to *re-member* the sacrificed daughters of Juárez. My objective for the conference was to focus not so much on "who is killing them," but instead, as Alma López's digital image suggests, on how we could reassemble the pieces of the puzzle of their deaths to help us understand why they died and why they were killed with such vicious vengeance against the brown female body. López's image suggests two other key questions: What war gods are being served by so many young women's deaths? and, What "mother/nation" or "father/land" are the killers, these modern-day Huitzilopochtlis who are wielding their own fiery serpents against their sisters, protecting?

I scheduled the conference during the Mexican Days of the Dead, October 31–November 2, 2003, and more than twelve hundred people from across Los Angeles, the United States, Mexico, and even Europe attended. We brought together scholars, journalists, artists, activists, writers, forensic investigators, and policy specialists, as well as mothers of the victims, in a series of roundtable discussions and presentations. Then Congresswoman Hilda Solis,[36] actress Eve Ensler, and U.C. Regent Dolores Huerta all gave keynote speeches. We screened Lourdes Portillo's *Señorita Extraviada*, followed by an interview with the filmmaker and a Q&A with the audience. There were literary and dramatic presentations; a multimedia student exhibition of written, aural, and visual materials collected in my research internship on the crimes; and a special altar of ceramic pieces commemorating the lives and losses of the Juárez women, featuring a "Tree of Death" by Puebla ceramicist Veronica Castillo.[37] There was also a live-stream audio broadcast of the conference via the Internet, courtesy of Coco Fusco and Operación Digna.[38]

I wanted the conference to expose an audience of university and high school students who were bused in from different schools across Los Angeles to the *testimonios* of the five mothers I had invited to tell their stories, and to the dangers and obstacles faced by the activists, journalists, and artists who had been raising consciousness about the femicides for a decade. I also wanted the researchers and scholars in the room to help us examine the social, political, economic, and cultural infrastructure in which the crimes were multiplying like another form of toxic waste on the border.

Just before I stepped up to deliver my welcome speech on the first morning of the conference, the office of the Chicano Studies Research Center received an urgent thirteen-page fax from the Mexican consulate, addressed to me, enumerating the official statistics of the crimes: 326 homicides of women, of which 72 percent were considered "common" or intrafamilial violence, and 28 percent were the result of sexual violence.[39] They also noted that there had been 4,633 disappearances reported over ten years, all but 43 of which had been satisfactorily resolved. I felt compelled to share some of these details with the audience in my opening remarks.

The fax went on and on, detailing all of the actions that had been taken; agencies and task forces formed; investigations launched by Mexican authorities at the local, state, and federal levels since 1998 in relation to the disappearances and murders of women in Ciudad Juárez, in reassurance of the fact that these crimes were a priority for the Mexican government under the different presidencies and administrations of the intervening ten years, and that all actions had been undertaken with the utmost openness and transparency (Juárez residents in the audience guffawed when I read that sentence aloud to the group). I plowed on through the lists of acronyms standing for names of committees and subcommittees, offices and programs, institutes and centers, the central and state governments had been busy implementing to coordinate actions to prevent and eradicate gendered violence in Juárez—the ICHIMU, the INMUJERES, the INDESOL, the SEDESOL, the UNIFEM, the ONUDD, the CIDH, the CEDAW. The part that really got people in the audience agitated was when I read that of the 326 cases of murdered women in Juárez since 1993, 92 of them had been resolved and their culprits punished, 13 had been sent to the Tribunal de Menores, or Juvenile Court, and 114 were under active investigation. The fax failed to account for the remaining 107. Moreover, of that 114, 85 were ready for trial, and 8 were under appeal. Most of the guilty parties had been sentenced to more than twenty years in prison, the report concluded. Charts and graphics were included to quantify the report. The most revelatory chart was the one that showed that 87 of the 326 victims were between the ages of eleven and twenty, 72 were between twenty-one and thirty, 53 were between thirty-one and forty, and 42 were of unknown ages. As befits the numerical conundrums of these crimes, these numbers don't add up.

There's so much we don't know. We don't know why—despite all of the actions supposedly taken by the Mexican authorities as detailed in that urgent fax—the murders continue and the numbers of bodies in the Juárez morgue increase exponentially. We don't know why there's a binational task force that includes immigration officers, border patrol agents, FBI agents, and police on both sides of the border that is engaged in the collective task of trying to solve the pernicious problem of *car theft*, but there's no similar binational effort to stop this epidemic of femicides. We don't know what role El Paso plays in either the investigation of the crimes or the protection of the perpetrators. We don't know how Mexico punishes sex crimes. We don't even know how many victims there actually are. The numbers change constantly, increasing or decreasing depending on whose report we're reading and what decade of the crimes we're talking about. In 2003, some sources reported 326 deaths, others 230, or 400, or 98. Today, activists assert that the body count (that is to say, the found bodies, not the missing ones, which number in the thousands) has now exceeded 800. While attention has focused on the tangible murders, cases in which bodies have been discovered, the actual number of victims may be more than twice as high.[40]

Another thing we don't know: Can the DNA-testing techniques employed by the Chihuahua state authorities be trusted? In a shocking revelation by a group of Argentine anthropologists and forensics experts who came to Juárez in 2005 to lend their expertise to the DNA investigations—the same team that "gained fame by using advanced DNA-study techniques to identify people killed in Argentina's 'dirty war' of the 1970s"[41]—the mothers of two of those eight victims found in the cotton field in November 2001 learned that the remains they had been given did not pertain to their daughters. Other irregularities the Argentine forensics team discovered were that clothes were mismatched with victims, and autopsy reports had been switched on some of the bodies.

"We declare that the kidnappings, tortures, and murders of girls and women in Ciudad Juárez and in the state of Chihuahua, committed since 1993 to the present, are *crimes against humanity* [emphasis added] and we demand that their solution become a high priority in the binational and international agendas for the defense of human rights" is the first of twelve resolutions[42] generated at the "Maquiladora Murders" conference, which called for "effective technical-legal cooperation" between the United States and Mexico through the formation of a binational human rights commission headed by Congresswoman Hilda Solis and Guadalupe Morfín Otero, the (at the time) newly appointed Subcommissioner for the Prevention and Eradication of Violence against Women in Ciudad Juárez,[43] and that this binational human rights commission be "designed in accordance with the human rights criteria established by the United Nations" to help bring an end to the crimes and justice to the murdered women and their families.

The resolutions became the "Ni Una Más" petition to "End Violence against Women and Children in Juárez and Chihuahua" addressed to both the U.S. Congress and the Mexican government, and still open for signatures online.[44] Although the petition has collected almost 15,000 signatures from across the world, many with strong comments of support like the one from a man named Jonathon from Pittsburgh,

"This is unbelievable, like the holocaust, only on a smaller scale," or the statement of solidarity from a Honduran woman in Maryland, "Es horroroso lo que está pasando en Juárez. Yo soy hondureña y vivo en los Estados Unidos. No quiero ver más víctimas. Todas son mi raza, y por lo mismo, las apoyo."[45] Or there's the remark from a woman named Virginia in Naples, Italy, who laments that she only recently found out about the murders and feels horrified and ashamed that this information isn't better known across the world. The heartfelt support is there, but logistically, there are not enough signatures from registered voters in any one state to have the petition presented before Congress.

In its 2003 report "Intolerable Killings: Ten Years of Abductions and Murders in Ciudad Juárez and Chihuahua,"[46] Amnesty International denounced the impunity of the Mexican government, as well as the apathy of the transnational corporations that, thanks to NAFTA, have brought so many hundreds of young women from southern Mexico to look for the yellow brick road of the American Border Dream: a job at a maquiladora, a paycheck, a shack of their own, money to send home. What hundreds of them have found instead is that Juárez is not the pass to the north or the ticket to a better life they were hoping for, but a ground zero of femicides where they and women who look like them find a gruesome and early death.

One little-known fact is that not all of the slain were Mexican citizens; at least six were U.S. citizens of Mexican descent from El Paso, Texas, and Las Cruces, New Mexico; one was from the Netherlands; and another was from Honduras. The Dutch woman was found under the bed in a seedy motel room on Juárez Avenue, raped, naked, and stabbed to death. Unlike the Mexican girls, Hester van Neriop was easily identified. Her documents were left in the room, which had been rented to a man believed to be an American citizen going by a Hispanic name, who was seen arriving at the hotel alone and on foot. No one knows how Hester got into the room. Of the *muchachas del sur*, only their body parts or their clothing serve as identity markers: a severed foot inside a tennis shoe, a piece of a spinal column inside a Mervyn's shopping bag, a bloodstained bra or a factory smock with a nametag attached, strewn in the mesquite.

To this day, despite all of the interventions previously discussed, as well as the involvement of Amnesty International, the United Nations, the Organization of American States, and the National Organization for Women;[47] despite the fact that in 2009 the Inter-American Court of Human Rights put the Mexican government on trial and ruled that

Mexico had violated "the American Convention on Human Rights and the 1994 Inter-American Convention on the Prevention, Punishment and Eradication of Violence against Women (Belém do Pará Convention) by failing to prevent the slayings and properly investigate the crimes,"[48] issuing a 167-page sentence and a list of actions that Mexico had to take to effect reparations to the families of the victims and to prevent future murders of women in Juárez (a decision that Mexico, as a member of the Inter-American Court of Human Rights, cannot appeal and is obligated to comply with, which it still has not done); despite continuing worldwide activism and all of the information and cultural production currently available on the crimes; and even despite the unanimous passage of House Concurrent Resolution 90 in May 2006,[49] spearheaded by Congresswoman Hilda Solis, no action has been taken by the U.S. government, and the femicides remain unsolved and apparently unstoppable.

Who Is Killing *las Hijas de Juárez*?

Who is killing the *Hijas de Juárez*, to allude to the title of an exhibition at the Social and Public Art Resource Center (SPARC) in Venice, California, in 2003?[50] Theories range from an American serial killer crossing the border to commit his crimes, knowing that even if he gets caught, there is no death penalty in Mexico; to a Satanic cult, because some of the bodies were found with ritual markings on the flesh; to snuff films; to the underground market for human organs; to the corrupt police force in Juárez; to that Egyptian chemist who was arrested in October 1995 for assaulting a prostitute, who was later thought to be masterminding the crimes from his jail cell. Other theories accuse the detrimental effects of Americanization on Mexican family life, causing the males to turn into good-for-nothing drunks and wife beaters, or worse, *cholos*,[51] and the females to leave their families and migrate north to work at the maquiladoras. Some accuse the factories themselves, not only of luring or recruiting hundreds of workers to this dangerous border each day with the promise of a good job, but also of the measly $3–$5-per-day salaries they pay, the unsafe working conditions, and the lack of protection they offer to their personnel.[52]

To answer the question of "who is killing the daughters of Juárez," both the authorities and the media employ the logic of blaming the victim. Accused of leading "una doble vida," the double life of a good girl (student or employee) and a bad girl (sex worker) who goes out drinking and dancing after her shift at the maquiladora, the victims are seen to be "asking for it," both because of the company they keep and the way they dress. Interestingly, not all of the murdered women were wearing short skirts, as was the popular accusation. The book *El silencio que la voz de todas quiebra: Mujeres y víctimas de Ciudad Juárez* was banned as a result of the public access the journalists who wrote the book had to the police files of the first five years' worth of cases. The book divulged information that the authorities did not want made public, such as the fact that although the victims were uniformly accused of dressing in provocative miniskirts, in actuality, 74 percent of the first 137 bodies that were found intact and still clothed were wearing long pants.[53]

When pressured to find a scapegoat to steer social attention away from their incompetence and apathy, the police arrest likely suspects. The first to be arrested was Abdel Latif Sharif Sharif, a well-off Egyptian chemist who had authored a number of important chemical patents for companies he had worked for in the United States, but who was employed at a maquiladora in Juárez. Sharif, tenacious journalists discovered, had a long record of sexual assaults in three U.S. states, and had even served six years in a Florida prison for rape and battery. Because he had three strikes to his name, he was to be deported back to his country, but at his deportation hearing in El Paso, his company's lawyers stepped in and got him removed to Mexico, instead, where he could help establish a twin plant for the company.

Sharif was Juárez's favorite scapegoat until David Meza, the cousin of one of the victims, Neyra Azucena Cervantes, stepped into the role in 2003.[54] From the time of Sharif's arrest until 1999, when he was moved from el CeReSo, the Juárez Social Rehabilitation Center, to the prison in Chihuahua City, the authorities attributed to the Egyptian a power of persuasion and mind control that made Charles Manson seem like the little man behind the curtain in *The Wizard of Oz*. For example, in May 1996, six months after Sharif's detainment, a gang of teenaged drug runners and *cholos* named Los Rebeldes and led by a charismatic, fully tattooed fellow called El Diablo, were arrested in a sting operation in a downtown discothèque. According to briefings made by Suly Ponce Prieto, the special prosecutor in charge of investigating the ongoing murders, Los Rebeldes had confessed that they were minions of the Egyptian, that Sharif was in fact paying them US$1,200 per victim when they brought him the girl's underwear and a newspaper report as evidence of death. Twelve hundred U.S. dollars is a lot of money for a dead *indita*, a lot of people thought, especially when narco-related executions didn't usually cost more than $500 a head.[55] Sharif held press conferences from el CeReSo, in which he denied any connection whatsoever with El Diablo and Los Rebeldes, although it was later discovered from a thorough perusal of the prison's visitors book, that one of the members of Los Rebeldes would come to visit a jailbird cousin of his quite regularly, and would at that time, also meet with Sharif. No doubt, this is when the exchange happened: greenbacks for evidence of the killing. At least, that was the story. When the press found out the teenagers were being beaten and threatened into "confessing," they had to drop the charges, and all but El Diablo were released. El Diablo was the only one who was not a teenager, and besides, his dental impressions matched the teeth marks on the breast of one of the bodies. Nothing more has ever been said about El Diablo.[56]

Three years later, the story changed and attention focused on a band of drug-addicted bus drivers called Los Choferes, who drove personnel buses that transported the workers back and forth between their shantytowns and factories; they got hauled in in 1999, when Nancy, a young woman they gang-raped, survived the attack and pressed charges. The supposed leader of Los Choferes was a violent alcoholic and crack addict who had two nicknames—el Tolteca and Dracula—who never got screened for drugs when he was hired for the bus-driving job. He left town after the attack on Nancy, but he was so nervous about what he had done that he had to take it out on his pregnant wife and beat her to a pulp. The wife's mother pressed charges against him, too, and the man with two nicknames was duly arrested, tried, and accused of all the murders that had taken place in Juárez, except those that had already been pinned on the Egyptian and Los Rebeldes. He named six or seven of his bus-driving buddies as accomplices, and all of them gave gruesome stories on the witness stand about how they would go out cruising for women to rape and kill after getting high.

But the conspiracy theories persisted. It wasn't that Los Choferes operated out of their own perverse power trips and misogyny, it was that they, too, according to the special prosecutor, had been hired by the Egyptian to do his bidding. By then, however, the rate had gone down to $1,200 per pair of victims, or $600 a head. Of course, neither the victims' families nor the general public, not to mention the local nongovernmental organizations and women's groups, bought the conspiracy theories. Then photographs of the suspects came out in the Juárez newspapers, their bared stomachs showing signs of torture. Apparently, police were using everything from cigarette burns to electric prods to elicit the bus drivers' confessions. Only Dracula's charges held because Nancy identified him in court as her perpetrator; the others were released and probably went back to driving personnel buses.

In 1999, the same year of the Choferes debacle, it was discovered that the Egyptian was living in luxury in the Juárez jail, his cell equipped with (among many other domestic conveniences) its own bathroom, a double bed, a small refrigerator, a microwave oven, a fax machine, and a cellular phone. A riot ensued in the jail when the Egyptian's privileges were made public. The warden resigned, a new warden stepped in, and order was restored, but the Egyptian was moved without explanation to the higher-security prison in Chihuahua. In 2000, charges were dropped against the Egyptian, on the basis of inconclusive evidence, which would have released him from his thirty-year sentence, but just as suddenly, the charges were reinstated, pending DNA analysis.

Sharif died in jail in 2006, of heart failure, we are told. His was the last in a series of mysterious deaths to plague the suspected perpetrators of the Juárez femicides. One of the two bus drivers who were arrested in 2001 for the murders of the eight women in the cotton field (and who were supposedly members of a convicted gang of rapists) died in jail in 2005. The official story was that he had died of complications from a hernia operation, which his wife, in a video interview after his death, asserted he did not need. In 2002, his lawyer had been shot down on a public street by police who said they had mistaken him for a fugitive. The organizations involved in protesting the policy of scapegoating that the police had been enforcing since the arrest of the Egyptian knew better, just as they knew that the bus drivers' "confessions" had been extracted under torture. The other bus driver had his charges dropped and was finally released after four years in jail, but only because the families of the victims and the families of the suspects had come together to decry the same injustice.

The Numbers Game

Any attempt at deciphering the mechanics of femicide on the U.S.-Mexico border must take the numbers game for what it is: a riddle intended to obfuscate the public as much as the authorities. To this day, no one really knows the exact number of victims. Diana Washington Valdez, in her 2002 *El Paso Times* exposé, "Death Stalks the Border" (nominated for a Pulitzer Prize), says her research shows 320 victims between 1993 and June of 2002; the Casa Amiga statistics showed 254 victims between

1993 and 2002; the Mexican Federal Attorney's office calculated the number at 258 for the same time period. In a conference presentation at New Mexico State University, Suly Ponce Prieto, the special prosecutor in the cases of the murdered women until 2001, reported that it was 222 women killed between 1993 and 2000. Other reports by other official entities of the state cited 232 murders, later revised to 233, while media reports cited 300 to 500 victims in the first ten years of the crime wave.[57]

Finally, in August 2003, the Instituto Chihuahuense de la Mujer (Chihuahua Women's Institute), under the leadership of Victoria Caraveo, released a glossy, detailed report with four-color pie charts and statistical analyses of the bodies found and processed by the Homicides Unit of the state of Chihuahua. Entitled "Homicidios de mujeres: Auditoría periodística," the report is an audit of press coverage of the crimes from January 1993 to July 2003, and it offers the "definitive" answer to the numbers game: 231 murders of women in ten years, of which 90 should be considered "sexual homicides," or rather homicides involving rape and other forms of sexual violation. Of these 90, according to the report, 43 percent (or 39 cases) were considered "resolved," while 56 percent (or 51 cases) were under investigation. Between 1995 and 1998, twelve to fifteen women were sexually murdered per year; after 1999, the number dropped to ten per year.

In a press release issued in September 2003, Amigos de las Mujeres de Juárez (Friends of the Women of Juárez), a Las Cruces, New Mexico–based NGO, countered the partial nature of the report and provided some important missing statistics.

> We have no desire to dispute the death of one more or one less woman, however, we would like to point out what is missing from the charts and statistics presented by the Chihuahuan Institute of Women. The homicide rate for women in Ciudad Juárez is at least 4 times that of any other border city. When one examines the rates by age, the difference is even more striking. For girls aged 5 to 14, Juárez has a murder rate 4 times that of El Paso and 20 times that of Tijuana. For women aged 15 to 24, Juárez has 11 times as many homicides as El Paso and 3.4 times as many as Tijuana.

The colorful charts and appendices of the "Auditoría periodística" report show statistics for a number of variables regarding the victims: how they died (28% sexual homicides, 17% crimes of passion, 14% vengeance, and only 7% narco-executions); how old they were (39% of the sexual homicides were between sixteen and twenty, 20% were between eleven and fifteen, and 10% were between twenty-one and twenty-five); where they were from (of the total number of victims, 31% were from Ciudad Juárez, 13% were from states outside Chihuahua, 41% had unknown origins); what their occupations were (36% of the total were employed, with their specific occupations listed in the appendices, the most common of which were dancer, factory operator, prostitute, and waitress; 20% were housewives; 9% were students); whether they were identified or not (86% identified, 13% not identified); and the number of cases investigated and resolved per year (102 resolved between 1993 and 1998, 103 resolved between 1998 and 2003). To this claim, Amigos de las Mujeres de Juárez responded with the following in the same press release:

> Generally, homicide has the highest clearance rate of any crime. This clear-ance rate is the number of cases solved and brought to trial by police forces. Generally, this rate is around 60 to 75%. While the Mexican government's study claims a similar rate, the conviction rate for the sexually motivated murders is only 0.05%. The claim that these cases have been solved is lu-dicrous in view of testimonies by those involved in the cases. One forensic expert resigned after being asked to manufacture evidence. There exists a recurring pattern of torture. The groups mentioned by the Chihuahuan Institute of Women as responsible for many of the crimes all allege they were forced to confess. There is credible evidence that this is the case. We, along with many of the family members and Mexican society as a whole, reject these people as the perpetrators of these crimes.

The "Auditoría periodística" report concludes that the actual number of sexual homicides is significantly lower than the numbers given in the local, national, and international media and that "the type of black legend woven around Juárez, the story that more than 300 women were 'kidnapped, raped, and murdered' over the last 10 years, has no basis in reality."[58] The appendices, however, contradict the findings of the report, as the total number of victims listed by the Fiscalía Especial para la Investigación de Homicidios de Mujeres between 1993 and 2003 is 321. What all the official channels seem to agree on is that 90 of the cases were sexual homicides. The methodology for determining that the *móvil*, or motive, of death was sexual, vengeance, family violence, theft, crimes of passion, fights, or narco-trafficking was attributed to criminological procedures and classifications utilized by the violent crimes unit of the FBI.

The Juárez femicides entry in the *Wikipedia* online encyclopedia provides yet another set of numbers: until 2004, there were 295 cases of kidnappings and murder of women. Of these, 108 were already under investigation by previous task forces, 175 were in the justice system, and 12 had been remanded to the court for crimes against minors. However, the entry also makes clear that there have actually been 332 female victims of femicide in Juárez, of which 218 have been resolved, supposedly, 104 of which resulted in sentencing, and 114 of which are still being investigated. The Nuestras Hijas de Regreso a Casa (May Our Daughters Return Home) website lists the names of 286 victims plus 75 unidentified cadavers, for a total of 361 murdered women as of 2004.

None of these numbers include the hundreds of women and girls who have disappeared without a trace. According to a report presented by the National Commission of Human Rights in Mexico on November 25, 2003 (the International Day for the Elimination of Violence against Women), two thousand women have disappeared in Mexico between 1993 and 2003. Other sources say the number of disappeared women in Juárez alone is over four thousand.

Amnesty International's 2003 report on the Juárez murders, "Intolerable Killings: Ten Years of Abductions and Murders in Ciudad Juárez and Chihuahua,"[59] concluded that 370 young women and girls had been killed on that border since 1993, "of which at least 137 were sexually assaulted prior to death." As reported in a Mexico City paper, the Chihuahua state government's response was that the Amnesty findings were "partial, slanted, distorted, and tendentious," and that the information presented in the report was both "inconsistent and decontextualized."[60]

In January 2006, the Mexican government issued its fourth and longest (four-hundred-plus-page) report, or "Informe,"[61] from the Office of the Attorney General of the Republic (Procuraduría General de la República; PGR) in which the Fiscalía Especial para la Atención de Delitos Relacionados con los Homicidios de Mujeres en el Municipio de Juárez, Chihuahua (Special Task Force on Crimes Related to Homicides against Women in Ciudad Juárez, Chihuahua), assigned to the task asserts that 63.1 percent of the 379 femicides committed between 1993 and 2005 have been resolved (for a total of 238 cleared cases) and that 177 perpetrators were arrested and sentenced in conjunction with these cases. Moreover, the report states, of the 379 murdered women, 345 of them have been identified and only 34 remain unidentified. The "Informe" also debunked the "myth" that over 4,000 women had been reported missing in Juárez, stating that only 47 missing women had actually been reported between 1993 and 2005, of whom 11 were found, 2 were dead, and only 34 were still under investigation.

Perhaps the most interesting of the charts presented in the "Informe" concerns the *móviles*, or motives, for the murders. Of the 379 cases, 119 appear to have been murdered as a result of "social violence," including revenge, theft, and gang violence; 106 were caused by domestic violence, including family violence and crimes of passion; only 78 (or 20.6%) are listed as a result of sexual violence; and 76 were determined to be of undetermined cause, which could include any or all of the previous motives. As Amnesty International notes in its February 2006 public statement in response to this fourth and final "Informe":

> The PGR appears to have concluded that only those crimes involving sexual violence—approximately 20% of the 379 murders documented—amount to gender violence. Domestic violence appears not to be considered gender-based violence and also appears to be necessarily excluded from the category of sexual violence. Other murders are classified as resulting from *social violence*, a concept which appears to necessarily exclude, without explanation, the gender of the victim as a factor in the murder. Another element not given proper consideration is the role played by the climate of violence against women and impunity which may have facilitated the commission of crimes.[62]

Overall, the discrepancy in all of these statistics and reports adds to the general confusion that surrounds the crimes, mystifying activists and authorities alike and increasing the sense that these cases are impossible to solve.

The Sex Offender Capital of the United States

Other than multinational corporations and an exploited poor Mexican female workforce that is rapidly becoming, as Eve Ensler puts it in *The Vagina Monologues*, "an endangered species"[63] in Mexico, whom else has NAFTA brought to the border? According to a 1999 article in the *El Paso Times*, "Since 1995, when sex-crime offenders were required by law to register with local law enforcement, more than 600 have registered in El Paso County."[64] A year later, police found a large number of the registered sex offenders in violation of the law. "El Paso police this week visited the residences of 620 registered sex offenders in El Paso County and found that 101 of them were not living where they had registered, as required by law."[65] If not living at their legal addresses, were all of these sexual predators running loose in El Paso, or crossing over into what Simon Whitechapel, in his troubling book about the femicides, calls "the serial-killer playground"[66]?

Indeed, while visiting the offices of the El Paso Police Department's Piedras Street Precinct, where I was interviewing Detective Andrea Baca as part of the research I was conducting for my novel on the Juárez femicides, I ran across a map of El Paso on which were marked the supposed addresses of all the registered sex offenders, and saw that many of them were conveniently clustered close to the downtown bridge that connects El Paso to Ciudad Juárez. "The 500 block of West Missouri Street in downtown El Paso is home to the largest concentration of registered sex offenders in the city. Out of 43 sex offenders registered in the 79901 zip code, 30 live in the 500 block of Missouri and nearby in the 300 block of Prospect."[67] Although sex offenders are not allowed to leave the state, much less the country, does this stop them from taking that five-minute walk over the Santa Fe Bridge and crossing into Mexico, especially when just across the border at any hour of the day or night they are sure to find at least one young woman walking alone in the desert? To what degree, I wonder, do U.S. immigration officials ignore or patently condone this illegal crossing of registered sex offenders, thus aiding and abetting their crimes?

By September 2000, the number of sex offenders living in El Paso had increased to 745, and the number had jumped to 751 in the next year. In November 2001, Alexandra Flores was kidnapped from a Walmart in the Lower Valley, and the perpetrator turned out to be a sex offender who had gone in to register at the Horizon City police station the day before he kidnapped, raped, and strangled the five-year-old girl. Diana Washington Valdez reported that "El Paso County Sheriff Leo Samaniego and other officials reeling from the Alexandra Flores case complain that El Paso has become a dumping ground for convicted sex offenders from other parts of the state."[68]

A January 2, 2002, letter to the editor of the *El Paso Times* decried the practice: "The number of convicted sex offenders paroled to El Paso County who are not from this community is a crisis. The system is failing us. Together, we must make some noise. I hope the outrage from El Paso County will be so loud that the echo of anger and disgust will reverberate from El Paso to Austin."[69] The wake-up call offered by the high-profile abduction and killing of Alexandra Flores motivated both community and state officials to oust sex offenders who were not from El Paso and send them back to their counties of origin. By February 2002, the number of sex offenders on parole in El Paso had gone down to 147, 112 of whom were not from El Paso.[70] The most chilling statistic, however, generated by city-data.com, is that as of April 25, 2013, the number of sex offenders in El Paso County has soared to 918, of whom approximately half live less than five miles from the border, as seen in the Google map that can be downloaded from the site. This means the ratio of residents to sex offenders in El Paso is 676:1.[71] Clicking on the red flags in the map brings up the names, addresses, and descriptions of the sex offenders domiciled at each location.

Is it a twist of fate that El Paso is the largest dumping ground for registered sex offenders in the country? Why are all of these sexual predators being sent to a place that is overpopulated with poor young women coming to work for the maquiladora industry who live in the most dangerous, desolate areas closest to the border, a place that, coincidentally, has been suffering the indignity of monstrous sex crimes against poor young women and girls since 1993? These are structural decisions made by the Texas Board of Pardons and Parole, not the personal choices of the perpetrators. I argue that the sex offenders, too, are part of the toxic fallout of the North American Free Trade Agreement, another type of vigilante army, like the Minutemen Project, against the infiltration of the porous border by fertile brown female bodies.

Mexican Penal Codes

How many of the victims were actually raped as well as slaughtered? Is it 137, as the Amnesty International report asserts, or 142, as Julia Monárrez Fragoso claims,[72] or 90, which is the official number given by the state of Chihuahua? Could it be more than that, considering that the Mexican penal codes define rape as nonconsensual penile penetration? We know there is no death penalty in Mexico, but what is the penalty for rape and other forms of gendered violence? The Mexican penal code makes a distinction between rape and sexual abuse. A sex crime is considered a "rape" if the "passive subject" is under fourteen years old or is a private citizen of sound mind or an infirm person, forced into vaginal, anal, or oral copulation and is unable to resist the attack. As per the August 2001 reforms to the Mexican penal code, rape is punished with a prison sentence of three to twelve years, and a fine of 50 to 100 times the assailant's salary. Cases in which a rape is perpetrated on a victim

younger than fourteen years old or is carried out by two or more assailants are punished with a five- to fifteen-year prison sentence and a fine of
80 to 200 times the assailants' salaries. However, if the victim is at least
twelve years old and is a "proven prostitute," no legal sanctions apply
to the "active subject." A caveat was added in the August reforms to
the penal code that diminished the punishment for rape to one to six
years in cases in which the victim led the attacker on and then later
refused to go through with the sexual act.

Sexual abuse is defined as a sexual act other than copulation that
takes place by force. The sentence for sexual abuse is six months to two
years in jail and a fine of 30–80 times the assailant's salary. Sanctions
increase to one to four years in prison and 50–100 times the salary when
the sexual abuse is perpetrated by two or more agents on nonprostitutes
under fourteen years old and on persons of sound mind over fourteen
years old. Cases in which vaginal or anal penetration occurs with anything other than the penis, or "*miembro viril*," are considered to be sexual abuse cases, and are punished with a two- to six-year sentence, or a
four- to twelve-year sentence if the crime is perpetrated on nonprostitutes
under fourteen years old and on persons of sound mind over fourteen
years old.

Under Mexican law, sexual abuse merits a lighter punishment than
rape. Although in 2003 the Mexican legal system categorized only 98 of
the then 320 violent murders of women and girls in Juárez as rape cases,
many more of the bodies were found sexually violated in ways other
than copulation. Victim #16, for example, a fifty-year-old woman who
was murdered in 1993 and found in her own home, had a deep wound
in the skull and a piece of wood inserted in the vagina. The body of a
much younger woman was found with a blanket inserted halfway into
the anus. Neither of these cases would be considered rapes according to
the Mexican penal code.[73]

Divide and Conquer

To make the drama of the femicides just a little more compelling, a rift
developed among some of the NGOs in Juárez, especially after 2001.
Despite lack of equipment; lack of funding; the ongoing accumulation
of bodies; and the daily struggle against apathy, legal impunity, and
incompetence, these grassroots organizations have helped raise social
consciousness about violence against women in Juárez and have decried
the complicitous role played by the media, the maquiladora industry,

and the Mexican government. In November 2001, when eight bodies were found in the cotton field across from the AMAC (Maquiladora Association) in the southeastern sector of the city, the teacher of one of the victims organized a separate NGO, Nuestras Hijas de Regreso a Casa. This organization has a comprehensive multilingual website that features a significant (though selective) bibliography of articles, reports, books, films, images, songs, plays, poems, and blogs on and about the femicides. The website also includes an archive of everything published by the Mexican newspaper *La Jornada* post November 2001, as well as the latest news, daily updates on what is and is not happening in the investigations, and links to other websites and other actions being taken on behalf of the women of Juárez around the world.[74]

Unfortunately, problems have arisen between Nuestras Hijas and some of the other mothers' collectives, primarily based on social class. Whereas the families of the victims are all poor or working class, the leaders of the umbrella organizations—the ones that raised funds and advocated for a number of the families, such as Victoria Caraveo's group, Mujeres por Juárez (Women for Juárez, established prior to her appointment as director of the Chihuahua Women's Institute), or Esther Chávez Cano's 8 de Marzo (March 8) and Casa Amiga, or the Las Cruces–based Amigos de las Mujeres de Juárez—are rich or middle-class women who are accused of using the femicides to draw public attention to their feminist causes and to make money for their organizations.

In a personal interview that I conducted with Victoria Caraveo in October 2002, she spoke about how the competition for resources had had a divisive effect among the different groups. "We're in pieces," Caraveo asserted.[75] When the state and federal government started "compensating" families for the losses of their daughters, not as a way of taking responsibility for the crimes but as a form of "humanitarian assistance" to the bereaved relatives, the mothers were also obliged to stop blaming the government for corruption or negligence in the matter of the investigations. Only those families who received no government funding, such as members of Nuestras Hijas and Amigos, have had the freedom to denounce their government the way Norma Andrade, Paula Flores, Eva Arce, and Ramona Morales have done.

Activism or "Hacktivism"?

On her web page, longtime Juárez activist, author, and performance artist Coco Fusco says that the Internet is the most effective site for activist struggle and consciousness raising in the case of the Juárez crimes. "The Internet has generated a community of interest from different places in the world . . . and is being used by a grassroots organization in Mexico to circumvent repression and censorship by the Mexican government. An international virtual community thus becomes a political force field."[76] Thanks to the Internet, people the world over have found out about what's happening in Juárez. The web techs who manage the Nuestras Hijas website wasted no time in tapping into that resource and eliciting that net-based activist support. For some of us, giving money to something is all we can think of doing or all we have time to do. But what if the money that is supposed to be a way of strengthening a cause is either mismanaged or ends up splitting a community of activists that should all be working together to end the violence and help provide a measure of support and solace? Is it just another example of divide and conquer?

Anything is possible in cyberspace. It serves the interests of victims and perpetrators alike. Notice what happens, for example, when you type the word "rape" into any search engine. Literally hundreds of sites come up with pages and pages of free pornography, many of them organized by ethnicity: Asian Girls, Latin Girls, Lolitas (girls under twelve years old). Available to anyone on the World Wide Web, these sites offer multiple images of eroticized extreme violence against young women and girls of color: women being raped with guns to their heads, women being penetrated by steel pipes, women being gangbanged by men in uniform, girls engaged in bestiality. Some of the sites provide written commentary as well, sadistic, misogynistic language about controlling and overpowering the female body. Who says snuff has to come packaged in celluloid, especially when anyone with a webcam and a computer can record a video and put it online?[77] So who profits from all of this "hacktivism," as Coco Fusco calls it? Is this yet another way of exploiting the poor brown female body?

When I was doing my research for *Desert Blood* in 1999, I found a tourist website on Juárez called "Border Lines" (not to be confused with *borderlines*, an online publication of the International Relations Center's Americas Program[78]), and there was a link on that page called "Those Sexy Latin Ladies" that took me to a listing of some well-known brothels in La Mariscal, as the red-light district in Juárez is called, complete with pictures of dancers named Brenda and Becky and Eunice. There were two things about that page that particularly disturbed me: the flashing neon-yellow message "Prostitution is legal here," and the little descriptive paragraph of the kinds of "girls" likely to provide that service:

Every week hundreds of young Mexican girls arrive in Juárez from all over Mexico. Most of these young ladies are looking for work that will be a primary source of income for their families back home. While many will begin their careers in one of the various *Maquiladora* factories in the area, often they end up in the many bars and brothels.[79]

There was even a map to the bars on Ugarte Street, with a downloadable coupon for a free drink at Club Panamá. That stretch of Ugarte Street, I later discovered, was precisely the area where a number of victims had last been seen. They'd been having a drink after work probably, or maybe moonlighting at one of those clubs to help supplement their substandard wages, and vanished into the night, to turn up days, weeks, months later with a neck broken, a right breast sliced off, a left nipple chewed off, a face beaten beyond recognition, legs spread-eagled, hands tied with cords or their own shoelaces.

Although it is possible that not every victim in the Juárez femicidal crime wave was raped, all of the victims—from the five-year-old who had her eyes removed to the seventy-year-old who died of twenty-three stab wounds—were brutalized, not "just" murdered. "In a significant number of cases, the brutality with which the assailants abduct and murder the women goes further than the act of killing and provides one of the most terrible examples of violence against women."[80] Another example of how women's lives are devalued on that border: a ninety-one-year-old woman was found strangled in her home after being sexually assaulted on February 17, 2006. Her attacker confessed that he'd intended just to rob her, but he decided it would behoove him to leave no witness, so he raped and killed her as well. The judge in the case ordered his release a few weeks later.

The Tres Marías Syndrome

The targets of the Juárez crimes are not "*güeras del norte*," or light-skinned girls from the north, but "*muchachas del sur*," or girls from the south, who in the patriarchal eyes of their society turn into Maqui-Locas, women who think they're independent because they work at a maquila, when all they really are is so far from God, so close to the United States. Who are these Maqui-Locas in the eyes of the society that has been witnessing their brutal slaying since 1993, and in what context can we read that social discourse to understand how these vicious crimes operate as part of a technology of female annihilation in the patriarchal paradigm? According to the popular misconception, a Maqui-Loca is a maquiladora worker who, as a result of her close contact with the libertine ways of "el norte":

- tries to behave like an American
- loses her good Mexican girl morality and, therefore, her value as a woman
- wears short skirts, high heels, and bright lipstick to attract or provoke men
- participates in beauty contests at her factory
- goes out with "*cualquiera*," that is, any man who approaches her
- dances at nightclubs in the downtown bars and brothels of the city
- drinks alcohol and probably uses drugs
- allows herself to be fondled and photographed
- engages in unsafe, premarital sex
- gets pregnant
- socializes with other "locas" like herself
- comes home in the early hours of the morning after staying out all night
- is asking for trouble and usually finds it.

Read within the context of the Tres Marías Syndrome, the patriarchal social discourse of Chicano/Mexicano culture that constructs women's gender and sexuality according to three Biblical archetypes—virgins, mothers, and whores—the Maqui-Locas clearly fall into the third category. Linked to the three Marys that attended Jesus Christ at his crucifixion—his mother, the Virgin Mary, who despite her pregnancy remained a virgin because she was both immaculately conceived and impregnated; the "other" Mary, who is referred to simply as the mother of James and Joseph; and the reformed prostitute Mary Magdalene, from whom La Malinche, another illustrious foremother of Mexicano/Chicano culture (also known by the upper-crust Mexican intelligentsia as "La Chingada," or the Fucked One), descended directly—the Tres Marías discourse outlines a code of ethics and behaviors that Mexican patriarchy prescribes for all of its women.

1. **María, la Madre**
- *La que vive por sus hijos y su familia*/She who lives for her children and family
- *La que siempre perdona*/She who always forgives

- *La que nutre, cuida y protege*/She who nurtures, cares for, and protects
- *La que hace todo*/She who does it all
- *La que da a luz al futuro*/She who gives birth to the future
- *La que participa en el sexo únicamente para procrear*/She who has sex only to procreate
- *La abnegada*/She who is abject and abnegated

2. María, la Virgen
- *La que obedece*/She who is meek and obedient
- *La que no se va con el novio*/She who does not run off with her boyfriend
- *La que se espera hasta que se casa para tener sexo*/She who waits till her wedding night to have sex
- *La que se viste y se porta decentemente*/She who dresses and behaves decently
- *La que vive con sus padres hasta que le piden la mano*/She who lives with her parents until someone asks for her hand in marriage
- *La que no conoce del sexo, ni consigo misma*/She who has no knowledge of sex, not even with herself
- *La que no llama la atención*/She who doesn't call attention to herself
- *La inocente*/She who is innocent

3. María, la Prostituta
- *La que tiene sexo por placer*/She who has sex for pleasure
- *La que tiene sexo por oficio*/She who sells sex
- *La que toma anti-conceptivos*/She who takes birth control
- *La que corrompe a los hombres*/She who corrupts men
- *La que avergüenza a su familia*/She who shames her family
- *La a que no le importa "el qué dirán"*/She who doesn't care what people say
- *La que se va con cualquiera*/She who goes out with whomever
- *La fácil*/She who is loose and easy
- *La que se merece lo que le dan*/She who deserves what she gets

For as archaic as it may seem, the Tres Marías Syndrome runs rampant in our twenty-first-century lives. My college-age Chicana students at UCLA, for example, straight and lesbian alike, continue to be plagued by the fear of "el qué dirán," or, rather, the gossip of wagging tongues constructing them as whores—bad girls, bad daughters—for enjoying sex with their boyfriends or, even worse, for desiring other women. They have internalized the message of the Tres Marías: there are only three ways to be a good Chicana or Mexican woman, and having sex for personal pleasure is not one of them.

> In patriarchy, a woman's sex is the site of her deepest power (creation, which must be controlled and monitored at all times) and her deepest weakness (penetration, which must be punished). In between the mother and the whore that is La Malinche, there is the virginal condition, that ethereal state of womanhood, which can be owned, traded, and renamed.[81]

A woman's function, in the revolution, the family, and the culture, is to procreate and produce sons for the father, not to be an autonomous entity with an active sex drive. Sex empowers the body, sex is agency, the enactment of desire, and in patriarchy, the only ones permitted to enact their desires are men; women's sexuality has to be scrutinized, proscribed, protected, or punished at all times. As Jane Caputi explains in *The Age of Sex Crime*, the modern-day prostitute (or someone accused of being a prostitute), like the medieval witch, is the "archetypal projection of the patriarchal *bad* woman"[82] who must be punished with torture, rape, and ritual destruction of the female body.

Why are the Juárez women being killed *the way* they're being killed? This is an important point, *the way* they're being killed, because we have to understand that these crimes are more than murder; they are ritual acts of pure and unadulterated hatred and brutality toward the poor brown female body. In "Femicide: Sexist Terrorism against Women," Caputi and Diana E. H. Russell explain the many expressions of violent misogyny that can result in femicide:

> Femicide is on the extreme end of a continuum of antifemale terror that includes a wide variety of verbal and physical abuse, such as rape, torture, sexual slavery (particularly in prostitution), incestuous and extrafamilial child sexual abuse, physical and emotional battery, sexual harassment (on the phone, in the streets, at the office, and in the classroom), genital mutilation (clitoridectomies, excision, infibulations), unnecessary gynecological operations (gratuitous hysterectomies), forced heterosexuality, forced motherhood (by criminalizing contraception and abortion), psychosurgery, denial of food to women in some cultures, cosmetic surgery, and other mutilations in the name of beautifications. Whenever these forms of terrorism result in death, they become femicides.[83]

Caputi and Russell's rubric for understanding the wide parameters of what constitutes femicide and sexual abuse in a patriarchal society helps underscore one fact: whether the victims in Juárez died at the hands of serial killers, sadistic policemen, or husbands and boyfriends, they are all victims of femicide. To argue that "only 90" of the over 500 murdered women in Juárez are victims of sexual violence, and that the majority of deaths are the result of "domestic violence" or "social violence," is to deny that all of these crimes are, as Caputi and Russell say, forms of sexual terrorism against women that ended in their deaths. Hence, they are all femicides.

The Juárez femicides are not a "leyenda negra" or "black legend" of the border. That there are cruel, bloodthirsty, greedy, fanatical men killing young Mexican women and girls on the border for sport or profit is not a myth or a legend or an exaggeration but the historical evidentiary truth. Collusions, conspiracies, trade agreements, drug trafficking, the human organ market, snuff films, serial killers, Satanists, a corrupt police force, the Partido de Acción Nacional (PAN; National Action Party) versus the Partido Revolucionario Institucional (PRI; Institutional Revolutionary Party)—above all of these, two institutions remain free and clear of any blame, responsibility, or accountability: the maquiladora industry and the U.S. Border Patrol. Therein, as Shakespeare would put it, lies the rub, and the rub, as Gloria Anzaldúa tells us, "*es una herida abierta* [is an open wound] where the Third World grates against the First, and bleeds."[84] Is it any wonder that "las hijas de Juárez" are mired in silence and a social apathy that has grown inured to the presence of slaughtered women on the border?

The Miller's Compensation, or, The Price of Free Trade?

In that complicity of silence in which all of us unwittingly partake, ignorance qualifies as innocence. As long as people don't realize or don't know what's going on in Juárez, it's not really happening and nobody has to do anything about stopping the killers or figuring out what the real motives are for killing this very specific population of young women. When the news is too sensational to keep quiet, such as when a woman's dead and mutilated body is discovered wrapped in a blanket and dumped at the intersection of two major streets in Juárez, then it's time to blame the victim, because as the city council's and the police department's "prevention campaigns"[85] imply, "she asked for it," trashy, slutty, ignorant *indita* that the media and the social discourse make her out to be.

The transnational corporations that employ the victims, the government structures that are selling their souls to Uncle Sam's Faustian "free trade" agreements, and the border watchdogs positioned at 20-yard intervals along the river with their infrared technology and their high-horse-power green trucks are all pretending they have no responsibility for the crimes. Emma Pérez explains where this devil-may-care attitude originates on the U.S. side of the line.

> Many people have surmised that a particular clause in NAFTA precludes the Mexican government from holding the maquilas responsible in any way. The chapter 11 provision of the NAFTA agreement allows U.S. companies to sue the Mexican government for any monetary losses, which include both actual profits and *anticipated* profits, incurred on account of protective environmental laws, labor laws, or labor strikes. U.S. companies may pollute the environment in Mexico and treat workers as disdainfully as they please, without retribution from Mexico. In the meantime, we in the United States can purchase inexpensive computers, cell phones, toys, and other products made in Mexico by women who have turned up dead.[86]

In "The Dead Women of Juárez," a chapter in *True Tales from Another Mexico*, Sam Quiñones comments on the anonymity of the victims, which renders their murders unimportant and therefore unsolved. "There is no resolution, no evil madman to pin it all on. The perfect murder is, it turns out, unusually easy to commit, especially when the victim is no one 'important,' an anonymous figure—and Juárez has enough of those."[87] Clearly, there is more wrong with the El Paso–Ciudad Juárez border than the systematic destruction of poor brown women.

> Pornographers, gang members, serial killers, corrupt policemen, foreign nationals with a taste for hurting women, immigration officers protecting the homeland—what did it matter *who* killed them? This wasn't a case of "whodunit," but rather of who was allowing these crimes to happen? Whose interests were being served? Who was covering it up? Who was profiting from the deaths of all these women?[88]

At the end of *Desert Blood*, Ivon Villa asks herself the questions above, concluding that the real criminals are not just the perpetrators of the crimes but the powers and interests that are being served by the brutal slayings of poor brown females. What is clear in Ivon Villa's mind is that the femicides are not just a Mexican problem; they are a border problem, and they implicate the Border Patrol as much as the Juárez police, the maquiladora industry as much as the Texas Parole Board. Under the stony gaze of Cristo Rey and the twin smokestacks of the American Smelter and Refining Company (ASARCO),[89] both of which stand guard over the trickle of water that separates the First World from the Third, Ivon realizes that Mexican women workers have become as expendable as pennies in the hungry slot machine of transnational capitalism, and that the tragedy of the dead women's lives did not begin when their bones were dumped in the desert but when they first set foot inside a maquiladora. As Melissa Wright notes in "Dialectics of a Still Life," "Their deaths are only symptoms of a wasting process that began before the violent snuffing-out of their lives."[90]

I am reminded of the etymology of the word *maquiladora*, which I found on a website called Maquila Portal, gateway to the latest news, developments, and statistics of Mexico's manufacturing industry.

> *"Maquiladora"* or "maquila" is derived from the Spanish word "maqui-lar," which historically referred to the milling of wheat into flour, for which the farmer would compensate the miller with a portion of the wheat, the miller's compensation being referred to as "maquila." The modern mean-ing of the word evolved from its use to describe any partial activity in a manufacturing process, such as assembly or packaging carried out by someone other than the original manufacturer.[91]

In Spanish, the title of the UCLA conference, "Maquilando mujeres en Juárez, o, ¿quiénes son los asesinos?," employed this double-entendre of the verb *maquilar*, which means to mill, grind, or crush as in wheat or grain, and also, to manufacture by machine, or to assemble manufactured goods in the maquiladora industry. Maquiladoras themselves can be seen as mills or processing plants where the slow, repetitive process of milling takes places, and where the women workers are "put through the mill" of exploitation, humiliation, objectification, and, sometimes, even murder.

If a *maquila* is what the miller earns for milling the wheat, and if the American corporations and the government behind them are the miller, and the farmer is the country that provides the grist for the mill, in other words, Mexico, are the victims, then, the wheat, the exploitable, dispensable cheap labor that is ground down and consumed? Are the murdered women and girls of Juárez the miller's compensation, the last ounce of profit in a system that already profits in the billions, or are they simply the price Mexico is paying for the privilege of "free trade"?

Flocking to Aruba[92]

North of the border, U.S. lawmakers' only response to this increased gender-targeted border violence has been to tighten the measures for Homeland Security. In 2003, upon returning from her fact-finding mission to the maquiladoras in Juárez with a delegation that included civil rights leader Dolores Huerta, Rep. Hilda Solis (D-CA) introduced a resolution in the House of Representatives calling for U.S. government intervention in the Juárez femicides, which did not pass. Not giving

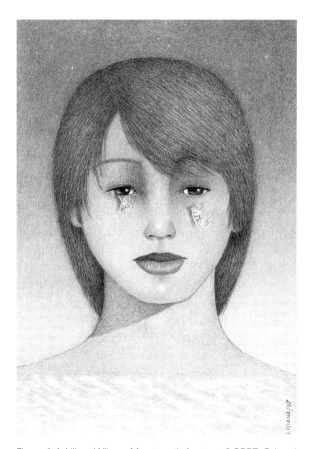

Figure 4.4. Liliana Wilson, *Muerte en la frontera*, © 2007. Colored pencil on paper, 7 x 10 in. Used by permission of the artist.

up, however, in 2005, Congresswoman Solis presented House Bill Concurrent Resolution 90 to the House, and Senator Jeff Bingaman (D-NM) presented Senate Bill Concurrent Resolution 16 to the Senate, "conveying the sympathy of Congress to the families of the young women murdered in the State of Chihuahua, Mexico, and encouraging increased United States involvement in bringing an end to these crimes." Slow at first in receiving the votes necessary for passage of the bill, in May 2006, Amnesty International announced that the concurrent resolution had at last been passed unanimously in the House. The Senate resolution has still not been passed, and has received only 18 bipartisan votes since its introduction in 2005 (as compared to the 143 votes the concurrent resolution got in the House), and is currently "referred to the Committee on Foreign Relations," where it may never be heard from again.

Why did it take three additional years and over three hundred poor brown women's bodies for U.S. lawmakers in the House of Representatives to even take a stand on the Juárez femicides? Why has the U.S. Senate decided to let the bill die in committee? And, why did former secretary of state Hillary Clinton, a longtime advocate for women's rights, not use the considerable international clout of her position to push for, at the very least, an investigation into this continuing crime wave that targets the poorest and most disenfranchised women of Mexico? "I believe that the rights of women and girls is the unfinished business of the 21st century," Hillary Clinton said in a much-publicized quote to *Newsweek* in April 2011.[93] "We see women and girls across the world who are oppressed and violated and demeaned and degraded and denied so much of what they are entitled to as our fellow human beings." Indeed, isn't that "the Hillary Doctrine?"[94] Didn't Hillary issue a policy brief titled "Advancing the Rights of Women and Girls: A Cornerstone of U.S. Foreign Policy," in which she stated, in no uncertain terms, that "the U.S. is committed to stopping violence against women in all forms, including rape as a tactic of war, domestic violence, and female genital mutilation/cutting"? If, indeed, the protection of women across the world is a "cornerstone" of this country's foreign policy, why haven't the femicides stopped on the U.S.-Mexico border after twenty years of rape, torture, mutilation, and misogynistic murder of poor brown women? Why hasn't the U.S. government done anything to stop this grisly genocidal violence?

And yet, when American high school student Natalee Holloway went missing in Aruba in 2005, there was an instant media frenzy about her disappearance, and hundreds of volunteers from the United States flocked to Aruba to search for her; thousands of civil servants were given the day off in Aruba to join the search; also involved in the search were American FBI agents and fifty Dutch marines, as well as three Dutch Air Force aircraft. Aruban banks raised $20,000 to support the search, and a reward for information was offered initially in the amount of $50,000, which increased to $100,000 and then $250,000. The reward for the girl's safe return was $1 million. At least two books were published about the case, one by the main suspect, Joran Van Der Sloot (captured in January 2012 for killing another teenager, Stephany Flores, in Peru, about whom we have heard nothing), and the other by Holloway's mother, Beth Twitty. Natalee's mother also appeared regularly on television talk shows and news shows and gave numerous interviews to the press, keeping her daughter's name and memory alive in the minds and hearts of both the national and international audience. To help memorialize Natalee even further, in 2009, the Lifetime Network aired *Natalee Holloway*, a movie about the mother's search for her daughter based on Beth Twitty's book. A sequel, *Justice for Natalee Holloway*, was released in 2011.

Although Holloway's body has never been found, and a judge pronounced her officially dead on January 12, 2012 (as announced on *Good Morning America*),[95] her name is synonymous with MWWS, or what *Wikipedia* calls "Missing White Woman Syndrome," which is when a disproportionate amount of media attention is paid to "a missing person case involving a young, attractive, middle- or upper-middle-class white woman, compared with cases concerning a missing male, or missing persons of other races or classes."[96] Meanwhile, the over eight hundred *"inditas del sur,"* or the Maqui-Locas of Juárez, have generated nothing but apathy for their disappearances, blame for their own demise, and impunity for their killers.

Five years after Holloway's disappearance, *Good Morning America* is still covering the latest developments in this case, after tourists discovered a jawbone with an attached tooth suspected of belonging to the missing teenager. Authorities speculate the remains may have been stirred up by a recent hurricane in Aruba, "it might have stirred up whatever container . . . [Natalee] was in, some of her small bones probably washed out and washed up to shore."[97] The test results confirmed that the remains did not belong to Holloway.

In "Mapping the Margins: Intersectionality, Identity Politics, and Violence against Women of Color," Kimberlé Crenshaw divides intersectionality into three categories to explain why sexual violence against women of color is often elided as a social problem: structural, representational, and political.[98] The poverty and legal status of the victims, the way the victims are represented in popular culture, and the color- and class-blindness of feminist groups in the United States, along with the similarly exclusionary agendas of antiracist groups that fail to acknowledge gender and sexuality as sites of oppression, all intersect to downplay the social problematic of sexual violence against women of color in the United States, says Crenshaw. Applying these same categories to the Juárez femicide victims, we see that the intersectionality formula holds fast. Structurally, the Juárez victims are among the poorest in Mexico, they earned miniscule wages relevant to their social status, and their demographic constitutes the largest number of "illegal aliens" to cross the border into El Paso—none of which does much to raise public empathy for their deaths or interest in stopping the violent crimes against them. Politically, there is dissension in the ranks, as feminist activists and NGO organizers come under attack for using the victims and their families to promote their agendas, and the families either accept money from the government to keep them quiet or try to proceed on their own without the support of an NGO, both of which put a quick end to their activism. Emblematically, the social discourse of "bad girls" and "bad women" espoused by the media and the Church against the victims, the Maqui-Loca profile attributed to them in the press, and the repetition of these representations in films and other popular narratives—all, in discrete and collective ways, devalue and disempower the femicide victims and at the same time reproduce social hierarchies that render their deaths, hundreds though they may be, much less important than the kidnapping of one good American girl, a college-bound rich, blond, blue-eyed, clean-cut high school student with a high GPA whose prom picture and Missing Persons poster saturated televisions, newspapers, and Internet sites, even years after her disappearance.

Maquiladora Goth

A new controversy developed in the ongoing crisis of the Juárez femicides when the well-respected MAC makeup company teamed up with a small fashion label called Rodarte from Los Angeles to promote a "sleepwalking girl aesthetic" (or what I call Maquiladora Goth) with products named "Factory," "Ghost Town," and "Juárez." The blood-streaked eye shadow, bone-white foundation, and fraying dresses look as though they were found in the Juárez desert, like the clothes of the victims. This is a good example of how cultural representation contributes to the desensitization of violence against women on the U.S.-Mexico border. As noted in the fashion blog *All the Rage*: "The designers were inspired by the idea of workers in Mexican maquiladoras walking half-asleep to the factories in Juárez, after dressing in the dark."[99]

The Juárez line was launched in February 2010, but the backlash didn't hit until the summer, with bloggers from fashion to social change sites clamoring for MAC and Rodarte to apologize for their insensitivity. After detailing the wage exploitations and inhumane living conditions endured by maquiladora factory workers, Sarah Menkedick observed in www.Change.org, "When embodied by thin, pale-skinned, wealthy young women in airy silk chiffon, I suppose these daily realities of life for the women in Juárez transition from terrifying to *romantic*."[100]

On the ColorLines.com website, Julianne Hing describes the "blood-streaked eyeshadows" and "pale nail polishes" of the new makeup line, noting that the first outcry against the new fashion statement came not from activists or feminists but from "beauty and fashion bloggers who were sent the press kits and preview photos of the makeup line, which [would] be available in stores in September [2010.]"[101] MAC apologized in a public statement issued on Facebook, which, comments Daniel Hernández, blogger for the *Los Angeles Times*, "came after a meeting in Mexico City between MAC officials and representatives of Mexico's commission on violence against women. The cosmetics company said, 'MAC executives reiterated their deep regret and reinforced that it was never MAC's or Rodarte's intent to minimize the suffering of the women and girls of Ciudad Juarez.'"[102] MAC also announced its intentions to rename the products and to donate $100,000 to a Juárez charity. MAC later amended this statement and promised to donate the full proceeds of their MAC-Rodarte products to "a newly created initiative to raise awareness and provide on-the-ground support to the women and girls in Juarez."[103]

While MAC creates a new initiative to raise awareness of the Juárez femicides, the academic world, or at least a bizarre sample of it that I witnessed in October 2011 at the "Vida y resistencia en la frontera norte: Ciudad Juárez en el entramado mundial" conference held at El Colegio de la Frontera (COLEF), has shifted its priorities: instead of continuing to theorize about, analyze, and denounce this twenty-year crime wave of deadly violence against women, some of the invited speakers at the conference were calling for broadening the analysis to include the much larger (and hence, more important?) number of murdered men in Juárez due to the narco-killing wars that have brought the Mexican military to occupy the streets of the city and terrorize the locals even more.

Although I acknowledge the grievousness of this occupation of Juárez by both organized crime and the military, and agree that the thousands of drug cartel–related executions that have plagued that border since the 2006 Mexican presidential election have completely transformed Ciudad Juárez into one of the most dangerous and deadly zones in the world outside of a war zone,[104] I disagree that these murders should eclipse the femicides just because there are more of them. I also differ profoundly with Spanish sociologist María Jesús Izquierdo's strange notion that "men kill women because they love them too much," as she stated in her keynote presentation, then going on to say that "women exploit men with love" and that to study femicide and exclude homicide is to "traicionar al feminismo."[105] To contain the outrage I was feeling during her presentation, I wrote the following comments for a future article in my notebook:

> What a weird direction femicide scholarship seems to be taking. How can this supposed feminist make such generalizations about male-female relations outside of any analysis of patriarchy? She seems to be agreeing with those who blame the women for their own murders because they participate in the competition for men and desire signifiers of power and status, which then leads men to kill them. Doesn't it actually demean and invalidate the work of femicide activists and scholars to say that focusing on the femicides is a "betrayal" to feminism? Hello!

After my own keynote presentation in which I denounced the maquiladora industry's egregious sexual exploitation of its female labor force and offered my genocidal/gynocidal theory about how the crimes "benefit" Free Trade initiatives on both sides of the border, a professor at the COLEF commented that he marveled at how I could make such indictments of NAFTA and the twin plant industry, as the maquiladoras are looked upon as a type of sacred cow in Mexico—untouchable and unimpeachable.

Gynocidal Imperatives

Femicide is the killing of women for being women, hence femicide is a hate crime, "motivated by misogyny as well as by masculinist notions of manhood, honor, love, pride, pleasure, religion, culture, and sense of ownership of women,"[106] asserts Jane Caputi in the afterword to my anthology *Making a Killing: Femicide, Free Trade, and La Frontera*. But

Caputi clarifies that the individual women aren't all that dies, nor is that the only objective of the crime. "I consider the murders a form of ritual blood sacrifice, a modern enactment of the core patriarchal myth of Goddess murder," says Caputi, pointing to examples of other patriarchal cultures across the world that encourage and condone misogynistic rituals such as witch hunts, widow burnings, public stonings of "bad women," and genital mutilations of girls—all of which are forms of goddess murder.

The way I see it, murdering the goddess means murdering the root of all female power, which is the power to create, the power to give life, the power to bring forth the future; hence, murdering those hundreds of poor brown women and girls in Juárez means annihilating the future that those female bodies would have had the power to create. More than femicides, then, Caputi classifies the Juárez crimes as "gynocides," whose intention is not to destroy all women per se, but rather "to destroy women as a spiritual, political, and cultural force and to obliterate women's group identity"[107] *We kill in this way because we can, we have the power, not just to kill you but to obliterate this entire society, and no one can stop us*—this is the message inscribed on those viciously slaughtered bodies. This, then, turns femicide into genocide. Says Jane Caputi:

> "Gynocide" resonates linguistically and politically with "genocide," and it is meant to. "Genocide" signifies not only the literal killing of a group of people, it also means the planned and systematic destruction of their traditions, language, spirituality, morale, memory, and sense of self and culture. This type of systematic violence, serving as a form of social control, also has been directed against women as a group in patriarchal cultures . . . "Gynocide" does not just sound like "genocide." The two are linked historically. First of all, the sexual violence that characterizes gynocide also is a basic component of genocide. Second, the motivation for genocide is sometimes rooted in gynocidal imperatives.[108]

What might be a "gynocidal imperative" on the U.S.-Mexico post-NAFTA border, when now, more than ever, "el norte," is the golden dream for thousands and thousands of young, poor, fertile women and girls from Mexico and Central America? When now, more than ever, the demographics revealed in the U.S. Census indicate that the Hispanic population in the United States has multiplied into the largest national minority, and in many places, particularly places located directly on the border like El Paso, Texas, Hispanics constitute the majority of the population? What Jane Caputi calls "gynocide," or rather, the ritual sacrifice of the female body, becomes a capitalist imperative when the border plays host to the only power that these young women have and that so threatens American homeland security: the reproductive power of all those young Mexican females whom NAFTA has brought too close to the chain-link fence, and whom the maquiladoras discard like so much industrial debris. They have no choice but to follow their American Dream.

Caputi urges us to re-member the modern-day Coyolxauhquis in Juárez, as Alma López has done in her logo for the "Maquiladora Murders" conference, by reassembling the goddess's pieces on a Tree of Life, because the suffering of *las hijas de Juárez* translates into a universal female suffering. Until we place these women in "their rightful place at the center of the world," Caputi argues, we will continue to replicate patriarchal myths that punish women simply for being women, that dispossess women of their lives as well as their voices, for "the word 'disarticulation' connotes both dismemberment and the loss of the power of speech."[109]

It is essential that we should *re-member* the dismembered Coyolxauhquis of Juárez, that we should do something to stop the violence; to end the impunity; to help the victims, their families, and the hundreds of others who come to Juárez on a daily basis and continue to live in the blissful ignorance of hope and desire that we call "the American Dream." But we must also remind ourselves that they are more than victims. Like the central figure in Figure 4.1, Alma López's *La Llorona Desperately Seeking Coyolxauhqui* (2003), which opens this chapter and graces the cover of *Making a Killing*, the victims were women and girls who lived and died among us. They had lives and names and histories imprinted on their bodies, they had dreams and troubles of their own. They left mothers desperate to find them, wailing like Lloronas at the indifferent desert to bring their daughters home. They deserve our remembrance, our activism, our outrage, and our voices yelling out "¡Ni una más!" Not one more femicide on the U.S.-Mexico border, not one more mutilated, disarticulated, violated brown daughter anywhere else in the world!

Figure 5.1. Alma López, *Desert Blood*, © 2003. Poster, 18 x 24 in. Special thanks to Anna Salinas. Used by permission of the artist.

Chapter 5

MAPPING THE LABYRINTH

The Anti–Detective Novel and the Mysterious Missing Brother

I have to confess: I am a novice when it comes to detective fiction, Chicano/a or otherwise. Until the year 2000, I didn't read detective fiction, much less write it, which is why my decision to write a mystery novel about the now twenty-year epidemic of murdered women of the El Paso–Ciudad Juárez border was, at first, such a daunting proposition. It wasn't until June 1998—five years after the crime wave had started— that I first read about the Juárez murders in *Ms.* magazine, and it would be two years more before I hit upon the idea of channeling my research on the crimes, my ontological speculations about the criminals, and my critiques of border politics into a mystery novel. Of course, I had read Lucha Corpi, Manuel Ramos, and Rolando Hinojosa-Smith, but I didn't think of their books as mystery novels per se. To me, their books are classified as Chicano/a literature with a detective protagonist.

Obviously, I had some homework to do, not only on the crimes themselves but also on the mystery genre. What is a mystery, exactly? Good researcher that I am, I bought shelves of mystery-writing manuals, books on forensics and serial criminals, and stacks of paperbacks by famous names like Patricia Cornwell, Marcia Muller, Sue Grafton, James Lee Burke, Sara Paretsky, Rudolfo Anaya, and Michael Nava. Anaya and Nava? Wait: two Chicano novelists in the popular mystery section of the bookstore instead of on the dusty bottom bookshelf devoted to "Hispanic Authors"? One whose sleuth was a shamanic private investigator tackling issues like nuclear waste and black magic in New Mexico; the other who wrote about a gay Chicano lawyer whose adventures included commentaries on AIDS, gay identity, and the complex negotiations of *familia*. Need I say I was hooked? Need I say I saw in the mystery genre a venue for social critique that prevailed in all of the books I was reading and that gave me precisely the vehicle I needed to comment on the social ills of the North American Free Trade Agreement and femicide on the border?

The trick was to apply the formula of a mystery without seeming formulaic. What did that formula consist of? I consulted the venerable

John G. Cawelti in *Adventure, Mystery, and Romance* (a book I had been forced to read in a graduate proseminar at the University of New Mexico back in 1990), and found a working definition:

> The classical detective story begins with an unsolved crime and moves toward the elucidation of its mystery [81]. . . . It seems to be important that the detective solve the crime or at least get on the right track from the beginning [83]. . . . The crime must be surrounded by a number of tangible clues that make it absolutely clear that some agency is responsible for it, and . . . it must appear insoluble.[1]

Clearly, each victim of the Juárez femicides constituted an unsolved crime surrounded by tangible clues that pointed toward murder, torture, rape, and other violations of the female body. What we didn't have, apparently, what we still don't have, despite the number of special task forces and investigators employed by the Mexican government to elucidate the mystery of the Juárez crimes since 1996, was the criminal. Not only did the crimes "appear insoluble," they actually were unsolved. Moreover, in the late 1990s and early 2000s, the crimes were unknown, at least in the United States. Through the popular medium of a mystery novel, I reasoned, I could bring this epidemic of femicides to the awareness of a broad English-reading American public, and in this way, I could help break the silence that continues to surround the crimes.

That left me with a significant conundrum: how does one write a mystery without a solution? What else does an effective detective do but identify the criminal? It is this quest for the criminal that gives detective fiction its ontological imperative, says Ralph Rodríguez, author of the groundbreaking *Brown Gumshoes: Detective Fiction and the Search for Chicana/o Identity.* Indeed, this ontological quest explains why detective fiction, as a genre, fits Chicana/o literature—concerned as it is with issues of identity politics—so well. Rodríguez writes that "detective novels are about discerning the mysteries of identity. At the heart of their narrative, after all, is the quest to reveal who the criminal is . . . Time and again the detective also unravels a mystery about him- or herself. The novel is as much his or her story as it is the story of the crime."[2] For Rodríguez, then, the act of solving a crime is analogous to unraveling the riddles of identity (ontology) and knowledge (epistemology), making detective fiction a natural genre for Chicana/o writers who ourselves are so obsessed with exploring, if not resolving, the bilingual, bicultural mysteries of our bifurcated lives.

But Ralph's book wasn't around in 2001 when I set out on the wild adventure of writing a mystery novel after two years of solid research on the femicides. A few articles had started to crop up on the burgeoning phenomenon of Chicana/o detective fiction.[3] I am thinking specifically of Klaus Zilles's work on Rolando Hinojosa-Smith's Rafe Buenrostro mysteries and Theresa Márquez's work on Manuel Ramos,[4] both of whom I had the pleasure of hearing in person at the first international conference of Chicana/o literature held in Granada, Spain, in 1998. However, that conference was held during Holy Week of 1998, and it wasn't until June 1998 that I read Sam Quiñones's "Maquiladora Murders" article in *Ms. Magazine*, which opened my eyes to the gravity of gendered violence in Juárez.[5] Had I been paying attention at that conference in 1998, my curiosity would have been piqued at Theresa Márquez's assertion in her paper that "within the past several years a modest yet vigorous 'boom' has set off what may well be the beginning of the Aztlán mystery tradition or the formation of the Chicana/Chicano detective persona."[6] I was a long way away from knowing anything about this "Aztlán mystery tradition," or even suspecting that I would be contributing to it one day.

By June 1998, when I realized there was a conspiracy of silence unfolding on the El Paso–Juárez border, buttressed by a social discourse of blaming the victim that was keeping border citizens in both countries from taking an active role in at least caring about the murdered women, much less joining the activist groups that had formed to bring attention to and stop the crimes, there were already 137 bodies of poor, brown, mostly very young Mexican women found dead in the desert.

Keep in mind that El Paso is my hometown, and that I have family living on both sides of the Córdoba Bridge, and yet nobody really knew anything about how or why these murders had started. Occasionally, speaking to my mother or grandmother on the phone, they would tell me about how "another girl" had been found dead, but there were no details, it was not a regular topic of conversation, nor did it grace the pages of the *El Paso Times*.

As I was to find out a year after I read the story in *Ms.* magazine, in the fall of 1999, while I was on a visiting professorship at my alma mater, the University of Texas at El Paso, and doing research on the crimes, the *El Paso Times* didn't cover Juárez news, only El Paso news, though the riverbed that separates the two cities, the two countries of that "herida abierta" (as Gloria Anzaldúa called the open wound of the border) "where the Third World grates against the First and bleeds,"[7] is in places as narrow as a hallway—and so dry you can walk across it without ever getting your shoes wet. We are two countries connected by long lines of traffic at the international bridges, but umbilically connected by a much longer history. How could it not be important to report these crimes in the *El Paso Times*?

My mistake was that I had been looking for information in English. But fortunately I had hired my niece Lizeth as my research assistant that fall semester of 1999, and thanks to her tenacious investigative skills, she compiled a thick archive of digitized stories from periodicals and journals all over Mexico that she had somehow managed to dig up at the Tec de Monterrey, a technological college in Juárez. It was from these reports that I gleaned the terrifying details of the first 137 crimes; that I read of the sadistic treatment of both the criminals against the victims and the authorities against the victims' families. A few books appeared; the first to be published was the disturbing pseudo-journalistic

Figure 5.2. Alma López, detail of *History in Our Hands*, © 2009. Mural in collaboration with Noni Olabisi at the Constituent Services Center, South Central Avenue, Los Angeles. Used by permission of the artist.

Las muertas de Juárez by Victor Ronquillo that fetishized the dead bodies, followed by *El silencio que la voz de todas quiebra*, written by seven women journalists in Juárez, which included details on the lives of the victims gleaned from the individual journalists' conversations with the victims' families, as well as forensic details about the murders that helped shed light on the lies and inconsistencies being reported in the media. In English, Charles Bowden had already published his exposé, *Juárez: The Laboratory of the Future*, where he clearly showed, through the work of Juárez photojournalists Julian and Gabriel Cardona and others, not just the horror of the mutilated bodies found in the desert but also the extremes of poverty that have resulted in the shantytowns that have sprung up just outside the city like so much industrial toxic waste or the detritus of drug cartels.

I don't remember when, exactly, it occurred to me to use the mystery novel as the methodology by which to convey my research on the crimes and the cultural context in which those crimes were taking place, a context that involved NAFTA, the deeply exploitative working conditions of the maquiladora industry, and the social discourse of the "bad woman." I saw a clear complicity between political and economic agencies in Mexico and the United States that I knew would make for a powerful detective story.

I have been asked why, when I am a tenured professor at UCLA, I didn't write an academic book instead. I tell them that more people read mysteries than academic books, even academics. I explain that the popular genre of the mystery novel can reach a wider audience and so can help break the silence surrounding the crimes, particularly north of the border, where, at the time that I was writing the book, so few people really knew that Juárez had become a playground for serial killers. The problem with my idea of raising consciousness through a mystery novel was that once I learned what the formal elements of a mystery novel were, once I organized all my research on the crimes into units of dramatic action, and once I had my cast of characters and their individual trials and tribulations figured out, I knew I had everything I needed for a good mystery except the most important thing for a mystery novel: a solution.

By 2001, there were already more than two hundred bodies in the morgue, the majority young women, indigenous looking and poor, found viciously murdered and mutilated in empty lots all over Juárez. I couldn't stop thinking about everything I didn't know. How many countless others have never been found? How many predators have never been brought to justice? How many families are still out there digging through trash in the desert looking for their daughters' bones? How many crimes have never been reported, much less solved?

So how, I asked myself on January 1, 2001, when I set my New Year's resolution to finish a draft of the novel that year, was I going to write a mystery about crimes that could not be solved? After all, finding the solution is why fans of this genre read mystery novels. The aim of these readers is to work alongside the sleuth or detective and put the pieces of the puzzle together, hopefully just ahead of the protagonist, to participate in the search for clues that might eventually identify the criminal. How could I write a mystery on the femicides without knowing who was actually massacring women in Juárez? All my "how-to-write-a-mystery" books emphasized this point: the satisfactory denouement at the end of a labyrinthine trail of clues sprinkled here and there with red herrings.

There are many clues in the story of the murdered women of Juárez, and even more labyrinthine trails winding through a terrain of silence. In fact, there is an area deep in the Chihuahuan Desert just on the southern outskirts of Juárez that is said to be popular with UFOs and now, also, dead women's bodies, known as "el laberinto del silencio" because the area is so vast and deserted that one can get lost in all that silence. The case of the femicides is equal to that labyrinth of silence, where all is lost or forgotten—the theories, the guilty, the names of hundreds of victims. Now even the femicides are forgotten, buried under the stacks of bodies that pile up daily as a social side effect of organized crime in Juarez.[8] No solution, no suspense, no satisfactory denouement—my novel was going to fail, I was sure.

It didn't matter that I had conceived of an airtight idea for an amateur sleuth who was both native and estranged from El Paso and as ignorant about the crimes happening in her own hometown as I had been (thus allowing her ample opportunities for employing her research and investigative skills); that she came with a complete genealogy of turbulent relationships and three-dimensional family members full of quirks and whims who could fill in the roles of the supporting cast; that she had solid, high-stakes personal reasons for getting involved in the investigation of the crimes in the summer of 1998. Everything related to characterization, motivation, setting, and conflict was compelling and good. But I had no structure. Not for a mystery novel that offered no way out of the maze. Beyond the Egyptian or El Tolteca or El Diablo— individual culprits who have been arrested, tried, and even indicted for some of the crimes—nobody seemed to know who the criminals or the masterminds actually were.

Luckily, in 2002, three years into my research on the crimes and at least two rough drafts of the novel later, the Universe provided a solution via my Cuban friend Sara Rosell, professor of Spanish at Iowa State University. An avid mystery fan herself, my dear friend Sara turned me on to a book that allowed me to understand precisely the kind of mystery I was writing. Authored by an Italian literary critic named Stefano Tani, and highly praised by one of my own gurus of writing, John Gardner, the book is *The Doomed Detective: The Contribution of the Detective Novel to Postmodern American and Italian Fiction*, which I had to special order through Amazon.com because the book was by then out of print. It was in *The Doomed Detective* that I learned that I had been trying to fit a modernist shoe—the structure of a classical detective story—on a postmodernist foot, or rather, what Stefano Tani called an "anti-detective novel."

Whereas the "constructive principle" of a classic detective story is the solution to the crime, Tani writes, the anti–detective novel inverts that principle by suspending the solution and emphasizing instead the detective's existential albeit fruitless quest. "The anti-detective novel, which frustrates the expectations of the reader, transforms a mass-media genre into a sophisticated expression of avant-garde sensibility, and substitutes for the detective as central and ordering character the decentering and chaotic admission of mystery, of non-solution."[9]

The main character in a classical detective story is the detective, who functions as the center and ordering principle of the story, whereas in the anti–detective novel, the main character is the mystery itself. An anti–detective novel has no center except for the labyrinth of the mystery, and it is the detective's job to "map the labyrinth."[10] In so doing, he or she gets emotionally caught up in the mystery and in the process of detection. Thus, the protagonist of an anti–detective novel becomes a kind of Theseus whose central function is to find a way out of the Minotaur's maze with the help of an Ariadne's thread. But though the thread gives our sleuth something to hold on to—a problem to solve and clues to analyze—that might perhaps guide her deeper into the maze or map her way out of danger, it does not solve the mystery that led her into the labyrinth in the first place.

Tani's study of Italian and American detective fiction leads him to conclude that there are three types of anti–detective novels: the innovative, the deconstructive, and the metafictional. Metafictional anti–detective novels are more like a literary game played loosely along the conventions of detective fiction but more concerned with the interactions between the reader, the writer, and the text. Deconstructive anti–detective novels tend to pit the detective against his/her own identity at the same time that they offer an outer mystery involving some sort of devil worship or evil magic that the detective is never able to decipher or even interpret. The only mystery a detective in deconstructive anti–detective novels is able to solve during the course of her investigation might be the one within herself, at no small cost to her sanity.[11]

The innovative anti–detective novel offered me the map out of my own labyrinth. In an innovative anti–detective novel, "the detective can find a solution," but it may not be the "real solution"; it may be "only the projection of his [or her] own desires, one of the multiple solutions that a puzzle may have."[12] In other words, it may be social protest rather than denouement. Indeed, the very lack of a denouement, which would imply in the case of the Juárez femicides not only an end to the state-sanctioned impunity of the perpetrators but also an end to the social apathy that has allowed these crimes to continue unabated and unresolved for twenty years, gives me much grist for the mill of my literary indictment of the corporate hunger of multinational capitalism that feeds on the bones of poor, young Mexican women on the U.S.-Mexico border.

Even if the detective of an anti–detective novel doesn't solve anything, the act of mapping the labyrinth leads her to ask questions, to connect loose ends, to divulge secrets, to survive dangers, to expose injustices, to awaken doubts—all of which may move the reader to initiate his/her own investigation. Thus, "a detective plot," in an innovative anti–detective novel, says Tani, "is ultimately a device to hold the reader's attention and to convey a social indictment in a concise and rational way."[13]

This is how the innovative anti–detective novel subverts and transforms all of the conventions of the classic mystery novel. Indeed, perhaps the most significant difference between a classic mystery and an anti–detective story is that while the purpose of the former is to reach the end to discover "whodunit," in the innovative anti–detective novel, "the purpose is beyond the reading (the end of the novel), and the 'solution' is the 'working out,' the assimilation of the novel's ingredients in the mind of the reader."[14]

It was the innovative anti–detective novel, such as *The Name of the Rose* by Umberto Eco, that offered me the Ariadne's thread I needed to escape from my own structural labyrinth. At least now I knew what kind of mystery I was writing and for what purpose: social protest against the Juárez femicides. I was also using the elements of this literary form to denounce the exploitations and inhumane treatment that the women workers must endure in the maquiladoras; to condemn the social discourse that converts the victims into "bad women"—or Maqui-Locas—and blames them for their deaths; and, finally, to expose the way the Internet facilitates the sale of women's bodies and so promotes sexual slavery. Theresa Márquez writes that "Raza writers are reshaping the mystery genre for specific cultural, political, and social purposes in order to comment on issues of class, gender, race, and sexual orientation. These writers are producing new literary models, which may be viewed as forms of social criticism and cultural representation."[15] So not only was I writing an innovative anti–detective novel, but also, the book was adding to the innovative social critique of Chicana/o detective fiction.

Who is the detective in an innovative anti–detective novel? It can be a policeman or policewoman, a private investigator who follows all of the techniques of professional investigation, or an Everyman or Every-woman who, due to circumstances out of his/her control, and by virtue of a constellation of conditions particular to his/her nature or situation, gets enmeshed in the mystery and becomes an amateur sleuth in his/her meandering journey through the labyrinth. Whatever the sleuth's vocation, she/he cannot rely on an objective or scientific process to analyze the facts, for the facts demonstrate that they make no sense, that there is no justice, no truth, no human compassion in the indifferent killing fields of the mystery.

Enter my brown detective, my labrys-tattooed, all-but-dissertation homegirl from the El Paso–Juárez border: Ivon Villa, protagonist of *Desert Blood: The Juárez Murders*. Ivon does not work in law enforcement nor is she a private investigator. She is an ABD (all but dissertation) visiting Women's Studies professor at a private Catholic university in Los Angeles. The novel opens with Ivon aboard an airplane en route to El Paso after a two-year self-imposed exile that resulted from a particularly nasty fight with her homophobic mother. Looking out the window as the plane prepares to land, she doesn't see a border divided into two sides, she sees one huge empty lot.

> Unless it's twilight, the only thing you see when you fly into El Paso is the desert—the brown, pachydermal, sagebrush-stubbled skin of the

desert. But at twilight what you notice right away is the sky, the green veil of sky that stretches between Mount Franklin and the Guadalupe Mountains. From the plane you can't see the boundary line, the cement riverbed that separates El Paso from Juárez. The borderland is just one big valley of lights. You can't see the chain-link fencing of the Tortilla Curtain, or the entrepreneurs in rubber inner tubes transporting workers back and forth across the Rio Grande, or the long lines of headlights snaking over the Córdoba Bridge—one of the three international bridges that keep the twin cities umbilically connected. For the locals on each side of the river, the border is nothing more than a way to get home.[16]

Ivon is returning home not because of anything having to do with the femicides (in fact, the date is June 1998 and she's reading the same "Maquiladora Murders" article in *Ms.* that was so instrumental to my own awareness), but because she's come to adopt the baby of a maquiladora worker who's on the verge of giving birth. After six years of resisting her lover Brigit's biological clock, Ivon overhears a little boy in a bookstore who awakens her own desire to have a son. She calls her cousin Ximena, a social worker in El Paso whose personal mission it is to help pregnant teenage girls on both sides of the border who are at risk for drugs or homelessness. Ximena has arranged everything for Ivon to come and meet Cecilia, the biological mother of the baby she and Brigit are going to adopt. But this is not the best moment for Ivon to be adopting a baby, since she only has two weeks to finish that dissertation or she'll lose her academic position. Nonetheless, in that charming self-sabotaging way of all ABDs, she chooses to go forward with the adoption.

When Ximena takes her to meet Cecilia, however, they discover that Cecilia has been murdered the night before, her baby carved out of her womb. Now, the Juárez femicides become personal for Ivon. Not only does she lose the child she was going to adopt, she is also brought face-to-face (literally) with the brutally mutilated body of the child's birth mother at the autopsy. The crimes hit a personal double whammy for Ivon when, later in the book, her own sixteen-year-old little sister, who fits the profile of the majority of the victims (young, short, dark-haired, dark-skinned Mexican girl), gets kidnapped from an Expo fair in the Juárez fairgrounds.

In the process of looking for her sister, Ivon will learn not only how privileged she's been in her ivory tower so far from the Rio Grande, how ignorant she's been about the misogynistic murders of all those impoverished Mexican girls and women in Juárez, but also how clueless she's been about the tragic exploitations of maquiladora workers that include slave wages, enforced birth control, and despotic monitoring of their reproductive systems.

In Ivon's map of the labyrinth of the Juárez femicides, she questions the vacuum of silence that surrounds the crimes, and reasons that the murders are not just a Mexican problem but a border problem that is purposely being kept quiet, which to her mind points to a binational collusion between the Border Patrol and the maquiladora industry, the first clues of which she finds scrawled in graffiti on the walls of a public bathroom.

> Someone had scrawled that old saying of Mexican president Porfirio Díaz: *Poor Mexico, so far from God, so close to the United States.* Underneath it, somebody else had written in red nail polish and shaky lettering: *Poor Juárez, so close to Hell, so far from Jesus.*[17]

The second time she returns to the Kentucky Club, now immersed in the Minotaur's maze of the mystery and the search for her little sister, and accompanied by her Mormon cousin, William, she finds that someone has added another line to the graffiti:

> *Poor Juárez, so far from Truth, so close to Jesus.* The old version, she could still see traces of it—*so close to Hell, so far from Jesus*—had been scratched out with something sharp.[18]

Ivon decides to participate in the dialogue that is obviously unfolding through this public form of communication:

> She drew a circle around *so far from the Truth*, and then an arrow pointing to a question: *Do you know the truth? Call me.* She wrote her cell phone number.[19]

Reading graffiti, or rather, performing a textual, semiotic, Marxist reading of graffiti, especially the glyphs doodled on the walls of public women's restrooms, is Ivon's expertise, the very subject of her dissertation. Her hypothesis is that public bathrooms are exhibition spaces wherein users communicate anonymously in graffiti. For Ivon, graffiti can be read as a type of public discourse unfettered by social boundaries of propriety, which functions at the same time like a closed discursive system, a language of its own. These marks on public walls are part of a structure of signification—phrases, drawings, and numbers that signify something very specific for the population that utilizes those spaces. The Kentucky Club is one of the most famous bars in Juárez, and because it's located on Juárez Avenue, one block away from the downtown bridge, it's a popular destination for American tourists and students of both sexes.

The Kentucky Club is also the portal to the sexual underworld known as La Mariscal. The bars and clubs of Jorge Mariscal Street, such as the Mona Lisa and the Panamá that lie behind Juárez Avenue, are heteronormative "gentlemen's clubs," places that have no age or hygiene controls, where some of the victims have disappeared. The only toilet facility available for women at such clubs is the back bathroom, meant for the female "staff," the waitresses and sex workers who ply their trade among the male clientele. Because she's a woman, because she's a lesbian with a history of sexual encounters in those very bars and clubs of the red-light district, Ivon knows these spaces and has access to the staff bathrooms of La Mariscal, and thereby, she is made privy to the graffiti scribbled on their walls, such as these lines that she finds when she and William visit La Casa Colorada:

> *Aquí no hay cholas ni maqui-locas.* "No Cholas or Maqui-Locas here," says one.
>
> *El nuevo gobernador le chupa la verga a la migra.* "The new governor sucks the Border Patrol's cock,"[20] says another.

To Ivon it's obvious that someone is leaving clues about the femicide victims in these public bathrooms. At the Kentucky Club, someone was hinting at a so-called capitalized Truth that evoked both Porfirio Díaz's notorious dictatorship as well as Uncle Sam's expansionistic policies that have already devoured half of Mexico. At Casa Colorada, someone was performing a political analysis of the complicity between the Chihuahua state government and U.S. immigration officials. In both cases, the graffiti appears in the women's bathroom, but the fact that the Casa Colorada graffiti is written in an insider space shows Ivon that the discourse here is private; it's not meant for outside eyes. It's a "*placazo,*" or tag, of protection for the women who work at Casa Colorada. By marking the difference between themselves, the workers, and "*cholas*" (considered Americanized wild girls who use drugs and run around in gangs) or

Maqui-Locas (maquiladora workers who supposedly are living a double life as good girls and bad girls), the graffiti suggests that here in this bar, the killers will find no prey for their sport.

It's as if the anonymous graffiti writers are speaking directly to the criminals, or to some female liaison of the killers that wanders clandestinely among them. Here, the first line of graffiti says, you'll find none of the Americanized, industrialized type of women you seek. We might be whores, but we're Mexican whores (not sellout Cholas or wannabe gringa Maqui-Locas), and we know our place in the social strata. The second line, written in tiny lettering near the bottom, communicates the writer's awareness of the political economy of the border. It's not just that the new PAN government of the state of Chihuahua is in bed with the Border Patrol, but more importantly, that in this relationship, the Mexican government is the one performing fellatio on Uncle Sam. "The positioning of the phrase under Díaz's words bemoaning the proximity of Mexico to the United Status," says Irene Mata in "Markings on the Walls: Writing in Opposition in Alicia Gaspar de Alba's *Desert Blood*," "functions to situate the current situation in Juárez within a longer history of U.S. imperialism in Mexico."[21]

As a stock plot element in noir mysteries, the sleuth must face extreme danger in her pursuit of truth or justice. Ivon and William are arrested on false charges by Mexican *federales*. She's caught by the Border Patrol with illegal pornographic material planted in her car. And near the end, she's about to become the midnight snack of two police-trained canines. When she receives a call on her cell phone from a blocked number, responding to her question "Do you know the truth?" Ivon starts connecting the dots, but it isn't until the mastermind of the "exxxtremely lucky penny" pornography ring captures her that she finally figures out where her sister is being held and for what reason.

> *Es una fábrica cerca de Jesús*, the voice had said on the phone. A factory close to Jesus. Close to Cristo Rey. What was close to Cristo Rey? She could see the smokestacks of the smelter up ahead . . . [22]

Irene Mata performs a fascinating analysis of the graffiti in the story as "oppositional writing," and deconstructs my use of local landmarks such as Cristo Rey, a Christ the King statue atop a mountain along the Rio Grande, and ASARCO, or the American Smelting and Refining Company:

A symbol of hope and faith, the [Cristo Rey] statue instead becomes a silent witness to the atrocities taking place in its shadow . . . By incorporating ASARCO into the narrative, Gaspar de Alba emphasizes the danger the refinery poses to the residents of the border area. As a result, the text situates the current crisis on the border within a long history of capitalist greed overruling the well-being of the border's citizens.[23]

For Ivon Villa at the end of *Desert Blood*, there are three self-evident truths: (1) that no matter who the actual killers are, multinational corporations through the maquiladora industry are making a killing from the globalization of poor brown female labor; (2) that the North American Free Trade Agreement has created an infrastructure that benefits from sexual terrorism of young, poor Mexican women and deadly misogynist violence on the border, and (3) that the lack of empathy from both Mexico and the United States is directly attributable to the social discourse of the "bad woman."

Finally, Ivon is able to see the way out of the maze. Connecting the extreme violence suffered by the victims, their complete exploitation within the twin plant industry, the mandatory pregnancy tests that accompany their job applications, their reproductive surveillance, the pervasive threat of dismissal due to pregnancy, and the sale of women on the Internet (an industry that is more lucrative for its "investors" than the combined profit of the three major broadcasting networks in the United States), Ivon asks herself: "What to do with all those fertile brown female bodies on the border? . . . What happens if they cross over? More illegal Mexican women in El Paso means more legal brown babies. Who wants more brown babies as legal citizens of the Promised Land?"[24] Who, indeed, would want all those fertile brown female bodies creating more anchor babies and future American citizens in a society that is already being overrun by Mexicans and other Spanish-speaking "illegals"? This is Ivon's final analysis as she exits the labyrinth of the Juárez femicides.

As befits the parameters of an anti–detective novel, Ivon does not find out "whodunit"; instead, she learns that the political complicity is so deep that there is no resolution to the femicides. Because of her relentless determination to find her little sister, however, she is able to track down the bus where she's being kept and prevent her from becoming yet another notch in the stick of the criminals. Somehow her sister survives the ordeal with her kidnappers, but not without getting raped, drugged, poisoned, beaten, and mauled by killer dogs. Some have criticized the "happy ending" to *Desert Blood*, the fact that Ivon does find her sister and saves her from getting killed, but how "happy" can a girl be after surviving such trauma at sixteen? Is death the only prerogative for empathy or commitment to social justice?

Ivon never solves the mystery of who is massacring the bodies of so many young women and girls in Juárez. In her harrowing journey through the labyrinth, however, she has learned that it's not just global capitalist greed that devours "*las hijas de Juárez*," exploiting their productivity until the last penny of profit. She is certain that there is a binational conspiracy that implicates the most powerful corporate interests of the U.S.-Mexico border, interests that include the deeply exploitative manufacturing industry, the online pornography industry that uses human trafficking for sexual slavery, and the Border Patrol with its informal army of sex offender vigilantes.

My contribution to what Theresa Márquez calls "the Aztlán mystery tradition," then, is not a brown detective tracking down a criminal; think of her as a Chicana lesbian Theseus mapping "el laberinto del silencio" in Juárez. That labyrinth encompasses a spectrum of violence that has femicide at one end and homophobia on the other, with racist immigration laws and neocolonizing trade agreements falling in between. All of it, Ivon comes to realize, impacts the social family that is created in the bleeding desert of the borderlands because, even if the body they find in the sand dunes of Lomas de Poleo isn't her little sister, "she's someone else's sister . . . someone else's daughter."[25] *Una hija más de la frontera.*

To this day, two decades after these heinous sex crimes began, and over eight hundred bodies later, the murders continue and remain unsolved, no matter how many cases the Mexican government alleges have been solved. Despite all the activism of the mothers and the relentless grassroots actions taken in Juárez and Chihuahua to denounce the impunity of the crimes, the botched investigations, the apathy of the state and the society on both sides of the border; despite all the task forces appointed by the Mexican government to solve the mystery of femicides since 1996 (however inefficient); despite the incarceration of several potential criminals and suspects through the years and the involvement of Amnesty International, the FBI, the United Nations, and the Inter-American Court on Human Rights; despite the community organizations around the world devoted to seeking justice for women in Juárez and the exponential growth of cultural products that exist to inform the world about the crimes—films, documentaries, songs, novels, journalistic books, academic conferences, poetry readings, art exhibits, websites and other cyber resources; despite the worldwide fund-raising campaigns to support the mothers in their activist work; despite all of the demonstrations and protests, the participation of movie stars Jane Fonda, Sally Field, Jennifer Lopez, Antonio Banderas, Eve Ensler, and Jimmy Smits in awareness campaigns and V-Day marches; despite, even, the joint resolution that was passed unanimously in the U.S. House of Representatives; despite an online petition that has been collecting signatures since 2003 with a list of twelve demands, including that the femicides be recognized as crimes against humanity, that a binational/international human rights commission be created specifically to investigate and put an end to these crimes, and that measures be taken to protect the mothers and families of the victims and the activists who are working to resolve these cases[26]— despite all of these local, national, and international efforts to put the Juárez femicides on the front page of a global social justice agenda, the murders continue unabated, hundreds more women wind up missing or turn up dead every year, and the criminals continue their march of impunity. Apparently, there is no solution. Definitely, there is no justice for the poor brown daughters of Juárez.

Under the watchful eyes of Christ the Redeemer and the poisonous maw of the ASARCO smelter,[27] perpetrators that could be anything from gangbangers to Border Patrol agents to policemen are getting away with femicidal murder in Juárez. We all have our theories as to why these crimes keep happening, but nobody really knows. All we have are questions and theories that multiply as fast as the bones in the desert. Could it be that the mythic story of Huitzilopochtli slaughtering his "bad sister," the sister who refuses to occupy her place of obedience and subservience, the sister who dares to act on her own desires and exercise her own agency, is not so far-fetched?

The Mystery of the Missing Brother

The legend of Coyolxauhqui, as it has been recorded in the *Florentine Codex*[28] and as it has been told and retold across the ages, in the academy as well as in the Chicano/Mexicano community, is the story of "la maligna media hermana de Huitzilopochtli,"[29] the malignant half sister and mastermind of the plot to commit matricide and fratricide with the help of her four hundred brothers.

According to the legend as it was written down in the *Florentine Codex*, when Coyolxauhqui, also known as Bells on Her Cheeks, found out about her mother's unexplained pregnancy, she felt shamed by her mother's transgression, as though the mother had committed a grievous sin against her family. Why would Coyolxauhqui and her brothers, the Centzon Huitznahua, have issues with their mother's pregnancy? Why would pregnancy be seen as a transgression to a people that honored childbirth, a people that had a goddess of childbirth, a people that saw women who died in childbirth as warriors? Would such a society judge a pregnant woman, a venerated old woman at that, a "bad woman," or a bad mother for being mysteriously with child? It makes no sense, no matter what is written in the *Florentine Codex* under the Catholic scruples and scrutiny of the evangelizing Bernardino de Sahagún and his ilk.

I agree with Grisel Gómez-Cano, who notes in *The Return to Coatlicue*:

> The logic of the plan and demand for matricide . . . is murky. Why would a daughter kill her pregnant mother? Many Mesoamericanists consider this legend not about murder but about the personification of the struggle between the sun, moon, and southern stars, and their mundane cults. Others propose that the theme of decapitation of Coyolxauhqui represents the annihilation of a female-led clan by the emerging patriarchal order ruled by a class of priests . . . The immaculate conception of Huitzilopochtli closely follows that of the Christ child, so Spanish missionaries could have rewritten this myth or influenced its native tellers . . . From a religious perspective, a major theme of this first Aztec century was the replacement of a lunar with a solar religious ideology. The birth of a solar god signaled the Aztecs' military expansion. He replaced the ancient agricultural moon deity known as Mecitli. Historically, this period could mark the emergence of the Mexica as an independent clan led by male warrior-priests and the extermination of a female kinship led by the Mexica warlady, Coyolxauhqhi.[30]

When we actually go to the *Florentine Codex* and read the story of Coyolxauhqui as it has been recorded in Spanish, we find an important element that never seems to make it into the retelling: the treacherous little brother named Cuahuitlicac who is the sole dissenter of Coyolxauhqui's plan to kill Coatlicue and prevent the birth of their new brother, who will become the god of war, Huitzilopochtli.

The three main characters in the legend are Coyolxauhqui, the bad daughter (in the mother's and brothers' eyes); Coatlicue, the bad mother (in the daughter's and family's eyes); and Huitzilopochtli, the youngest but strongest of Coatlicue's sons, destined to rule the Aztecs and the Fifth Sun. The four hundred siblings, also known as the four hundred Southerners or Centzon Huitznahua, play a role in the story, as well, mostly as textured background to the warrior goddess's gruesome tale. So what accounts for the mystery of the missing brother? When did Cuahuitlicac get left out of the oral tradition? Why does he disappear completely from the story, although his name is inscribed in the codex, along with the names of his older sister, brother, and mother, and his agency in the drama was instrumental to the total destruction of Coyolxauhqui *and* Coatlicue?

As the only one of the Centzon Huitznahua named in the narrative, Cuahuitlicac has a role in the unfolding of events as central as Coyolxauhqui's, for it is he who reveals Coyolxauhqui's plans to Huitzilopochtli (speaking to him through his mother's womb) and helps Huitzilopochtli time his birth at the precise moment that Coyolxauhqui and the Centzon Huitznahua storm into the temple. Huitzilopochtli's sudden, full-grown delivery from Coatlicue's womb provides the dramatic twist to Coyolxauhqui's matricidal plot, and it is the sister rather than the brother who ends up being killed; more than killed, *la hermana maligna* is beheaded, stripped naked, dismembered, her body parts kicked down the temple steps, and humiliated for eternity. Coatlicue's death, though never described in the *Florentine Codex*, is conveniently ascribed to the evil sister.

I believe that *Coyolxauhqui was framed*. For nearly seven millennia, Coyolxauhqui has been blamed for her disloyalty and her anger, for plotting the unforgivable sins of mother and brother murder. She has been seen as the treacherous, rebellious daughter, the unmanageable, disobedient, moody, crazy sister, who got what she had coming because of her own selfish interests and bad temper. Cherríe Moraga and Gloria Anzaldúa have both written about Coyolxauhqui and have reinterpreted her story within a Chicana lesbian feminist frame.

Moraga writes that Coyolxauhqui's actions are political, not personal, that the warrior goddess "hopes to halt, through the murder of her mother . . . the birth of slavery, human sacrifice and imperialism (in short, patriarchy)."[31] And yet, Moraga doesn't question the idea that Coyolxauhqui was attempting to "murder her mother." My interpretation of Coyolxauhqui is more aligned with Gloria Anzaldúa, who sees her as a "symbol not only of violence and hatred against women but also of how we're split body and mind, spirit and soul . . . when you take a person and divide her up, you disempower her. She's no longer a threat."[32]

Indeed, for Anzaldúa, understanding the warrior goddess's actions as activism, as a response to a call to right an injustice, leads to "Coyolxauhqui consciousness," one of the seven steps in the process of *conocimiento*, or self-knowledge. This call to action, however, can be a dismembering process, like the act of writing about the self. "This process or struggle, where a piece of experience is worked on, is connected to the soul, connected to making soul . . . You have to destroy, tear down, in order to put together and rebuild."[33] For me, this process is also related to teaching, to helping draw out the Coyolxauhqui consciousness in my students through a keen and often painful analysis of their own lives and choices.

So let me summon my storyteller's skills here, and try to rewrite and rebuild the myth from the perspective of another "bad sister," a Chicana lesbian feminist who is invested in putting the pieces of Coyolxauhqui back together.

Unframing Coyolxauhqui

Long ago, in a sacred place called Coatepec, or Snake Mountain, Coatlicue, the Mother of the Gods, was performing her seasonal sweeping of her temple when she came upon a ball of bright blue hummingbird feathers, which she picked up and nestled between her breasts. Stray feathers were dangerous, she knew, but at her age, and after giving birth to 401 children, Coatlicue wasn't worried about the mystical consequences of a few floating feathers.

It wasn't long before she realized that she was wrong, for the feathers had (as feathers always did) mysteriously impregnated her. The voice in her womb told her she was to give birth to Hummingbird to the South, or Huitzilopochtli, the sun god and god of war and sacrifice.

Coatlicue summoned her eldest child, her daughter, Coyolxauhqui, or Bells Painted on Her Cheeks, to the temple to give her the news of her pregnancy. Fearless and loyal and hot-tempered, Coyolxauhqui had chosen the warrior's path, not the scribe or the priestess path more common to the eldest child of a powerful goddess.

"Tonantzin, did you go out looking for feathers again?" Tonantzin was the name Coyolxauhqui and her four hundred siblings called their mother.

Coatlicue shrugged. "I'm thousands of years old. How was I supposed to know I could still get pregnant? And they were so tiny, nothing but hummingbird feathers. Who could suspect they would be so powerful? And they were so beautiful, too, bright iridescent blue. You know I can't resist beautiful feathers."

"Yes, Tonantzin, but feathers are dangerous for you. Especially the pretty ones. You always want to touch them and put them next to you.

That's why we want you to stay inside the temple, so that the wind and the feathers don't find you and make you pregnant."

"I didn't leave the temple, *hija mía*. It was right here, while sweeping under Ometeotl's altar that I found the ball of feathers. Just like the time I found that long, single quetzal feather in the temple of the moon in Aztlán and it brought me you, my brave warrior daughter."

Coatlicue stared silently across the lake, remembering their peaceful life in Aztlán, the trees heavy with white herons. She still could not understand what a quetzal bird had been doing that far north. If anything, it should have been a white heron feather that produced her eldest child. But that one had been second, followed by the eagle quintuplets and the gray owl twins.

"Did you hear me, Tonantzin? I am worried about this hummingbird. Always moving, always hungry, and that long sharp beak always taking the nectar out of the flowers. Is it a good omen or a bad omen?"

"What a strange question, my daughter. You know that there can be no good without bad, no light without darkness. We have lived in harmony for generations. Your reign during the Sun of Water has been good to us, and our people have grown fertile and strong. But lazy, too, lazy and greedy. Now, the time has come for balance. And the balance to all this fertility is war, for through war, and the death it will bring to our people, will we be reborn. Your new brother has told me his name. He will be Huitzilopochtli, Hummingbird to the South. He will be the god of war and sacrifice."

"War and sacrifice?" Coyolxauhqui removed her turquoise helmet, crowned with quetzales and marigolds. "Our people are not warmongers. They're poets and artists and musicians. They study the stars and the planets. They grow flowers and cultivate fruits. Why would they make war, when war is the opposite of what the Nahui Atl is all about? The Sun of Water is one of growth not death."

Coatlicue stroked the scars her daughter had carved into her cheeks when she chose the warrior's path. Now the scars looked like bells tattooed on her cheeks. The jagged nail of Coatlicue's thumb caught on the rough skin of her daughter's face. "A new sun is coming, my daughter. The Nahui Ollin, the Sun of Movement. And this child I carry inside me will be the ruler of that new sun, the supreme deity, who must be fed with the ripe fruit of the human heart. If we fail to keep him fed, the fire will go out of the sky and the people will be plunged into darkness and despair. He tells me a great change is coming, and that our people will have to move from Coatepec and find another place on which to build his temple."

"Build his temple?" Coyolxauhqui rose to her feet, incensed at the idea of this upstart little brother. "Who does he think he is! We already have a temple in honor of you, Tonantzin, our Great Mother. Does he mean to displace the great goddess of life and death? Does he mean to crush our Serpent Skirt, Coatlicue, this hummingbird trespasser?"

"Don't be jealous, my daughter. You're still the firstborn and no matter what happens, the quetzal feather will never be displaced in my heart."

"Jealous? You offend me, Tonantzin. I'm not thinking of myself. It's you who is being dishonored. How can you be so calm about it? The Centzon Huitznahua are going to be very unhappy with this news. Our people wandered for more than two centuries since leaving Aztlán. They've been so happy here on Coatepec."

"There is a prophecy that the people will be divided," said Coatlicue. "Those who follow Huitzilopochtli will travel for many more years until they find an island in the middle of a wide lake. On the island they will see an eagle perched on a cactus devouring a snake. That will be their sign that they have found their new homeland. They will build a great civilization on this island, with pyramids and temples and schools."

"And those who don't?" asked Coyolxauhqui. "What happens to those who don't follow Huitzilopochtli?"

Coatlicue turned her eyes away from her daughter's face. "They will be conquered."

Coyolxauhqui got to her feet, resplendent in her turquoise armor, her copper-colored skin turning silver in the last rays of the sunset. "I won't let him do this to you, or to our people, Tonantzin," she threatened, hand on the hilt of her obsidian sword. "This hummingbird trespasser will destroy everything we have built for thousands of years. He will bring down the Nahui Atl. He will sow conflict and hatred, he will wreak havoc and destruction. I will not stand for it."

"We must accept that life changes, *hija mía*. Every sun runs its course." Coatlicue tried to soothe Coyolxauhqui, but even the bells on her daughter's cheeks were flaming with a white rage. Her eyes glistened with angry silver tears. Coatlicue had never seen such ferociousness in her daughter, and it frightened her, the depth of Coyolxauhqui's fury, which had turned her normally copper skin white as a bone.

Coatlicue felt a sharp kick in her womb. She doubled over with pain. Already the child was fighting back.

"Leave me now," Coatlicue instructed. "This conversation has tired me. I need my rest. Tomorrow we will discuss how to tell your four hundred brothers about the birth, and then they will have to break the news to the people."

That night, Coyolxauhqui's wrath would not be quelled, and her body emitted a silver halo of livid rage. She paced and paced at the base of the temple, not realizing she had worn a groove into the red earth. She couldn't stop thinking about the prophecy, about the insult that was to be perpetrated on their Great Mother. If she didn't stop this travesty, it would mean the end of the Fourth Sun. In truth, the solution was simple, but she couldn't carry it out alone, so she went to her secret cave and blew on her conch shell and called her four hundred brothers together to tell them about the prophecy, about her ruse to kill Hummingbird to the South.

She told them about their mother's pregnancy, about the birth of the god of war and sacrifice, about the prophecy that he would divide the people and bring death and mayhem into their lives. At first, the fury of the Centzon Huitznahua matched her own. How dare he! That upstart! That maniac! Then one by one the heart went out of them, and they grew bitter and morose at the thought of having to leave Serpent Mountain. Coyolxauhqui admonished them.

"Don't let your sadness defeat you, my brothers. We cannot allow this birth to take place. We must kill this hummingbird brother. It is the only way to protect Tonantzin. The only way to preserve our life on Coatepec."

And so Coyolxauhqui incited her brothers' courage again, and they agreed to help her carry out her furtive plan. Only one of them, the scribe they called Cuahuitlicac, disagreed with Coyolxauhqui. He was a liar and a meddler, and Coyolxauhqui had no patience for his objections. She kicked him out of the meeting and didn't give him a second thought as she turned her attention back to her other 399 brothers to plan their attack.

Cuahuitlicac ran to the Great Mother's temple and found her sleeping deeply on her *petate*. Quietly, he approached her swollen belly and whispered to his little brother the plans that their sister Coyolxauhqui and the Centzon Huitznahua were plotting for his demise.

A sound rumbled from the Great Mother's belly, and Cuahuitlicac heard his brother's manly voice.

"Worry not, little uncle. I know what must be done."

Why had his brother called him uncle? Did that mean one of the Centzon Huitznahua was the father? A son coupling with his own mother? Immediately, Cuahuitlicac felt ashamed. Was it right to doubt his mother? Had he been right to betray his sister?

Coatlicue stirred fitfully in her sleep. From beneath her serpent-like skirts that wrapped around her in different colors, the young god was moving himself into position.

"Where are they now?" asked the hummingbird brother.

From the top of the temple steps, Cuahuitlicac had a clear view over the valley and saw the cloud of warriors moving quickly toward Coatepec.

"They're getting closer. They're moving fast."

"Worry not, little brother. Where are they now?"

Now he could hear the whooping sounds of the Centzon Huitznahua as they approached.

"They're almost here. Wake up, Tonantzin, wake up!"

"Where are they now?" asked the unborn brother for the third time, still calm.

Cuahuitlicac heard the army of his siblings swarming up the temple steps. "It's too late!" he cried, "they're here!" He ran to hide in the darkest part of the temple.

Coyolxauhqui and the Centzon Huitznahua stole into the temple like shadows. In the light of the full moon slicing down from the opening in the temple roof, Cuahuitlicac could see that his brothers were fully arrayed for battle. Their hair gathered in topknots, their insignias pinned to their padded tunics, they wore long streamers of colored paper tied from their girdles, and bells tinkled from their armored calves. The barbed tips of their arrows gleamed with poisoned oil. Coyolxauhqui led the way, fully armored in turquoise, gold paint on her face and body, her obsidian sword raised high over her quetzal-feathered headdress. A strange white light emanated from her, brighter than the moon.

Cuahuitlicac squeezed his eyes shut to block the horror of what was about to happen.

"Put your weapons down," he heard Coatlicue say. "How dare you raise your hand to your own mother?"

"It is not you we are here to kill, Tonantzin," said Coyolxauhqui. "We protest the birth of the one you carry inside. It is he whom we will not allow to be born."

But Coatlicue could say no more, for the pain churning in her womb was worse than all 401 of her previous births put together. She felt herself being cut open and pecked apart by a sharp beak, and she cried out to the Tzitzimine to come to her aid and ease what she knew were the death pangs of labor.

Suddenly, there was a great quake in the earth below Coatlicue. Cuahuitlicac would record later in the Song of Huitzilopochtli how Coatlicue's screams shook the temple as the god of war exited from her womb, nothing but a hummingbird, so small he made Coyolxauhqui laugh.

"That's the great god of war?" she taunted, swatting at the hummingbird with the tip of her sword and maiming the tip of its left wing. The Centzon Huitznahua laughed with her.

Instantly the little hummingbird transformed himself into a full-grown god, taller than Coatlicue or Coyolxauhqui, his arms and legs painted blue, yellow war paint striped on his face, holding a shield of eagle feathers and wielding the fiery serpent, Xiuhcoatl, like a thunderbolt in his left hand.

In horror, Cuahuitlicac and all of his brothers watched the mortal combat between Huitzilopochtli and Coyolxauhqui. Never had they seen their elder sister fight more fiercely, her obsidian sword deflecting the flames of the thunderbolt, her turquoise shield smashing down on Huitzilopochtli's withered left foot, the wing tip that she had maimed earlier. Hobbled, Huitzilopochtli let out a war bellow louder than the combined cry of the Centzon Huitznahua.

In one sudden move, quick as a hummingbird, Huitzilopochtli darted behind Coyolxauhqui and sliced off her head with one blazing sweep of the fiery serpent. Just as swiftly, he chopped off her arms and legs, pulled the breastplate off her torso and exposed her naked breasts, and kicked her body parts down the temple stairs. He chased and killed all but a few of his 399 brothers and turned them to embers with his fiery serpent sword. The survivors ran for their lives as far south as they could get from Coatepec and were never heard from again.

In her last moments of life, Coatlicue, greatly weakened from the birth and devastated by the carnage she had just witnessed against her firstborn, cradled her daughter's head to her breast, kissed each of the tattoos on her cheeks, and threw the head into the night sky to become the moon. She dragged herself to the embers that her other children had been reduced to, blew on them with her last breath, and sent their immortal souls up to join their sister, and the sparks became the southern stars.

Cuahuitlicac would say later that the worst part was seeing what Huitzilopochtli did to their Great Mother. She was close to dead already, so there was no need to do what he did, but he had not finished asserting his dominion, and Cuahuitlicac dared not stop him.

The young god, resplendent with victory and vengeance, the blue blood of his siblings dripping from his entire body, approached the prostrate Coatlicue. "Because you allowed her to threaten me," Huitzilopochtli pronounced, "because even after she attacked me you still loved her and kissed her face, and have immortalized her in the night sky, you do not deserve to be my mother. Know this. This is how I will commemorate my malevolent sister. At the base of my temple, there will be a stone carved with her dismembered image, to remind my enemies what happens to those who dare to defy Huitzilopochtli."

With a cold anger that terrified Cuahuitlicac more than the massacre he had just seen, Huitzilopochtli swung his fiery sword down the middle of the Great Mother's head in an attempt to hew her body in half. But Coatlicue was the All-Powerful Mother of the Gods, and she would not be smitten by her own son. Her head cleaved, but instead of destroying her, the blow released the two great serpents that lived in her being, the serpent of life and the serpent of death. Monstrous eagle talons emerged from her fingers, crocodile claws from her feet, and a necklace of hearts and hands hung over her sagging breasts. A cape of multicolored feathers—eagle feathers, owl feathers, the long green feathers of the quetzal bird, the white heron, the black raven, the red cardinal, the yellow parrot, the blue hummingbird, and so many more—the feathers that had fathered all her children, hung from the Great Mother's shoulders.

"For your disrespect and dishonor," spoke Coatlicue's voice through the mouths of the two serpents that now lashed their red and black tongues at Huitzilopochtli's face, "shall you remain hobbled on the left side, shall you be doomed to fight this battle with your sister, the Moon, and your brothers, the Stars, every night for eternity. And, though you will slay them day after day, they will come back to me every night, while you lick your wounds in the cave of sorrow and regrets. Yes, you will be the most powerful ruler, and many nations will fall to your fiery sword and render tribute in your honor. But because you have disgraced your mother, and dismembered your sister, and killed your brothers, because you have no one now save the traitor who will tell your story, your sun will be destroyed by those who come with a far more powerful weapon than the silly toys you wield now. I pity you, my son, for you will have no one to help you stop the invaders."

With that, the monstrous creature that Coatlicue had become turned to stone.

Huitzilopochtli laughed at his mother's curse. What did a shriveled foot matter when he would have the world at his feet? He spotted Cuahuitlicac cowering behind a bundle of sticks and ordered him to compose a song about what had just happened, so that the people would always remember that it was she, Coyolxauhqui, the treacherous daughter, the evil sister, who had plotted to kill their mother, and that it was he, Huitzilopochtli, who had saved her, though the mother would always be blamed for having transgressed against her children and her family's honor.

Huitzilopochtli then collected the weapons of his victims, donned their armor, decorated himself with their insignias and colored streamers, hung the bells off his own calves, and placed the feathers in his own headdress. He stood with his legs wide open, shaking his fiery serpent bolt at the sky just as the bright orb of the new sun, the Nahui Ollin, cleared the horizon.

Among the people known as the Mexica, one of the eight tribes whom we call Aztec left the sacred hill of Coatepec in the year of Huitzilopochtli's birth, heeding their god's ordainment to build a new temple in his honor on an island upon which they found an eagle perched atop a nopal devouring a snake. For the Aztecs, movement became a way of life. They wandered for hundreds of years in search of their promised land, making war, making enemies, taking spoils, living and dying until at last they came to the Valley of Mexico and saw the sign of the eagle perched on a nopal devouring a snake in the middle of a marsh. Upon that marsh they settled and founded a city that eventually became the Aztec Empire of Mexico-Tenochtitlan. The great Templo Mayor was dedicated to Huitzilopochtli, and in honor of the god's birth, the high priests of Tenochtitlan placed a stone carving of the dismembered Coyolxauhqui at the foot of the temple stairs as a clear warning to the enemies of the Mexica: if he could do this to his own sister, imagine what he will do to you? The goddess's breasts are exposed as a sign of ritual humiliation for having been conquered in battle, "since nakedness for the ancient Mesoamericans was a sign of submission," as Grisel Gómez-Cano points out. "When soldiers conquered regions, both men and women were undressed to show they had been dispossessed."[34] It was upon the Coyolxauhqui stone that the broken bodies of sacrificial victims would fall and be dismembered after their hearts had been offered to Huitzilopochtli, for the only food that would appease Huitzilopochtli was the sacrificed human heart.[35]

I end this chapter with this retelling of Coyolxauhqui's story not because I simply want to shift the blame from the sister to the brother, not because I hate men or think the Aztecs were more violent than we are today, and not because I think pointing the finger at patriarchy is all it takes to change history. I end by exposing the mystery of the missing brother and unframing Coyolxauhqui as the bad sister because it crystallizes my mission as an academic and a writer. In my research, my teaching, and my scholarship, I will continue to question dominant narratives, to unframe the lives of "bad women" in history, and reframe their stories within the chronicle of revolutionary females, just as I will continue to break down sexist, heterosexist, and homophobic paradigms, and prioritize the lives of Mexicans and Chicanas/os.

Because I believe in activist scholarship and social justice, I remain committed to both the pedagogy and the methodology of the oppressed.[36] Writing novels of social protest, teaching students how to reframe the knowledge and stories by which we shape our worldviews, engaging in research for the sake of community and personal empowerment—these are my "decolonizing *movidas*," my forms of praxis in the academy.

At UCLA, I have exercised what Jennifer Bickham Mendez calls "strategic duality," in which I have used my "position within the academy to contribute to social justice struggles, while at the same time working to place at the center alternative voices and ways of knowing."[37] One of those is the voice of Coyolxauhqui, who, for cosmic reasons, I'm sure, was stirred back to life in 1978, and whose rebellious vibrations continue to emanate from the Templo Mayor to the City of Angels.

Like Coyolxauhqui, Chicana feminists and Chicana lesbians have also been accused of betraying our *familias*, rebelling against our fathers, attacking and hurting our brothers in struggle, of shaming our mothers and breaking our family's hearts. As Gloria Anzaldúa, Cherríe Moraga, Alma López, and other writers and artists have shown, we have a lot in common with this warrior daughter, this *rebelde con causa*.

Figure 6.1. Alma López, detail from *Lady/Virgen: Comparisons*, © 2003–2012. Acrylic on canvas, 12 x 12 in. Used by permission of the artist.

Chapter 6

DEVIL IN A ROSE BIKINI

The Inquisition Continues

On February 25, 2001, the *Cyber Arte: Tradition Meets Technology* exhibition opened at the Museum of International Folk Art (MOIFA) in Santa Fe, New Mexico, showcasing the work of four Chicana/ Hispana/Latina artists who combine folk iconography with computer technology in the creation of their digital media artworks. One of the pieces in the show was Alma López's *Our Lady*, a 14" x 17.5" digital collage representing the artist's interpretation of the Virgin of Guadalupe, dressed in roses, held on high by a bare-breasted butterfly angel, and draped with a cloak engraved with symbols of the Aztec moon goddess, Coyolxauhqui. Several months before the show opened, the museum sent out invitations to the show's opening featuring *Our Lady*, and almost immediately started receiving calls from community activists and representatives from the Catholic Church protesting the image and demanding that it be removed from the exhibition. For months after the opening, protest rallies and prayer vigils were organized outside the museum, spearheaded by a volunteer chaplain for the city's police department, a deacon of the Guadalupe Parish, and the archbishop of the Santa Fe Archdiocese. Like the three witches of *Macbeth* invoking toil and trouble over their cauldron of curses, the three men agitated and inflamed the protestors, who grew more and more belligerent at what they saw as the museum's patent disregard of New Mexico's religious beliefs and, in particular, Alma López's "blasphemy" of their holy symbol, which the newspapers had labeled the "bikini Virgin." Not only did the protestors demand the removal of *Our Lady* from the exhibition, they also demanded a public apology from the Museum of New Mexico and the immediate resignations of the exhibition curator, Tey Marianna Nunn; the MOIFA director, Joyce Ice; and the director of the Museum of New Mexico, Tom Wilson.

So much did the archbishop and his flock of outraged protestors blow López's 14" x 17.5" artwork out of proportion that she cast a huge shadow over Santa Fe and conveniently dwarfed the pedophilia scandal that the archbishop was doing his utmost (to the point of nearly bankrupting the archdiocese) to contain. Indeed, the more *Our Lady* loomed as the foremost outrage in Santa Fe, the less heat there was for the archbishop from the press, the public, and the Vatican.

On Sunday, April 1, 2001, *Journal North*, a Santa Fe newspaper, published a very telling cartoon by Jon Richards. The cartoon showed a caricature of Archbishop Michael Sheehan standing next to an Ayatollah Khomeini–like figure, the image of Alma López's *Our Lady* in the background.[1] The men appear to be looking at the image on the wall of the museum, and the Sheehan character asks, "So just how do you go about issuing a fatwa?" The cartoon is alluding to the infamous diktat of the Ayatollah's in which he called for the assassination of Salman Rushdie for having allegedly blasphemed against the prophet Mohammed in his 1988 novel, *The Satanic Verses*. Calling the fatwa a "religious duty for Muslims" because of the novel's great offense against Islam, the Ayatollah deputized any Muslim in the world to "send [the writer] to Hell."[2]

Given its publication date, the cartoon could be taken as a sardonic April Fool's comment on the cultural climate in Santa Fe at the time of the *Our Lady* controversy, but I think the cartoonist aptly illustrates the zealotry with which the archbishop and his holy army of protestors attacked the constitutional rights of Alma López and sought to punish her for her alleged offense against the Mother of God.

Anther cartoon by Jon Richards lampooned the big fuss being made over this innocuous art piece by showing *Our Lady* as the equivalent of the 50-foot Woman, or perhaps the archetypal Lady of the Apocalypse; in comparison, the tiny archbishop is depicted as barely reaching the height of the angel at the bottom of the picture. In another cartoon, *Our Lady* is taking the place of the Statue of Liberty, with a thought bubble that reads "Personally, I'm in favor of the separation of Art and State," to underscore the fact that in conflating the art piece with a religious artifact and attacking the artist for her representation, the protestors were flagrantly trampling the artist's First Amendment rights.

As I will show in this chapter, the "irreverent apparition" that the archbishop and his cronies and their followers were protesting was of their own making. Blasphemy, in other words, was in the eye of the beholder.

Over the eight months of the controversy, hundreds of articles were published in local newspapers and independent publications; countless news broadcasts kept talking about Alma López and showing *Our Lady* on TV, panning in close-up, filming over the image from head to foot, pausing at the sensational spots, like the angel's bare breasts at the bottom, *Our Lady's* strong abs, and her direct gaze at the viewer. National newspapers like the *New York Times* and the *Washington Post* covered the controversy, and it was featured as well in mainstream magazines such as *Art in America*, *Art Papers*, and *Ms.* The BBC online and *Reforma*, the major newspaper out of Mexico City, also participated in the media frenzy, all of which had the unintended effect of placing Alma López on the world map as an artist and forever embedding Alma's *Our Lady*, or as some called her, "Our Lady of All This Fuss"[3] and "Our Lady of Eternal Conflict,"[4] in the colonial imaginary of New Mexico.

In this chapter, I want to look more closely at the popular reception of *Our Lady*, the social discourse that surrounded and indeed engulfed the piece in waves of gossip, scandal, and religious fanaticism. Some saw the work as evil incarnate and protested vehemently against displaying it in a state-funded museum. Some saw evil incarnate in the protestors and found unacceptable their demand for censorship in the name of religion.

Figure 6.2. Alma López, *Our Lady*, © 1999. Giclée on canvas, 14 x 17 1/2 in. Special thanks to Raquel Salinas and Raquel Gutiérrez. Used by permission of the artist.

What is interesting to me in examining the protest over this 14" x 17.5" digital photo collage is how an action of disapproval and denunciation by hundreds of "faithful" Catholics was converted or, rather, inverted into a procession and then a pilgrimage, such as those that follow miraculous appearances on a tree or a tortilla. At the heart of the protest was the miracle of the appearance of the Virgin of Guadalupe to a lowly Aztec Indian in 1531, a story that has won the hearts and souls of millions across the centuries and that is credited for single-handedly converting the "bloodthirsty heathens" in Mexico to Christianity and the Catholic faith.

My contention in this chapter is that in their apocalyptic protest of an artwork that they saw as profaning the miraculous image of Our Lady of Guadalupe, the protestor-pilgrims, as I will refer to them throughout, virtually witnessed a second miracle, transforming Alma López's *Our Lady* into an irreverent apparition to which a multitude of believers and disbelievers flocked in witness.

The dictionary defines *apparition* as "1. Anything that appears unexpectedly or in an extraordinary way; esp., a strange figure appearing suddenly and thought to be a ghost. 2. The act of appearing or becoming visible." The second meaning presupposes that what has suddenly become visible used to be invisible or could not be seen. This quality of the unseen and the invisible suggests something else, that what has become visible was not really there in the first place but came into being at the moment it was "seen." To see, however, is not just to perceive something visually but also to understand, to learn, and to believe. To see an image of the Virgin Mary in the charred cornmeal of a tortilla or on the bark of a cottonwood is more than just to observe the form in an unusual location; it is also, and more significantly, to witness a miracle, something that not everyone can perceive or believe. Thus, miracles and apparitions are created by the eye/I of the believer.[5] The viewer's subjective beliefs inscribe the image with connotative meaning, be it sacred or sacrilegious.

While clamoring for the censorship of López's "sacrilegious" image from the *Cyber Arte* exhibition at MOIFA, the protestor-pilgrims— most of whom did not even witness *Our Lady* with their own eyes but were spurred by the technology of *chisme*/gossip—actually created an apparition, that is, they perceived something that was not visible. They did not see *Our Lady*, a photo-based digital collage giclée on canvas of a rose-clad woman named Raquel Salinas created by Alma López. They saw something that wasn't there. Some saw their mother. Some saw the

Virgin Mary or the image on Juan Diego's *tilma*/cloak. José Villegas, the first instigator of the protest, saw "the Devil" with "her bosoms sticking out," while Archbishop Michael Sheehan saw a "tart," a "call girl," and a "streetwalker." One outraged letter to the editor in the *Albuquerque Tribune* spells it out:

> Sacrilege consists in profaning persons, places, and things consecrated to God. No one of God's creatures is more totally consecrated to God than the most holy virgin mother of God, Mary Immaculate. Thus, to portray the mother of God in bikini attire is to desecrate her in a most outrageous and sacrilegious manner.[6]

In essence, this argument is based on the miraculous transubstantiation of Raquel Salinas into the Mother of God. And so, what started as a protest became a collective witnessing of a miraculous, albeit unholy, transformation that sparked a procession and then a pilgrimage of believers, skeptics, and holy inquisitors.

Another interesting transformation occurred at the level of the museum, which, in some of the protestor-pilgrims' eyes, had been turned into a "cyber-chapel," as it was called in some of the e-mails; a "New Age chapel"; a "parody of a chapel"; and, most intriguing of all, an "occult" or "Satanic chapel." In a hand-delivered memo to his "excellency," Archbishop Sheehan, Henry Casso entreated the archbishop to seek the return of all sacred art that was in the custody of the Museum of New Mexico. Casso's objection was that the museum desecrated sacred art, as could be seen, he argued, in the way that MOIFA had parodied the holy architecture of a chapel in the installation of the *Cyber Arte* exhibition. As he stated in his memo:

> Given the pervasive use of symbols that parody a Catholic Chapel it would be fair to say that the Museum has designed the Cyber Arte Exhibit as an Occult Chapel. The "chapel" consists of 13 pictures to the side in parody of the Stations of the Cross. Although there are 14 Stations of the Cross the number 13 is favored among occultists . . . There is a prie-dieu [a kneeler], and an altar. On the "altar" is a computer monitor. The computer monitor is situated on the "altar" in parody of the Tabernacle. Above the tabernacle on the wall is an image of a cross with a black snake wrapped around it. At one time during the exhibit there was a sign asking visitors to leave their "*Ofrendas.*" . . . We are very much aware of the pagan revival and

the animosity of the occult movements toward the Catholic Faith and the People of God. . . . Indeed the extensive use of parody raises suspicions of a Satanic Chapel.[7]

Casso's memo falls short of accusing the museum of staging Satanic Masses, but the implication is clear: if the installation itself is a Satanic space, then *Our Lady* must be the equivalent of its reigning anti-Christ, its Devil in a rose bikini, and viewers who support the work and the exhibit are probably devil worshippers themselves. What did that make the artists, I wonder? Particularly since their work summoned those demonic technologies that issued from the unholy computer/tabernacle in the occult virtual universe known as cyberspace. Indeed, part of the outcry was directed at the perceived threat of new-millennium technologies and irreverent art practices on the redemptive, protective, and revered image of their "Nuestra de Guadalupe," as she was called in José Villegas's first e-mail to the artist on March 19, 2001.

> Some people say it is alright to do your own onda [your own thing] in art expression, however, when you cross the sacred boundaries of our gente [*sic*] traditional values of over five hundred years, you cannot impose and/ or provoke thought on an issue that will inflame emotions against your own gente. Our Nuestra de Guadalupe does not belong to the new age interpretation of the millenum [*sic*] century and never will.[8]

If she does not belong to the New Age artist, if she has nothing to do with computer technology, how can we have Virgin of Guadalupe websites[9] through which we can send e-cards emblazoned with different images of La Virgen, and hear a virtual Mass from within the Basílica de Guadalupe in Mexico City? Are the video homages on YouTube any more or less "holy" than Alma López's *Our Lady*? Or was there something else about *Our Lady* that "inflamed the emotions" of the Catholic "gente" of New Mexico and spurred them to perform a particularly virulent brand of "disruptive religion"?[10]

Mis/Reading and Meta-Ideologizing the Sign

In "Whose Lady? Laying Claim to the Virgin Mary," freelance journalist Hollis Walker summarizes the controversy as an insider-outsider conflict that was also riddled with class and sexuality issues.

While on the surface the controversy was about a piece of art that offended the devout, it was more complex than that. Protesters repeatedly and consistently posited their argument as one of outsider/Anglo versus native/Hispano (though this argument ignored the fact that the exhibit's curator and all four exhibiting artists were Hispana). Another "underground" issue was López's sexuality. She is openly lesbian, and her Web site depicts imagery that is decidedly lesbian. Protest leaders used those images to incite opposition. The controversy also posed as class conflict, in which museum officials were elite, wealthy, and educated, while protesters were uneducated peasants.[11]

As Hollis Walker's title asks, whose lady is Our Lady? Does she belong to the offended community of protestor-pilgrims? Does she belong to the Catholic Church, which has used the image to disseminate a miraculous legend of conversion and colonialism for over four hundred years? Does she belong to the native people of Mexico and their descendants, for whom she represents the syncretized face of their Aztec creation goddess, Tonantzin? Does she belong to Alma López and any other Chicana/Mexicana/Latina artists who choose to represent her in ways that signify their own lives? Does she belong in a museum? Ultimately, these are semiotic questions of interpretation, of the perception, reception, and negotiation of meanings inherent in cultural signs. Even more, however, these are also questions about power.

For people of color, women, and other oppressed and marginalized groups, says Chela Sandoval in *Methodology of the Oppressed*, "the semiotic perception of signs in culture as structured meanings that carry power is a basic survival skill necessary to subordinated and oppressed citizenry."[12] We will see that it was Alma López's exploration of the way her own life fit into the structured meaning of the Virgin of Guadalupe that led her to "meta-ideologize"[13] the image and create a different sign with an altered meaning that most challenged the powers that claim ownership of the sign. Sandoval defines meta-ideologizing as "the operation of appropriating dominant ideological forms, and using them whole in order to transform them."[14] Although Alma López did not reproduce the exact image of the sign known as the Virgin of Guadalupe, she did appropriate key elements of the sign, such as the Virgin's brocade gown and the folds of her starry cloak in the background, the black crescent moon upon which the Virgin stands, the aura of rays around the Virgin's body, the cherubic angel at her feet, and, most importantly, the roses that are said to signify the miracle of her apparition.

"In Encoding/Decoding," Stuart Hall posits that there are "three hypothetical positions from which decodings of a [visual] discourse may be constructed,"[15] three sets of codes by which a cultural text is coded and in which it can be read, or received: the dominant, the negotiated, and the oppositional. We could say that, despite their ethos and pathos of opposition, José Villegas, Deacon Trujillo, Archbishop Sheehan, and their congregation of protestor-pilgrims were reading *Our Lady* within the dominant reference code of a patriarchal, misogynistic Catholicism that teaches not only that the Virgin of Guadalupe is the immaculately conceived "mother of God," but that, as a pure vessel of love, she is an abnegated, submissive, all-suffering, all-forgiving, asexual, maternal figure to which all "good girls" and "respectable women" should aspire and which men have the authority to control. In this reference code, a woman who stands ostensibly naked in front of a camera covered only in roses does not constitute a pure vessel. Nor does she suggest the archetypal Eve in the Garden of Eden before the fall, but rather, the fallen Eve, the shameful, sinful, disobedient Eve who listened to the serpent and partook of the secret knowledge that God the Father had forbade her to learn, and who tempted Adam to his own fall from grace. Thus, *Our Lady* is that same shameful, sinful, disobedient woman who leads men into temptation and who was reincarnated as Mary Magdalene and then as La Malinche.

The archbishop's objection to *Our Lady* was "not on the basis of morals," he said in a statement to the *Ottawa Citizen*.

> My objection is on the basis of the insult to the religious beliefs of a very large number of people that look at the Virgin Mary as being very holy. She is depicted in a floral bikini as if she were a tart.[16]

The idea that *Our Lady* is dressed in a "floral bikini" did not originate with the archbishop. Rather, as Hollis Walker points out, a March 17 article in the *Albuquerque Journal North* by staff writer Morgan Lee describes the artwork as "the Virgin of Guadalupe in a floral bikini."[17] This description sensationalized the image and "helped fuel Villegas' complaints into a firestorm; the image was thereafter referred to in media accounts as 'the bikini Virgin.'"[18] Never mind that the rose wreaths are neither "itsy-bitsy" or "teeny-weeny . . . or even a two-piece bathing suit," says Hollis Walker; it "may as well have been a G-string as far as some people were concerned."[19]

These sensationalized sentiments were echoed in some of the remarks left in MOIFA's comment books. Although there were more comments in support of *Our Lady* than in opposition to it, some viewers called the work "trash," "offensive," a "centerfold picture," "sacrilegious," and "blasphemy," and two offered to pray for the artist and the curator.

> I pray for the soul of Alma López, Dr. Wilson and Dr. Nunn, may the Lord have mercy on you! I can only hope the regents of this museum rightly take it down and *send it back to California* [emphasis added].

> You should not show Jesus' mother like that. Would you dipict [*sic*] your own mother in such a manor [*sic*]? It was very disrespectful. Mary was a virgin not a stripper!![20]

This, then, constitutes the dominant domain or reference code in which *Our Lady* was decoded and in which the protest took root and flourished, bringing hundreds of angry spectators to the door of the "master's house" to express their outrage at the museum's decision to display what they saw as an intentionally disrespectful rendering of "their" Virgin of Guadalupe by an outsider. For this contingency, Margaret Montoya explains, Guadalupe "is not anatomically correct; she has no breasts, no nipples, no pubic hair, no vagina, and no erogenous zones."[21] Still, the protestor-pilgrims saw all of that in *Our Lady*. Out of their subjective perception of what was not actually on the walls of the museum, the protestor-pilgrims were able to transmute an Absence (of faith) into a Presence (of body) while at the same time justifying the reactionary bludgeoning of an artist's constitutional right to represent the meaning of the Virgin of Guadalupe in her own life. In this bizarre turn of events, the act of censorship can be likened to a sacrifice, and indeed, Alma López was racked, pinioned, and crucified under the scrutiny of the archbishop.

The Mexican-born Sinaloense artist from the El Sereno barrio of northeast Los Angeles occupies the other end of the spectrum, the oppositional reference code, which "deconstructs and decontextualizes the dominant code and reinterprets the message through an alternative context."[22] For Alma López, that alternative context is the positionality of a Mexican immigrant, Chicana, lesbian, feminist, working-class artist who opposes all of the misogyny of the dominant code and instead sees the beauty of the female form, the nurturing breasts, the fearless stare, and the strength of women's collective survival in patriarchy. Says the artist in the statement she delivered at MOIFA on April 4, 2001, at the first meeting of the museum's Board of Regents, which was stormed by protestors:

> Even if I look really hard at my work and the works of many Chicana artists, I don't see what is so offensive. I see beautiful bodies that are gifts from our creator. I see nurturing breasts. I see the strong nurturing mothers of all of us. I am forced to wonder how men like Mr. Villegas and the Archbishop are looking at my work that they feel it is "blasphemy" and "the Devil." I wonder how they see bodies of women. I wonder why they think that our bodies are so ugly and perverted that they cannot be seen in an art piece in a museum? . . . [These men] self-righteously believe that they have the authority to dictate how a particular image should be interpreted. They believe they can tell me as well as other Chicanas how to think. I am a woman who has grown up with La Virgen. Who are these men to tell me what to think and how to relate to her? . . . This museum, like other museums, is a site of learning. Museums are not churches or sites of spiritual devotion . . . If my work is removed, that means that I have no right to express myself as an artist and a woman. It means there must be something wrong and sexually perverted with my female body. It means it's okay for men to look at our bodies as ugly. It means that as Chicanas we can only be sexualized or only be virgins. It means that only men can tell us how to look at the Virgen. It means that we cannot look upon the Virgen as an image of a strong woman like us.[23]

Well aware that *Our Lady* contested La Virgen's "structured meanings" of docility, modesty, and humility to signify the sacred feminine, and choosing to depict her instead as a strong, liberated, revolutionary image, which challenged the "power" of men to confer negative and abusive meanings on women's bodies, Alma López catalyzed and harnessed the oppositional consciousness of a social movement.

As MOIFA's comment book shows, month after month, from March to August 2001, visitors left messages applauding the museum's decision to show *Our Lady*, entreating people to "stop fearing art" and to "censor censorship," expressing dismay and surprise at the "ruckus" and the "fuss" being stirred up over this "beautiful," "respectful," and "innocuous" image, which none of them saw as dressed in a bikini.

Thank you for bringing this most creative & thought provoking show. If it hadn't been for the protest *against* art I might have missed this wonderful exhibit!!!

Local Catholics acting too much like Taliban!!! Miss Guadalupe is dressed with more modesty than young "ladies" in public places today.

As a devout Catholic & New Mexican, I believe we exhibit our faith individually. "Censorship in the name of God" is unacceptable.

Guadalupe is shown with love, with respect, with humor. "Thank God" the museum allows that vision to reach the good people of New Mexico. My tax money has been spent well, very well. Viva Guadalupe y Viva el Museum de International Folk Art.

I gave my rosary to the computer altar as a symbol of my appreciation for this great show. I believe that Alma López is expressing all her respect for women's bodies and the Lady of Guadalupe cult in her work. Congratulations to the museum for this instigative exhibition.

Blasphemy is in the eye of the beholder.

Me da berguenza [*sic*] pensar que todavía estamos en la epoca de la Inquisición![24]

In addition to these viewer comments, there were many positive reviews that appeared in the local New Mexican newspapers and national periodicals like the *New York Times*, the *Los Angeles Times*, *Ms.* magazine, *Art Papers*, and *Art in America*. At least two-thirds of the nine hundred e-mails[25] López received in support of her vision of Our Lady, which inspired her to create a website specifically devoted to the controversy, attest to the power of oppositional discourse. Other forms of what Chela Sandoval calls "the politics of the Other-in-opposition"[26] included the militant feminist artworks of *Las Malcriadas*, an exhibition that opened in Santa Fe in July 2001, organized by New Mexican artist Delilah Montoya in response to the threat of censorship experienced by Alma López.[27] In a speech to the American Women Artists organization, which was hosting its annual show in Santa Fe in June 2001, Judy Chicago, creator of the famous installation *The Dinner*

Party, called for solidarity with Alma López in the maelstrom of this male-led crusade against *Our Lady*, urging the women artists in the room to stage counterprotests to "support the right of women artists to create 'the art they want to make.'"[28] Taken together, all of these actions and the numerous other tactics and strategies of oppositional consciousness deployed by individuals and organizations like the American Civil Liberties Union and the National Coalition Against Censorship in support of Alma López and *Our Lady*, which have been discussed by other writers over the last several years since the controversy,[29] constitute the equivalent of a "differential social movement," which Sandoval defines as a "global decolonizing alliance of difference in its drive toward egalitarian social relations and economic well-being for all citizenry."[30]

What were the negotiated readings of this "miracle" that was created by the protest? The negotiated discourse is the tricky middle ground between the dominant and the oppositional registers of meaning. "A negotiated reading occurs when the viewer acknowledges and even, on an abstract level, adopts the message of the dominant code, but also contradicts that message by restricting or applying it to what Stuart Hall calls 'situational logic,'"[31] the logic of any given situation that has the power to invert or subvert the meaning of a cultural text. We can say that the Museum of New Mexico itself applied that negotiated reading when in response to the initial community outcry against *Our Lady*, and after meeting with city officials, community members, and representatives from the Catholic Church after the show's opening, the museum agreed to hold a community forum to allow both protestors and supporters to express their views about the piece. The gathering was originally scheduled to take place at the museum on April 4, at the meeting of the museum's Board of Regents, and it was at the press conference that followed the meeting that Alma López presented the statement quoted above. As shown in López's video that accompanies *Our Lady of Controversy*, hundreds of protestor-pilgrims showed up, too many to be safely contained within the museum without posing a fire hazard. The forum had to be postponed and rescheduled for a week later in the Sweeney Center in downtown Santa Fe, which could accommodate up to twelve hundred people. Sack lunches, bottled water, and even day care were provided for those in attendance, supporters and protestor-pilgrims alike. According to some reports, between six hundred and one thousand people attended this second attempt at democratizing the protest. If the old adage about putting your money where your mouth is tells us anything, the fact that the museum spent $12,000 on the forum and only $4,500 on the exhibition should indicate its sincerity in trying to assuage the inflamed emotions of the community.

Summoning the curative qualities of the traditional Virgin of Guadalupe and her compassionate interventionist skills, Museum of New Mexico director Thomas Wilson stated in a press release that the forum could have a "healing" effect for all of the stakeholders.

> We have an opportunity to be a national model of what can work when a community explores its differences from a standpoint of cooperation. The format we have proposed will allow all sides to hear and understand each other's points of view ... I also want to take this opportunity to apologize to anyone who has been hurt by the contemporary depiction of Our Lady of Guadalupe in the *Cyber Arte* exhibition. The museum meant no disrespect, and I regret any distress that this issue has caused . . . This forum can be just the first step toward healing in a way which leaves no one out.[32]

While acknowledging the religious concerns raised by the protestor-pilgrims, and even issuing an apology to the community for any pain that the exhibition may have caused inadvertently, Tom Wilson, along with MOIFA director Joyce Ice and Tey Marianna Nunn, the exhibition curator, applied the situational logic of the museum's "mission to present changing ideas and concepts, a mission shared with other museums accredited by the American Association of Museums and one that is central to the educational responsibility of museums in today's world."[33] Nevertheless, the museum made some compromises. It posted bilingual warning signs outside the exhibit stating, "Some objects in this exhibit may be disturbing to certain viewers." And instead of extending the run of the show by four months, museum officials decided to close the show on October 28, 2001, as had been originally scheduled.[34]

Why were Catholics so deeply disturbed by this image? "Perhaps, time and place play prominent roles in this controversy," said Alma López in her April 4, 2001, statement. "This is Lent, a time of devotion between Ash Wednesday and Easter. Santa Fe is a place with deep spiritual and traditional roots, and the Museum of International Folk Art is the place where many images of saints reside."[35] Lent in Santa Fe, a time of sacrifice and pilgrimage for the Catholic community, a time of *penitente* reenactment of the passion of Christ from flagellation to crucifixion, is the "situational logic" of the controversy. As one viewer comment expressed in defense of the protestors' call for the removal of *Our Lady*:

We are not censoring! We are protesting sacrilegious rendering in the land of the penitente, the matachine, and Chimayo.

Here are the three ruling planets that align over Northern New Mexico: the brotherhood, or *hermandad*, of Jesus of Nazareth emulators "credited with preserving the sacred traditions of New Mexico and southern Colorado as early as the eighteenth century . . . through acts of *caridad* (charity), *oración* (prayer), and *el buen ejemplo* (the good example),"[36] for whom the performance of corporeal penitence constitutes a form of sacrifice akin to Christ's; the northern Mexican and New Mexican native Matachine dancers who perform their most sacred dance reenacting the conquest of the Aztecs, complete with a Malinche figure, in December in honor of Our Lady of Guadalupe; and the Santuario de Chimayó, located 25 miles north of Santa Fe, considered the "the most important Catholic pilgrimage center in the United States." *Wikipedia* tells us that because of its "reputation as a healing site (believers claim that dirt from a back room of the church can heal physical and spiritual ills), it has become known as the 'Lourdes of America,' and attracts close to 300,000 visitors a year, including up to 30,000 during Holy Week (the week prior to Easter)."[37] It is in that logic of the Lenten season, in the convergence of the penitent, the conquered, and the miraculous, and the consequent drama of their interaction, that the inversion occurs, the chiastic transformation of a protest into a procession and a pilgrimage.

Protest as Performance Art

In *Symbol and Conquest: Public Ritual and Drama in Santa Fe*, Ronald Grimes explains the difference between processions and pilgrimages, two popular forms of public spectacle in Santa Fe. Although both forms are "ritualistic movement[s] through space,"[38] their difference is dictated by their purpose. Whereas "the typical activities involved in processions are walking, carrying, showing, viewing, praying, singing, and being seen"[39] through the city streets and, typically, through the center of the city as a way of reenacting the status quo, pilgrimages are more "goal-oriented" in that their ultimate purpose is to reach a particular site in which something miraculous or holy has been manifested. Processions are more spectator driven. Their objective is not to reach a particular location, but rather to display the journey itself as a ritual reinforcement of the community's beliefs and values. "One way to interpret a procession," writes Grimes, "is by selecting and reciting a story—a historical or myth-ical narrative."[40]

I attended the Virgin of Guadalupe procession held in East Los Angeles in 2009 and had the opportunity to take hundreds of pictures of La Virgen's devout followers on their mile-long journey down historic Cesar Chavez Avenue. Their destination was the football stadium at East Los Angeles College (ELAC) where a Mass would be offered by a number of priests and bishops, complete with smoking copal incense and communion wafers for the multitude. The theme of this year's procession was "No Tengas Miedo," or "Don't Be Afraid," taken from the myth narrative of the miraculous apparition of an indigenous Mother of God to the Aztec convert to Christianity Juan Diego. According to the myth, the Lady's apparition frightened Juan Diego, and the divine mother reassured him by saying "Don't be afraid, aren't I who am your mother here with you?" Several floats in the procession—dioramas and installations staged on the back of pickup trucks—echoed this theme, as did the clumps of women walking under a variety of standards of the Guadalupana and praying the rosary. They were followed by barefoot Matachine dancers with elaborate headdresses; women and girls enacting Native American dances and wearing face paint and pleated red skirts emblazoned with sequined Guadalupes; charros on horseback carrying huge Mexican flags adorned with Guadalupe images in the place of the Mexican eagle; masked figures that could have been *brujos*, or wise men, in baroque costumes and crowns; children in miniature Juan Diego *tilmas* with hand-drawn and hand-colored pictures of Guadalupe; people in wheelchairs and on crutches; high school students in matching blue Guadalupe T-shirts—all paying homage to their holy mother. Parishes across Los Angeles were represented, and the flags of all of the Americas flew in the wind. The ELAC stadium was almost full as the bilingual Mass was kicked off on the 30-yard line.

The historical or mythical narrative that the protestor-pilgrims in Santa Fe had selected for their community action was also the Virgin's apparition to Juan Diego, a "miracle" that catalyzed the conversion of nine million native people only ten years after the Spanish invasion and conquest of Mexico. It was this "miracle" that they felt was being defiled by *Our Lady* and this story that was on the lips and in the minds of the protestor-pilgrims who had come as if on procession to the center of Santa Fe. For, as Grimes notes, "processions inevitably pass through the central plaza of the city . . . Passing through this center usually symbolizes, and requires as a prerequisite, the sanction of civil authorities, many of whom actually participate in the processions."[41] Indeed, all but two of the New Mexico state legislators agreed with the protestor-pilgrims that *Our Lady* blasphemed the holy image and myth of the Virgin of Guadalupe.

On March 31, José Villegas organized a procession in the parking lot of the museum. In the video *Bikini Virgin on Trial* by Cynthia Buzzard—a compilation of video clippings about the controversy and footage of the protests—the protestor-pilgrims are seen arriving in cars and buses and starting to assemble for the procession. Although small in comparison to the mob that showed up on April 4 to manifest their anger at the museum and at the artist, the gathering has all the trappings of a procession, and indeed is called a procession by its organizer. Heading the procession is a shrine to the Virgin of Guadalupe carried on a small palanquin, followed by the faithful carrying placards demanding "Stop Blasphemy Now!" and "Honor Thy Mother!" The standards of other saints are also being carried, the most visible of which is a life-size image of the resurrected Christ in his flowing white robe. The Virgin shrine is placed on a table at the steps leading up to the museum, and an altar is quickly assembled. On the altar, the Virgin is flanked by an archangel and surrounded by votive candles and blue containers of generic salt. Perhaps the salt is intended to "protect" the Virgin from the "evil" the protestor-pilgrims perceive as emanating from the museum. Henry Casso, the author of the letter to Archbishop Sheehan about how the *Cyber Arte* show was installed like a satanic chapel, sits at the head of the Media Table next to the "real" Guadalupe. Musicians are playing guitars and tambourines, and people are praying the "Hail Mary." Speeches are given, petitions are signed, and off to the side, five women docents of the museum are gathered in a small counterprotest in support of the artist.

By April 4, the peaceful procession had given way to a more threatening presence of hundreds of protestor-pilgrims demanding to be let into the auditorium where the museum's Board of Regents had agreed to open its meeting to a civil debate that did not happen. The facilitator of the meeting called it a "dangerous situation," as more and more people jammed the museum grounds. "Alma López was taken away by security as soon as the meeting ended because museum officials feared for her safety," stated a reporter for Santa Fe's Channel 13 News.

When Frank Ortiz, the only museum board member who opposed *Our Lady*, announced that the meeting had been cancelled and would be rescheduled in a larger venue, a "small group of musicians started playing harmonicas, and prayers in Spanish along with clapping and cheers broke out among the crowd."[42] But there were more than prayers and *alabanzas* in praise of the Virgin Mary being uttered by the protestor-pilgrims. Soapbox speeches rang out from the microphone, and chants of "Crucify the artist!" were heard at both gatherings.[43] A writer for the *Santa Fe Trend* described the protest "event" at the Sweeney Center as a "mix between a crudely produced public access television talk show and a bad open-mike poetry reading . . . the participants . . . delivering common folk testimonials normally relegated to infomercials."[44]

Praying, singing, chanting, and testimonials bearing witness to the sacred healing and life-saving interventions of the Virgin of Guadalupe—was this activism or performance art? In "Staging Prisons: Performance, Activism, and Social Bodies," Peter Caster distinguishes between "activist performance" and "staged activism." Activist performance is theater that unambiguously defines itself as theater and "associates itself with a particular social project" and "makes its alliances explicit." Staged activism "employs theatrical strategies of representation," yet the event is considered "really real"—it is not performed by actors but by activists. Indeed, "one of the fundamental goals of staged activism is *telling the difference* between the two [experience and performance], as oppressed people describe their positions in their own words, communicating as fully as possible the circumstances and actualities of their oppression."[45]

I argue that the protestor-pilgrims engaged theatrical modes of representation both to communicate "the actualities of their oppression" by the Museum of New Mexico and Alma López's "irreverent apparition" and also, paradoxically, to enforce imperializing right-wing ideologies, or "structured meanings," about the Virgin of Guadalupe and the role of women in relation to both Church and state. Indeed, one journalist described the protestors as "elderly men . . . standing like St. Peter fending off evil-doers from the pearly gates" and demonstrating "the kind of fervor reserved for abortion clinics against this female artist's appalling depiction of 'their' Virgin Mary."[46]

This analogy reminds me of what Peggy Phelan has written in *Unmarked: The Politics of Performance* about the tactical uses of performance art in antiabortion demonstrations, whose purpose is "making a spectacle *for* the sake of publicity."[47] Staging rescues of fetuses that need to be saved from the maws of abortionists, male rescuers at a demonstration play the part of the unborn "baby" crawling around on all fours and "yell[ing] out in a strange falsetto, 'Mother, please don't murder me,'"[48] while a choir of women nearby chant and pray with their arms in the air. "The spatial separation between the men and the women rescuers mimics the situation often found in mainstream Western theatre: speaking men and observing women."[49]

This describes exactly the protest against *Our Lady*: men like Villegas, Trujillo, Casso, and the archbishop taking the microphone, and women observing their submissive role in patriarchy, doing the praying, the chanting, and the crying. Because the protest was ultimately about determining not just who owns the Virgin of Guadalupe, who has the power to dictate what the Mother of God looks like, but more importantly how faith will be exercised, and how women are supposed to behave within the faith, it was men who initiated the protest against *Our Lady* and took center stage in the spectacle. Like the "speaking fetuses" of Operation Rescue, the male defenders of the City of Faith wanted to manifest their predetermined right to control women's bodies, particularly the body of the woman they were all claiming as their mother. "In excessively marking the boundaries of the woman's *body*, precisely in order to make it thoroughly visible, patriarchal culture seeks to make *her* subject to legal, artistic, and psychic surveillance."[50]

By casting themselves in the role of the oppressed children of a maligned mother, the protestor-pilgrims performed the social discourse of a people clamoring for salvation and in need of deliverance from evil, which in turn created both a physical and a virtual community of offended Catholics and angry taxpayers demanding that their faith be respected. "Social protests that either deliberately or inadvertently draw on the conventions of theatre produce the unity through political investment that makes the audience a social body joined in affect,"[51] writes Peter Caster. In other words, in both staged activism and activist performance, a social body, a "we," is produced that recognizes its responsibility to act.

Although the original purpose of the protest was to express the Catholic community's indignation and offense over what they saw as a vilification of "their" sacred symbol, the protestor-pilgrims turned the "cyber chapel" of the exhibition into a pilgrimage site, as visitors flocked to the museum in droves in a crusade that continued for months. MOIFA records estimate that over 14,000 viewers came to see *Cyber Arte* and that attendance averaged 344 people per day after the March 17 article by Morgan Lee, which launched the Helen of New Mexico, or rather, the "bikini Virgin."[52] As Ronald Grimes reminds us, pilgrimages "are usually characterized by images rather than relics, and . . . [pilgrimage sites] are liminally located beyond the centers of cities and towns and beyond the centers of economic, political, and ecclesiastical power."[53] All of those visitors; the constant gathering of protestor-pilgrims outside the Museum of International Folk Art located miles away from the downtown plaza, in the periphery of the city off Old Santa Fe Trail and Camino Lejo; the pilgrimages taken by Catholics from outside of New Mexico, namely the America Needs Fatima group that came from Philadelphia (a group that stands for Tradition, Family, and Property)[54] to bring word of the "true" image of Mary; and all of the protestor-pilgrims who walked and drove and were bused in from towns outside Santa Fe—all contributed to transforming MOIFA and the *Cyber Arte* show into a pilgrimage site: "Pilgrimage sites are not necessarily established only through the official sanction of a church or a religious tradition. Rather, pilgrims may in fact 'create' a pilgrimage site simply by flocking in large numbers to a place believed to be imbued with the sacred."[55] In the case of the *Our Lady* controversy, however, the Museum of International Folk Art was believed to be imbued with the opposite, the antisacred. Ironically, the protest was inverted into its opposite, a pilgrimage, spurred by the social body's miraculous transformation of a photo-based digital collage into an irreverent apparition.

In a final performance of the controversy, six long months after the hullabaloo erupted, on October 28, 2001, the last day of the *Cyber Arte* show at MOIFA, Deacon Anthony Trujillo of the Guadalupe parish "staged a mock burial ceremony" of *Our Lady*.

> Trujillo instructed the 20 or so people who turned out to write down on pieces of paper whatever animosity [about the work or the exhibit] they wanted to bury, and place it in a hole he dug outside the church . . . Trujillo also participated in the burial, throwing into the mock grave court documents from his attempts to stop the exhibit . . . A mariachi band was joined by a church choir that sang before the ceremony began. After the burial, the paper-filled hole was covered with dirt.[56]

A photo accompanying the article shows a woman and a child casting their notes into the small hole, which has been dug beside a sign that reads "Our Lady of Guadalupe Parish." How nice of Trujillo to have "buried" *Our Lady* in hallowed ground.

What were the actual gains of these different manifestations of staged activism? For one critic of the protest (and there were many, as the articles, editorials, and letters to the editor collected in the *Cyber Arte* archives show), all the "idolaters" protesting *Our Lady* actually did was call attention to themselves, so that instead of letting the issue slip quietly into oblivion, the ruckus they made brought more and more people to see the show and lured the spotlight of sensationalism directly over Santa Fe—and perhaps they even broke a commandment or two.

> If the Catholics and other Christians protesting this piece of art were truly devout, they would understand that God made a complete ban of all art in the second commandment. They would not, therefore, have icons of any kind that depict angels, Christ, or the Madonna . . . I would even suggest that they are, by their protest, also breaking the third commandment against taking the Lord's name in vain; that is, they are using the Lord's name as a means to bring notoriety and/or power unto themselves.[57]

One more performative-protest event deserves some attention, as it shows the nationalistic rather than the religious side of the controversy. Pedro Romero Sedeño, a Santa Fe artist who left his own Chicano cultural nationalist comment in the museum's comment book early on, organized in June what he called a "performance art intervention" titled the "Santa Fe Ofrenda Project," which was to be staged every Sunday, beginning June 2, at MOIFA.[58] The purpose of the intervention was didactic as well as nationalistic. Said Sedeño: "We as human *ofrendas* enrobed with the Mexican flag, will offer the Museum of New Mexico, its docents and Alma López . . . education as to the profound cultural significance of, and devotion to, the traditional image of Our Lady of Guadalupe to the Mexican people, and its sovereign place as the banner for Mexican cultural identity."[59] Completely stripping his "human *ofrendas*" project of religious overtones, Sedeño's performance art of protest nonetheless had ideological dogma embedded in its intention. Rather than point fingers at how Alma López had desacralized the image of Our Lady of Guadalupe, Sedeño *assumed* that the artist (not to mention the museum staff) was ignorant of the "cultural significance" of the Virgin as a symbol for "Mexican cultural identity."

Sedeño was not the first or the only Chicano who fixed the Virgin of Guadalupe's meaning in the realm of Mexican history and Mexican national identity politics and claimed her as a sign of Chicano cultural nationalism. Chicano protest processions have been using the banner of La Virgen to champion their cause since the 1960s, and Mexicanos before them since Father Miguel Hidalgo rang the bell of Mexican independence in 1810 and pronounced "¡Viva México! ¡Viva la Virgen de Guadalupe! ¡Muerte a los Gachupines!"[60] The Guadalupe standard was one of four flags that were carried in the 250-mile farmworker march from the fields of Delano to the steps of the capitol in Sacramento in 1966, which was led by UFW leaders César Chávez and Dolores Huerta. Because it included not only farmworkers but also students, teachers, activists, artists, actors, politicians, and urban professionals from across the Southwest who sympathized with the farmworker "*causa*," the Delano march, under the banners of the U.S. flag, the Mexican flag, the UFW flag, and the standard of the Virgen de Guadalupe, is considered the beginning of the Chicano civil rights movement. Similar Guadalupe banners were carried by the millions of undocumented immigrants who marched on Los Angeles in 2006 in an attempt to bring national attention to their desire to remain in the United States, to have their lives legitimized through citizenship, and to be free to work for the American Dream. In 1993, the Virgin of Guadalupe was used as an emblem in the student-led protest at the University of California, Los Angeles, that led to a two-week hunger strike and demands for the institutionalization of a Chicano and Chicana Studies Department at UCLA.[61] Indeed, every May 1, International Workers' Day, the hundreds of workers and laborers who gather in downtown Los Angeles march in the Virgin's wake.

More than a symbol for Mexican cultural identity, La Virgen signified for Sedeño and other Chicano cultural nationalists[62] the mythological Aztlán, the original homeland of the Aztecs said to be located in the conquered Mexican North (now the American Southwest). To reconquer or reclaim Aztlán, in cultural if not territorial ways, was considered one of the goals of the Chicano movement, and the Virgin of Guadalupe, like the Mexican flag, was a signifier of that struggle. Indeed, by wrapping his human offerings in the Mexican flag—the term human offering itself is reminiscent of Aztec sacrifices—Sedeño's performance was alluding to the legendary Niños Héroes, or child heroes, of Mexico who, according to the myth, wrapped themselves in the Mexican flag and jumped from the ramparts of the castle at Chapultepec to protest the Anglo takeover of Mexico in 1848.

In Sedeño's worldview, Alma López was ignorant of that history and ignorant as well of the "true" significance of the Virgin of Guadalupe for Mexicans and Chicanos; therefore, she could be neither Mexican nor Chicana. Furthermore, as a feminist and a lesbian who dared to strip the traditional image of its vested purity and maternity, thereby robbing Chicanos of their cultural mother, she had betrayed her brothers in Aztlán and aligned herself with the Anglo conquerors who continued to colonize New Mexico.

The Embodied Aesthetics of Alma López

In "There's No Place Like Aztlán: Homeland Myths and Embodied Aesthetics" (Chapter 3 in this volume), I argue that the concept of Aztlán, with its twin tropes of loss and recuperation, functions as a place-based aesthetic in the work of Chicano and Chicana artists. Place-based aesthetics is the name I give to an artistic practice that expresses the artist's connection to place, and place is represented in the theme and content of the artwork not as landscape, but rather as homeland, culture, region, community, neighborhood, family, and even memory. Over and over in the course of the controversy, Alma López stated that as a Mexican-born Chicana who grew up with the Virgin of Guadalupe in her East Los Angeles home, the Virgin "belonged" to her as much as and even more so than to men like José Villegas and Archbishop Sheehan. "Catholic or not, Chicana/Latina/Hispana visual, literary or performance artists grew up with the image of the Virgen de Guadalupe, therefore entitling us to express our relationship to her in any way relevant to our own experiences."[63] Her connection to the Virgin is based on a notion of place that is more than a homeland or site of origin (Mexico), more than culture (Chicano), more than religion (Catholic), and more than class (community)—although all of them intersect in *Our Lady*. For Alma López, the place at which she connects most intimately with the Virgin of Guadalupe is her own sex, that is to say, her body.

> Rather than expressing their attachment to place as either dispossessed of or exiled from their native land, Chicana artists have a more intimate and embodied connection to place. . . . Chicanas are actively deconstructing and reconstructing . . . a politics of the body and of self-creation. . . . Transmuted into art, this politics of the body produces an *embodied aesthetic*, one that frees the Chicana artist from the shackles of a relational identity as some man's wife, mother, daughter, or mistress. Instead of dispossession, ownership, or reclamation of a place outside the self, embodied aesthetics uses the body as the signifier for place. As such, the body functions as site of origin, bridge between worlds, and locus of liberation.[64]

Our Lady disrupted the conservative Hispano community's expectations of a cultural icon; the Mother of God was not just humanized but depicted as a second-rate human, that is, as a woman, flaunting her sexuality rather than submitting to the biological imperative of her gender. Interestingly, depicting the Son of God as a baby boy suckling at his mother's exposed breast with his genitals exposed does not insult Catholics because the naked breast is performing its biological function and the holy being attached to his mother's lactating nipple has been incarnated in the male form, that is, he was made into first-class flesh, male flesh, a masculine and therefore universal subject. Nor does his nearly naked body on the cross offend anyone, as what we are taught to see in the image of the crucified Christ is not a sexual being, not a dead body with an erection under his loincloth, but a battered, tortured redeemer of our sins. Indeed, the suckling baby Jesus and the erect penis of Christ are semiotic signs of his humanity, of the "Word made flesh," as Tey Diana Rebolledo, paraphrasing Leo Steinberg's thesis in *The Sexuality of Christ in Renaissance Art and in Modern Oblivion*, points out. "This iconography is not meant to be salacious, but rather to reflect the fact that God has become a male human"[65] and has bodily needs like eating and ejaculating, like any other son of God.

In "Sons of La Malinche," Octavio Paz exemplifies what Chicana historian Emma Pérez calls "the colonial imaginary"—a way of imagining history that reifies the male colonizer—by describing the quintessential difference between two female icons of Mexicano and Chicano culture, both from the colonial period, and both of which serve the interests of patriarchy in the social construction of the feminine gender: the Virgin of Guadalupe and La Malinche, the interpreter and slave of Hernán Cortés who, it is rumored, willingly offered herself to her conquerors and for that is eternally blamed for the downfall of the Aztec Empire. In short, the Virgin represents the good mother, the obedient daughter, the passive wife—all of the qualities that Mexican and Chicana girls are taught to desire and become. La Malinche, or "la Chingada," as Paz calls her, on the other hand, is the bad mother, the violated whore, the betrayer of her culture—the bearer of the most negative qualities of womanhood that have the power to destroy not only the family, but the community as well.

> The Virgin is the consolation of the poor, the shield of the weak, the help of the oppressed . . . The Virgin is pure passivity . . . she consoles, quiets, dries tears, calms passions . . . [La Chingada] is even more abject . . . she does not resist violence, but is an inert heap of bones, blood, and dust. Her taint is constitutional and it resides . . . in her sex . . . She loses her name; she is no one; she disappears into nothingness; she *is* Nothingness. And yet she is the cruel incarnation of the feminine condition."[66]

When the protestor-pilgrims performed their "staged activism" against Alma López's *Our Lady*, they were protesting what they saw as La Chingada in the halo of La Virgen de Guadalupe. Who can respect, much less worship, a nameless, violated "Nothingness," who wears nothing but a bikini of roses and is held aloft by a naked-breasted butterfly angel rather than a cherub with a dangling participle between his wings? Even worse, the woman in the image is anything but an "inert heap of bones, blood, and dust." She is not immobilized by her long embroidered tunic or weighed down by the Coyolxauhqui stone that she wears tossed over her bare shoulders like the lightest of capes. Her defiant gaze, her confrontational stance, her bare feet and legs practically walk off the canvas. We can almost see her kicking her head back to challenge the viewer. "I am woman, hear me roar," said singer Helen Reddy. "Ain't I a woman, too?" asked Sojourner Truth. "*Soy mujer, y ¿qué?*" says *Our Lady*. Who can feel consoled and nurtured by this rebellious woman, this shameless woman whose unabashed exposure of her female flesh invites one and all to partake of it?

One of the religious activists in the *Bikini Virgin on Trial* video speaks to this issue clearly. Holding up an image of the traditional Guadalupe, the man says, "We want to keep her dressed . . . Why does she need to be undressed? . . . Would you call it good judgment if two people undressed right here in front of us and started copulating each other?"[67] To this viewer, *Our Lady* represented an unspoken desire; the female body signified for him the sexual act of copulation, something that should never be ascribed to the Virgin of Guadalupe, for she is beyond sex, beyond desire, and certainly beyond pleasure. The only sexual act the body of the Virgin is allowed to perform, or, rather, the only act she is allowed to perform with her sexual organs, is giving birth to her half-human, half-divine hybrid son. Pregnancy as a result of copulation is not the issue, although the fact that Raquel Salinas is not portrayed as a pregnant Madonna is problematic for these male defenders of the faith. It is the all-too-real digital photo collage of Raquel Salinas and her muscular abs and thighs posing as La Virgen that animates *Our Lady* and makes the image both so threatening and so desirable. This is no miraculous imprint of a meek brown pregnant woman on a *tilma*.

The protestor-pilgrims were selective, however. They did not object to any and all artistic renderings of the Virgin of Guadalupe, nor, apparently, to the myriad applications of their sacred symbol on consumer products from mousepads and light-switch covers to beach towels and tattoos. Indeed, even Archbishop Sheehan was selective about what he considered a promiscuous image. Three years earlier, the cover of the Winter 1998 issue of *La Herencia del Norte* (a newsletter from Northern New Mexico) featured a photograph by Miguel Gandert of a Guadalupe tattoo on a young woman's bare back. The photo accompanied a story inside called "The Lady Has Many Faces," by Jacqueline Orsini, author of *Viva Guadalupe!* In the article, Orsini explains that

> Nuestra Señora de Guadalupe is a lady with many faces, and each one finds favor with followers according to their personal needs. Guadalupe reaches out to friars, pilgrims, artists, lowriders, scholars, housewives, prisoners and *street women* [emphasis added]. Guadalupe is especially sought by those who fall short of ideal Christian conduct, for she does not condemn sinners; she offers compassion, pardon, understanding. Nuestra Señora de Guadalupe's first words at Tepeyác were an offer of care for all folk of every kind without reserve, without retribution.[68]

The model in the photo looks like either a Mexican American or a Native American young woman in baggy jeans who has removed her shirt to show off the tattoo. In fact, she is identified in the title of the photograph: *Teresa Gutiérrez of Juárez, Mexico*. Neither Chicana nor indigenous to New Mexico, she is a Mexican from the border. Also pictured in the frame is a pair of men's hands that seem to be pulling down the young woman's halter-top to show the Virgin tattoo more clearly. The man's hands on the girl's waist suggest a familiarity with the girl's body, a nuanced sense of ownership or entitlement that communicates that he has the right to pull down her shirt and, possibly, her pants as well. Also, there's a friendly coquettishness about the girl's smile and sexy sidelong gaze that suggests a heterosexual relationship between her and the man (not to mention the male viewer), who are represented synecdochically by the hands.

The following year, in the Spring 1999 issue of the same newsletter, Archbishop Sheehan wrote the following short letter to the editor:

> I was intrigued by the picture of the young girl on the cover of the Winter 1998 issue with the Guadalupe tattoo on her back. It seems like Our Lady of Guadalupe is a very friendly and understanding spiritual image that many people can relate to, even those who have terrible problems.[69]

What does the young woman in Miguel Gandert's photo represent that the archbishop seems to be able to relate to? Perhaps, as Orsini

Figure 6.3. Miguel Gandert, *Teresa Gutiérrez of Juárez, Mexico*,
© 1992. Black-and-white photograph. Used by permission of the
artist.

alludes to in her article, she is one of those "who fall short of ideal Christian
conduct," not a pilgrim or a housewife but a "street woman," openly
offering herself to men and their cameras. Or perhaps she is someone
with "terrible problems," as the archbishop's letter euphemistically states,
who has found spiritual friendship with or forgiveness from Guadalupe.

If, as Orsini claims, the Virgin of Guadalupe "find[s] favor with
her followers according to their personal needs" and also "offers
compassion, pardon, understanding" to "all folk of every kind without
reserve, without retribution," then why is it that the archbishop could not
seem to follow in the Virgin's footsteps when it came to the incorrigible
Alma López? If he can absolve pedophile priests;[70] if he could bring

his archdiocese to the brink of bankruptcy as he did in 1993 to pay the $50 million settlement that would help in some measure to atone for the rape, sodomy, and illicit sexual relationships that New Mexican priests were perpetrating on girls and boys in their congregations, beginning with the former archbishop, Robert Sánchez;[71] if he could find visual gratification in the image of a Guadalupe tattoo on a young Mexican woman's naked back—why did the archbishop react so violently to *Our Lady*? What changed for Archbishop Sheehan between 1999— when he was so "intrigued" by Miguel Gandert's photograph that he felt compelled to send a letter of praise to the editor of *La Herencia del Norte*—and 2001, when he summarily condemned Alma López for turning Our Lady into a "tart and a street walker"? What difference did the archbishop perceive between Teresa Gutiérrez in Gandert's photo and Raquel Salinas in *Our Lady*?

The answer, I think, is obvious. *Our Lady* is not flirting with anyone. The hands on her waist are her own, not some anonymous male hands about to pull down her floral garment. Nor is she winking in coquettish response to the male gaze. And despite her naked breasts, the butterfly angel that sustains *Our Lady* offers no lactating solace to believers. The two Raquels of *Our Lady* form an interpretation of the Virgin of Guadalupe that refuses to be objectified or appropriated. By calling her a "tart" and a "street walker," Archbishop Sheehan not only gave permission to male viewers to bring their own illicit desire for the not-so-naked Virgin to the surface, but he also gave her an identity that the men could control. Just as the protestor-pilgrims created an irreverent apparition, the archbishop created an inversion of the woman with "terrible problems" who "intrigued" him in 1999. He simultaneously sexualized *Our Lady* and punished her for not being [hetero]sexual enough.

Not only did López's digital depiction of *Our Lady* as a real live Everywoman "cheapen" the Virgin of Guadalupe in the eyes of López's detractors, that is, reduce the Virgin's value in the pantheon of sacred Catholic icons, but worse (and here is the key to the vituperative community response that was instigated by men), she was the tempting Devil in the rose bikini, the evil twin of the Lady of the Apocalypse. The bare belly, the bare legs and feet, the hidden cleavage vividly present in their absence—all aroused the unspoken heterosexual desire of her penitent male progeny. But it was the unseen parts, *Our Lady*'s breasts and vulva covered demurely with roses, coupled with that defiant stance and the butterfly angel's pierced nipple that terrified and yet gave rise to other perversely pleasurable Catholic sentiments such as guilt and shame. As Luz Calvo tells us in "Art Comes for the Archbishop," Alma López's "images seduce the spectator into new desiring positions by exposing Chicano/a libidinal investments—conscious and unconscious—in the Virgin of Guadalupe. Her images mobilize and disturb these investments, channeling Chicano/a desire in queer directions."[72] It is this seductive quality that is at the heart of López's "embodied aesthetic," or rather, her use of the place-based Aztlán aesthetic to deconstruct and transform longings for an imaginary conquered homeland, which La Virgen de Guadalupe represents, into a reclamation and celebration of a brown female body that will not submit to any conqueror, which is *Our Lady*.

In trying to understand how the cultural icon of the Virgin of Guadalupe could signify her own life, Alma López sought the help of two of her friends, performance artist Raquel Salinas and writer-performer Raquel Gutiérrez. Together, they fleshed out Alma's vision of an embodied Virgin, not encumbered by the heavy robes that hide her limbs and keep her tethered to a one-dimensional existence. *Our Lady* showed a powerful, actual woman liberated from the yoke of a relational identity. Neither the "Mother of God" nor the "deliverer of the faithful," the Virgin in this artwork literally stands on her own two feet, which are rooted as much to the land (the earth, the continent, and the nation from which she sprang) as to the mysteries signified by the dark moon. *Our Lady* is anchored in the history of her Aztec past, which is encoded into her racial memory, just as the Viceroy butterfly's migrant journey between Mexico and the United States is encoded into its genetic DNA.

By engaging in semiotics, deconstruction, and meta-ideologizing—the first three technologies in Chela Sandoval's "methodology of the oppressed"[73]—Alma López transformed the meaning of the Virgin of Guadalupe to more accurately signify her own experience as a sexed, gendered, raced, and classed body in patriarchy. Hers is what Margaret Montoya calls "a spirituality animated by transgression [that] makes us come to terms with different forms of repression."[74] Her unshakable faith in the dignity of her creation, and her abiding love and respect for the revolutionary image that the Virgin of Guadalupe represents, gave Alma López the spiritual and political wherewithal to refuse to apologize, refuse to be stigmatized, and refuse to do penance. "When I see *Our Lady* as well as the works portraying the Virgen by many Chicana artists, I see an alternative voice expressing the multiplicities of our lived realities. I see myself living a tradition of Chicanas who, because of cultural and gender oppression, have asserted our voice. I see Chicanas creating a deep and meaningful connection to this revolutionary cultural female image. I see Chicanas who understand faith."[75]

The Shadow of *Our Lady* in the City of Faith

So large was the shadow cast by Alma López's one-and-a-half-foot *Our Lady* that it could only be eclipsed seven years later by a 12-foot, 4,000-pound bronze statue of the Virgin of Guadalupe. Standing at the corner of Guadalupe and De Vargas Streets (an appropriate crossroads, indeed), perhaps over the very spot on which *Our Lady* received her mock burial in the ancient Catholic tradition of building Christian temples over pagan ruins, the statue is surrounded by offerings of roses on a platform of memorial bricks stenciled with the names of the parishioners who donated to her shrine and who now compose the Guadalupe Family.[76]

> She came to Santa Fe covered with bubble wrap and a blue tarp, lying on a flatbed trailer pulled by a red Dodge Ram truck. The sirens signaled her arrival at the Cathedral Basilica of St. Francis of Assisi . . . When the procession came to a stop, Deacon Anthony Trujillo of Our Lady of Guadalupe Church and José Villegas, the police chaplain, began unwrapping the 12-foot, 4,000-pound bronze statue of Our Lady of Guadalupe. The parish, which is the oldest Marian shrine in the United States, raised the money and commissioned the work from a Mexican artist.[77]

It is no surprise that two of the most vocal protestor-pilgrims, indeed the instigators of the protest—José Villegas and Deacon Trujillo—were involved in welcoming the statue to Santa Fe, undressing her, as it were, from her bubble-wrap veil and raising her from her flatbed repose to her place of honor in front of the Guadalupe Santuario, as the church is called. As a consequence of the *Our Lady* debacle, no doubt, the parish's nonprofit Guadalupe Historic Foundation launched a campaign to build a permanent shrine to the "true" Virgin of Guadalupe in Santa Fe. Although the Santuario is considered the oldest church dedicated to Our Lady of Guadalupe in the United States,[78] and is itself a historic landmark as well as a shrine, parishioners felt it necessary to reassert the power of the traditional Guadalupe image in a sizable and public way. Fund-raising for the shrine project began in 2001, the same year as the *Our Lady* controversy, and Deacon Trujillo was on the board of advisors for the nonprofit.[79] Anne Constable, a journalist for the *Santa Fe New Mexican*, tracked the July 2008 twelve-day pilgrimage of the statue and its *peregrino*/pilgrim escorts from Mexico City to Santa Fe, where the statue was greeted with all the fanfare of a triumphal entrance reminiscent of another New Mexico Virgin, La Conquistadora, who was carried into New Mexico by the armored conquistador Diego de Vargas in 1692 when he reconquered New Mexico in the name of the Spanish Crown and the Catholic faith.[80]

There is a reason that the protests against *Our Lady* took place in New Mexico, and not, say, Mexico or Texas or California, where *Our Lady* has also been shown. Of all of the states of the Southwest, New Mexico is probably the most tricultural or mestizo—blending Spanish, Anglo-American, and Native American cultures—and yet, also, the most attached to its Spanish ancestry and the most celebratory of its Catholic colonization. Every year just after Labor Day, for example, Santa Fe observes its annual Fiestas de Santa Fe. Instituted in 1712, this popular celebration and tourist attraction second only to Spanish Market and Indian Market offers a reenactment of the Catholic colonial takeover of New Mexico from its indigenous inhabitants, who in the Pueblo Revolt of 1680 had burned down the Catholic mission and driven out the Spaniards and their Conquest Virgin. In 1692, Diego de Vargas and his army of conquistadores reentered Santa Fe carrying the Virgin of the Conquest and effected a peaceful and bloodless "reconquest" of New Mexico. Since 1712, New Mexicans have been commemorating the Spanish subjugation of the Indians and occupation of their homeland in an annual festival, complete with royal processions of La Conquistadora through the downtown streets followed by a Conquistador King, a Virgin Queen,[81] a noble court of ladies and gentlemen, special Masses in the Cathedral Basilica, native dances, an effigy burning, and a "historical/hysterical" parade, in which the floats fall into the category of history or humor.[82]

A city that commemorates its history of conquest; a landscape of faith-healing earth, ancient adobe churches and brotherhood *moradas*, a miraculous staircase,[83] a medieval cathedral elevated to basilica status by a pope, saint-carving *curanderos*, Easter pilgrimages and *penitente* re-creations of the Via Crucis and the Passion of Christ in the isolated communities of the Sangre de Cristo Mountains; an archbishop, a deacon, and a chaplain who rouse the Catholic community into a punishing rabble over an irreverent apparition of their own making; and a 12-foot Virgin of Guadalupe city mascot—need we wonder at the City of Faith's historical/hysterical response to *Our Lady*?

As fate would have it, what the protestor-pilgrims most wanted to remove from the walls of the Museum of International Folk Art has now etched itself permanently into the cultural memory of the Land of Enchantment. Because of the protest's processions and pilgrimages, because of the media blitz, because of the way the controversy drew communities together in defense of their faith or in support of an artist's constitutional right to make personally relevant art, Alma López is now a household name in New Mexico. Her fame to some may be along the lines of the atom bomb or the UFO,[84] but to others she is "da bomb," that is, the example of an artist living true to her faith in the transformational power of her work. Along with La Conquistadora and the Virgin of Guadalupe, *Our Lady* forms a trinity of Virgins that preside over Santa Fe. Everyone finds solace now: the penitent, the conquered, and the queer.

"It's Blaaaasphemy!": The Inquisition Continues from Oakland to Ireland[85]

The publication or utterance of blasphemous, seditious or indecent matter is an offence which shall be punishable in accordance with law.

—*Irish Constitution, Article 40.6.1.i, Defamation Act, 1961*

A decade after the Santa Fe debacle, the witch hunt against Alma López resumed, and the America Needs Fatima (ANF) clan started stalking her again and harassing her with hate mail. For ten years, *Our Lady* had been reposing quietly in López's studio, until February 2011 when she appeared again in a small exhibition called *Contemporary Coda* at the Oakland Museum of California (OMCA). The preceding fall, López had received an invitation from Drew Johnson, curator of photography at the OMCA, to exhibit *Our Lady* in *Contemporary Coda*, which the museum had organized as a companion installation to *Splendors of Faith/Scars of Conquest: The Arts of the Missions of Northern New Spain, 1600–1821*. A large international exhibition on the arts of the Franciscan and Jesuit missions of the colonial period in what used to be "*el norte*" of New Spain, *Splendors of Faith* originated at the Antiguo Colegio de San Ildefonso in Mexico City and would be traveling to two museums in Mexico and two in the United States.[86] The original purpose of the mission artwork displayed in the *Splendors of Faith* show was to convert the indigenous people of the northern provinces (which included the areas we now know as California, New Mexico, Arizona, Sonora, Sinaloa, Chihuahua, and Zacatecas) to Catholicism, and much of the work consisted of two-dimensional paintings and *retablos* of saints and representations of Virgins and Madonnas. Other pieces were three-dimensional sculptures and objects used in liturgical rituals as well as the finely embroidered vestments used by the missionary priests. According to Johnson, the OMCA had conceptualized of *Contemporary Coda* as "a counterpoint in the form of contemporary works which share or comment upon some of the historical and religious themes of the [colonial] pieces."[87] Aware of the controversy that *Our Lady* had sparked in New Mexico, the OMCA specifically invited López to display the piece in *Contemporary Coda*. The OMCA "considered it vital to include voices other than those represented by the mission artwork alone. It became apparent that contemporary artists had much to say about the colonial and Catholic experience in North America," and the museum hoped the contemporary work by mostly Chicana/o artists, commenting on issues such as faith, immigration, and identity, would help "stimulate dialogue among visitors and . . . encourage the community to weigh in"[88] on the discussions.

Somehow, the ANF watchdogs were alerted about this new appearance of *Our Lady* on the secular horizon. Armed this time with social media and Internet technology, they cranked up their zealot base again, and sent thousands of e-mails to the Oakland Museum (all blasted from the same website and saying exactly the same thing) to protest the hanging of this "blasphemous" image in the museum, calling the piece "pornography of the highest order," and staging a prayer protest outside the museum, which they scheduled on May 29, the same day that had been prognosticated by some self-ordained prophet and announced on billboards as the Day of Rapture.

Although bothered by the inconvenience of the e-mail barrage, the OMCA staff was not surprised by the response; I contend, actually, that they wanted to summon the specter of the controversy, both to draw a larger audience and media attention to the two shows and to stir up the community and get them to think about precisely those issues of conquest and conversion that lay at the heart of the *Splendors of Faith* show.

As it turned out, *Our Lady of Controversy: Alma López's "Irreverent Apparition,"* the volume that López and I put together about the Santa Fe controversy, was slated for release on April 1, 2011,[89] while *Our Lady* was on display in *Contemporary Coda*. A few protestors had already posted negative reviews of the book to the website for Powell's Books in

Figure 6.4. Howard Thornton, *ANF Protest at Oakland Museum of California #2*, © 2011. Color photograph. Used by permission of the Oakland Museum of California.

San Francisco. On the same day, ANF cronies posted forty-six negative reviews of the book on Amazon.com, driving the ratings of the book to below one star. Clearly, none of the so-called reviews were about the book, as none of the "reviewers" had actually bought it or read it. But all of them condemned López, *Our Lady*, and the book to the eternal fires of damnation. When I wrote to Amazon to complain about this heckling posing as reviews, and posted a counterpoint to their attacks, Amazon simply removed all (including mine) but the few comments that stayed focused on the content of the book.

Part of the programming for the *Contemporary Coda* show was a panel titled "Art, Religion and Censorship in Museums," to which López was an invited speaker, along with UCLA art historian and colonial Mexican art specialist Charlene Villaseñor Black, whose talk I discuss in more detail below. The panel was scheduled for the end of April, two months after the opening, followed by a book signing of *Our Lady of Controversy* at the museum bookstore (for which the bookstore had ordered extra boxes of books). Although the museum anticipated a large crowd because of the ANF e-mail blasts and the media attention on *Our*

Lady, museum staff spoke to the Museum of International Folk Art in Santa Fe to get their advice on how to handle conflict and violence in the crowd, should such develop in Oakland. They even hired a bodyguard for López's protection during her day at the museum.

Nothing happened, however. No pilgrimage of outraged Catholics or rabid protest outside the doors of the museum occurred on the day of the panel. No outbursts from the audience during López's presentation. López sold two *Our Lady* giclées that day, and we signed and sold a fair number of books but not as many as the museum had ordered. May 29, the Day of Rapture, came and went, but the world did not end. A small group of praying protestors stood outside the OMCA with their banners and posters decrying the "blasphemous and impure depiction of 'Our Lady' in the museum." But it was a tame spectacle in comparison to Santa Fe.

Needless to say, *Our Lady* was not censored from the exhibit, even though the bishop of San Francisco did drive across the Oakland Bridge to see *Our Lady* in person and took umbrage not only with López's piece but also with the other work displayed in the *Contemporary Coda* exhibition (perhaps Ester Hernández's piece, installed next to *Our Lady*, depicting the Virgin of Guadalupe as an "illegal" on an ICE [U.S. Immigration and Customs Enforcement] poster). The irate bishop demanded an apology from the museum director, Lori Fogarty, who responded that she and the museum had nothing to apologize for because the work fell within the museum's parameters for exhibition and education.

In June 2011, the ANF fund-raising protest machine hit Ireland. Alma López and I had been invited, along with Cherríe Moraga and Celia Herrera Rodríguez, to give keynote presentations on our work at the "Transitions and Continuities in Contemporary Chicano/a Culture" conference, organized by the Hispanic Studies Department's Centre for Mexican Studies at University College Cork, where López was also going to exhibit *Our Lady* and four of her *Queer Santas* banner paintings. Ten days before we even arrived on the Emerald Isle, the ANF blog posted this: "Here in America, we pray that Catholics in Ireland will rise up in a massive and immediate spiritual and peaceful protest and petition the University College Cork to CANCEL this blasphemy now!"[90] Five days later, the message got a little stronger:

> In our globalized world, blasphemy can cross the oceans and airwaves with more ease than in previous ages. And that is now the case with the blasphe- mous art exhibit "Our Lady and Other Queer Santas," by the self-avowed

lesbian Alma López, which will be on display at the University College Cork and is open to the general public—America Needs Fatima opposes blasphemous 'Our Lady' exhibit in Ireland. Twitter this! Blog this! Share to Facebook! Share to Google Buzz![91]

In their frenzy to bring down this "bad girl," the ANF's rumor-mongering cyber tsunami slammed University College Cork with thousands of e-mails to the university's head of events, Chloe Kerins, whose contact information was posted prominently in the ANF blogsite. A few days before we boarded our flight to Ireland, in a surreal quantum physics, López and I sat in our studio in Los Angeles and listened to a live stream of Joe Duffy's "Liveline" show on Radio RTE 1 in Ireland, and the complaints of one holier-than-thou native son named Dennis, who was enjoining listeners to protest a blasphemous "painting" that was going to be exhibited later that week at University College Cork. Although he admitted to not knowing the full story behind the Virgin of Guadalupe's apparition, Dennis pontificated that he knew very well Our Lady's sacred image was being disrespected and desecrated by a self-avowed Mexican lesbian. Thus, Dennis was asking listeners to protest the showing of *Our Lady* and the discussion of our sacrilegious book as well—all of which would be taking place at a state-funded university. According to the Network for Church Monitoring Blog, other callers to the Joe Duffy show

> told how "Microsoft and NASA" had recently used a special microscope which had proved the miraculous nature of the image of Mary that had appeared on the poncho of Juan Diego. Their calls for bans and protests were countered by Michael Nugent of *Atheist Ireland*, who later commented: "It was like discussing the rules of quidditch with people who believe Harry Potter was a documentary."[92]

In yet another radio interview, the morning of our departure, López was asked to respond to the rumor that she was a "self-avowed lesbian," to which she responded, "You say that like it's a bad thing. Yes I am, and I'm very proud of it. In fact, Alicia and I are legally married in California." A self-named atheist on the radio program called the protestors irrational and sycophantic (thank you). The one woman who called in toward the end of the show stated that only people who were insecure in their beliefs would be alarmed by López's representation (thank you). The only caller who had obviously taken the time to log on to López's website to see the image for himself described the piece to the listening audience and opined that López was probably breaking the blasphemy laws of the country.

Really? Blasphemy laws?

I used the few hours left before we had to be at the airport to research the Irish blasphemy laws, as I could just imagine the two of us being arrested upon alighting from the plane. I discovered that an old Defamation Act of 1961 was, indeed, still in the Irish Constitution, which had been modified in 2006, and again in 2009. For my reading pleasure en route to Ireland, I downloaded the thirty-four-page 2006 Defamation Bill that I found on the Internet. In his address to the Committee on Justice, Equality Defence and Women's Rights on Wednesday, May 20, 2009, Dermot Ahern, the Irish Minister for Justice, Equality, and Law Reform, proposed a new amendment to the law on Libel Speech:

> As regards the offence of blasphemous libel, I think we would all agree that the optimal approach, and certainly the one that I find most preferable, would be to abolish it. As a Republican, my personal position is that Church and State should be separate. But I do not have the luxury of ignoring our Constitution. . . . Until the Constitution is amended, it is necessary that blasphemy remain a crime and that the relevant legislation must make provision for punishment of this crime. There is no alternative to this position. . . . My revised proposal now includes a defence for proceedings for an offence under this section for the defendant to prove that a reasonable person would find genuine literary, artistic, political, scientific, or academic value in the matter to which the offence relates.[93]

We got busy asking friends, colleagues, and allies to write letters of support to the UCC to vouch for the artistic and academic merit of López's work so that, just in case an arrest was threatened, we would have written evidence that would uphold this proviso to the Irish Constitution. No matter what the Irish protestors' religious beliefs dictated, the image was protected as a work of art, which had not been intended to cause outrage to any religion; thus, *Our Lady* was not breaking the blasphemy laws of Ireland.

But the ANF was just getting started. They sent such an onslaught of complaints and protest e-mails to the president and the head of events at the UCC that they ended up crashing the university's server and seriously undermining the online registration process of the conference. University officials were surprised, to say the least, especially when members of the Garda, or National Guard, came on campus to look at a copy of

Our Lady for themselves and determine whether or not the piece was breaking Ireland's blasphemy laws. Rumor had it that a Senior Garda had reported that a file (maybe an X-File?) about *Our Lady* was being sent to the Director of Public Prosecutions.

A small group of protestors formed outside the university gates on the day the conference and the exhibit opened to the public. Holding their placards, rosaries, and umbrellas, and led by a young priest in his old-school cassock, the protestors demanded that the university censor the piece from the show on the grounds that it was an offensive depiction of the Virgin Mary. One protestor even suggested to the president of the university that he should resign for allowing *Our Lady* to be exhibited on university grounds and that the university should be investigated by the Garda for contravening the blasphemy laws. In a usually quiet town, spectators driving by the university yelled out support or scorn for the protestors.

An online university poll showed that the vast majority of students at UCC supported López's right to exhibit *Our Lady*. The university's student Atheist Society formed a counterprotest with makeshift signs declaring, "My free speech is not negotiable" and had their photo taken with the artist in front of *Our Lady*, which later appeared on Facebook. López and I were very clear with the conference organizers and said that if the university caved in to the protestors' demands and censored the piece, we would withdraw our participation from the conference. After an entire day of no response from the UCC president's office, during which time Professor Nuala Finnegan, chair of the Centre for Mexican Studies,[94] was bombarded with phone calls and e-mails and requests for media interviews, campus administrators finally issued their statement to the press:

> Having given due consideration to all viewpoints, UCC has confirmed the conference will go ahead as planned and the image will be exhibited in a position where only those who personally choose to view it may do so . . . It is understood that notices will be placed on the doors of the room where it will be displayed, warning people that the exhibition features images that may provoke or offend.

In Figure 6.5, taken by one of the local papers, the *Evening Echo*, we can see that *Our Lady* is not in fact sequestered off in a private room but hanging front and center in López's exhibition space in the O'Rahilly Building. Warning signs saying "Some of this art may be offensive to

Figure 6.5. Sample coverage of the *Our Lady* controversy at University College Cork in Irish newspaper *Evening Echo*, June 29, 2011, Life, 23.

some people" were posted in the elevators and close to the doors. The few locals who did wander in to see the "naked Virgin Mary," as *Our Lady* was being billed by the media, came away feeling defrauded. "That's it?" they asked. Yes, indeed, that was it. As had happened in Santa Fe with the other three artists who were in the *Cyber Arte* exhibit along with López, the manic spotlight on *Our Lady* ended up eclipsing the work of Celia Herrera Rodríguez, whose art was on display just down the hall from López's show.

Our Lady of All This Fuss. *Our Lady* that launched at least one newspaper article every day that we were in Ireland, with López's picture in it, under sensationalist headlines such as "UCC Suffers the Wrath of the Bishop" and "The Holy Mother of All Rows." López's own statement was printed in a two-page spread, under the melodramatic headline: "I never intended to offend." She was also interviewed for television, radio, and some online journals. In fact, the discussions lasted long after Alma López left the Emerald Isle, in letters to the editor, websites, and blogs such as Cork Student News, Cork Politics, *Cork News*, the *Irish Examiner*, Irish Central, *The Independent*, the *Hibernia Times*, the Catholic Lawyers Blog, Jesus In Love Blog, the *Irish Times*, the *Guardian*, the *Free Irish Press*, and the National Catholic Reporter Blog.[95]

What confounded me about this latest smear campaign against Alma López and *Our Lady* was not that the ANF minions are everywhere, or that yet another white male bishop was passing judgment on the artist, or that those callers to the radio show wanted to censor the artwork before it even landed on Irish shores. What confounded me was that the protestors, by virtue of their Catholicism, claimed ownership of La Virgen de Guadalupe, an image that pertains to Mexican and Chicano cultural iconography, and yet they knew nothing about the icon save for the barest-bones version of the story of La Virgen's apparition to Juan Diego. They knew nothing about the history of that image in the genocidal moment of the Spanish Conquest, or how the Catholic Church converted the apparition narrative of what was actually a syncretic image into a representation of a fully catechized indigenous population. Much less did they know that Chicana artists like Yolanda M. López and Ester Hernández had reinterpreted the image in the 1970s, almost twenty years before *Our Lady* ever appeared in López's computer, or that Chicana and Chicano artists continue to work in this tradition today. Those Irish protestors knew nothing about the artist, or about the book, or even about the conference that the Centre for Mexican Studies at University College Cork had been working very hard for two years to organize. All Dennis and the rest of those Orwellian sheep standing in the rain with their protest signs knew was that the ANF had told them to keep saying "It's Blaaaasphemy, it's blaaaasphemy." I am reminded of George Orwell's *Animal Farm,* where the pigs have taken control of the farm and are greedily consuming more food than the other animals on the pretext that they think more. The greedy pigs, under the leadership of Napoleon, are turning the puppies on the farm into attack dogs and training the sheep to bleat out whatever the party line is; apparently, "It's Blaaaasphemy" is the party line of these reactionary Catholics, Napoleonesque defenders of tradition, family, and property.

Even within that strange and archaic Irish orthodoxy, with blasphemy laws on the books, *Our Lady* could not be considered "blasphemous matter . . . that is grossly abusive or insulting in relation to matters held sacred by any religion, thereby causing outrage among a substantial number of the adherents of that religion"; nor had López set about "to cause such outrage."[96]

Moreover, because reasonable people (as evidenced by the many letters that were sent to Nuala Finnegan and the University College Cork administrators on López's behalf) could find "genuine literary, artistic, political, scientific, or academic value in the matter to which the offence relates,"[97] the image was protected as a work of art, and López, as an artist whose work has genuine artistic and academic value.

No matter what the ANF wanted people to think, *Our Lady* was not blasphemy, and López was not a criminal. Although the image caused outrage among certain members of the Catholic community, their hornet's nest stirred by an organization known for its worldwide demonstrations of intolerance and zealotry, the artist never intended to outrage or defame anybody. In fact, as she declared in her statement published in the *Irish Examiner*, her purpose in making *Our Lady* was "not to address Catholics at all [in other words, "It's not about you!"] but to portray a strong Chicana in the position and honor of the Virgin of Guadalupe," and to urge Chicanos to show the women in their lives the same love and respect they have for Our Lady of Guadalupe. Alma urged the Irish people "to unite to remove the blasphemy laws from their country in order to be free of the threat it poses to their freedom of expression and other rights granted in a democratic society."[98]

There's another question at the root of all this sanctimonious indignation. Is a woman's body sacrilegious? Is rendering *La Virgen's* human female body any different from portraying Jesus in a loincloth or Adam's penis on the Sistine Chapel? Are paintings of Christ's postmortem erection pornography? What about images depicting the Christ child's circumcision? Surely, that should outrage somebody. The "holy foreskin" is considered the most sacred relic in Christendom. What about the "holy nipple?" Shouldn't the nipple that fed the Christ child be just as holy as his foreskin? What makes the male body sacred and the female body obscene?

In Charlene Villaseñor Black's talk on the Censorship panel at the Oakland Museum, she placed the *Our Lady* controversy within a long history of protest against nudity in female religious art, beginning with Inquisition cases against images of lactating Madonnas, or Maria Lactans iconography depicting the Virgin Mary nursing the baby Jesus—known as the *"virgen de la leche"* controversy. In the mid-sixteenth century, the Council of Trent prohibited female nudity in art. To work within the restriction, some painters depicted the baby Jesus reaching into Mary's cleavage, fondling but not exposing the breasts. Others, namely Francisco de Zurbarán, Bartolomé Esteban Murillo, and Alfonso Cano, painted lactating Madonnas squirting long arcs of divine milk into the mouths of adult male saints.

Another colonial tradition that *Our Lady* would have fit into perfectly, argued Villaseñor Black, was the tradition of demonizing or paganizing powerful female saints, like St. Anne, Mary's mother, who used to be depicted as the matriarch of her family. The Church wanted

Figure 6.6. Alfonso Cano, *St. Bernard and the Virgin*, seventeenth century. Oil on canvas, 267 x 185 cm. Museo del Prado, Madrid, Spain. Photo credit: Album/Art Resource, NY.

a patriarchal family depicted, headed by a male saint. The Church also shunned attempts to humanize holy images and was particularly fearful of recognizing female saints as fully human. Jesus, however, could be depicted as a fully human male with a postmortem erection, as the erect phallus only proved his humanity (that is, his maleness, which, of course, is a sacred thing in patriarchy). The lactating breast of the Madonna, however, which ostensibly proved that the Virgin was a human mother feeding a human child, was forbidden. As Villaseñor Black's presentation made abundantly clear, the ANF and the Catholic Church's response to *Our Lady*, as much in Santa Fe as in Oakland and Ireland, is part of a centuries-old tradition of dogmatic attempts to control depictions of women in art, going all the way back to the Inquisition.

The controversy, in other words, can and should be seen as a modern-day reenactment of an Inquisition trial. Ultimately, this censorship tradition and its contemporary manifestations amount to one thing: misogyny. Only those who despise women, especially strong, older, Mexican women with a proud attitude and a fearless gaze, only those who find this type of female body inherently sinful, could be offended by Alma López's image.

And so, the *Our Lady* controversy reared its ugly head again, ten years later: the same excoriating diatribes against the artist; the same attacks on her First Amendment rights; the same fear- and hate-mongering tactics on behalf of the America Needs Fatima organization and its worldwide army of sycophantic sheep to slander her reputation as an artist, spoil the ratings of the book, and tar and feather López's soul in the afterlife.

In the closing chapter of *Our Lady of Controversy*, López's "It's Not about the Santa in My Fe, but about the Santa Fe in My Santa," written in the tradition of the *Nican Mopohua*, which recounts the apparition of the Virgin of Guadalupe from an indigenous perspective, tells her own version of the Virgin of Guadalupe apparition and deconstructs the "codex" represented by the different symbols that appear on the original image of La Virgen. It is also the story of the evolution of her work as a digital artist and of how *Our Lady* came into being. In reading the story of *Our Lady* from the artist's perspective, and learning about the personal meaning and history of each detail in the piece, we understand how mistaken were and are the lurid interpretations of the protestors, how the furthest thing from the artist's mind was irreverence or disrespect.

La Virgen de Guadalupe is a Mexican icon. Alma López is a Mexican Chicana artist. Who has more of a vested interest (pun intended) in re-searching and studying, questioning and understanding, deconstructing and reconstructing, that icon, which is woven into the DNA of the artist's Chicana identity and her Chicana/Mexicana culture? López's re-vision of the icon strips away Our Lady's colonized trappings and docile attitude to reveal the strong brown woman, the look-you-in-the-eye woman, woman-loving woman, border-crossing Viceroy-butterfly woman that the artist sees underneath those robes. *Our Lady* represents everything López loves, which, apparently, is everything the protestors seem to hate: strong women, brown women, queer women, and roses. I wonder: is that how you define blasphemy?

Figure 7.1. Alma López, *La peor de todas*, © 2013. Acrylic on wood, 12 x 12 in. Used by permission of the artist.

Chapter 7

THE SOR JUANA CHRONICLES

I am not the one you think,
your old world quills
have given me another life,
your lips have breathed another spirit into me,
and diverse from myself
I exist between your plumes,
not as I am, but as you
have wanted to imagine me.

—Sor Juana Inés de la Cruz[1]

My first encounters with Sor Juana did not take place in school, but rather at home, witnessing the drunken poetry recitals that my uncles and father used to engage in back in the early 1960s. They liked to challenge each other to see who could declaim the full text of Sor Juana's "Philosophical Satire" about "Hombres necios que acusáis a la mujer sin razón." Sor Juana was not on the curriculum of the Catholic grade schools I attended in El Paso, so I didn't know the text of "*hombres necios*" the way my cousins from Juárez did. Nonetheless, I learned it quickly, listened to it carefully, and without knowing it, completely internalized the organic feminism of those seventeenth-century lines. It didn't occur to me at the time to be jealous that I wasn't getting this knowledge in school because I learned it anyway, at home, in Spanish, from my loquacious (and liquoracious) family, who unwittingly planted in me Sor Juana's rebellious seed. Three decades later, while sweeping my apartment in Boston, trying to figure out how to write a novel that would incorporate my two favorite but seemingly unrelated subjects—Sor Juana and the Salem witchcraft trials—I saw, as they say, the whole story flash before my eyes, beginning to end. It took me ten years to put flesh on that subject, to read and know Sor Juana not from "*los dientes para fuera*," as the men in my family knew her, from a mnemonic recapitulation of her words, but from within Sor Juana's feminist mind and female-centered desire.

Before I go on to discuss my fleshing-out of the subject in *Sor Juana's Second Dream*, let me recap some of the highlights of Sor Juana's material existence as a criolla daughter of colonial New Spain.

"Hija de la Iglesia"

Born in 1648, in a small town on the outskirts of present-day Mexico City, Juana Inés was the third "natural" daughter of Doña Isabel Ramírez and was registered in the baptismal records of her parish as a "daughter of the Church," a euphemism for illegitimacy. She learned to read at the age of three, and at six requested that her mother dress her as a boy so that she could attend the University of Mexico. At eight, she was sent to live with relatives in Mexico City, and eight years later, Juana Inés had secured a post as lady-in-waiting to the vicereine, La Marquesa de Mancera, soon to become the favorite of the viceregal court of New Spain. Her reputation as a girl-scholar won her the admiration of nobles, scholars, and clergy across the realm, and yet it would prove to be a double-edged sword that both empowered and endangered her throughout her life. In an age when learning was the exclusive domain of men, she was viewed simultaneously as a prodigy and an aberration to her sex, a distinction that compromised her "salvation," as she put it, which may explain why she donned the habit of the Order of Saint Jerome at twenty years of age.

She writes in her autobiographical *Respuesta a Sor Filotea de la Cruz*,[2] penned in response to the bishop of Puebla's admonition in "Letter Worthy of Athena,"[3] that she joined the convent because of the "total antipathy [she] felt for marriage,"[4] and because it was possible there to pursue a life of learning, regretting that her own education resulted from her singular efforts rather than from a formal teaching environment, and yet warning against the "perilous association"[5] between male teachers and young girls. In her two-story cell, she led a scholar's life devoted to study, contemplation, and analysis, as well as a writer's life of commissioned plays, poetry, and musical scores, not to mention her own prose and endless correspondence. In her twenty-six years as a nun, she amassed a library of nearly four thousand books, and her prolific pen produced a body of work that included poetry, prose, and plays, both secular and profane, and now anthologized in four separate volumes. Of these, her more famous pieces are *Respuesta a Sor Filotea*—her defense of a woman's right to learn, discourse, and publish, which critics refer to as Sor Juana's intellectual autobiography—her *Primero sueño*, and her "Philosophical Satire" on "stubborn men who malign / women for no reason / dismissing yourselves as the occasion /for the very wrongs you design, / if with unmitigated passion / you solicit their disdain / why do you incite them to sin / and then expect them to behave?"[6] It is in her love poetry to the two vicereines[7] that we discover the true nature of what she calls her "negra inclinación," her "dark inclination[, which] has been so great that it has conquered all else!"[8]

Two years after scandalizing her superiors in religion with her *Respuesta*, in which she brilliantly rebutted the clergy's mandate to keep women silent and ignorant save for biblical scholarship, she grew even more notorious, more dangerous in the eyes of the Church patriarchs. Her first book, a compilation of poetry, was published in Spain in 1689, followed soon after by a second expanded edition of the same volume. Her books were popular in both Spain and New Spain; indeed, in our day, we might even call Sor Juana an international bestseller. By 1693, there were two volumes of her collected works and two editions of the first volume along with her second volume in circulation. Her celebrity, however, was also the final noose that would silence Sor Juana forever.

A year later she celebrated her Silver Jubilee, an event that marked her twenty-fifth anniversary as a bride of Christ and required her to sign a new testament of faith, to offer a "general" confession that examined in excruciating detail the quarter century she had lived as a nun, to live a year of approbation as though she were reentering the novitiate, and, ultimately, to renew her vocation to the Order of Saint Jerome. Considered a "formality" in the life of nuns, a milestone in their profession, an early form of post-tenure review, if you will, the Jubilee presented a convenient opportunity for the Church Fathers to issue their ultimatum to Sor Juana: either renounce her worldly ways and her scandalous writer's life and prostrate herself to the Rule or have her petition for reinstatement into the Order rescinded and get cast out of the sorority of nuns, perhaps even suffer the Inquisition, or worse, excommunication. Not, I believe, that the archbishop had any intention of releasing Sor Juana from her vows, as that would have given her the very freedoms he was adamant about curtailing. Because her body and, by extension, her life belonged to the Church by virtue of those vows of poverty, chastity, obedience, and enclosure that she had taken twenty-five years earlier, she could be demoted to the status of a "*beata*"[9] and still be forced to remain in the convent. She had no choice but to submit to all of the Church's demands, selling her library and musical and scientific instruments and donating the proceeds to the poor, and forfeiting everything that had once given meaning to her life and been the source of her passion, her devotion, and her enlightenment. That's my interpretation of what happened.

Stripped of the work that constituted her identity, bereft of the only outlet wherein to communicate not only to the world but also with herself, Sor Juana suffered the general confession, went through the motions of her year of approbation, and signed three documents to renew her faith and her vows in the Order of Saint Jerome. In one, she called herself "la más indigna e ingrata criatura de cuantas crio nuestra Omnipotencia . . . que ha tantos años que yo vivo en Religión, no solo sin Religión si no peor que pudiera un pagano."[10] Not only does she admit to living without religion in a religious community, but more, to living worse than a pagan. In the convent's *Book of Professions*, beneath her first testament of faith that she wrote in 1669, when she joined the convent, she pledged anew her devotion to the Virgin Mary and the Passion of Christ, and signed her new testament with her own blood on February 8, 1694. Here, her pen always poised for the double entendre, she called herself "la peor que ha habido . . . la peor del mundo."[11] The worst there has ever been, she wrote, but the worst of what? Not just "the worst of all," as María Luisa Bemberg's film is titled, but the worst of all women, the worst of all nuns, the worst woman who has ever existed, the worst nun in the world. Appropriating the discursive trappings of a nun's confession, Sor Juana subverts the self-contempt and humiliation of the genre into a declaration of autonomy and difference. My translation of what she meant is this: I am the worst of women and worst of nuns because I reject and have always rejected the social construction of my gender. I refused to be the kind of woman that my society and my superiors (the world) wanted me to be. By writing with her blood, Sor Juana was writing *with* the body to inscribe the body's submission to patriarchy,[12] at least on the discursive level; but she was also encoding her rebellion *through* the body, choosing a protracted form of suicide (she died a year later, in 1695) by devoting herself to the care of her terminally ill and highly contagious convent sisters, which could be interpreted as an act of contrition, humility, and holy service that would demonstrate how insignificant her life was and how much she wanted to prostrate her body and soul to the Church.

What happened to Sor Juana? Did she experience the equivalent of an open-heart transplant on her mind, or was this a final strategy she employed to put an end to an abject life? To help answer this question, and using the frame of Chicana lesbian feminism, which rewrites feminist epistemology by intersecting race, class, gender, ethnicity, language, and decolonial theories with the lesbian/queer standpoint, I would like to compare four Sor Juana chronicles: Dorothy Schons's unpublished novelized biography of Sor Juana (circa 1930s); Estela Portillo Trambley's three-act play *Sor Juana* (1983); my historical novel *Sor Juana's Second Dream* (1999); and Canadian writer Paul Anderson's epic rendition of the same historical figure in *Hunger's Brides* (2004). Always hovering above these texts, of course, is the ghost of Octavio Paz, self-appointed guru of all things Mexican, and his magnum opus on the life and times of our Tenth Muse, *Sor Juana Inés de la Cruz, o, Las trampas de la fe* (1982), which many consider to be the Sor Juana Bible, if you will, even more of a primary source than Sor Juana's own writings.

The Conquered Sor Juana

Buried in the Nettie Lee Benson Latin American Collection at the University of Texas is the typescript—part original, part carbon copy—of the first English-language novel on the life of Sor Juana Inés de la Cruz, titled "Sor Juana: A Chronicle of Old Mexico," by Dorothy Schons,[13] professor of Latin American literature at U.T. Austin and the first North American Sorjuanista. Although the manuscript is undated, Georgina Sabat Rivers believes the novel was probably written in the 1930s,[14] as it was in 1925 that Schons coined the epithet "first feminist in the New World" for Sor Juana.[15] In the foreword to the manuscript, Schons places Sor Juana in the genealogy of American feminists: "Two hundred years before Susan B. Anthony initiated the feminist movement in this country, there appeared in the New World a woman who was undoubtedly one of the earliest American feminists. Strange as it may seem, this woman was a Mexican nun, Sor Juana Inés de la Cruz."[16] Schons admits in the "Apologia" that her book is a novelized version of Sor Juana's biography, constructed as it is on the limited documentation of Sor Juana's life beyond Sor Juana's own work and the brief secondary materials that were available at the time.

Schons's motivation for writing Sor Juana's story is to "interpret for American readers the Mexico of the past," showing how Sor Juana's three-fold genius, as an artist, a poet, and an intellectual, represented the Mexican people themselves. "What [Sor Juana's] environment did to her, [is what] Mexico's past has done to the Mexican people." There is an overtly political purpose to her text. "Mexico's plea for social justice," Schons writes, "arises out of social inequalities inherited from colonial times." Thus, Sor Juana's story serves as a "chronicle of old Mexico," a signifier, perhaps, of the social inequities that have plagued Mexico since the Spanish Conquest. The chronicle is also an intimate account of Sor Juana's inner life that aims to recover the Mexican nun's "hidden motives" and "seeds of action."

There is a love story in Schons's narrative, a very brief unrequited love that Juana experiences with an Inquisitor while a lady-in-waiting at the court, but the real love that we see represented in Schons's book is Juana's love of learning and, to some extent, the narcissistic love she feels upon seeing her works in print. Although Schons also writes about Sor Juana's friendships and allegiances with the two vicereines who were her protectors, Sor Juana's primary relationship in this story is to her father confessor, Padre Antonio Núñez de Miranda. There are intimations of his admiration and desire for Juana, but they are thickly cloaked under the paternalistic guise of his role as her spiritual advisor. In fact, Schons paints him as a surrogate father for Sor Juana and depicts Sor Juana not as the illegitimate "daughter of the Church" that she was, but as a member of a nuclear family, complete with a Basque father, a criolla mother, and a pair of siblings. What scholars know about Sor Juana's father, other than his name and his origin, is that he was absent from her life and that her mother was not married to him, and yet Schons has chosen to add him back into the story, just as she has chosen to portray a vanquished Sor Juana at the end, one who ultimately sees the errors of her ways and willingly accedes to the archbishop's demands that she give up her worldly correspondence, sell her vast library and her collection of jewels and instruments to feed the poor, and devote herself to a saintly life of service and corporeal punishment.

Indeed, Schons's Sor Juana is liberated, not devastated, by her renunciation of everything that gave meaning to her life. Although she admits to being a woman conquered in a world of men (just as Mexico was conquered by the Spaniards), her victory is in having conquered her own desire for fame and glory. "She had achieved true wisdom at last," writes Schons. Let us see if in the other three chronicles, Sor Juana was indeed wrestling with a desire for fame and glory or with a deeper desire for a forbidden "*conocimiento*,"[17] or wisdom about her sexual self.

The Penitent Sor Juana

Fellow El Paso native Estela Portillo Trambley creates a darker and more tormented depiction of Sor Juana Inés de la Cruz in her three-act play *Sor Juana* (1983). Beginning the play in 1693, the year of Sor

Juana's General Confession before renewing her vows for her Silver Jubilee, Portillo Trambley presents a penitent, self-flagellating Sor Juana, mourning the death of her relationship with her father confessor. "She beats her breast, lowers head to floor, begins to unbutton top of her garment," state the stage directions in the script. "There is the sound of a whip descending upon bare flesh . . . Another whip lash, the sound of suffering sobs."[18] The city is in ruins, as the Indians have been protesting the high price of grain, and they have taken to the streets to burn the market and the palace, looting warehouses and granaries for food. But the real source of Sor Juana's suffering is the absence of Padre Antonio, who has been forbidden to visit Juana by the Inquisition Tribunal. "I wait for you, Father, and a tenderness grows inside of me—the resurgent language of the heart."[19] Heartsickness is not all that ails Juana, for a physical illness caught from the sisters she has been attending to, and spurred by her physical mortifications that are part of her purification process, has given her a delirious fever.

In this delirium, Sor Juana's mind flashes back to her childhood in Panoayan, reading books in her grandfather's library, playing in the gardens with her mulatto and Indian friends. She remembers life at court as lady-in-waiting to La Marquesa de Mancera; her short stay at the Carmelite convent; the tournament with the forty professors; her two-timing suitor, Bernardo, a courtier who confessed his undying love for the erudite and beautiful Juana Inés even though he was already betrothed to a highborn lady in Spain. Despondent about losing Bernardo, about being illegitimate, about not being allowed to enter the university, and knowing that she is "only a woman incapable of changing worlds" with her "imperfect scribblings,"[20] she waxes melancholic until, finally, Padre Antonio persuades her to turn to God to find salvation and join the Hieronymite Order, where she will be allowed to study.

Rather than the court's father confessor, Portillo Trambley's Padre Antonio is an activist priest, one who advocates for and ministers to the Indians and the poor of Mexico City. As such, he encourages Sor Juana to join his cause, to learn about how poverty and social injustices in New Spain are connected to racial status—a reality that, as a privileged member of the court, Juana Inés did not have to experience. In *With Her Machete in Her Hand*, Catrióna Rueda Esquibel interprets Portillo Trambley's representation of Sor Juana as a "play about political and racial consciousness," and argues that through Padre Antonio, Juana must learn "that her social position has a human cost."[21] Indeed, in Act II, Scene 2 of the play, Padre Antonio explains to Juana where her loyalties should lie: "For almost two decades you have spent your life writing, singing the praises of the masters. *Villancicos* for a long parade of Viceroys, Vicereines—loas and sonnets about the Spanish great. Your praises have been bountiful for those who have conquered your people, exploited them."[22] While she celebrates the exploits of the conquerors and laments the limitations of her life as an illegitimate woman of the upper caste, she fails to "hear the sad songs of the zambo slaves living in the hovels behind the rich man's house," and ignores the cries of the "women whose children are in pain because of the hunger."[23] Service to the people, Padre Antonio tells her, is the only solution.

I see a slightly different political narrative here. Knowing that Portillo Trambley came of age during the Chicano movement, I clearly hear a loyalist narrative in *Sor Juana*. Like the male leadership of El Movimiento and the female loyalists who supported them, Padre Antonio ranked race and class oppression on a higher scale than gender oppression; hence, the social consciousness Padre Antonio inspires in Sor Juana is not that of an autonomous woman with a right to self-determination via an education, but instead the race and class *conciencia* of the Chicano movement, whose goal was to liberate the working-class base of the social structure from oppressive racial discourses and material inequalities. The Chicana loyalist slogan "The problem is the *gabacho*, not the macho," or rather, we want to fight racism not sexism, is echoed in *Sor Juana*.

Rueda Esquibel finds that Portillo Trambley's *Sor Juana*" is also defined by the patriarchy and the nun's heterosexuality, or rather, the fact that her relationships with men determine her course of action in the story. This, too, establishes Portillo Trambley's standpoint as a Chicana loyalist rather than a feminist. Paraphrasing my own argument about the double standards employed by the Sorjuanistas, Rueda Esquibel states that "Sor Juana's biographers consistently try to prove her heterosexuality without evidence while at the same time arguing against her lesbianism in spite of the evidence."[24]

On joining the convent, the flame of Sor Juana's unrequited love for Bernardo gets transferred to Padre Antonio (who, in reality, was at least three decades her senior). In one particularly intimate scene as she prepares to sign the *Book of Professions*, Padre Antonio expresses concern that she will not be able to live up to the vows of poverty and enclosure required by the Rule, but she assures him that she loves him more than anybody and that he must "help [her] be what [he] want[s] her to be." He tries to clarify that it is God's will, not his, that she become a bride of Christ, and that she will become his "daughter" in religion, but she

tells him that to her, he is "[m]ore than father—brother, lover." Padre
Antonio attempts to silence her, but she continues. "I'm not saying sinful
things. My heart says this and I merely speak it. It says you are my other
self—the one still unborn (*She embraces him*)."[25]

Seeing her innermost self, her unborn self, reflected in the figure
of the activist Padre Antonio, Portillo Trambley constructs a Chicana
nationalist version of Sor Juana, whose ultimate purpose in life is not to
leave a legacy for women writers and future feminists of the Americas,
but to renounce her worldly connections and possessions and devote
herself to a life of service and subservience to the Church. "This is Sor
Juana's salvation [in Portillo Trambley]," writes Rueda Esquibel, "her
racial/class consciousness . . . [This] salvation proceeds not through
religion so much as through her *recognition* [emphasis added] of her duty
to Mexico."[26]

Re-Conocimiento, or, The Lesbian Sor Juana

Without a doubt, the longest and most difficult part of my research for
Sor Juana's Second Dream was reading Sor Juana's primary documents
in their original baroque Spanish. But, auditory learner that I was, I
loved reading her work aloud, listening to the rhythm and the meter
of her poetry, the convoluted syntax of her prose, the clear grammar of
her logic. Part of what I learned to discern as I heard Sor Juana's own
words was the difference between her *homenajes*, commissioned works
that paid tribute to the king and queen or other nobles of the court,
full of deference and obsequious praise; her religious poetry honoring
different saints, both male and female, as well as the Virgin Mary's
Immaculate Conception, written for the Church; her *romances*, akin to
English sonnets, themselves divided into ditties and panegyrics that she
used to demonstrate the genius of her wordplay with her literary friends
and admirers; her plays and performance pieces in which she employed
stylistic innovations, from integrating black and Indian dialects and
cultural customs into the narrative to cross-dressing and transgendering
some of her characters; and her bona fide love poems that spoke of the
secrets and silences of Sor Juana's heart.

Not surprisingly, those that fall into the latter category were all directed at two women, vicereines both: the earlier ones to "La Marquesa,"
Leonor Carreto, Marquesa de Mancera, whom Juana Inés attended as
a lady-in-waiting when she lived at court (1664–1669), and the later
ones dedicated to "La Condesa," María Luisa Manrique de Lara,

Condesa de Paredes, with whom Sor Juana shared a deeply intimate friendship, both during La Condesa's eight-year stay in Mexico (1680–1688) and even later, when the countess returned to Spain, carrying with her a trunk filled with whatever "scribblings" Sor Juana could collect, which La Condesa intended to see published in Spain. Indeed, La Condesa became the editor of the first two volumes of Sor Juana's collected works.

In an "interview" I constructed with Sor Juana as part of my final paper for a graduate class on Chicana feminisms at the University of New Mexico,[27] I asked Sor Juana specific questions based on issues in feminist theory, and she "answered" with excerpts from her writings, including her poetry, her autobiography, and a letter she wrote to dismiss her father confessor. Asking Sor Juana to "speak" about her subjectivity, her desire, her sense of pleasure, her views on male teachers, her attitude toward marriage, her reasons for joining the convent, her rationale for studying and writing—to name a few of the subjects we touch on—the interview helped me to recognize and unveil what kind of a "sister" she really was.

Eight years later, as an assistant professor of Chicana/o Studies at UCLA preparing my dossier for tenure, I published my historical novel *Sor Juana's Second Dream*, in which I construct Sor Juana as a lesbian nun.[28] After my very long and careful perusal of Sor Juana's primary documents—the prose, the plays, and especially the love poetry she left behind as evidence of her existence in the world—I came to the conclusion that Sor Juana was, in fact, not just a lesbian nun, but a separatist feminist cross-dressing as a nun to inhabit an identity that we now call lesbian, but that in seventeenth-century Spanish America did not exist as a discursive reality. That the word to describe that identity did not exist, however, does not mean the desire did not exist, for as John Boswell has shown,[29] same-sex desire was not born in the twentieth century or in the New World. To admit to that desire in the rigid patriarchy of the colonial world in which women's submission and domination were absolute would, no doubt, have been interpreted as heresy; and we all know what the Inquisition did to heretics. To disguise that desire using the literary conventions of the day, to refuse to submit to the heteronormative fate of marriage and child-rearing by joining a convent, to use her social location as a criolla nun to expand her education and at the same time safeguard her identity—these actions would have been very consistent with Sor Juana. She specialized in wordplay, in puns and double entendres. Already persecuted for her "negra inclinación" toward learning, she knew that the only path to her salvation as a body came from veiling her subjectivity in the drag of a "bride of Christ."

Sor Juana left behind a legacy of colonial feminism and a cloistered identity that was begging to be let out, a request that I happily obliged in *Sor Juana's Second Dream*. Engaging queer and Chicana feminist methodologies of disidentification, decolonization, *conocimiento*, and what I call "the politics of *re-conocimiento*,"[30] or radical recognition, I see my novel as part of a larger enterprise being deployed by Chicana lesbian theorists like Gloria Anzaldúa, Emma Pérez, and Deena González, whose revisionist task it is to write Chicana, Mexicana, and mestiza lesbians back into history.

José Esteban Muñoz, writing in 1999 about queer Latina/o disidentification in performance studies, argues that the politics of identifying "on and against" dominant ideological formations of gender or sexuality "is a strategy that tries to transform a cultural logic from within."[31] Rather than assimilating or overtly rejecting (and thereby reifying) a dominant politics of identity, disidentification aims to hold on to that identity while imbuing it with a new meaning. Muñoz's idea of disidentification is a counterpoint to Jean Laplanche and Jean-Bertrand Pontalis's definition of identification as "a psychological process whereby the subject assimilates an aspect, property, or attribute *of the other* [emphasis added] and is transformed, wholly or partially, after the model the other provides. It is by means of a series of identifications that the personality is constituted and specified."[32] To *dis*-identify with the Other, then, means to not assimilate aspects of the Other that ideologically restrict the development of what Chela Sandoval calls "differential consciousness" (or consciousness born out of difference) and contradict the subject's "identity-in-difference" (as articulated by Anzaldúa, Moraga, Alarcón, and other Third World feminist thinkers). My question: Who is "the Other" referenced in the above? Typically, in postmodern discourse anyway, "the Other" has been the domain of identities-in-difference or marginalized, oppressed, differential subjects in heteronormative white patriarchal constructions of subjectivity or citizenship. To *Otherize* the dominant is, first, to subvert the status quo, but second, to hegemonize difference, to make difference the central rather than the marginal point of reference. Thus, a disidentification from this dominant Other (and dominance can be coded by any combination of race, class, gender, sexuality, nationality, language, and other vectors in what Patricia Hill Collins terms "the matrix of domination") is a return to or reification of differential consciousness, which becomes the fundamental identificatory site for what Muñoz calls "minoritarian subjects."[33]

Perhaps more importantly, the politics of disidentification as imagined by Muñoz involves "read[ing] oneself and one's own life narrative in a moment, object, or subject that is not culturally 'coded' with the disidentifying subject."[34] While Sor Juana has not been "coded" as a lesbian nun by the homophobic dominant cultural logic of Octavio Paz and the Sorjuanistas, I read my own disidentificatory lesbian subjectivity within Sor Juana's love poetry to other women (and within other texts in which she articulates and disarticulates her "negra inclinación") as well as within the Sorjuanista discourse that conflates the mystery of Sor Juana's desire with her identification with her Enlightened mind or her Catholic nun's habit; thus I disidentify Sor Juana from either a purely intellectual or a purely spiritual existence—both realms that deny her embodiment as well as her identity as a woman-loving woman.

In *Refusing the Favor*, Deena González argues that part of the work of Chicana feminist historians is to disidentify and therefore recover women like Sor Juana and Malintzin Tenepal (better known in Chicano/Mexican history as La Malinche) from the Eurocentric constructions that male historians and critics have imposed on them. For González, disidentification is not driven by either a Freudian or a psychoanalytic impulse, as we see in Muñoz, but rather by history and place: the history of conquest and colonization of the Americas. Colonization, argues González, imposes two identities on colonized subjects: of belonging and not belonging to their own place of origin. Their forced identification with the Other—in this case, the colonizer, who does not belong—in essence alienates colonized subjects from the Other and from themselves. Colonized people can no longer identify with their place of origin (which implies cultural, linguistic, and racial identification) in the same way; thus, González's take on disidentification sees it as a much more ontological rather than strictly psychological process.

By engaging in "complex and multidimensional interactions of inscription and creating identities based on what *they* (the previously disidentified and the unknown) were not, that is, non-European," says González, it becomes possible "to acknowledge their replacement of an identity based on a recovered self."[35] For the Spanish Mexican women of nineteenth-century New Mexico who were the subjects of González's study, this meant showing how their political identity before and after the U.S.-Mexico War was produced in resistance to and accommodation of both Catholic patriarchy and Anglo colonization.[36] For Sor Juana in seventeenth-century New Spain, disidentification entailed not only appropriating, as Audre Lorde would say, "the master's tools"—rhetoric, enlightenment, discourse—to "dismantle the master's house" but also constructing a new veiled identity as a lesbian located in the interstices between being a bad nun/woman ("la peor del mundo") and the best poet of the Golden Age (La Décima Musa).

My theory of *re-conocimiento* builds on the Anzaldúan notion of *conocimiento*, which she defines in an interview with Inés Hernández-Ávila as "an overarching theory of consciousness, of how the mind works. It's an epistemology that tries to encompass all the dimensions of life, both inner—mental, emotional, instinctive, imaginal, spiritual, bodily realms— and outer—social, political, lived experiences."[37] While *conocimiento* is the seven-stage process of self-knowledge and consciousness-raising about the inner and outer dimensions of the self,[38] *re-conocimiento* takes that process outside the self and involves perceiving, naming, knowing, accepting, acknowledging, and identifying the Other in whom you see a reflection or expression of yourself.

Re-conocimiento can only occur after the conscious opening of the self to all of its many feelings and "subversive knowledges,"[39] through which the self recognizes its own image in the Other. Here we can hark back to Foucault's notion of similitude, finding the resemblance between the self and the Other. This process of identification between self and Other is at the root of the adage "It takes one to know one." Gaydar, or the inner radar that helps us locate the other gay person in the crowd, is *re-conocimiento*. Even more profoundly, so is the Mayan concept of *in lak'ech ala k'in*: I am another you, you are another me. *Re-conocimiento* is a dialectical process, knowing the Other by knowing the self, knowing the self by knowing the Other. It is reciprocal, a constant mirroring, reflecting the hidden parts of both selves.

"Although all your cultures reject the idea that you can know the other," writes Anzaldúa, "you believe that besides love, pain might open this closed passage by reaching through the wound to connect. Wounds cause you to shift consciousness."[40] It is my recognition of Sor Juana's wounded warrior heart, survivor of what Yvonne Yarbro-Bejarano, elaborating on Cherríe Moraga's concept of the "woman-wound," describes as "all the interconnected forces that inflict both psychic and physical damage on women on the global, national, and 'community' levels and within the family, the couple, and the self,"[41] this intimate knowledge I have of how the wounds perpetrated by sexism, misogyny, family, and community are deepened by homophobia, that allows me to know Sor Juana as lesbian.

Anzaldúa offers us two ways by which to recognize Sor Juana's pain: as her Shadow-Beast that both terrorized her and inspired her to rebel, and as her agonizing and ultimately transformative passage through the Coatlicue State,[42] that immobilizing pause in the journey toward *cono-cimiento* that we refer to as an identity crisis.[43] It is this repressed identity, this hidden Other within herself, the outlawed lesbian, that I recognize in my *re-conocimiento* of Sor Juana, and that constitutes Sor Juana's politics of location in my literary and critical interpretations of her life. When I say that I recognize Sor Juana, then, I am saying that I name, know, acknowledge, identify, accept, and allow her to speak as a lesbian. As tatiana de la tierra wrote in a poem: "lesbian texts are passed from hand to hand and mouth to mouth between lesbians. they are located on the skin, in the look, in the geography of the palms of the hands."[44]

In *Reading Chican@ Like a Queer: The De-Mastery of Desire*, Sandra Soto expounds upon the expansiveness she sees in the "mere two-letter prefix" that the term "de-mastery" signifies for her as she attempts to explain how the process of unlearning the discourses that promote mastery over knowledge (even epistemologies of identity) can lead to "reading like a queer." In essence, I think, my recognition of Sor Juana as lesbian is an example of this kind of reading, as this *re-conocimiento*, also employing a "mere two-letter prefix," in front of an Anzaldúan theory of self-awareness separates Sor Juana from the master narratives by which she has come to be known as the Golden Age Intellectual or the Mexican Phoenix or even the First Feminist of the Americas, and knows her again through another kind of reading, one that marks her embodied lesbian desire as the wellspring for Sor Juana's creativity and "revolutionary subjectivity."[45]

This type of recognition is akin to Aristotle's theory of anagnorisis, the moment in a play when the protagonist "recognizes his or her or some other character's true identity, or discovers the true nature of his or her situation."[46] Specifically, Aristotle defined anagnorisis in his *Poetics* as "a change from ignorance to knowledge, producing love or hate between the persons destined by the poet for good or bad fortune."[47] This discovery, or recognition, marks a shift in the protagonist's consciousness from ignorance to awareness, and establishes a bond ("of love or hate") between the protagonist and the character or situation being recognized.[48]

I see ample evidence of anagnorisis in Sor Juana's own texts, where she clearly leaves clues to her real self in the drama of her existence, coded

Figure i.1. *Woman with Frames*, © 2010. UNAM Sculpture Garden, Ciudad Universitaria, Mexico City. Color photograph by Raymond Meier. Photo credit: Trunk Archive.

Figure i.7. Leonardo Da Vinci, *St. Jerome*, circa 1480. Oil on wood, 103 x 75 cm. Pinacoteca, Vatican Museums, Vatican State. Photo credit: Scala/Art Resource, NY.

Figure 1.1. Teyali Falcón, *Athena among Calla Lilies*, © 1999. Oil on canvas, 14 x 18 in. In the collection of Alicia Gaspar de Alba.

Figure 3.1. John Gast, *American Progress*, 1872. Oil on canvas, 11 1/2 x 15 3/4 in. (29.2 x 40 cm). Autry National Center, Los Angeles; 92.126.1.

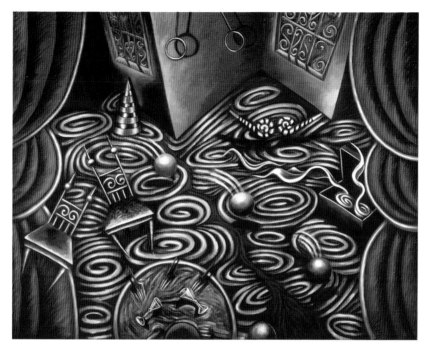

Figure 3.3. Patssi Valdez, *The Magic Room*, © 1994. Acrylic on canvas, 96 x 119 5/8 in. Smithsonian American Art Museum, through the Smithsonian Institution Collections Acquisitions Program.

Figure 5.2. Alma López, detail of *History in Our Hands*, © 2009. Mural in collaboration with Noni Olabisi at the Constituent Services Center, South Central Avenue, Los Angeles. Used by permission of the artist.

Figure 6.6. Alfonso Cano, *St. Bernard and the Virgin*, seventeenth century. Oil on canvas, 267 x 185 cm. Museo del Prado, Madrid, Spain. Photo credit: Album/Art Resource, NY.

Figure 7.3. Yreina D. Cervantez, *Mujer de Mucha Enagua, Pa' Ti, Xicana*, © 1999. Serigraph (SHG), 22 x 30 in. Used by permission of the artist.

references to her true identity or to the reality of her doubly cloistered life: the "dark inclination" she tries to explain in her *Respuesta*; the Dark Queen of Night in *Primero sueño*; the "secret" from La Condesa that she shredded and "swallowed . . . lest one scrap escape [her] breast"; the "Tenth Muse" epithet on her first book; the sign of "la peor del mundo" she inscribed in her own blood.

Indeed, the fact that I can decipher these and so many other clues, recognize this similitude between us, and therefore *know* Sor Juana as a lesbian establishes a bond of love between us, one that motivates me to disidentify and decolonize Sor Juana and write a radical new interpretation of her life, a radical recognition based in love of self and Other. "It is love that can access and guide our theoretical and political 'movidas,'" writes Chela Sandoval in *The Methodology of the Oppressed*, "revolutionary maneuvers toward decolonized being."[49] *Sor Juana's Second Dream*, then, is my revolutionary *movida* to liberate Sor Juana from the ghostly grip of Octavio Paz and the Sorjuanistas' colonial imaginary.

Decolonizing Sor Juana

Ever since the 1999 publication of *Sor Juana's Second Dream*, a year after the death of Octavio Paz, I have found myself jousting again and again with the 1990 Nobel prizewinner, particularly with his stubborn refusal to entertain Sor Juana's lesbian identity. Everywhere I go with my lesbian Sor Juana in hand, I run into the ghostly Paz. Be it the annual conference of Chicana/o Studies in Mexico City or a festival of multicultural arts at a small private college in upstate New York or at a reading of my work at the now defunct Midnight Special Bookstore in Santa Monica, there he is, wagging his crooked finger at me, shaking his wooly head at my audacity.

How dare I contradict the word of this venerable patriarch, this self-ordained high priest of the Mexican psyche? How dare I question his meticulous dissection of this Mexican cultural icon and give more weight to Sor Juana's own words than to his own enlightened interpretation? Then, with a condescending shrug, Paz retreats into the shadows of his self-righteous upper-class, heteronormative Mexicanness. What can be expected of a Chicana, a polluted Mexican, I can almost hear him saying.[50] The implication: a true Mexican, not one corrupted by foreign, libertine ideologies about sex and gender, would never disrespect him in that way, would never seek to look beneath or beyond Sor Juana's habit to imagine her sexuality, and a deviant one, at that. A true Mexican would never invent illicit desires for La Décima Musa that, he knows for a fact, did not exist.

Although Octavio Paz (may he rest in *paz*) needs to explain Sor Juana's "Sapphic tendencies"[51] as excessive libido that had no outlet in the opposite sex, or a consequence of her "illegitimacy," or an overt "identification with her grandfather . . . [which led to] masculinization and neutralization of the libido . . . and always an exalted narcissism";[52] although psychoanalytic critics such as Ludwig Pfandl and Fredo Arias de la Canal attribute her (what today Judith Halberstam would call female) masculinity to penis envy,[53] masochism, an Oedipal complex, or just basic neurosis brought about by the absent mother, it is evident from reading her own primary documents that Sor Juana not only refused to submit to the social construction of her gender but also rejected altogether what Adrienne Rich calls "compulsory heterosexuality"[54] by joining a cloistered community.

In a poem to La Condesa, she states "that you are a woman / that you are absent / none of these impede my love for you / for the soul ignores / gender and distance."[55] In response to a Peruvian correspondent who suggested in a poem that she should have been born a man, anticipating feminist icon Simone de Beauvoir's famous line "One is not born a woman"[56] by three hundred years, Sor Juana provides an etymological argument for why she should not be seen as a woman:

> for here [in the convent] we have no Salmacis,
> whose crystal water, so they tell,
> to nurture masculinity
> possesses powers unexcelled.
> I have no knowledge of these things,
> except that I came to this place
> so that, if true that I am female,
> none substantiate that state.
> I know, too, that they were wont
> to call wife, or woman, in the Latin
> *uxor*, only those who wed,
> though wife or woman might be virgin.
> So in my case, it is not seemly
> that I be viewed as feminine,
> as I will never be a woman

who may as woman serve a man.
I know only that my body,
not to either state inclined,
is neuter, abstract, guardian
of only what my Soul consigns.[57]

And she is equally unequivocal about her desire for María Luisa, her "divina Lysi," whom she confesses to adore in various poems, to whom she wants to belong like a slave belongs to her master, a crime whose punishment would be a reward:

I love you with so much passion
neither rudeness nor neglect
can explain why I tied my tongue,
yet left my heart unchecked . . .
Let my love be ever doomed
if guilty in its intent,
for loving you is a crime
of which I will never repent.
This much I find in my feelings—
and more that I cannot explain;
but you, from what I have said,
may infer what words won't contain.[58]

My favorite, though, of the lesbian-coded poems Sor Juana wrote to her beloved Condesa is this one, which gives us a glimpse into how secrets were transported and shared between the two women, a communion of secrets, if you will.

The page, discreetly, will relate
how, the moment it was read,
I tore your secret into shreds
that shreds be not the secret's fate.
And something more, inviolate,
I swallowed what you had confessed,
the tiny fragments of your note,
to guard the secret that you wrote
and honor thus your confidence, lest
even one scrap escape my breast.[59]

Rather than "speak" the secret delivered by a page from the palace, Sor Juana consumes the secret, La Condesa's confession, and thus makes it a part of her own body. The note, like the wafer at Holy Communion, becomes transubstantiated into the body of the beloved, the Savior, in this case, La Condesa. Rather than the Word becoming Flesh, however, we have the Flesh (La Condesa) becoming Word (the secret) to redeem Sor Juana.

In the eight years that La Condesa remained in New Spain, until the time of Sor Juana's death in 1695, they no doubt shared many secrets with each other, just as they exchanged letters and gifts. Sor Juana wrote love poems and other odes to María Luisa, and received favors and visits from the palace in return. As the editor of the first two volumes of Sor Juana's collected works, it was La Condesa de Paredes who gave Sor Juana the epithet "La Décima Musa," or "the Tenth Muse"—a play on words that harked both to the *décima* poetic form, at which Sor Juana excelled, and to what Plato had called Sappho two millennia earlier.[60] Surely, the allusion to the woman-loving poet was not lost on Sor Juana. Always there was the intimacy of discourse between them, a camaraderie of souls, if not bodies. It's all there, in the primary documents, the chronicle of this friendship, this love story, and yet, the Sorjuanistas have been denying, explaining, justifying, ignoring, or pathologizing Sor Juana's sexuality for a good part of the twentieth century.

In his magnum opus, Octavio Paz asserts that the love that Sor Juana and La Condesa shared was a "Platonic love-friendship," and that the "only thing we know for sure is that their relationship, although impassioned, was chaste";[61] moreover, he adds, we have no documents to prove that Sor Juana was, in fact, of the Sapphic persuasion.[62] Even if it were true that Sor Juana had joined the convent because she "felt a clear aversion to men and an equally clear attraction to women," Paz's logic goes, she was, first of all, too young to know her "true inclinations," and second, too ignorant about sex to have made such a "cold-blooded" decision. Hence, his colonial patriarchal imaginary finds the possibility of Sor Juana's lesbian desire "absurd," and more appropriate to the licentious heroine of a French Enlightenment writer than to a decent criolla girl of New Spain.

Although Sor Juana herself said in *La Respuesta a Sor Filotea* that she had joined the convent because of her "total antipathy toward marriage," which to me speaks pretty clearly about the kind of desire she did not feel, Octavio Paz argues vehemently that Sor Juana could not have known what she did and did not desire when she joined the convent.

"It is futile to try to learn what her true sexual feelings were," he writes. "*She herself did not know*" (emphasis added).[63] Hence, his male mind knows for a fact that the relationship between Sor Juana and La Condesa was chaste, and negates not only Sor Juana's desire, but more, her own knowledge of her desire. He, of course, omniscient Mexican patriarch that he is, knows what Sor Juana could not possibly have known and, thus, authorizes himself to speak for her. To say Sor Juana didn't know what she desired, *but he does*, is the colonial imaginary at work, the male authority speaking for a woman who was the epitome of literate and articulate and perfectly capable of speaking for herself. It is also a paternalistic dismissal of Sor Juana's subjectivity and an arrogant denial of her existence as a fully human being.

At nineteen years of age, while still serving at the viceregal court as lady-in-waiting, Juana Inés Ramírez de Asbaje was the intellectual equal of forty scholars from diverse fields at the University of Mexico. Yet, Paz assures us, she did not know "her true sexual feelings." Is it really that much of a stretch to admit that at the age of nineteen, she *did* know what she desired and did not desire, what she wanted as well as what she did not want to do with her life and her body? Is it truly so difficult to imagine that Sor Juana had a body as well as a mind, and to grant that both her body and her mind desired what supposedly only belonged to the male gender: knowledge, autonomy, fame, and, why not, women? Short of videotapes in the seventeenth century, there was sex, there were lies, and the "proof" was in the pudding, as they say, or rather, in Sor Juana's own "scribblings," as she called her writings.

But no, say her critics, her primary documents do not count, for they reflect the literary conventions and limitations of her day; in other words, Sor Juana's own words don't speak for the "real" or the "true" Sor Juana. Although Sor Juana's descriptions of the female body, her divina Lysi's body in particular, are quite erotic, Paz nonetheless asserts that "it is not possible to extract any conclusions about her personal erotic tendencies from an examination of the poems."[64] Early feminist though she was, and the one who baptized Sor Juana "the first feminist of America," Dorothy Schons asks in the "Apologia" to her unpublished novel, "Who shall vouch for what went on in that mind and heart?" Feminist or sexist, Schons and Paz may represent opposite ends in the continuum of the colonial imaginary, but they both fail to give Sor Juana the dignity of her own authority, the power to speak, or vouch, for herself.

The problem is that for most of the last century, Sor Juana's mind and heart have been interpreted, appropriated, and vouched for primarily by a cadre of scholars, critics, translators, and historians (even feminist ones) who are homophobic in the extreme. It would be difficult for critics who deny the validity of a queer reading to see, much less recognize, the lesbian desires in Sor Juana. Our reliance on critical interpretations of Sor Juana is partly due to the baroque difficulty of much of Sor Juana's language, and the fact that it's slightly less challenging to read twentieth-century literary criticism than it is to decipher the intricate locutions of the Golden Age. We assume, moreover, that the critic has already done that deciphering for us, and thus we authorize that critic to speak for the documents themselves. This is, in large measure, also the task of the historian, the analysis of primary documents rendered in a "contemporary" voice and filtered through the particular politics and ideologies of the author and her times. History is, after all, as much interpretation as it is translation, as much a chronicle of "what happened" as a narrative construction answering the question "How should I tell the story of what happened?" There is no such thing as "objective" or impartial history, for history, as Howard Zinn has proven, is either the story of the conquerors or the conquered.[65] It is the subjectivity of the discursive practice of history that interests me as a cultural critic and a historical novelist, both the historian's subjectivity, which informs her analysis of the primary documents, and the subjectivity of the figure who has authored the primary documents.

Emma Pérez argues that traditional history—the white male narrative of the past that Chicano historians were taught and continue to practice—is a colonial imaginary, a way of imagining the past that emerges from and contributes to a male colonial agenda. It is, in other words, a history of "great events" and "great men," that is, a *seminal* history, in the biological and figurative meanings of the word, history written from the point of view of those in power, which glorifies and perpetuates that power while at the same time eliminating perspectives that fail to contribute to that view (read: feminist, lesbian, and queer readings). Thus, even though Chicano history is not a history written by the white colonizer, it is nonetheless a male-privileged history granted, by patriarchy, the authority to include and exclude, to select what is important and not important in the historical narrative, and to speak for others. Pérez sees Chicana history as an archaeological practice that excavates gender and sexuality from the gaps and crevices of Chicano/Mexicano history through a process she calls the "decolonial imaginary."[66]

In the colonial imaginary, Pérez explains, women are "spoken about, spoken for, and ultimately encoded as whining, hysterical, irrational, or passive women who cannot know what is good for [them], who cannot know how to express or authorize [their] own narratives."[67] This is exactly what has happened to Sor Juana: she has been spoken about, spoken for, and ultimately encoded by a patriarchal colonial imaginary that dictates that women, especially idealized women in Mexican history such as Sor Juana and the Virgin of Guadalupe, are not supposed to have any knowledge of sex (especially not lesbian sex).

The critics and historians who have written about Sor Juana have, in the main, been writing out of a colonial imaginary that privileges the Eurocentric Hispanic heteronormative construction of knowledge and the male conquistador's view of history, a perspective that not only Otherizes women and queers but would also negate that a queer reading of Sor Juana is either plausible or possible.

For Emma Pérez, Octavio Paz is an excellent example of the colonial imaginary, a historical narrative that is centered in and narrated from the perspective of the colonizer and the colonizer's male offspring, who shares the father's male privilege and yet is shamed by his Indian mother's color and language. In order to be more like the father and less like the mother, the colonial son adopts the father's language, customs, and political ideologies and reviles the mother by hating in himself the irreducible differences that she has biologically encoded in him; in this way, the mestizo son reinforces the colonial imaginary, which cannot imagine women as full human beings with their own agency and subjectivity.[68] The "decolonial imaginary" is the constant questioning and challenging of the colonizer's authority, particularly his discursive authority and his sense of entitlement.

Critics like Octavio Paz allow Sor Juana a discursive subjectivity (indeed, the four thick volumes of her collected works circulating through the ages attest to her existence and her genius) but not a physical one. Sex and desire are the two male domains that the Sorjuanistas will not allow Sor Juana to access; in essence, they erase her body from history. Thus, they effectively bind her to a strictly intellectual existence, a life entirely of the mind, devoid of the knowledge of sexuality, much less the experience of it. Through her habit, she died to the world as a body; through the Sorjuanista discourse, she died as a woman.

If we read Sor Juana as the colonized object of knowledge upon which the Sorjuanista regime has imposed its colonial imaginary, then it follows that we have to decolonize her "Otherness" if we expect to find the speaking subject. How do we do this? Emma Pérez suggests finding the subject's "*sitio y lengua*,"[69] in other words, she situates historical agency in and through the tongue in all three of its forms: (a) the linguistic tongue (through language); (b) the literal tongue (through the body); and (c) the sexual tongue (through the body's desire).[70]

The decolonial, as Emma Pérez enacts it in the kind of history that she writes, is the colonized's resistance to erasure. Building on Luce Irigaray's theory of a "female symbolic," a female discourse in which women are the center and the perspective from which the world is imagined, a language of desire rooted in the female body, Pérez proposes a Chicana lesbian imaginary that makes Chicana lesbians the center and the perspective from which the world is imagined. Pérez calls this "historically tracking women's agency on the colonial landscape"[71] to reveal the trappings of sexual power that are embedded in colonial acts such as the conquest of the Americas, the occupation of a foreign territory, the mapping of a civil rights movement, and the writing of history. This rewriting of the colonial narrative from a Chicana lesbian female symbolic is how I track Sor Juana's agency across the colonial landscape of both New Spain and the Sorjuanista imaginary.

"The [Chicana lesbian] historian's political project, then, is to write a history that decolonizes otherness,"[72] writes Emma Pérez. To do this, Pérez argues, requires exercising "strategic essentialism" and transforming what Luce Irigaray calls the female symbolic into the Chicana lesbian symbolic, a culturally and historically specific matrix from which to view the world and rewrite our/"her" story. "A strategic essentialist," explains Pérez, "is one who exercises political representation, or identity politics, within hegemonic structures,"[73] one who asserts all of her differences in the face of prevailing colonialism, not to exclude others, but to claim the "*sitios y lenguas*," the positions and intersections, in which the speaking subject is located.

To help clarify the point even more, I turn to Gayatri Spivak, who asserts that "[it] is not possible to be non-essentialist . . . the subject is always centered. . . . Since it is not possible not to be an essentialist, one can self-consciously use this irreducible moment of essentialism as part of one's [deconstructive/critical/narrative] strategy."[74] Indeed, this strategic use of essentialism is crucial to the politics of *re-conocimiento* that I practice in *Sor Juana's Second Dream*.

In the unfinished and undated poem written in homage to the "inimitable pens of Europe" that I quote from in my epigraph to both this chapter and my novel, a poem that scholars believe to be among the last pieces that Sor Juana was working on before she succumbed to the illness that took her life, Sor Juana talks about the dialectics of discourse and identity, subject and critic:

> I am not the one you think,
> your Old World quills
> have given me another life,
> your lips have breathed another spirit into me.[75]

Originally, she was writing these lines to a group of seven Spanish theologians and men of letters who had written glowing endorsements of her critique of a Jesuit priest's analysis of Christ's "Sermon on the Mandate."[76] Antonio de Vieyra's analysis, not just the original sermon, was thought to be Holy Writ by some members of the Church, but especially by the archbishop of Mexico, the avowed misogynist Francisco de Aguiar y Seijas, Sor Juana's archenemy. Without her consent, Sor Juana's critique was published by the duplicitous bishop of Puebla, Manuel Fernández de Santa Cruz, who commissioned the critique in the first place, bearing the title "Carta Atenagórica," or, "Letter Worthy of Athena,"[77] preceded by an admonition from the bishop (his identity disguised as a nun named Sor Filotea de la Cruz) for Sor Juana to devote her time to reading Scripture rather than engaging in polemical discourse with a Portuguese priest. This publication catalyzed the downfall of our Tenth Muse. It set the stage for what Octavio Paz calls the "traps of faith" that punctuated the last five years of her life, leading eventually to Sor Juana's rebuttal to her transvestite sister, "Response to Sor Filotea de la Cruz" and her soon-to-follow fall from grace.

What interests me about those lines dedicated to "the inimitable pens of Europe" that are the epigraph of this chapter is how succinctly they show Sor Juana's awareness of the dialectics of writing. "Diverse from myself," she writes, prefiguring discussions of difference and *differánce* by three centuries, "I exist between your plumes / not as I am, but as you / have wanted to imagine me," acknowledging the role that critics play in the construction of her identity, as well as the way that the writer's imaginary becomes a mirror to her life. Not the Cartesian "I think, therefore I am," but instead, the postmodern "You think, therefore I exist as you imagine me or as you want me to be, and I remain *between* your discursive constructions as someone different than who I am." This brings me back to Emma Pérez, as she explains how the historical narrative becomes the mirror projection of the historian, and how the process of decolonizing Otherness allows for the existence of multiple reflections between the colonial self and the colonized Other:

> The imaginary is the mirrored identity where coloniality overshadows the image in the mirror. Ever-present, it is that which is between the subject and the object being reflected, splintering the object in a shattered mirror, where kaleidoscopic identities are burst open and where the colonial self and the colonized other both become elements of multiple, mobile categoric identities. . . . One negotiates within the imaginary to a decolonizing otherness where all identities are at work in one way or another.[78]

Three hundred years before postmodernism, feminist theory, deconstructive praxis, and decolonial theory, Sor Juana was writing about not only the social construction of gender and the gendered construction of knowledge but also about representation, subjectivity, fragmented identities, and the power of the imaginary. Well she knew that, as a subject of scrutiny or an object of critical praise, she existed not as she was, but as her critics, biographers, historians, defenders, or chroniclers wanted to imagine her through their/our own discourse, a product of our plumes as much as of our imaginations, a reflection of our times and our own identities, for, as Gayatri Spivak reminds us, "No representation can take place . . . without essentialism."[79]

Thus, in my humble opinion, Sor Juana authorizes us to imagine her any way we want to, which, of course, we're going to do anyway. She or we might not agree with Jaime Manrique and Joan Larkin's translation of some of her love poems, for example, but we have Sor Juana's blessing to read her as we will.[80] To that end, I have used the narrative techniques of novel writing to reimagine Sor Juana's life through a subjectivity more akin to her own—that of a lesbian, feminist, writer, scholar; daughter of upper-caste, light-skinned Mexicans, Catholics, and colonialist minds—and more capable of recognizing the coded language of her lesbian ethos and eros. Perhaps, as Lee Bebout argues, I have simply invented a "mythohistorical" lesbian past for Sor Juana:

> In *Sor Juana's Second Dream*, Gaspar de Alba challenges the archival limitations of history, the limitations that have foreclosed the possibilities of a Latina/Chicana lesbian past. Through the novel, Gaspar de Alba deploys an innovative mythohistorical intervention to present a queer ancestress to modern-day Chicana lesbian feminists . . . Lacking a historical record,

Gaspar de Alba fictionalizes an archive . . . [that] does not merely challenge heteronormative history by creating a record of lesbian consciousness and desire, but also by showing how that record is vulnerable to erasure. . . . That is, through exploring the creation and destruction of archival records of lesbian desire [such as Sor Juana's Sapphic diary entries, which at the end are burned by her niece], Gaspar de Alba exposes that the very foundation of historical knowledge is limited.[81]

Using a New World computerized quill, I have authored the second English-language historical novel (though the first to be published) about our Mexican Tenth Muse in which I pull off her habit and put the flesh back on her bones. To hark back to the poem, I have "breathed another spirit" into Sor Juana. I use that poem as the epigraph to the novel because in these lines, she has given me license to imagine her the way I want her to be, or perhaps the way she might have imagined herself, had she had the language and the discourse by which to name and theorize her desire.

The Hungry Sor Juana

In 2004, five years after the publication of *Sor Juana's Second Dream*, a new Sor Juana novel in English was published in Canada by a male Canadian writer named Paul Anderson.[82] It was published the following year in the United States and came packaged as an "international event" with a media blitz that included a national author tour; national television, radio, and periodical interviews; four-color posters; a viral e-mail campaign; and a DVD available for in-store displays that depicted the story behind the book. It was a featured title at both the *Los Angeles Times* Book Festival and Book Expo America in New York City, and was graced with a glowing review on the front page of the *New York Times* Arts section (among others).[83] The book also had its own website, filled with baroque imagery and Aztec glyphs, and conceptualized as a portal to Sor Juana's seventeenth-century convent.[84] It was, in short, the superstar of a Sor Juana novel, more rococo than baroque, with the heft of two *Da Vinci Codes*. Titled *Hunger's Brides*, Anderson's book is structured as a double frame story, that is, a story within a story within a story. Sor Juana's is the interior story, which itself is framed by the contemporary story of Beulah Limosneros, a graduate student of Mexican descent (perhaps a Mexican Canadian or a Canadian Latina?) so obsessed with her research on Sor Juana that she disappears into Mexico for two years to indulge her archival obsession. Another layer of the framing story is narrated by Beulah's professor (first-person author's alter ego?) and erstwhile lover, Donald Gregory, who is forced into early retirement when he's accused of having an affair with his student and possibly even harming her. He must now wade through Beulah's journals, research notes, and an unfinished novelized biography that she had been writing on Sor Juana to vindicate himself and find out what really happened to Beulah. Why was she found bleeding in her apartment upon her return from Mexico City? Did the professor have anything to do with the violence perpetrated upon a woman whose name means Married Beggars? Although the frame story weaves in and out of the main narrative, which is Sor Juana's biographical story told in chronological order,[85] Sor Juana's poetry, fragments from her plays, and other baroque and ancient Greek poesies serve as interludes between the chapters, many translated by the brilliant B. Limosneros. There are also footnotes that show the range and depth of Beulah's erudition, though many are in the voice of the professor.

Anderson's Sor Juana, imagined as Beulah's Sor Juana, or rather as a Sor Juana steeped in the baroque shards of a disturbed Latina mind and distilled into clear narrative form by her forty-two-year-old retired, two-timing professor, is primarily a *hungry* Sor Juana: hungry for knowledge, hungry for freedom, hungry even for celebrity. She is so hungry, in fact, that rather than see herself as a bride of Christ, which her condition as a cloistered nun entails, her subjectivity is wedded to the absence of that which would satisfy her hunger, and thus, like a spiritual anorexic, she must deny herself sustenance of the soul in order to feed her "voracious hunger for learning."[86] Indeed, Sor Juana's very voraciousness is baroque, which Professor Gregory defines as "an era of monstrous vitality and tension, of florid camouflage and violent contradictions—of unbridled license and brutal censure. Of a craving that yields to disgust."[87] Joining a passion for myth with the irreverent scribblings of Sor Juana's own pen, and the nun's own research into Goddess and other arcane lore, Beulah's baroque musings on Sor Juana grow to engulf her completely in the same way that Sor Juana herself was engulfed by her own myth. It is Professor Gregory's task, then, to plumb his pupil's journals and figure out the puzzle of Beulah, the riddle of Sor Juana, and what truly became of them both.

One of the riddles that Beulah attempts to resolve is the question of why, at nineteen years of age, the prodigious lady-in-waiting Juana Inés Ramírez de Asbaje would resign her very promising worldly existence[88] and enclose herself in a convent for the rest of her life, subjected to the vows of poverty, chastity, obedience, and silence (none of which, I argue, she observed very devoutly). Underneath that riddle, which scholars from Dorothy Schons to Octavio Paz and beyond have attempted to discern for nearly a century, is an even more compelling question: Was Sor Juana being targeted by the Inquisition? Finding the answer to this question, it seems, becomes Beulah's raison d'être as well as the elusive smoke she chases into the mirrors of oblivion.

With all of Beulah's preoccupation with quantum physics at the beginning of the novel (the professor reproduces long sections of a research paper she wrote on the subject) and the use of Beulah's journals that reveal she was raised by her mother and her Spanish father's best friend after her natural father died in an accident, and with hints of sexual abuse the adoptive father perpetrated on her and the tendentious relationship with her mother, it becomes evident that Anderson's conceit is meant to establish a contemporary Sor Juana in the body of Beulah Limosneros and the historical Sor Juana that so obsesses her; indeed, the Hebrew word Beulah (which appears once in the Bible)[89] means "to be master of, or, to be married," and is used symbolically to indicate the sacred marriage of faith, of Christians to Christ, so perhaps the author's intent is to master/marry Sor Juana through Beulah, or to marry Beulah to Sor Juana. To intensify the quantum parallelism of their stories, both narratives are told in first person. Even the alleged abuse that Sor Juana intimates in her *Respuesta*, where she discusses the danger of allowing men to teach young girls, is reproduced in the sexual liaison that develops between Professor Gregory and his student.

But there are other quantum parallelisms that disturb me. Not between the character of Beulah and Sor Juana, but between *Hunger's Brides* and *Sor Juana's Second Dream*, which Paul Anderson tells me when we meet at the *Los Angeles Times* Book Festival on the UCLA campus in 2005 that he has not read, did not even realize it existed, he says. I tell him I find that hard to believe, as my book has been out since 1999, and I would imagine that writing a Sor Juana novel is so rare an endeavor that as a writer he would research whether or not there were any other novels on Sor Juana already published (as I did). Still, I must take him at his word. He knew not that *Sor Juana's Second Dream* existed. What, then, I wonder, accounts for the several similarities in our stories, not the details that can be confirmed by research into Sor Juana's life and times, but the parts that resonate too closely to the fictional aspects of my story? Quantum physics? Here are but a few of these resonances:

- The gift of a secretary who lives with Sor Juana, in my book named Concepción and given by a Mother Superior, in Anderson's, Antonia, given by the bishop of Santa Cruz—in both, a copyist whose good handwriting redeems Sor Juana's "masculine penmanship." An intriguing fact about Anderson's Antonia is that she hails from a village of refugee slaves called San Lorenzo de los Negros, the same village that Concepción's enslaved *cimarrona* friend, Aléndula, hails from and to which they escape in *Sor Juana's Second Dream*.

- Anderson's book also includes a Concepción, shown to be one of the Indian maids who live in Sor Juana's cell and who was devoted to Sor Juana. Perhaps Concepción is the name Anderson has given to Sor Juana's mulata slave, Juana de San José?

- The indigenous stories Juana Inés learned in her childhood in Panoayan, in my book told by a Mayan gardener, in Anderson's by a Nahua Indian woman named Xochitl.

- The mention of Plato's *Symposium*, in which Aristophanes explains what love is by expounding upon the legend of the three sexes, the male-male, the female-female, and the male-female, who were split by Zeus when they grew too arrogant, and were destined for eternity to look for their other half. Compare:

    ◦ Anderson: "Plato's *Symposium* was another such night, another such dream. . . . The guests Plato has assembled are to make speeches in praise of love. As the others discourse, Aristophanes sits silent until Socrates enjoins him to speak . . . To this challenge and this banquet we owe a lovely legend of the sexes. You see, first there were three: male, female, and hermaphrodite . . . it is from this third sex that we are descended, says Aristophanes, as can be plainly seen in our lurching about half our lives in search of our lost half."[90]

    ◦ Gaspar de Alba: "But it was Aristophanes' definition that nearly choked Juana Inés, for . . . once upon a time . . . there had been three sexes: Man was composed of two male bodies, Woman of two female bodies, and Man-Woman, or the Androgynous One, was made of a male and a female . . . Forevermore, Man, Woman, and Man-Woman have searched for their other half, and this, said Aristophanes, this pursuit and desire for wholeness was what constituted Love. . . . Fantastic as Aristophanes' story seemed, at least it explained the origin of her feelings, at least it brought her desire out of the deep mire of shame in which she'd been wallowing for more than a year. And yet, she realized that la Marquesa was not her other half, for if Aristophanes was right, when the two halves met, they *recognized* [emphasis added] each other and clung to each other and tried to become one again."[91]

- The coded reference to the masculine woman known as "la Monja Alférez," or the "Lieutenant Nun," Catalina de Erauso, the famous female-to-male cross-dresser of colonial New Spain who wrote a memoir about her life that showed she had been both a good woman (meaning she retained her virginity) and a good man (meaning she protected the interests of the Spanish Crown), which earned her the privilege of living the rest of her days in whatever gender she chose.[92] Lieutenant Nun is referenced in dialogue in my book, and in Anderson's story as a play that Juana attends while living with her aunt and uncle in Mexico City; in both stories, it serves as an allegory for Sor Juana's unspoken lesbianism.
- Sor Juana's Sapphic diary, or "Pandora's Box," in *Sor Juana's Second Dream*, and the nun's "Sapphic Hymns" in *Hunger's Brides*, both "lost" to posterity (or rather, invented by their authors).
- The epistolary sections, especially Sor Juana's letters to La Condesa, by which the intimacy of their relationship unfolds.
- The trial that Sor Juana undergoes in front of the Tribunal of the Inquisition, which is completely a product of my imagination in *Sor Juana's Second Dream*, and yet reappears in Anderson's novel, structured as a screenplay depicting the forty days of Sor Juana's confession to Padre Antonio ordered by the Inquisition. We also see an Inquisitorial prosecutor named Dorantes in both books.
- In *Sor Juana's Second Dream*, as part of his Machiavellian plot to entrap Sor Juana at the time of her Silver Jubilee, the archbishop assigns Padre Antonio, in his capacity as Chief Censor for the Holy Inquisition, to go to Sor Juana's cell and make an inventory of any and all banned books that might be in her library. A similar inventory is requisitioned by Master Examiner Dorantes in Anderson's novel.
- The narration of Sor Juana's final demise of the unnamed disease plaguing the convent, written as a diary by Sor Juana's duplicitous niece, Belilla, in my novel, and as a journal by Sor Juana's duplicitous secretary, Antonia, in Anderson's.
- The strained relationship between Padre Antonio, the viceregal court's father confessor, and this recalcitrant lady-in-waiting, in whom he perceives not only a great talent, but also a great temptation that he would be required to quell by incarcerating her in a convent. Here is an

example of a "confession" that Juana Inés, while still at court, makes in both novels; in mine, the confession is secret, addressed to but never shared with Padre Antonio. In Anderson's book, the confession takes place in the palace chapel, after Padre Antonio comes upon the weeping and distraught *doncella*. Her description, in Padre Antonio's point of view, from *Hunger's Brides*:

- ○ Anderson: "Her skin, already pale, was ashen, the more so in contrast to her black hair. Her large eyes, black in the dim candlelight, were wide, filled with tears and what seemed, from where I stood, like horror. . . . The child spoke of an evil that followed her everywhere, saw visions of a black beast that stalked her, dogging her every step."[93]

- ○ Juana Inés's confession in *Sor Juana's Second Dream* is structured as a letter she writes just before the tournament with the forty professors, addressed to Padre Antonio, in which the girl scholar admits to an "ugliness" that she cannot name or talk about but that is aroused in her whenever she is in the vicereine's presence. "Punish me as you would punish the vilest sinner, but do not make me say this to you. Pull out my tongue, Padre, poke out my eyes, lock me up in a convent."[94] After burning the confession over the flame of a candle, Juana Inés looks in the mirror and sees how pale and frail she looks. "She knew that the pallor of her face and her red-rimmed eyes and quivering voice betrayed her, made her seem the vapid, frightened girl whom the professors had come to patronize or to embarrass."[95] As the tournament gets under way, the narrative trifurcates between the professors' questions and Juana Inés's answers and an inner monologue in which she continues her confession to Padre Antonio: "*Bless me, Father, for I cannot keep from sinning, deep and terrible sins that flourish like poisoned mushrooms in my dreams.*" It is in this private confession that we learn the true nature (the first anagnorisis of the novel) of this "sin," this "ugliness" that she hopes a cloistered life in the convent will veil if not remove: her desire for another woman, Leonor Carreto de Mancera, the vicereine. "*There is love in my heart, Father, but it is a vile love, an unnatural, unnameable love, and yet, so deep, so pure it feels almost holy.*"[96]

- • In Anderson's novel, Juana Inés's sin is the girl's penchant not just for learning but also for gnosticism and Egyptian goddess worship.

Anderson's Juana Inés is a secret devotee of Isis, whose dark aspect she sees reincarnated in the Virgin of Guadalupe. Indeed, it is through her epistolary friendship with Don Carlos (though Anderson lets us read only his letters to her, and not vice versa) that we learn of the ways she has occulted pagan ideology within her seemingly Christian writings, such as in her play *Divine Narcissus*, which, Sigüenza y Góngora warns her, borders on heretical ideas sure to raise the eyebrows and interests of the Inquisition. In the private diary of her Pandora's Box in my novel, Sor Juana writes observations of a lunar eclipse that not only gives her the conceit for *Primero sueño* but also shows the nun's knowledge of arcane goddess lore:

○ Gaspar de Alba: "Clearly, the moon is Athena, and the lunar eclipse is also her eclipse . . . The moon is the goddess incarnate. To be sentenced to darkness is to live eternally in the presence of the goddess. Is darkness, then, a punishment or a reward? . . . If . . . my soul were to take flight through the diaphanous spiral of the skies, it would be a foot soldier in Athena's army, its quest to uncover the moon and release her light again over the night."[97]

One of the most troubling similarities I find between my novel and *Hunger's Brides* is the spiritual break that takes place between Sor Juana and her father confessor. In *Sor Juana's Second Dream*, I've borrowed from an undated letter of Sor Juana's titled "Carta de la Madre Juana Inés de la Cruz a el R. P. M. Antonio Núñez de Miranda de la Compañía de Jesús." The letter was discovered in 1980 by Sorjuanista scholar Father Aureliano Tapia Méndez in a folio of colonial documents housed in the library of the Archdiocese of Monterrey in Mexico; the document was studied, authenticated and dated to 1680, and published as *Autodefensa espiritual de Sor Juana Inés de la Cruz*.[98] In this letter, Sor Juana dares to denounce Núñez de Miranda for the sundry ways in which he has maligned her name and sought to subjugate and oppress her God-given free will, and actually dismisses him as her father confessor. To depict this key moment in Sor Juana's life, I have borrowed lines verbatim from this "*autodefensa espiritual*" and interpolated them as lines of the letter that she is dictating to her amanuensis, Concepción. In *Hunger's Brides*, the scene is constructed as a face-to-face confrontation between Sor Juana and Padre Antonio, the verbatim lines from Sor Juana's letter interpolated into an angry dialogue between the two. This may not be a novel idea, the integration of primary materials into a fictional account to structure a scene of critical importance to Sor Juana's life, but the parallelism (quantum physics?) of the two scenes is more than resonant.

As already mentioned, Juana's sin in *Hunger's Brides*, the "evil" that Padre Antonio perceives in her even as a young lady-in-waiting in the viceregal palace, is her pagan veneration for the occult and particularly for the occult power of women such as Isis, the Virgin of Guadalupe, and Malintzin Tenepal. Among these, of course, is Sor Juana herself, to whom Beulah ascribes the identity of "psychic masochist," one more in the long line of psychoanalytic theories devised to explain the paradoxes of Sor Juana: "theories of psychosis, narcissism, lesbianism, masochism and even penis-envy [that] account for Sor Juana's prodigious hungers and accomplishments."[99] For Beulah, then, the notion that Sor Juana may have been a lesbian is as ludicrous as her having penis envy, though the attributes of a psychic masochist seem to fit Beulah better than Sor Juana. Still, Anderson uses the word "lesbian" in its modern application throughout the novel, and he makes multiple references to some scandalous "Sapphic Hymns" that Sor Juana is said to be writing. Indeed, Book III of *Hunger's Brides* is titled "Sappho," and shows the intimate friendship between Sor Juana and La Condesa de Paredes, which coincides with the years that mark Sor Juana's apogee as New Spain's most famous and celebrated poet, 1680–1690. The section in my novel that deals with this intimate friendship and the rise of Sor Juana's celebrity is called "The Onyx Queen" and covers the years 1680–1688.

In "The Onyx Queen," I develop the Sapphic love story between Sor Juana and La Condesa, covering all of the significant events that transpired in Sor Juana's life between 1680 and 1688, which I've embellished with Sor Juana's leaving the convent to attend her mother's funeral in Panoayan, and her overnight stay at La Condesa's house upon her return to the convent, with niece Belilla in tow. After dinner, Belilla and La Condesa retire for the evening, leaving Sor Juana and Don Tomás (the former viceroy) to enjoy each other's company over several bottles of wine. The evening ends with a sexual consummation of the two women's mutual desires. At the close of that section, the viceroy and vicereine bid farewell to Sor Juana as they prepare for their departure back to Spain. La Condesa insists on taking with her copies of all of Sor Juana's writings, which she plans on compiling into a book.

It is this first book to which La Condesa gave the elaborate and allegorical title of *Inundación castálida de la única poetisa, musa décima, Sóror Juana Inés de la Cruz, religiosa profesa en el monasterio de*

San Gerónimo de la imperial ciudad de México, que en varios metros, idiomas, y estilos, fertiliza varios assumptos; con elegantes, sutiles, claros, ingeniosos, útiles versos: para enseñanza, recreo, y admiración.[100] After the subtitle describing the different styles, languages, themes, and uses of the poetry, the title continues into the florid dedication to Her Excellency, Doña María Luisa Manrique de Lara, clearly acknowledging La Condesa's role in bringing the book to light. The adjective *"castálida"* refers to the sacred fountain Castalia, consecrated to the Muses and located near Apollo's temple in Delphi. As Sor Juana has been baptized the "Tenth Muse" and "Only Poetess" of Mexico by La Condesa, then it is Sor Juana's poetic verse that makes the Muses' fountain overflow, hence, the *Inundación castálida*, or Castalian Inundation, of the title.

In *Hunger's Brides*, Sor Juana refers to the book as "our daughter, Castalia," meaning the intellectual offspring of Sor Juana and La Condesa; thus, Anderson makes of their relationship a productive "Beulah land," or marriage union, a tacit lesbian motherhood of two hungry brides, though the word "brides" presupposes the presence of a "husband," and hence constitutes a relational identity between a man (Anderson, perhaps, in the character of the professor?) and a woman (Sor Juana?).

In *Sor Juana's Second Dream*, commenting in her diary on how she feels upon holding her first book, Sor Juana writes: "Now I understand a mother's pride in her firstborn, how she must hold it constantly, stare at it, caress it, wonder at its presence, for surely this is the product of the fertile loins of my own mind and La Condesa's persistence, which was, in truth, the instrument of delivery."[101]

But Anderson, too, was wrestling with the ghost of Octavio Paz, which he depicts at one point as Professor Gregory musing on how Beulah pushes Octavio Paz to go "beyond the limits of good taste"[102] (assuming that a discussion of lesbianism is perhaps in bad taste?). The professor concedes the following points about Sor Juana's sexual identity:

In the past half-century, much has been made of Sor Juana's emotional instability, and more recently of her sexual orientation, or orientations . . . Her writings refract and redouble facets of her sexual persona. Donning poetic masks by turns ironic, allusive, and sincere, the author variously portrays the 'I' of her verses as essentially male in her rationality, as virgin and therefore sexless, as a woman transformed into a man by Isis (the etymology of Isis in turn being *doubly man*), as a disembodied soul in amorous rapture, as double-sexed, as hermaphrodite, androgynous . . . And still the fact remains that Sor Juana's most impassioned and erotic poems have other women for their object. To lesbianism, Paz proposes an alternative reading; passionate but platonic; whereas in Pfandl's account, Beulah finds Sor Juana's fall describing a long-charted trajectory: from the inversions of Sapphism to a libidinal leap into the mythic abyss of mania, depression, and paranoia . . . The sympathetic reader will perhaps see how desperate to refute Pfandl's diagnosis, hating herself for feeling its temptations, Beulah would find it increasingly difficult to resist a martyrology.[103]

After several pages discussing Beulah's growing obsession with Octavio Paz, however, we are made privy to the unraveling of Beulah's mind as each new letter she writes to Paz becomes increasingly incoherent, so that whatever cogent meditations she might have been writing regarding Sor Juana's sexuality degenerate into psychobabble:

> Hunger is sex hunger is love hunger is rage it's revolting . . . Hunger is love but they build a wall around it. It's behind the wall they say but the wall's too high to see over too smooth to climb. How do I know it's behind the wall I can't FEEL it PLEASE—We promise! It's there we told you—have faith—but how do I get over it?[104]

Using the point of view of the unreliable narrator, the babbling Beulah, whose work is being interpreted by Professor Gregory, a nonspecialist on Sor Juana, as obsessed with Beulah as she is with Sor Juana, Paul Anderson never really answers the question (shall we call it a riddle?) of Sor Juana's sexuality, and thus avoids being accused of having created a Sapphic Sor Juana at the same time that he has indulged his male authority in the Sapphic language play of the Tenth Muse.

Perhaps the most disquieting of parallelisms between my novel and Anderson's is the appearance of a foreign spy, an allegorical device I added to my narrative as a way of planting an undercover subjectivity that serves as a mirror to both Sor Juana and myself (the anagnorisis of his deceit gets the spy sentenced to the gallows). In my book, he is a Dutch artist named Jorge de Alba who accompanies Archbishop Fray Payo on a visit to Sor Juana's locutory, and who will be in charge of fleshing out artistically the images of the triumphal arch that Sor Juana has described in great detail in her *Neptuno alegórico*, which the Church council commissioned from her to welcome the new viceroy and vicereine to their realm in New Spain. In the course of their conversation, Don Jorge equates Sor Juana with the cross-dressing Catalina de Erauso, the notorious Lieutenant Nun, and intimates his own queer identification with the nun's veiled identity. Later it turns out that he is none other than the Flemish spy known as "El Tapado," the Cloaked One, condemned to hang for his treason against the king of Spain.

Imagine my surprise when I find a foreign spy in *Hunger's Brides*, one French viscount, whose secret mission in New Spain is to "buy" Sor Juana as well as her close friend, Don Carlos de Sigüenza y Góngora, for the French court. In the scene where Don Carlos brings the viscount to visit Sor Juana in her locutory, the three discourse at length about a new literature that has blossomed in France, women's literature, the viscount calls it, of whom the most notorious and brilliant example is one Madeleine de Scudéry. The viscount relates that she is known as Sappho in France because of her erudition and popularity; he then proceeds to correlate one Sappho to another by noting that in New Spain, Sor Juana is called "the tenth muse," Plato's allusion to Sappho. It seems this de Scudéry has even written a book in which Sappho is the protagonist, and is said to be the daughter of an androgynous entity. "To her discerning readers, it's very clear that all creators—humanity really, not just artists, *sont au fond bisexués*," says the viscount. To which Don Carlos guffaws, though Sor Juana encourages the viscount to go further, seeing in his performance a sly probing to learn of Sor Juana's own sexual inclinations. The viscount waxes poetic about de Scudéry's artistry in transforming "even the basest of passions—the insatiate inversions *du sapphisme*—into pure elegance. The signs are all there for those willing to probe a little—Louis would never stand for open talk of *l'amour lesbien*."[105]

Apparently, Anderson's foreign spy serves a similar purpose in *Hunger's Brides*, for he is the tool through which the subject of Sor Juana's lesbian identity is broached to the reader, presenting the mirror of this Madame de Scudéry in which Sor Juana can see her Sapphic face. Leaving aside that the word *lesbian*, as a derivative of Lesbos (the island associated with Sappho) was not coined until the twentieth century, and that the term "Sapphism" or "Sapphic" was not used as a qualifier to connote female-to-female desire (part of the poetic license of novelists is the anachronistic turn of phrase) until the nineteenth century, this dialogue suggests that one of Sor Juana's unrequited hungers is, indeed, her lesbian desire, but to be too direct about it would perhaps be in bad taste, the kind of "grotesque and debased" behavior that aroused the Holy Inquisition. Hence, the teasing occlusion of Sor Juana's sexual identity in *Hunger's Brides*.

It is not just in content that Anderson's novel mirrors *Sor Juana's Second Dream* but in structure as well. The weaving of the historical figure's original poetry and other writings with the fictional narrative is a standard feature of historical novels; however, the selections chosen and the way the content in Anderson's book echoes the content in mine is a little too close for comfort. As we learn on the *Hunger's Brides* website:

> *Hunger's Brides* establishes the Inquisition as a spectre hovering ever near, from the earliest days of Sor Juana's life until its last. It emerges that *Sor Juana's chapters are the telling of her life story in response to and rebellion against a demand that she give a full accounting of her every sin* [emphasis added]. There must be no gaps, her interrogator insists. But her story is fashioned precisely here, in the gaps between the warp of her sins and the weave of her destiny.[106]

Ostensibly, then, the "essential story" framed within the 1,357 pages of *Hunger's Brides*, and between the covers of the 736-page abridged version, *Sor Juana, Or, The Breath of Heaven* (sans notes), like the bulk of *Sor Juana's Second Dream*, constitutes Sor Juana's General Confession that the Tribunal of the Inquisition required that she submit as part of the process of renewing her vocation as a bride of Christ in the Order of Saint Jerome. In the "Prologue" to *Sor Juana's Second Dream*, which I have structured to mirror the first scene in *Macbeth* where the three witches, in my novel dressed as three priests, come together to cast their hex over Sor Juana, the public confession in front of the Tribunal of the Inquisition is the "something wicked [that] this way comes," the denouement toward which the plot of the book moves chronologically in Sor Juana's life from 1664, when she was first taken to the palace as a lady-in-waiting, to 1694, when she renewed her vows in blood.

An even more interesting formal resemblance is the conceit of a chess game to structure the representation of Sor Juana's defeat. "The [section] titles in Gaspar de Alba's *Sor Juana's Second Dream*," writes Paul Allatson in his 2004 review of the novel, "are drawn from the game of chess, and proceed from the Fianchetto opening gambit to Middle and Endgames, before the final, Inquisitional Check and Mate. This organizing principle . . . serves as a salutary reminder that the task of textual-sexual revision presents particular hazards with regard to Sor Juana."[107] Not only is Sor Juana in danger from the outset of the book, posits Allatson, but perhaps I, too, as the author, am risking the "particular hazards" of censorship and other forms of textual marginalization that might come my way as a result of lesbianizing the venerated figure of Sor Juana.

In this chess game between Sor Juana and the Church Fathers, the bishops—Archbishop Aguiar y Seijas and the bishop of Puebla—make their first move in the "Fianchetto," using Sor Juana's father confessor, Padre Antonio, as their Bishop's Pawn. The subsequent parts show the correspondence of her life to the different stages of the game: "Castling" when she goes to live at the viceregal court as lady-in-waiting to La Marquesa de Mancera; "The Middlegame," which covers her early years in the convent of San Jerónimo; the love story between Sor Juana and La Condesa de Paredes in "The Onyx Queen," and the beginning of the three ending "actos" of Sor Juana's life: "The Endgame," which covers her attack on Vieyra, her remonstrance from and response to Sor Filotea de la Cruz, as well as the publication of her first collected works in Spain; "Check," which returns to the three bishops poised to entrap her in 1693, the year before her Silver Jubilee; and finally, "Mate," after she's renounced her writing, given away her books, and submitted to the Church by way of a General Confession, renewing her vows in blood, and surrendering her life to the plague that was infecting the convent.

Marion Rohrleitner, in "Recovering Afro-Mestizaje in Contemporary Latina/Chicana Historical Fiction," notes that "Fianchetto is a chess opening in which the mobility and power of the bishop is privileged over that of the knight."[108] To underscore the deviousness of the bishops, the original cover for the novel, a colored pencil drawing titled *Sor Juana* (1999), which I commissioned from Chilean artist Liliana Wilson before my novel was published, showed Sor Juana seated at her desk in front of a chessboard, while behind her in the doorway to her cell, a mitred bishop stood with the staff of Inquisitional power with which he would bludgeon Sor Juana into submission.[109] In the black-and-white version of the drawing that we see in Figure 7.2, the mitered bishop is shown as the duplicitous masked bishop hiding his identity behind the pseudonymous Sor Filotea, who conspired with the nun's father confessor and the archbishop to orchestrate the "Fianchetto" that finally checkmated Sor Juana.

We see Paul Anderson employing a similar organizing principle of a chess game in the title to the final subsection of Book III of *Hunger's Brides*, "Bishops and Queens," in which Sor Juana becomes aware that everything from the bishop of Puebla inciting her to write down her critique of Vieyra's Sermon to the General Confession has been a

Figure 7.2. Liliana Wilson, *Sor Juana*, © 1998. Lead pencil on paper, 12 x 12 in. Used by permission of the artist.

stratagem in a chess game orchestrated by the Church Fathers to cut the Tenth Muse down to size. "A bishop blocks a priest, a vice-queen holds an archbishop in check. Then she leaves, the bishop wants promotion, it all collapses."[110]

Since the entire structure of *Sor Juana's Second Dream* is based on a chess game between Sor Juana (represented by the onyx queen in my novel) and her three male antagonists, Padre Antonio, the bishop of Santa Cruz, and Archbishop Aguiar y Seijas, I remain highly skeptical of the quantum physics that I am supposed to believe accounts for the similarities in these two (and, I think, only) published English-language Sor Juana novels.

Rather than a disidentificatory or revolutionary project, *Hunger's Brides*, for all its poesy, is yet another example of the colonial white male imaginary's catholic appropriation of resources that he mined for content but did not feel the need to credit or acknowledge. Anderson's Sor Juana, it turns out, married to two long-winded interlocutors, Beulah and the professor, is hungry only for her own voice.

La Segunda Vez Rebelde

A fascinating thing happened to me when I learned of Octavio Paz's passing. I felt a little sad, like I had lost a member of my family, a great-uncle several times removed but a relative nonetheless. And then I figured it out. The source of my sadness was this: he wasn't going to be around to read my novel on Sor Juana, to enter her psyche, not from his magisterial Mexican perspective, but from the perspective of a Chicana lesbian (read: polluted Mexican female in the extreme) who shared with Sor Juana the several subjectivities that he staunchly refused to grant her in his biography—that of a woman-identified, woman-loving, woman-defending lesbian feminist who believed to the death in her innate right to choose her own destiny and to exercise her inmost desires, be they to write, to study, to challenge the patriarchs of her day to a tournament of minds, or, simply, to fantasize about making love to another woman. That fantasy, I argue, was Sor Juana's female symbolic, her language of desire rooted in her veiled, cloistered, hidden lesbian body. I recognize it. I vouch for the lesbian mind and heart of Sor Juana.

Because Sor Juana's experience as an outlawed lesbian body was written out of Mexican history, it has been my self-imposed mission to rescue that story from the cracks and fissures of the master narratives of the Sorjuanista colonial imaginary. In the cosmic chess game that I employ as the architecture for *Sor Juana's Second Dream*, Sor Juana loses the game of her life but wins the battle between her heart and her mind. By isolating those poems and phrases from her prose that Sor Juana left as testaments to her lesbian desire, by creating fictive letters and journal entries in which we see the *second dream* of her true self, by weaving a third-person narrative perspective with Sor Juana's first-person voice, I have pulled Sor Juana's lesbian identity out of the closet of the colonial imaginary. "The Onyx Queen" is not just an allusion to a chess piece, but to the Dark Queen that Sor Juana herself wrote about in *Primero sueño*, symbol of the warrior goddess of nightly passions—the Moon—who battles with (and ultimately loses to) the bright harbinger of reason—

the Sun. As Luis Harss says in his annotated translation of this most cryptic of Sor Juana's works: this figure is the "Queen of Night—the dark questioner," who, although driven off by the rays of Helios, or rather the enlightened rationality of sunrise, "remains in the wings, awaiting her chance to bloom again."[111]

In *Sor Juana's Second Dream*, it isn't only the imaginary documents that speak for themselves, but also, the poems and sentences that Sor Juana wrote with such grace and clarity about who she was, what she believed, and what she did and did not want to do with her life, her mind, her body, and her tongue. Unlike the outcome of Dorothy Schons's *Chronicle of Old Mexico*, Estela Portillo Trambley's *Sor Juana*, Paul Anderson's *Hunger's Brides*, or even Sor Juana's *Primero sueño*, in my *Second Dream*, the Onyx Queen, the Queen of Night that Sor Juana names "*la segunda vez rebelde*," and whom Luis Harss calls "the rebel Empress who retains her power over 'the dark half of the globe'"[112]— indeed "blooms again." To me, this *segunda vez rebelde*, this second-dream rebel, is the trope Sor Juana invented to name her lesbian desire, the anagnorisis of the poem, and in this perhaps "impossible dream," it is the dark forces of her rebellious passion that triumph over "el Mundo iluminado" of male enlightenment by which Sor Juana has been constructed as a mind devoid of a body. In this way, *Sor Juana's Second Dream* is a counterpoint to both *Primero sueño* and the colonial imaginary interpretations of Sor Juana's life. By filtering Sor Juana's *First Dream* through a Chicana lesbian feminist optic that draws on pre-Columbian symbols of feminine empowerment, I see the work as a baroque version of the Coyolxauhqui story, in which the forces of the sun god, Apollo/Huitzilopochtli, or the masculine world of rationality, vanquish the dark armies of the Moon goddess, Athena/Coyolxauhqui, or the occult world of the divine Feminine. In my novel, I wanted Sor Juana to have a "second dream," a reversal of the first; rather than the god of the Sun cutting his sister's head off and chopping her to pieces (the Aztec version of that eternal battle of the sexes), I wanted the Moon goddess, Sor Juana's "Queen of Night," to be the victor. Instead of the eye of reason opening and thus occluding the rebel forces of passion, as happened at the end of *Primero sueño*, I opened Sor Juana's third eye, what Anzaldúa calls the "reptilian eye" of her *conocimiento*, or rather, her sexual awakening. I wanted to show the triumph of passion over reason, the secret, lesbian passion that she braided so eloquently into her love poems, the "sweet fiction for which [she] happily died / beautiful illusion for which [she] painfully lived."[113]

Borrowing the double entendre that Sor Juana signed in her own blood upon renewing her vows to the convent a year before she died, Alma López, in Figure 7.1, synthesizes the essence of Sor Juana's coded nickname into a layered image of Chicana/Mexicana oppositional consciousness. In honor of Sor Juana, López constructs a genealogy of iconic "worst of all" women, which includes the prolific Sor Juana, passing her quill to the Chicana feminist/lesbian revolutionary, the activist who wields the weapon of her art and her education, and Coyolxauhqui, the warrior goddess in the background. The unifying resemblance they all share is their noncooperation with patriarchal gender dictates about what constitutes a "good woman."

In Figure 7.3, *Mujer de Mucha Enagua, Pa' Ti, Xicana*, Yreina Cervantez constructs a similar revolutionary genealogy for Chicanas, connecting the Zapatista struggles for autonomy, embodied by the indigenous revolutionary mother and activist, with Sor Juana's feminist struggle for equality and the right to self-expression. The artist's own hand in the middle of the picture represents the bridge between criolla, mestiza, and *indígena* as much as between activism, history, and art—a combination that contributes to the "mucha enagua," or power of women. "Una mujer de mucha enagua, a woman with a lot of petticoat, is comparable to the idea of a person with a lot of strength, a person that is empowered,"[114] by self-love and revolutionary love for the courageous, creative, and transcendent women in her culture.

As a first-generation, Mexican-descended poet, novelist, and academic, I place myself in the intellectual genealogical tree of Sor Juana Inés de la Cruz, and, knighted by poetic license, I authorized myself to bring our "décima musa, poetisa americana, fénix de México," out of the epistemological ashes of the closet. In an age when there was no word to attach to her identity, Sor Juana Inés de la Cruz could only identify through her desire, through her discourse, and through her rebellion. "If this is a sin," she writes, "I confess it, / if a crime, I must avow it; / the one thing I cannot do / is repent and disallow it."[115] Indeed, I, too, confess my sin, avow my crime of having committed Sor Juana's life and body to the lesbian archives. I remain unrepentant in my *re-conocimiento*. Somehow, however, I don't think she'll mind, and I don't think she'll sue me for having snuck into the pages of her imaginary Sapphic diary and copied the following:

> I remember how my mind seemed to separate from me, like a yolk from the egg white, and how in my imagination I watched my hands and mouth

Figure 7.3. Yreina D. Cervantez, *Mujer de Mucha Enagua, Pa' Ti, Xicana,* © 1999. Serigraph (SHG), 22 x 30 in. Used by permission of the artist.

demonstrate the knowledge of my desire, as if I have always known what to do to another woman's body. Is it the harmony of our sex, the fact that we are both women, that gives me this knowledge? Or is it an epistemology long buried in my bones, a knowledge I was born with?[116]

When *Sor Juana's Second Dream* hits the silver screen in Mexico in the next couple of years, under the title *Juana de Asbaje*, the title role played by Mexican actress par excellence Ana de la Reguera, how will that innate lesbian *re-conocimiento* of Sor Juana's be enacted and received? Will the audience recognize her, I wonder, as "their" Sor Juana, the intellectual "madre" they use as currency in their daily lives, the second most important cultural symbol of Mexico next to La Virgen de Guadalupe? I think Sor Juana would appreciate the poetic irony of this resignification of her life through the New World quill of a Chicana lesbian author-academic.

"Óyeme con los ojos," she said in a poem, inviting me to listen to her with my eyes, to know her with my tongue, to "breathe a new spirit into [her]," with my lips and words. Imagine me, and I exist, she says. *In lak'ech. Ala k'in.*

Figure e.1. Annie Valva, *Making Waves*, © 1992. Black-and-white photo of Gloria Anzaldúa, Santa Cruz, CA.

To Your Shadow-Beast: In Memoriam
(for Gloria E. Anzaldúa, 1942–2004)

You loved water
as only a cactus or a campesina
bred on the thirsty earth
of South Texas
can love water.

Everyone knows about your kinship
with the Goddess,
the One of many names
and the nameless one you called
the Shadow-Beast.

You traded dirty secrets with Tlatzolteotl,
swapped *nopalito* recipes with Tonantzin,
re-membered body parts with Coyolxauhqui
and borrowed shadows from Cihuacoatl.
La Llorona gave you voice lessons.

You were Yemayá's child.
In white shirt and blue jeans you laugh
Into the camera, frolic in the waves, at one
with the element foaming around your knees.
You walk into the holy cross of the Pacific
gathering conch shells and sea horses
for the secret lover that dwells within.

Once, the tepid tide of the Gulf of Mexico
drew you down into its green depths
and you were reborn in the corpus of the Goddess.

Oshún, too, claimed you.
Mother of the sacred cave where desire
flames into words, where words become flesh
and flesh becomes the dark Goddess of Love,
it was her crescent moon that throbbed in your cunt,
turning pain into amber, blood into gold
in the fiery gush of your *tres lenguas*.

Some say you had thunderbolts in your eyes,
but it was just Changó sparking your warrior spirit
the same way Coatlicue tested
your Facultad and forked your tongue.

Straddler of rivers, you bridged
the dark brown currents of the Rio Grande,
the two-fold consciousness of eagle and serpent,
the split in the psyche between English and Spanish,
between Texas and California.

When I met you for the first time in Iowa City,
your *tejana* accent and Náhuatl vision
your Virgen de Guadalupe earrings
brought me home to that *frontera*
I had abandoned like an old lover.

You moved the margins to the middle,
the border to the cordillera of my own spine
and taught me what it means to be a *fronteriza*.
Lover of trees, you spoke
to rattlesnakes and watermelons,
the red and black of Eleguá
guiding you at every *cruzada*.

Nepantlera de aquellas,
you have joined Sor Juana, La Malinche, and Isis
on the black lacquered boat of the dead,
your last passage on the water
where the toll to *el otro mundo*
is paid with the left hand.

NOTES

Preface

1. In this piece, I combined and expanded on two previously published short personal essays. See Alicia Gaspar de Alba, "Crop Circles in the Cornfield" and "How the CARA Exhibition Saved My Academic Career." The structure of the piece is modeled on Gloria Anzaldúa's "Speaking in Tongues: A Letter to 3rd World Women Writers."

2. See Chmaj, "A Decade of Déja Vu."

3. Anzaldúa, "Border arte: Nepantla," 110. *Nepantla* is a Nahuatl word that means "place in the middle," like the Midwest. It is also the name of the town just outside of Mexico City where Sor Juana Inés de la Cruz was born in 1648.

4. Anzaldúa, *Borderlands*/La Frontera, 39.

5. Ibid., 78–79.

6. Of course, I wouldn't have survived even the nine months without the queer *familia* that welcomed and sustained me with great food, laughter, and stimulating discussions from the political to the absurd. *Gracias* to Rusty, Papusa, Tina, Luis (Fefita), Liliana, Sara, Raúl (La Bruja), Virginia, Bridget, Alexis, and my Italian roommate, Maria.

7. Anzaldúa, "Speaking in Tongues," 173.

8. Kerber, "Diversity," 421.

9. Davis, "Politics of American Studies," 370.

10. Anzaldúa, "Haciendo caras," xxv.

11. See Mechling, "If They Can Build A Square Tomato."

12. Orwell, "Politics and the English Language," 92.

13. For more about this discovery of my border Chicana identity, see Gaspar de Alba, "Literary Wetback" in *La Llorona on the Longfellow Bridge*, 40–43.

14. *CARA* was the acronym for the exhibition titled *Chicano Art: Resistance and Affirmation, 1965–1985.* My dissertation focused on the Chicano Art Movement and the politics of multiculturalism in the museum world at the time of the Columbus Quincentennial.

15. To see a picture of the supposedly mainstream "house of popular culture studies," see the cover of *The Popular Culture Reader*, 3rd ed., edited by Christopher

D. Geist and Jack Nachbar (Bowling Green, OH: Bowling Green University Popular Press, 1983).

16. The *CARA* archives are now housed in the UCLA Chicano Studies Research Center Archives. It was one of the research initiatives I spearheaded when I served as associate director of the CSRC from 2002 to 2004.

17. Native Americans were in on the Quincentennial action as well, as protest and counternarrative to the prevailing euphemisms of "discovery," "exchange," or "encounter" between Europeans and the indigenous peoples they conquered, colonized, dispossessed, and killed off. See Smith, "Outside and Against the Quincentenary."

18. Along with Cherríe Moraga, Gloria Anzaldúa edited *This Bridge Called My Back: Writings by Radical Women of Color*, now considered "the bible" of Chicana and Third World feminisms. In 2002, she coedited a follow-up text with AnaLouise Keating, titled *This Bridge We Call Home: Radical Visions for Transformation*. And in 2000, AnaLouise Keating edited a volume called *Gloria Anzaldúa: Interviews/ Entrevistas*. Gloria also published two children's books: *Friends from the Other Side/ Amigos del Otro Lado* and *La Prietita y La Llorona/Prietita and the Ghost Woman* (Emeryville, CA: Children's Book Press, 1993 and 1995 respectively).

19. Anzaldúa, "Speaking in Tongues," 170.

20. See Gaspar de Alba, *Chicano Art Inside/Outside the Master's House.*

21. See Chapter 4 of my *Chicano Art* book.

22. In spring quarter 1993, nine protesters (six of them students) waged a two-week hunger strike in front of the administration building to garner more administrative support and resources for Chicana and Chicano Studies at UCLA, the outcome of which was a new academic unit, a CII, or Center for Interdisciplinary Instruction, that would function like a department in everything but name. In 2005, the CII earned its stripes as a department, and in 2007, the department was named in honor of César E. Chávez.

23. Anzaldúa, "Speaking in Tongues," 172–173.

24. While I was working on this piece, Chavela Vargas, another icon of the Mexicana/Chicana/Latina lesbian world, died on August 5, 2012, at the age of ninety-three. A few days later, tatiana de la tierra, militant lesbian poet and lover of women, also passed into spirit.

25. Anzaldúa, "Speaking in Tongues," 169.

Introduction

1. See Gaspar de Alba, *Sor Juana's Second Dream*; *Desert Blood: The Juárez Murders*; *Calligraphy of the Witch.*

2. See Gaspar de Alba, *Chicano Art Inside/Outside the Master's House*; *Velvet Barrios*; Gaspar de Alba with Georgina Guzmán, *Making a Killing*; Gaspar de Alba and Alma López, *Our Lady of Controversy.*

3. See Foucault, *The Order of Things*, 17–44.

4. Hall, "New Ethnicities," in *Stuart Hall: Critical Dialogues*, 446.

5. Ibid., 447; emphasis in original.

6. Ibid.

7. Ibid., 443.

8. In 1963–1964, five years after I was born, the hundred-year-old border dispute between Mexico and the United States was settled by the Chamizal Treaty. To stabilize the course of the Rio Grande/Río Bravo, the Chamizal Convention isolated 796.5 acres of land along the El Paso–Juárez border, 193.2 of which were transferred to the United States, and 603.3 to Mexico. It is the only piece of "el Norte," lost to the United States in the Treaty of Guadalupe Hidalgo of 1848, ever returned to Mexico.

9. See Pérez, "Sexuality and Discourse."

10. See Wilson Gilmore, "Public Enemies and Private Intellectuals."

11. Pulido, "FAQs," 342.

12. Hale and Calhoun, *Engaging Contradictions*, 4.

13. Spivak, *The Post-Colonial Critic*, 103.

14. Hale and Calhoun, *Engaging Contradictions*, 3.

15. Foucault, *The Order of Things*, 29.

16. Ibid.

17. See Gaspar de Alba, "Literary Wetback," 40–43.

18. Anzaldúa, *Borderlands*/La Frontera, 104.

19. For more about the Tres Marías Syndrome, see Chapter 4, "Coyolxauhqui and Las 'Maqui-Locas': Re-Membering the Sacrificed Daughters of Ciudad Juárez," in this volume.

20. Paz, "Sons of La Malinche," 197–208.

21. Adam's punishment was work, or rather, that he would have to toil for the rest of his life to be able to feed and shelter himself and his belongings, as he had lost the privilege of divine keep.

22. De la Cruz, Poem 146, "Quéjase de la suerte: insinúa su aversión a los vicios, y justifica su divertimiento a las Musas," in *A Sor Juana Anthology*, 94, 96. This is my own translation of the opening quatrain of the poem.

23. Ibid., Poem 92, or "Philosophical Satire," 110.

24. Harss, *Sor Juana's Dream*, 7.

25. See Caputi, *Age of Sex Crime*.

26. To read more about the 2010 MAC-Rodarte controversy, see Chapter 6 in this volume. For a more detailed description of how the Rodarte designers came up with this "sleepwalking" aesthetic, see Nicole Phelps's piece on www.Style.com, "Rodarte," February 16, 2010, at http://www.style.com/fashionshows/review/F2010 RTW-RODARTE.

27. Whereas my novel on Sor Juana is a lesbian-feminist reconstruction of the life and work of the famous foremother of Chicana feminism, *Calligraphy of the Witch* explores a facet of Mexican American identity that rarely gets discussed in Chicana/o or American Studies and that has yet to be imagined in Chicana/o literature: the historical rivalries and gothic connections between the English and the Spanish, the Protestant and the Catholic, the Enlightenment and the Inquisition.

28. Foucault, *The Order of Things*, 19, 21, 23.

29. Holland, *Misogyny*, 8.

30. *Webster's New World College Dictionary*, 4th ed. (Cleveland, OH: Wiley Publishing, 2004), 561.

31. Kennedy, "Generation Mex," 88.

32. Ibid., 88.

33. Foucault, *The Order of Things*, 64.

34. Anzaldúa, *Interviews/Entrevistas*, 238.

35. See Erving Goffman, *Frame Analysis*.

36. Noakes and Johnston, "Frames of Protest," 2.

37. See Snow and Benford, "Master Frames," 133–135, 137; and Benford and Snow, "Framing Processes."

38. Benford and Snow, "Framing Processes," 613.

39. See Oliver and Johnston, "What a Good Idea!," where the authors argue that although the importance and usefulness of frame theory to social movement research cannot be denied, it should not substitute for a thorough analysis and deconstruction of ideology. "Understanding ideology as a system of meaning that couples assertions and theories about the nature of social life with values and norms relevant to promoting or resisting social change opens the door to serious investigation of ideologies and the social construction of ideologies" (200).

40. Tadiar and Davis, Introduction to *Beyond the Frame*, 3.

41. Kendall, *Framing Class*, 7.

42. Ridgeway, *Framed by Gender*, 7.

43. Collins, *Black Feminist Thought*, 299.

44. Ridgeway, *Framed by Gender*, 190–191.

45. Personal side note: In 1980, I completed my B.A. in English at the University of Texas at El Paso, divorced my Anglo husband, and came out as a lesbian, a triple molting of identities that plunged me into my first Coatlicue State. Not that I had yet heard of Gloria Anzaldúa in 1980. We didn't read her work in the Chicano Literature course I took at UTEP, so I didn't even know she existed. I did know, however, that two years earlier, in Mexico City, an ancient Aztec artifact had been discovered under the Templo Mayor known as the Coyolxauhqui Stone: a representation of the fierce warrior goddess who, according to legend, was dismembered by her brother, the war god Huitzilopochtli, when she and her four hundred siblings had attempted to kill their mother, Coatlicue, to prevent the birth of the god of war. In retrospect, the discovery of the Coyolxauhqui Stone to me signifies the rising of an indigenist/feminist moon in the Americas. That Helen Escobedo, the only woman of the seven artists to have a sculpture installed at the UNAM's Espacio Escultórico, created *Coatl* two years after the discovery of the Coyolxauhqui Stone in Mexico City makes sense to me, seems part of that indigenist/feminist vibration emanating from the Templo Mayor from Mexico to Aztlán. Also in 1980, a 7.0-magnitude earthquake with its epicenter in Oaxaca shook Mesoamerica from Mexico to Guatemala. North of the border, Chicana lesbian poets Gloria Anzaldúa and Cherríe Moraga were working on what is now the foundational text of Chicana feminist studies, *This Bridge Called My Back: Writings by Radical Women of Color*, published originally in 1981 by Persephone Press, and reissued in 1983 by Kitchen Table Press—a text that would cause shock waves through both Chicano Studies and Women's Studies.

46. Although Anzaldúa suffered a near-fatal snakebite as a young girl, and saw visions of serpents throughout her life, it took her years of consciousness work to connect the serpent with what she calls her animal soul. *Borderlands*/La Frontera, 48.

47. Ibid., 34.

48. Ibid. Another ancient Aztec goddess is Cihuacoatl, or Serpent Woman, earth goddess of both war and childbirth. She walks the street weeping at night, crying out

for her lost children, and is believed to be the precursor to the legendary Llorona, or Weeping Woman.

49. Ibid., 46–47.

50. The "new mestiza," says Anzaldúa, is one who "undergoes a struggle of flesh, a struggle of borders, an inner war . . . The coming together of two self-consistent but habitually incompatible frames of reference causes *un choque*, a cultural collision . . . The new mestiza copes by developing a tolerance for contradictions, a tolerance for ambiguity . . . In attempting to work out a synthesis, the self has added a third element . . . that third element is a new consciousness—a mestiza consciousness—and though it is a source of intense pain, its energy comes from continual creative motion that keeps breaking down the unitary aspect of each new paradigm." Ibid., 78–80.

51. Ibid., 35.

52. The UNAM was the first university in the Americas and was founded in 1551. It is a government-financed educational institution. Although no longer located in its original site near the Plaza Mayor, the university was declared a UNESCO World Heritage Site in 2007.

53. Marin, "Frame of Representation," 79. Marin explains that framing is one of three "mechanisms of presentation . . . the background, the field, and the frame . . . which properly understood, constitute the general framing of representation" (80).

54. Ocho Conejo, or 8 Rabbit, represents a specific year on the Aztec calendar, and *colotl* is the Nahuatl word for scorpion.

55. See "Helen Escobedo, Obituary: Mexican Sculptor Who Strove to Integrate Her Art with Nature and the Environment," *The Guardian*, Art and Design section (October 29, 2010), http://www.guardian.co.uk/artanddesign/2010/oct/29/helen-escobedo-obituary.

56. Duro, *Rhetoric of the Frame*, 1.

57. Ibid., 4.

58. The sculpture space itself was created to honor the quincentennial of the university's autonomy in Mexico.

59. My translation. See Canseco Rodal et al., *Espacio Escultórico de Ciudad Universitaria*, http://culturaycomunicacionfi.blogspot.com/2007/11/espacio-escultrico-de-ciudad.html. Original quote:

> Son esculturas de formas geométricas, de varios metros de desarrollo en cualquier sentido, hechas para moverse en torno de ellas y, en algunos casos, para ser penetradas por el caminante, lo mismo que por el aire del lugar, porque la continuidad formal y espacial es parte del propio ámbito que cada una de ellas condiciona, es decir, que las esculturas no terminan en los límites de los materiales de su construcción sino que cada una sugiere su propia prolongación, el aire las recorre y sigue a través de ellas.

60. The bloggers also note that climate and vandalism are seriously damaging the pieces as much as "fecal matter and trash—primarily bottles and alcoholic beverage containers—and noxious [perhaps dead?] fauna." Original: "De las siete esculturas del paseo, seis están seriamente dañadas por grietas en su estructura, pintas, graffitis, materia fecal, basura—principalmente botellas y empaques de bebidas alcohólicas—y fauna nociva."

61. Original: "la vanguardia de nuestro país para apoyar la modernización de México." See Canseco Rodal et al., *Espacio Escultórico*.

62. This is what Ignacio García called Chicana feminists, whom he saw as dividing the Chicano movement and separating the field of Chicano Studies from what he perceived to be the "original goals" of *El Plan Espiritual de Aztlán* and *El Plan de Santa Barbara*. "These gender nationalists find the lurking 'macho' in every Chicano scholarly work" (190). See his essay, "Juncture in the Road," 181–203.

63. López, "It's Not about the Santa in My Fe," 257.

64. Pinkola Estes, *Untie the Strong Woman*, 19.

65. Sandoval, *Methodology of the Oppressed*, 147.

66. Ibid., 142.

67. Ibid., 140.

Chapter One

AUTHOR'S NOTE: Originally published in *Living Chicana Theory*, ed. Carla Trujillo (Berkeley: Third Woman Press, 1998), 136–165. I wrote this piece while simultaneously working on my dissertation at the University of New Mexico and trying to finish *Sor Juana's Second Dream*. It was my own struggle between passion (the novel) and reason (the dissertation, the PhD, the tenure-track job). Although reason ended up dominating my life for five more years, I eventually returned to the novel and finished it in 1998.

1. Peden, *A Woman of Genius*, 28. This is the first English translation of Sor Juana's *Respuesta a Sor Filotea de la Cruz*.

2. Ibid., 30.

3. López-Portillo, *Estampas*, 57–65.

4. Quoted in Paz, *Sor Juana*, 98.

5. In the class and caste superstructure of colonial New Spain that we know as the "sistema de castas," or the caste system, *criollos/as* were first-generation Spanish Americans and their descendants born in the colonies. Criollos/as were socially and racially superior to all the other castes in New Spain, except for the immigrant (and supposedly pure-bred) *españoles* from Spain.

6. Paz, *Sor Juana*, 99.

7. Peden, *Woman of Genius*, 30.

8. Paz, *Sor Juana*, 217.

9. Peden, *Woman of Genius*, 65.

10. Harss, *Sor Juana's Dream*, 7.

11. Rich, "Notes toward a Politics of Location," 214.

12. Hurtado, "Relating to Privilege."

13. Paz, "Juana Ramírez," 81.

14. Rich, "Compulsory Heterosexuality."

15. Though it can be argued that not all Chicana lesbian feminists are, in fact, academics, it is the academics who are more likely to claim these three labels as signifiers of their difference and identity. I am, therefore, alluding not to the *empirical* Chicana lesbian feminist whose politics of location is shaped by *experience* and not necessarily framed by terminology or schools of thought, as much as to the Chicana lesbian

feminist who creates her various identities and political locations through participation in academic discourse communities, particularly the intellectual history of Chicanas. But as Chicana historian Deena González argues, if we extend feminism outside the walls of the academy, Sor Juana is not, in fact, "the first feminist of the Americas." If feminism is primarily about female agency and resistance to male domination, and not necessarily a written discourse, then the "first feminist of the Americas" was the woman who brokered between European domination and indigenous resistance, that is, La Malinche. See Deena González, "Encountering Columbus."

16. María R. González, "El embrión nacionalista," 252.

17. See Anzaldúa, *Borderlands*/La Frontera.

18. Paz, *Sor Juana*, 111.

19. Ibid., 217.

20. In fact, in Judith Brown's hagiography, *Immodest Acts: The Life of a Lesbian Nun in Renaissance Italy*, we learn of one of the first documented cases of a lesbian nun, in this case, a fifteenth-century Italian abbess named Benedetta Carlini. Benedetta's relationship with Bartolomea, another nun, was unwittingly discovered in a Church investigation of Benedetta's supposed mystical visions (Coatlicue States?).

21. See Anzaldúa, "Entering into the Serpent" and "La herencia de Coatlicue/The Coatlicue State."

22. Alarcón, "The Theoretical Subject(s)," 32.

23. Trueblood, *A Sor Juana Anthology*, 1.

24. Beauvoir, *The Second Sex*, 249.

25. Wittig, "One Is Not Born a Woman," 49.

26. AUTHOR'S NOTE: At the time I was writing this essay, I was still doing the research for the novel that would become *Sor Juana's Second Dream*, which would be published eight years later by the University of New Mexico Press. In the novel, I wanted to focus on Sor Juana's veiled subjectivity as a lesbian. Drawing together historical facts about Sor Juana's life (such as the tournament sponsored by the viceroy between Juana Inés and forty scholars of the university, and the documented conflicts between Sor Juana and her father confessor) and critical insights gleaned from Sor Juana's own "scribblings," the novel traces the quest of Sor Juana's self-acceptance through a maze of struggles between logic and passion, employing the narrative technique of first-, second-, and third-person perspectives to characterize Sor Juana's multiple selves and conflicts. See Gaspar de Alba, "Excerpts from the Sapphic Diary" and "Juana Inés."

27. Foucault, *History of Sexuality*, 61, 62.

28. Weedon, *Feminist Practice*, 40.

29. See Franco, *Plotting Women*.

30. Lavrin, "Values and Meanings," 382.

31. See Aguirre, *Del encausto a la sangre*.

32. Anzaldúa, "*Tlilli, Tlapalli*," 71.

33. Most of the responses in the subsequent interview are taken from Margaret Sayers Peden's translations of Sor Juana's work, particularly the translation of *Respuesta a Sor Filotea de la Cruz* published in *A Woman of Genius* (1987). Use of the translated material does not constitute Professor Peden's (or anybody else's) alliance with my view of Sor Juana or my interpretation of her writings. The construction of Sor Juana's sexuality and politics of location is strictly my own.

34. Paz, *Sor Juana*, 499.

35. Trueblood, *A Sor Juana Anthology*, 93.

36. Peden, *Woman of Genius*, 52, 56.

37. Ibid., 50, 52.

38. Ibid., 46.

39. Paz, *Sor Juana*, 497.

40. Trueblood, *A Sor Juana Anthology*, 31.

41. Weedon, *Feminist Practice*, 32.

42. See "In Reply to a Gentleman from Peru, Who Sent Her Clay Vessels While Suggesting She Would Better Be a Man," in *Sor Juana Inés de la Cruz: Poems*, 23.

43. Peden, *Woman of Genius*, 30.

44. Ibid., 42.

45. Ibid., 26.

46. Ibid., 43.

47. Ibid., 32; Latin phrase in italics in original.

48. Ibid., 58.

49. Ibid., 62.

50. Ibid., 62.

51. See "Appendix, Sor Juana: Witness for the Prosecution," in Paz, *Sor Juana*, 491–502.

52. Ibid., 501.

53. Trueblood, *A Sor Juana Anthology*, 95.

54. Peden, *Woman of Genius*, 40.

55. Ibid., 76.

56. Ibid., 74, 76.

57. The following is my own translation of these lines. For the full text of the "Philosophical Satire," see Peden, *Sor Juana Inés de la Cruz: Poems*, 28–32; hereafter cited as *Sor Juana: Poems*.

"Stubborn men who malign
women for no reason,
dismissing yourselves as the occasion
for the very wrongs you design:
if with unmitigated passion
you solicit their disdain,
why expect them to behave
if you incite their deviation?"

58. Again, this is my own translation of these lines from the "Philosophical Satire."

59. Peden, *Woman of Genius*, 30.

60. Peden, *Sor Juana: Poems*, 21.

61. Trueblood, *A Sor Juana Anthology*, 51.

62. Peden, *Sor Juana: Poems*, 45.

63. Ibid., 23.

64. Trueblood, *A Sor Juana Anthology*, 78.

65. Peden, *Woman of Genius*, 20.

66. Foucault, *History of Sexuality*, 27.

67. Trueblood, *A Sor Juana Anthology*, 45.

68. See De la Cruz, *Obras completas*, Vol. 4, 518–519: "Protesta que, rubricada con su sangre, hizo de su fe y amor a Dios la Madre Juana Inés de la Cruz, al tiempo de abandonar los estudios humanos para proseguir, desembarazada de este afecto, en el camino de la perfección." For the original document in the convent's Book of Professions, see the Dorothy Schons Archives at the Nettie Lee Benson Library's Latin American Collection, University of Texas at Austin. See also María Luisa Bemberg's filmic treatment of Sor Juana's life, *Yo, La Peor de Todas* (1990), which was showcased at the 12th annual Gay and Lesbian Film/Video Festival in Los Angeles in 1994.

69. Trueblood, *A Sor Juana Anthology*, 89.

Chapter Two

AUTHOR'S NOTE: "Malinche's Revenge" by Alicia Gaspar de Alba is reprinted with permission from the publisher of *Feminism, Nation, and Myth: La Malinche*, edited by Rolando Romero and Amanda Nolacea Harris (Houston: Arte Público Press, University of Texas, 2005).

1. See Pérez, *The Decolonial Imaginary*.

2. See Paz, *The Labyrinth of Solitude*.

3. Pérez, "Sexuality and Discourse," 167.

4. Ibid., 168.

5. This essay was originally written for the Malinche conference at the University of Illinois at Urbana-Champagne, which was held in 1999. Although the *María Isabel* example itself is dated, the caste system as represented in Mexican *telenovelas* remains the same.

6. Cope, *Limits of Racial Domination*, 24.

7. This is one of the stories associated with the Mexican volcanoes of the same name. Popocatéptl is the name of the active (thus, male) volcano, and Ixtaccíhuatl is the name of the dormant (thus, female) one. Indeed, her name means Sleeping Lady.

8. Martínez, *De Colores*, 175.

9. Quoted in Moraga, *The Last Generation*, 157.

10. Martínez, *De Colores*, 166.

11. See Alma García, *Chicana Feminist Thought*; see also Chapter 3, "Out of the House, the Halo, and the Whore's Mask: The Mirror of Malinchismo," in my book *Chicano Art Inside/Outside the Master's House*, 119–157.

12. Beauvoir, *The Second Sex*, 249.

13. See Peden, *Poems, Protest, and a Dream*.

14. Beauvoir, *The Second Sex*, 253.

15. Paz, "Sons of La Malinche," 208.

16. See Moraga, "A Long Line of Vendidas," in *Loving in the War Years*, 90–144.

17. This is an allusion to Helena María Viramontes's story "Growing" in *The Moths and Other Stories*, 35–42. In the story, the female protagonist has to come to terms with the fact that growing up, or becoming a woman, automatically wins her the distrust of her machista 'Apá.

18. Moraga, *Loving in the War Years*, 112.

19. Trujillo, *Chicana Lesbians*, 186–194.

20. Moraga, *Loving in the Way Years*, 109.

21. Cypess, *La Malinche in Mexican Literature*, 35.

22. Deena González, "Encountering Columbus," 19.

23. Castillo, *Massacre of the Dreamers*, 16.

24. Lorde, *Sister/Outsider*, 110–113.

25. Pérez, "Sexuality and Discourse," 169.

26. The "Shadow-Beast" is Gloria Anzaldúa's term for a contradictory psychic energy that lives in all colonized peoples, but especially women and queers. It is a two-faced beast: one is the face of internalized hatred, the monster that aids our conquerors in keeping us oppressed by making us hate ourselves, our skin color, our sexuality, our desire; the other is the face of rebellion, the liberating force that gets us to rebel against the cultural tyranny of homophobia, linguistic terrorism, racism, sexism, and other forms of bigotry and internalized oppression. See Chapter 2, "Movimientos de rebeldía y las culturas que traicionan," in *Borderlands*/La Frontera, 15–23.

27. Ibid., 49.

Chapter Three

AUTHOR'S NOTE: An earlier version of this essay was published in *The New Centennial Review* 4, no. 2 (Fall 2004): 103–140. I revised the piece substantially in 2012. Part of the early research for this piece was supported by a Rockefeller Fellowship for Latino Cultural Study at the Smithsonian that I received in 1999.

1. Baum, *The Wonderful Wizard of Oz*, 80.

2. The word *utopia* comes from the Greek *ou* (not) + *tóp(os)* (place).

3. *Webster's College Dictionary*, 2nd ed. (New York: Random House, 1997), 622. One of the definitions of *place* is "the portion of space normally occupied by a person or thing" (994).

4. Baum, *The Wonderful Wizard of Oz*, 91.

5. "I do not know where Kansas is, for I have never heard that country mentioned before. But tell me, is it a civilized country?" [the Witch of the North asks Dorothy]

"Oh, yes," replied Dorothy.

"Then that accounts for it. In the civilized countries, I believe there are no witches left; nor wizards, nor sorceresses, nor magicians. But, you see, the Land of Oz has never been civilized, for we are cut off from all the rest of the world." Ibid., 11–12.

6. Believed to be the Aztecs' place of origin prior to their migration into present-day Mexico City, Aztlán means "place of herons" or "place of whiteness" in Nahuatl.

7. Bhabha, "Beyond the Pale," 62.

8. Ibid., 62.

9. Ibid., 63.

10. Gómez Peña, *Warrior for Gringostroika*, 85.

11. I conducted much of this research in the archives of the Smithsonian's National Museum of American Art (now renamed the Smithsonian American Art Museum) in Washington, DC, in spring 1999, as part of my Rockefeller fellowship.

12. Frueh, "The Body through Women's Eyes," 192.

13. Driskell, "Introduction," 7.

14. Morrison, "The Global Village," 39.

15. Ibid., 38.

16. Quoted in Baerwaldt et al., *Memories of Overdevelopment*, 55.

17. Barkan and Shelton, *Borders, Exiles, Diasporas*, 5.

18. Quoted in Baerwaldt et al., *Memories of Overdevelopment*, 86.

19. Viera and Morris, "Juan Boza," 186.

20. Elleguá, the trickster god of the crossroads, likes to hide behind the mischievous Santo Niño de Atocha; Changó, the fierce lightning rod of social justice whose colors are red and white, has chosen Saint Barbara as his Catholic alter-ego; Changó's wife, Oshún, sexy goddess of fertility, creativity, and love, likes the disguise of the Virgin of Charity, patron saint of Cuba, with the three little figures in the canoe at her feet staring up at her in absolute adoration.

21. Lindsay, *Santería Aesthetics*, xvii.

22. The most notable of these Santería artists were the Cubans Wifredo Lam and Juan Boza and the Cuban American Ana Mendieta.

23. Rushing, "Authenticity and Subjectivity," 13.

24. Leuthold, *Indigenous Aesthetics*, 3.

25. Ibid., 31.

26. Mithlo, *Our Indian Princess*, 98.

27. Passed in the state of California in 1994 by an overwhelming majority vote, Proposition 187 denied basic health care and educational rights to undocumented immigrants and their children. It was repealed in 1999.

28. Moctezuma was the reigning emperor of the Aztecs at the time of the Spanish conquest of Mexico in the sixteenth century; Geronimo led a band of insurgent Apaches who fought off Anglo invasions of their homeland in Arizona in the nineteenth century.

29. See Gaspar de Alba, "A Theoretical Introduction."

30. Although I have issues with José Vasconcelos's eugenic treatise *La raza cósmica*, I recognize the value of this term to denote the hybridity of races that converge in the Americas, and that early Chicano/a activists saw as an ideal metaphor for our Spanish/Indian/African *mestizaje*.

31. See Chávez, *The Lost Land*, Chapter 1. Certainly, an analysis of the prevalent leitmotifs in the art and literature produced by Chicanos, that is, by Chicano *men*, in the early years of the Chicano movement substantiates Chávez's point. José Antonio Villareal's *Pocho* (1959), Corky Gonzales's *I Am Joaquín* (1969), Armando Rendón's *Chicano Manifesto* (1971), Tomás Rivera's *Y no se lo tragó la tierra* (1971), Ernesto Galarza's *Barrio Boy* (1971), Aristeo Brito's *The Devil in Texas* (1972), Oscar Zeta Acosta's *The Revolt of the Cockroach People* (1972), Rudolfo Anaya's *Bless Me, Ultima* (1972), and Ron Arias's *The Road to Tamazunchale* (1975)—whether through fiction, memoir, or poetry, all represent Chicano identity as a process of loss and recuperation, as a consciousness that is native to and yet dispossessed of the cultural homeland of Aztlán. The names of the first Chicano art groups and galleries reflect the same allegiance to cultural nationalism: Los Toltecas en Aztlán, Congreso de Artistas en Aztlán, Los Artes Guadalupanos de Aztlán, Los Pintores de Aztlán, El Grito de Aztlán Gallery, El Centro Cultural de Aztlán, Casa Aztlán. Not to mention the name of the flagship journal of the field of Chicano Studies, *Aztlán: A Journal of Chicano Studies*, housed at the UCLA Chicano Studies Research Center, and of which I served as coeditor from 2002 to 2004 while the associate director of the CSRC.

32. See "Overview of Race and Hispanic Origin: 2010," 2010 Census Briefs, accessible online at http://www.census.gov/prod/cen2010/briefs/c2010br-02.pdf.

33. Chabot, "Framing," 21.

34. For a history of the development of the framing perspective as applied to social movement research, see Noakes and Johnston, "Frames of Protest."

35. Baud and Rutten, "Introduction," 2.

36. Rutten and Baud, "Concluding Remarks," 198.

37. Chávez, *The Lost Land*, 1.

38. Moraga, *The Last Generation*, 150.

39. Ibid., 149.

40. Ibid., 148–149.

41. See Henry Nash Smith, *The Virgin Land*; Perry Miller, *Errand into the Wilderness*; Leo Marx, *The Machine in the Garden*; and Patricia Limerick, *The Legacy of Conquest*.

42. O' Sullivan, "Great Nation of Futurity." This quote is taken from an excerpt of that article, accessible online at www.mtholyoke.edu/acad/intrel/osulliva.htm. See also "Manifest Destiny" by Robert E. Mays on the PBS website for the program *U.S.-Mexican War, 1846–1848*. http://www.pbs.org/kera/usmexicanwar/prelude/md _manifest_destiny2.html.

43. Turner, *Frontier in American History*, 3.

44. Ibid., 4.

45. Martínez, *De Colores Means All of Us*, 43, 45.

46. Downloaded from http://siris-artinventories.si.edu/ipac20/ipac.jsp?&profile =all&source=~!siartinventories&uri=full=3100001~!219837~!0#focus on 4/15/2013. The painting has been purchased by the Gene Autry National Center, which gave me permission to reproduce it here.

47. Lippard, *Lure of the Local*, 134.

48. O'Sullivan, "Annexation." An excerpt is accessible online at http://www.his torytools.org/sources/manifest_destiny.pdf.

49. Vasconcelos, *La raza cósmica/The Cosmic Race*. The first English translation was published by the Department of Chicano Studies, California State University, Los Angeles, 1979. The first Spanish edition was published in 1925.

50. Ibid., 26.

51. Ibid., 20.

52. Rendón, *Chicano Manifesto*, 10.

53. Ibid.

54. For more on alter-Nativity, see my *Chicano Art Inside/Outside the Master's House*.

55. Padilla, *My History, Not Yours*, 232.

56. Rendón, *Chicano Manifesto*, 337.

57. Vasconcelos, *La raza cósmica*, 21. The full sentence aptly describes both the historical conflict between the English and the Spanish, and the outcome of the U.S.-Mexico War: "If Latin America were just another Spain, to the same extent that the United States is another England, then the old conflict of the two stocks would do nothing else but to repeat its episodes on a vaster territory, and one of the two rivals would end up prevailing and imposing itself."

58. I added this section in 2012. Special thanks to Alma López for helping me conceptualize the graph of the four quadrants of Aztlán.

59. I place the word "chose" in quotation marks to indicate that the vast majority of the Mexicans who remained in the conquered territory were not exercising a choice between staying or leaving, but rather between losing or retaining their land. I see this as a type of inverted diasporic condition, where the body remains but the land, the rights to the land, and eventually the memory of nativity in the land are all taken away.

60. Gómez, *Manifest Destinies*, 7

61. Ibid.

62. McWilliams, *North from Mexico*, 43–53.

63. Ibid., 33.

64. O'Sullivan, "Great Nation of Futurity," which may also be accessed at http://www.pbs.org/kera/usmexicanwar/resources/manifest_destiny_sullivan.html.

65. For more about Santa Anna's role in the loss of Texas, see the PBS website for *The West* series at http://www.pbs.org/weta/thewest/people/s_z/santaanna.htm.

66. Chávez, *The Lost Land*, 67.

67. Doss, "'I *Must* Paint,'" 210.

68. Erika Doss describes John Gast's *American Progress* (1872) as a "true" icon of the West, a romantic construction "where Native Americans and bison are beset by the onslaught of advancing Anglo civilization—wagon trains, railroads, prospectors, and farmers—guided overhead by a gigantic Gilded Age female clad in loosely flowing drapery and carrying a schoolbook and a rope of telegraph wire." Ibid.

69. Kaminsky, *After Exile*, 6.

70. Pérez, *Decolonial Imaginary*, 122.

71. To read the primary documents of early Chicana feminists and their struggles in the male-dominated Movimiento, see Alma M. García, *Chicana Feminist Thought*.

72. Borrowed from Chicana historian Deena J. González. For a feminist historical analysis of native women's accommodation and resistance to colonization in the nineteenth century, see her book, *Refusing the Favor*.

73. Gaspar de Alba, *Chicano Art*, 144.

74. The triptych refers to Yolanda M. López's Guadalupe series (1978), which includes *Margaret F. Stewart: Our Lady of Guadalupe*, depicting the artist's mother as a seamstress Guadalupe sewing her own mantle of stars, and *Portrait of the Artist as the Virgin of Guadalupe*, which depicts López as a marathon runner in Guadalupe drag stepping off the Virgin's dark crescent pedestal. According to the artist, the angel trod under the Virgin's foot in the marathon image "got in the way" (personal conversation).

75. Ester Hernández's works are *La Ofrenda* (1985), *La Virgen de Guadalupe Defendiendo los Derechos de los Xicanos* (1975), and *Libertad* (1976), respectively.

76. *Las Tres Marías*, a mixed-media installation by Judith Baca, is owned by the Smithsonian American Art Museum.

77. Gaspar de Alba, *Chicano Art*, 139.

78. Ignacio M. García, "Juncture in the Road," 190.

79. Muñoz, *Disidentifications*, 11.

80. Pérez, *Decolonial Imaginary*, 7.

81. For a similar approach to place, gender, and aesthetics in the visual art of Chicanas, including a very helpful comparative chart on the characteristics and experiences of artists from three different regions, see Stoller, "Peregrinas with Many Visions."

82. Kun, "The Personal Equator," 356.

83. Ibid., 360.

84. Although Valdez also paints more stable interior landscapes, with windows opening out to gardens, patios, or ocean views, the chaotic aesthetic remains a benchmark of her work.

85. To see more of the work of Patssi Valdez, go to www.patssivaldez.com.

86. The New Mexico Office of the State Historian explains the Penitente Brotherhood as a "Catholic lay men's organization whose beliefs and practices center around re-creating the passion and death of Jesus of Nazareth." See http://www.newmexico history.org/filedetails.php?fileID=21554.

87. From a talk delivered by the artist at the "Puro Corazón: Chicana Art Symposium" held at Pomona College, February 1995.

88. To see more of the work of Delilah Montoya, go to www.delilahmontoya.com.

89. I wasn't able to secure permission to reprint Lomas Garza's work in my book. To see examples of her work, go to www.carmenlomasgarza.com.

90. From the brochure for *Directions: Carmen Lomas Garza*, an exhibition of her work held at the Hirshhorn Museum and Sculpture Garden, Washington, DC.

91. Yarbro-Bejarano, "Laying It Bare," 300.

92. The exhibit of eleven women artists working in the traditional altar medium ran from October 1999 through December 2000 and was installed at Tufts University in Medford, Massachusetts; Santa Clara University in the Silicon Valley, California; and Texas Tech University in Lubbock, Texas.

93. Cortez, "Imágenes e Historias," 3. The paper was first given at the College Art Association Annual Meeting in February of the same year (2001).

94. Mieri, "Latino Representation at the Smithsonian," 3.

95. See the catalog *The Road to Aztlán: Art from a Mythic Homeland*, edited by Virginia M. Fields and Victor Zamudio-Taylor. In "Queer Aztlán," Cherríe Moraga writes that on a desert road just east of San Diego she saw the word AZTLAN "in granite-sized letters etched into the face of the mountainside" (151).

Chapter Four

AUTHOR'S NOTE: This chapter combines, reorganizes, and expands portions of two essays previously published in 2010 under the titles "Introduction: *Feminicidio*: The Black Legend of the Border" and "Poor Brown Female: The Miller's Compensation for 'Free Trade,'" in *Making a Killing*, edited by Alicia Gaspar de Alba with Georgina Guzmán, 63–93. Although I cowrote the introduction to *Making a Killing* with Georgina Guzmán, I have used only the first part, which I authored.

1. Blake, *Chicana Sexuality and Gender*, 30.

2. See Sahagún, *Florentine Codex*. As of October 31, 2012, this text became digitized and available online through the World Digital Library, and may be accessed at http://www.wdl.org/en/item/10096/#languages=spa&item_type=manuscript.

3. Milbrath, "Decapitated Lunar Goddess," 186.

4. Ibid., 202. "During a New Fire Ceremony there was a perceived threat to the state, for the Aztec world could end in eternal darkness. Around the time of the festival, the Aztecs may have focused on observations of the day the moon disappeared, because the new [dark] moon could eclipse the sun. An eclipse at the time of the New Fire ceremony could bring the downfall of the Aztec empire" (203).

5. Blake, *Chicana Sexuality and Gender*, 32.

6. Anzaldúa, *Interviews/Entrevistas*, 257.

7. See Diana Washington Valdez, "Decapitated Body among 100 Girls, Women Killed in Juárez in '09," *Elpasotimes.com*, October 14, 2009, http://www.elpasotimes .com/ci_13555924?IADID=Search-www.elpasotimes.com.elpsaotimes.com.

8. Russell, "Defining Femicide," 13.

9. The second half of the quotation is taken from Radford and Russell, *Femicide*, 6.

10. "According to the latest reports in the Ciudad Juárez and El Paso press, some of them based on statistics maintained by the Chihuahua state attorney general's office (PGJE), at least 750 women were murdered in Ciudad Juárez and the neighboring Juárez Valley between the beginning of 1993, when women's murders first began to get serious public attention, and the first week of May 2010 . . . If subsequent homicides reported in the press are added to [Diana Washington Valdez's] figures, then at least 808 women have been murdered between 1993 and the first week of May 2010." See *Frontera NorteSur*'s report "Mexico Is Accountable for Femicides: European Parliament," May 10, 2010; accessed August 29, 2012, http://mexidata .info/id2659.html.

11. These crimes should not be confused with "narco-killings," which are crimes committed in the turf and power struggles of local drug cartels and target mainly male victims.

12. See Borunda, "Woman's Body Found."

13. "Juárez" by Tori Amos on the album *To Venus and Back* (Atlantic, 1999); "Invalid Litter Department," CD single by At the Drive-In (EMI International, 2001); "La Niña" by Lila Downs on the album *Border/La Linea* (Narada World, 2001); "Las Mujeres de Juárez" by Los Tigres del Norte on the album *Pacto de Sangre* (Fonovisa, 2004); "Madera" by Jaguares on the album *Crónicas de un Laberinto* (Sony International, 2005).

14. See www.youtube.com/watch?v=o5mlgmqy9oI&mode=related&search=.

15. HBO's *The Virgin of Juárez* (2006), directed by Kevin James Dobson and starring Minnie Driver; *Bordertown* (2007), directed by Gregory Nava and starring Jennifer López, Antonio Banderas, Martin Sheen, and Sonia Braga.

16. *Las Muertas de Juárez*, directed by Enrique Murillo (Laguna Productions, 2002).

17. In February 2009, Paramount released a Mexican production titled *El Traspatio/Backyard*, written by Sabina Berman, directed by Carlos Carrera (*The Crime of Padre Amaro*), and starring Ana de la Reguera and Jimmy Smits. For more details on the movie, see http://news.newamericamedia.org/news/view_article.html?article_id =910ba01693bec5c05fb4cd25a32d06fe.

18. *Bajo Juárez: A City Devouring Its Girls*, directed by Alejandra Sánchez Orozco and José Antonio Cordero (Indymedia, 2006); *On the Edge: Femicide in*

Ciudad Juárez, directed by Steev Hise (Illegal Art, 2006); and *Border Echoes*, directed by Lorena Méndez (Documentary Films, 2006).

19. See Bard, *La Frontera*; Gaspar de Alba, *Desert Blood*; Agosín, *Secrets in the Sand*; Pope Duarte, *If I Die in Juárez*; Hawken, *The Dead Women of Juárez*. Part 4 of Roberto Bolaño's massive *2666* is a laundry list of all the femicides in Juárez from 1993 to 2003, an almost verbatim transcription of details and statistics about each murdered woman that up until 2010 could be found on the website of Casa Amiga. Carlos Fuentes has also written a novel about the border, parts of which focus on maquiladora workers; see *The Crystal Frontier: A Novel in Nine Stories*. For an analysis of *Desert Blood*, *Crystal Frontier*, and other popular cultural representations of the Juárez femicides, see Volk and Schlotterbeck, "Gender, Order and Femicide."

20. See González Rodríguez, *Huesos en el desierto*; Washington Valdez, *Cosecha de mujeres*; and Rodríguez, Montoné, and Pulitzer, *The Daughters of Juárez*.

21. See Staudt and Coronado, *Fronteras No Más*; Wright, *Disposable Women and Other Myths of Global Capitalism*; Staudt, *Violence and Activism at the Border*; Monárrez Fragoso, *Trama de una injusticia*; Piñeda-Madrid, *Suffering and Salvation in Juárez*; Luevano, *Woman-Killing in Juárez*.

22. Monárrez Fragoso and Tabuenca Córdoba, *Bordeando la violencia*; Fregoso and Bejarano, *Terrorizing Women*; Gaspar de Alba with Guzmán, *Making a Killing*.

23. The most recent of these is Bowden, *Murder City*.

24. To name a few: Lourdes Portillo, Coco Fusco, Rubén Amavisca, Alma López, Laura Molina, Rigo Maldonado, Victoria Delgadillo, Daisy Tonantzin, Ester Hernández, Yreina Cervantez, Consuelo Flores, Favianna Rodríguez, and others.

25. Agosín, *Secrets in the Sand*, 25.

26. See http://www.elpasoredco.org/regional-data/ciudad-juarez/twin-plant/maquiladora-faq.

27. Wright, "Dialectics," 456.

28. For more on this sexual surveillance, see ibid., 467. See also the "Women on the Border" website, http://www.womenontheborder.org/sexdiscrimination.htm.

Indeed, this illegal practice is endemic to the maquiladora industry across the Americas, as we learn from the 2002 Human Rights Watch report, "From the Household to the Factory." Also, at http://hrw.org/reports/2002/guat/guato102A.jude-03.htm#P646_139924, "Human Rights Watch found widespread sex discrimination in the maquila sector, in the form of questions or testing to determine reproductive status, post-hire penalization of pregnant workers, and failure to enforce maternity protections . . . Although factories can be fined and even closed down for this blatantly illegal practice, ineffective monitoring by the social security system itself means that most factories never suffer any consequences. Even when they are affiliated with the system, many workers are unable to get permission from their employers to seek health care. This means that pregnant workers may not receive the prenatal care they need."

29. Dillon, "Sex Bias Is Reported," A8.

30. See Monárrez Fragoso, "Serial Sexual Femicide."

31. Quiñones, "The *Maquiladora* Murders."

32. Sagrario was the daughter of Paula Flores, who has been very active in the mothers' struggle to end the femicides in Juárez and whose *testimonio*, "The Government Has Tried to Divide Us," is published in my anthology *Making a Killing*.

33. For some of the earliest scholarship on the femicides, see Wright, "Dialectics" and "A Manifesto against Femicide"; Fregoso, "Voices without Echo"; Monárrez Fragoso, "La cultura del feminicidio." For early pre-NAFTA scholarship on the maquiladora industry, see Iglesias Prieto, *La flor más bella de la maquiladora*. For early feminist scholarship on sex crimes, see Caputi, "The Sexual Politics of Murder."

34. For more about my process of writing this novel, see "Mapping the Labyrinth: The Anti–Detective Novel and the Mysterious Missing Brother," Chapter 5 in this volume.

35. The conference, whose title in Spanish was "Maquilando mujeres en Juárez, o, ¿quiénes son los asesinos?," was cosponsored by the UCLA Chicano Studies Research Center, Amnesty International, and a number of departments and student organizations on campus. The full program of the conference and related programming may be accessed at http://www.sscnet.ucla.edu/maqui_murders/.

36. Hilda Solis served as the U.S. Secretary of Labor from 2009 to 2013. Prior to her appointment in the Obama administration, she represented the 32nd Congressional District of California from 2001 to 2009.

37. The altar was commissioned from the Esperanza Peace and Justice Center in San Antonio, Texas, for the purpose of a silent auction, the full proceeds of which were donated to the mothers' NGOs whose representatives attended the conference.

38. To read the Operación Digna press release announcing the live-stream audio broadcast of the conference and support of other protest actions planned for Days of the Dead, 2003, see http://www.sscnet.ucla.edu/maqui_murders/operaciondigna.htm.

39. The fax may be viewed in its entirety at the conference website: http://www.sscnet.ucla.edu/maqui_murders/MexicanConsulFax.pdf.

40. By 2003, copycat killings started to crop up in other border cities such as Nogales, Matamoros, Mexicali, Nuevo Laredo, and Chihuahua City, where over one hundred women and girls had already been slain in the "Juárez style."

41. Braine, "Argentine Experts."

42. Access the resolutions online at http://www.sscnet.ucla.edu/maqui_murders/resolutioneng.htm.

43. Morfín Otero only occupied that position for three years, between 2003 and 2006. She is now an independent lawyer and human rights consultant. To read her statement upon being charged with the position in 2003, see http://www.rnw.nl/espanol/article/comisi%C3%B3n-para-prevenir-y-erradicar-la-violencia-contra-las-mujeres-en-ciudad-ju%C3%A1rez. The Mexico City newspaper *El Universal* reported on June 1, 2009, that the Juárez Commission had been recommissioned by presidential decree as a national rather than a local entity to prevent and eradicate crimes against women in the nation of Mexico and promote equality between men and women, all files, archives, and financial resources to be transferred to the new entity. See the online article at http://www.eluniversal.com.mx/notas/601697.html.

44. Access the petition at http://www.petitiononline.com/NiUnaMas/petition.html. As of June 28, 2007, four and a half years after the petition went online, it had garnered 10,700 signatures from supporters in Europe, Latin America, and the United States. On August 22, 2012, the number was up to 14,585 signatures.

45. Comments have been corrected for grammar and spelling.

46. Access the report online at http://www.amnesty.org/en/library/info/AMR41
/026/2003.

47. NOW has renamed its "Women of Juárez—Stop Femicide" campaign to "Stop
the Killings of the Women of Juárez." Please see http://www.now.org/issues/global
/juarez/.

48. See the *Frontera Norte-Sur* report, "International Court Holds Mexico Responsible for Femicides"; accessed August 29, 2012, at http://news.newamerica
media.org/news/view_article.html?article_id=f6cf95102528733a5ffe81c487a02fdf.
See also Diana Washington Valdez and Aileen B. Flores, "Court Blasts Mexico for
Women's Murders"; accessed August 29, 2012, at http://www.elpasotimes.com/news
/ci_13981319.

49. To see the full text of the bill, accessed August 7, 2013, see http://www.lawg
.org/storage/documents/house%20concurrent%20resolution%2090%20juarez%20
resolution.pdf. It is identical to Senate Concurrent Resolution 16, which was presented
to the Senate by Senator Jeff Bingaman (D-NM) but has still not passed.

50. For more information on the exhibition and reproductions of some of the
artwork displayed in the show, see Delgadillo and Maldonado, "Journey to the Land
of the Dead." See also the SPARC website archives at http://www.sparcmurals.org/.

51. Seen as criminals, gangbangers, drug addicts, and drug pushers, *cholos* embody and represent the Mexican imaginary of what happens to Mexicans under the
corrupting influence of the United States. *Cholismo*, or the practice of turning into
cholos, is seen as a negative consequence of living too close to the border. The attitude
is related to the long-standing Mexican animosity toward Chicanos and Chicanas,
who, from the perspective of Mexican nationals, are said to have sold out their allegiance to Mexico and to pollute their native language and culture with Americanisms.

52. For a breakdown on salaries versus cost-of-living expenses for *maquiladora*
workers, see the Women on the Border website, particularly Elvia Arriola's "Voices
from the Barbed Wire of Despair," 66. The full text of this article can be accessed
online at the Women on the Border website at http://www.womenontheborder.org
/Articles/Voices%20From%20Barbed.pdf. See also Arriola's "Accountability for Murder in the Maquiladoras: Linking Corporate Indifference to Gender Violence at the
U.S.-Mexico Border," in *Making a Killing*, 25–61. Finally, check out the charts in
my online Powerpoint on the Juárez Femicides, on my Desert Blood site, http://www
.desertblood.net.

53. Benítez et al., *El silencio que la voz de todas quiebra*, 18. The chart on this
page shows that only 10 percent of the victims were wearing skirts or dresses, and 16
percent, miniskirts.

54. David Meza was accused of killing his cousin, even though he was in Chi-
apas at the time she was murdered. He spent close to three years in jail on false
charges. To find out more about his story, see the documentary *Bajo Juárez: A City
Devouring Its Girls*. To read about Neyra Azucena Cervantes's abduction and the two
families' joint struggle for justice, see "Feminicide and Torture in Ciudad Juárez and
Chihuahua," available online at the Witness homepage: http://www.witness.org/index
.php?option=com_rightsalert&Itemid=178&task=story&alert_id=38.

55. See Ortega, *Las muertas de Ciudad Juárez*.

56. In *Bordertown* (2006), a Hollywood feature about the crimes, directed by Gregory Nava, the loose end of "el Diablo" is put to dramatic use by the local indigenous population of Juárez, who are depicted as naïve and superstitious in their belief that "the devil" is killing the women of Juárez.

57. To view tables for these statistics, see Gaspar de Alba with Guzmán, *Making a Killing*, 70–71.

58. "La suerte de leyenda negra tejida en torno a Juárez en el sentido de que más de 300 mujeres fueron 'desaparecidas, violadas, y asesinadas' en el transcurso de los últimos 10 años, no encuentra sustento en la realidad." See Otero Calderón, "Homicidios de Mujeres," 12.

59. For an online summary of the report, see http://www.amnesty.org/en/library/info/AMR41/026/2003. For an updated list of femicides in Juárez between 2004 and 2006, see the website of the Washington Office for Latin America (WOLA) at http://www.wola.org/index.php?option=com_content&task=viewp&id=474&Itemid=2.

60. See "Ciudad Juárez: Gobierno de Chihuahua desacreditó informe de AI," *Mujereshoy* (August 15, 2003), available online at http://foro.univision.com/t5/Asesinatos-de-Mujeres-en-Ju%C3%A1rez-close/Ciudad-Ju%C3%A1rez-Gobierno-de-Chihuahua-desacredit%C3%B3-informe-de-AI/td-p/167738247.

61. For the full text of the "Informe Final," see http://www.pgr.gob.mx/Temas%20Relevantes/Casos%20de%20Interes/Muertas%20de%20Juarez/Informe%20Final.asp.

62. Amnesty International USA no longer has its "Justice for the Women of Juárez and Chihuahua" statement available, nor does it appear as a campaign, but I was able to find the campaign's report at Amnesty International and locate the statement's document in Spanish under the title "Sigue la lucha por la justicia en relación con los homicidios y secuestros de mujeres en Ciudad Juárez y la Ciudad de Chihuahua." Please see http://www.amnesty.org/en/library/info/AMR41/012/2006/es.

63. Ensler, *Vagina Monologues*, 110.

64. Ramírez, "Police Look to Track Sex Offenders."

65. Cruz, "101 on Sex Offender List Violated Rules."

66. Whitechapel, *Crossing to Kill*. Although this is a problematic book on many counts, not the least of which is the author's last name, which alludes to Jack the Ripper's Whitechapel murders, it was one of the first books published on the Juárez femicides, and one of the first to pose the question of serial killers crossing into Juárez from El Paso.

67. Gilot, "Some Neighbors Wary of Sex Offenders."

68. Washington Valdez, "Officials Say State Dumps Sex Offenders in El Paso."

69. Letter to the Editor, *El Paso Times*, January 2, 2002.

70. Gilot, "Sex Offenders Trickle Out of El Paso."

71. Accessed April 28, 2013. See http://www.city-data.com/so/so-El-Paso-Texas.html.

72. See Monárrez Fragoso, "Serial Sexual Femicide," 169.

73. The sections of this chapter on the discrepancy in numbers and on the Mexican penal code, as well as the chart on theories about who the perpetrators are, appeared originally in a policy brief I wrote entitled "The *Maquiladora* Murders, Or, Who Is Killing the Women of Juárez?" *Latino Policy and Issues Brief*, no. 7 (August 2003),

1–4, published by the UCLA Chicano Studies Research Center. Used by permission of the UCLA Chicano Studies Research Center.

74. See the Nuestras Hijas de Regreso a Casa website at http://nuestrashijasde regresoacasa.blogspot.com/.

75. Personal interview with the author, October 2002.

76. See Coco Fusco's Virtual Laboratory, http://www.thing.net/~cocofusco/.

77. While writing this chapter, and surfing the Nuestras Hijas website, an advertisement for Passion.com popped up on my screen showing pictures of half-naked "naughty" girls in Southern California looking for sexy men.

78. See www.irc-online.org/americaspolicy/borderlines/index.html; site discontinued.

79. Although the Border Lines Juárez tourist site has been discontinued, it may still be accessed at http://web.archive.org/web/20000605023811/http://blines.com/page 9.html. The link to "Those Sexy Latin Ladies" is still available on the drop-down menu.

80. See the Amnesty International report, "Intolerable Killings."

81. Gaspar de Alba, "Malinche's Revenge," 52. Also, Chapter 2 in this volume.

82. Caputi, *Age of Sex Crime*, 95.

83. Caputi and Russell, "Femicide."

84. Anzaldúa, *Borderlands/La Frontera*, 25.

85. For more on the "prevention campaigns," see Tabuenca Córdoba, "Ghost Dance in Ciudad Juárez," 100.

86. Pérez, "So Far from God," 148.

87. Quiñones, *True Tales*, 152.

88. Gaspar de Alba, *Desert Blood*, 333.

89. The ASARCO smokestacks are no more. They were brought down and ASARCO closed permanently on April 14, 2013. "One cannon-like, reverberating boom was followed several seconds later by another reverberating boom. Those were the sounds produced after about 300 pounds of explosives were detonated inside the bases of two huge concrete smokestacks. They slowly fell like giant trees onto cushioned dirt beds on the former 126-year-old Asarco copper smelter site in West-Central El Paso," wrote journalist Vic Kolenc in "El Paso's ASARCO Smokestacks Gone in 35 Seconds," *El Paso Times* online, http://www.elpasotimes.com/newupdated /ci_23015235/el-pasos-asarco-smokestacks-demolished.

90. Wright, "Dialectics," 467.

91. From "Maquila Overview," http://www.maquilaportal.com/Visitors_Site.

92. I added this section in 2012. New and updated statistics were added in 2013.

93. See www.thedailybeast.com/newsweek/2011/03/06/the-hillary-doctrine.html.

94. To read more about the Hillary Doctrine, see http://www.theworldofhillary clinton.com/2011/04/hillary-doctrine.html. To read about Clinton's most recent speech, now billed as "Hillary Doctrine Unplugged," see http://www.cfr.org/women /hillary-doctrine-womens-rights-national-security-issue/p30407.

95. To listen to the story online, see abcnews.go.com/News/judge-pronounces -natalee-holloway-dead/story?id=15346993#.UX2EaoJAtQY.

96. See the MWWS entry in *Wikipedia*, en.wikipedia.org/wiki/Missing_white _woman_syndrome.

97. To see the full transcript for the show, go to http://transcripts.cnn.com /TRANSCRIPTS/1011/22/ijvm.01.html.

98. Crenshaw, "Mapping the Margins," 1245.

99. See Booth Moore, "New York Fashion Week: Rodarte, Derek Lam, Go Wild with Western Themes"; accessed February 27, 2010, http://latimesblogs.latimes.com /alltherage/2010/02/new-york-fashion-week-rodarte-derek-lam-go-wild-with -western-themes.html. See also Jessica Wakeman, "MAC/Rodarte Make-Up Collaboration Names Nail Polish after Impoverished, Murdered Women"; accessed July 15, 2010, http://www.thefrisky.com/2010–07–15/tasteless-but-chic-mac-names-makeup -after-impoverished-murdered-women1/.

100. Sarah Menkedick, "Rodarte and MAC Create Collection 'Inspired by' Women in Ciudad Juárez"; accessed July 29, 2010, http://news.change.org/stories/rodarte -and-mac-create-collection-inspired-by-women-in-ciudad-juárez; site discontinued.

101. Hing, "Beauty Bloggers." See also ColorLines, "MAC, Rodarte Say Sorry."

102. Hernández, "Fashion, Make-up Lines," http://latimesblogs.latimes.com/la plaza/2010/07/juarez-fashion-label-rodarte-women.html. This site has pictures of what I call the MAC-Rodarte "maquiladora goth" look.

103. Quoted in Bustillos, "When PR Goes Wrong."

104. Indeed, a number of invited speakers to the conference ended up canceling their trip because their institutions refused to cover their travel to one of the ten most dangerous cities in the world in 2010, 2011, and 2012, along with such places as Baghdad, Iraq; Bogotá, Colombia; Caracas, Venezuela; Guatemala City, Guatemala; Cape Town, South Africa; and Grozny, Chechnya, Russia. Crime statistics reported on the Urban Titan website for Ciudad Juárez listed 1,400 drug-related murders in 2008 and 2,500 in 2010, for a total of 8,330 since 2007—a ratio of 130 murders per 100,000 inhabitants. See http://urbantitan.com/10-most-dangerous-cities-in-the -world-in-2011/.

105. From my notes taken during the presentation of María Jesús Izquierdo's keynote presentation at the conference "Vida y resistencia en la frontera norte: Ciudad Juárez en el entramado mundial," El Colegio de La Frontera, Cd. Juárez, Chih., Mexico, October 20–22, 2011.

106. Caputi, "Afterword," 280.

107. Ibid.

108. Ibid.

109. Ibid., 281.

Chapter Five

1. Cawelti, *Adventure, Mystery, and Romance*, 85.

2. Rodríguez, *Brown Gumshoes*, 8.

3. In fact, a conference called "La Página Roja" (in reference to the title of the crime page in Mexican newspapers) was organized at the University of New Mexico in 1999, the proceedings of which were going to be turned into an anthology, though that text has not yet been published.

4. See Zilles, "Postmodernism and Discourses," and in the same volume, Márquez, "The Manuel Ramos Mile-High Murders." See also Zilles, "Microstructure and Macrostructure."

5. See Quiñones, "The Maquiladora Murders."

6. Márquez, "Manuel Ramos Mile-High Murders," 219.

7. Anzaldúa, *Borderlands*/La Frontera, 25.

8. In 2011, I attended an international conference in Juárez about the femicides, organized by Colegio de la Frontera (COLEF), and left feeling completely besotted by the new turn of events. The message from many of the conference participants' presentations, even from feminists, was that now, with all the narco-related killings happening in Juárez on a daily basis, we act irresponsibly if we pay attention only to the murders of women; we must now look at the murders of men as well, especially since there are more men killed than women on a daily basis. Once again, under the pretext of numbers, the femicides are brushed aside like yesterday's news.

9. Tani, *The Doomed Detective*, 40.

10. Ibid., 48.

11. The deconstructive anti–detective novel, says Tani, "is basically characterized by a more ambiguous perception of reality from the point of view of the detective. The detective is unable to impose meaning, an interpretation of the outside occurrences he is asked, as a sleuth, to solve and interpret. . . . The detective risks his sanity as he tries to find a solution . . . At the end he (or she) quits sizing up clues and admits the mystery: he discovers that in the meanwhile, even if he has not found an objective solution, he has at least grown and understood something about his own identity" (76).

12. Ibid., 52.

13. Ibid., 61.

14. Ibid., 74–75.

15. Márquez, "Manuel Ramos Mile-High Murders," 219.

16. Gaspar de Alba, *Desert Blood*, 7.

17. Ibid., 98.

18. Ibid., 186–187.

19. Ibid., 188.

20. Ibid., 211.

21. Mata, "Markings on the Walls," 63.

22. Gaspar de Alba, *Desert Blood*, 286.

23. Mata, "Markings on the Walls," 66–67.

24. Gaspar de Alba, *Desert Blood*, 332.

25. Ibid., 249.

26. The petition was generated after the conference I organized at UCLA in 2003. As of this writing, the petition has only garnered 14,585 votes (even after a decade of circulating in the World Wide Web. See http://www.petitiononline.com/NiUnaMas /petition.html.

27. The ASARCO smelter was shut down permanently and the smokestacks demolished on April 14, 2013, forever altering the landscape of west El Paso.

28. The *Florentine Codex*, also known as *Historia general de las cosas de Nueva España*/General History of the Things of New Spain*, for which Fray Bernardino de Sahagún (1499–1590) is usually given authorial credit, was a massive ethnographic project undertaken under Sahagún's supervision and created by unnamed Mexica *tlacuiles* (scribes) and pupils of Sahagún who were responsible for the images and Nahuatl text of the bilingual codex, made for the purpose of preserving the history,

culture, and cosmology of the indigenous people of Mexico after the Spaniards deci-
mated the Aztec temples and libraries. Sahagún's underlying motive was a religious
one; he wanted to catechize and evangelize the Indians, and to do so he needed to
establish a linguistic bridge between Spanish and Nahuatl and between the picto-
graphic narrative form of native codices and the written form of European books.
Hence, the *Florentine Codex* represents an early form of not only conceptual/visual
and linguistic *mestizaje*, but also a hybridity of the beliefs, myths, and legends of
native memory and Catholic interpretation. For more about the *Florentine Codex*,
see the *Wikipedia* entry: http://en.wikipedia.org/wiki/Florentine_Codex. The full text
of the *Florentine Codex* has been digitized into three volumes by the World Digital
Library, and may be accessed at www.wdl.org/en/item/10096/#languages=spa&item
_type=manuscript. The Coyolxauhqui legend is in Vol. 1, Book III, 413–420.

    29. Nicholson, "New Tenochtitlan Templo Mayor," 77.

    30. Gómez-Cano, *Return to Coatlicue*, 104.

    31. Moraga, *Loving in the War Years*, 147.

    32. Anzaldúa, *Interviews/Entrevistas*, 220.

    33. Ibid., 226.

    34. Gómez-Cano, *Return to Coatlicue*, 107.

    35. The Coyolxauhqui stone was unearthed in Mexico City in 1978 under the
Zócalo, site of the ruins of the Templo Mayor of Tenochtitlan.

    36. I am alluding here to Paulo Freire's *Pedagogy of the Oppressed* and Chela
Sandoval's *Methodology of the Oppressed*.

    37. Bickham Mendez, "Globalizing Scholar Activism," 138.

Chapter Six

    1. To view the cartoons and other images discussed but not shown here, see the
original publication of this chapter in Gaspar de Alba and López, *Our Lady of Controversy*, 212–248.

    2. "Even if Salman Rushdie repents and becomes the most pious man of all
time, it is incumbent on every Muslim to employ everything he has got, his life and
wealth, to send him to Hell." See the Ayatollah Khomeini entry in *Wikipedia*, www
.wikipedia.org.

    3. Nelson, "Our Lady of All This Fuss," A3. *Cyber Arte* Collection, Museum of
International Folk Art Archives.

    4. Allen, "Our Lady of Eternal Conflict," 14. *Cyber Arte* Collection, Museum of
International Folk Art Archives.

    5. The "eye" part of this construction functions as a synecdoche to represent
the body of the viewer and the material conditions that inform the experience of the
body—race, class, gender, age, sexuality, ethnicity, language, etc.—and that consequently shape the subjectivity of the "I" that filters what the eye sees. For more about
how the eye/I constructs positionality, see my *Chicano Art Inside/Outside the Master's
House*, 23–28.

    6. Linton, "'Our Lady' Artwork Is an Offense," C2.

    7. Henry Casso, letter to Archbishop Michael Sheehan, June 20, 2001. *Cyber Arte*
Collection, Museum of International Folk Art Archives.

    8. See "Our Lady Controversy" page on www.almalopez.com.

9. See www.sancta.org.mx; www.virgendeguadalupe.org.mx.

10. McVeigh and Sikkink, "God, Politics, and Religion," 1426.

11. Walker, "Whose Lady?," 43.

12. Sandoval, *Methodology of the Oppressed*, 131.

13. Ibid. Meta-ideologizing is the third of five technologies of the methodology of the oppressed. The first two are semiotics and deconstruction, and the last two are democratics (or the hermeneutics of love) and differential consciousness. In actuality, *Our Lady* is a representation of the five technologies working together.

14. Ibid., 83.

15. Hall, "Encoding/Decoding," 100. Although this essay is about the reading of televised images, the same three readings or reference codes can apply to all cultural texts.

16. Benke, "Bikini-Clad Virgin Mary," A12. *Cyber Arte* Collection, Museum of International Folk Art Archives.

17. Quoted in Walker, "Whose Lady?," 43.

18. Ibid., 43.

19. Ibid., 42.

20. *Cyber Arte* Collection, Museum of International Folk Art Archives.

21. M. Montoya, "Un/braiding Stories," 9.

22. Gaspar de Alba, *Chicano Art*, 162.

23. López, "The Artist of *Our Lady*," 14–16. This artist statement was originally published online on April 2, 2001, as "The Artist of 'Our Lady,'" www.lasculturas.com.

24. "I'm embarrassed to think that we're still living in the age of the Inquisition." *Cyber Arte* Collection, Museum of International Folk Art Archives.

25. To read the full text of all of these e-mails, see the "Our Lady Controversy" page at www.almalopez.com.

26. Sandoval, *Methodology of the Oppressed*, 183.

27. The show opened at Emanations Studio Gallery in Santa Fe. The six artists in the show were Delilah Montoya, Pola López, Goldie Garcia, Vivian Marthell, Ana Rivera, and Alma López.

28. Sharpe, "Artist Calls for Backing," B1, B4. *Cyber Arte* Collection, Museum of International Folk Art Archives.

29. Indeed, because we discovered how much interest there was in the *Our Lady* controversy panel that López, Luz Calvo, and I organized for the 2008 annual meeting of the National Association for Chicana and Chicano Studies, which also included Cristina Serna and was moderated by Antonia Castañeda, we decided to put together a teaching tool in the form of an anthology of feminist interpretations of the controversy, which resulted in the book *Our Lady of Controversy: Alma López's "Irreverent Apparition."* López's 47-minute video, *I LOVE Lupe*, featuring a historic conversation between Ester Hernández, Yolanda López, and herself about their respective interpretations of La Virgen and their ensuing controversies, accompanies each copy of the book.

30. Sandoval, *Methodology of the Oppressed*, 182.

31. Gaspar de Alba, *Chicano Art*, 162.

32. Museum of New Mexico press release, April 6, 2001. *Cyber Arte* Collection, Museum of International Folk Art Archives.

33. "Museum Director Denies Appeal: *Our Lady* Stays," Museum press release, July 13, 2001. *Cyber Arte* Collection, Box 1, folder 3, Museum of International Folk Art Archives.

34. This explains the rumor that the museum had to close down the show four months early, which is inaccurate.

35. López, "The Artist of *Our Lady*," 15.

36. López Pulido, *Sacred World*, xiii–xiv.

37. See the "Chimayo, New Mexico," entry at www.wikipedia.org.

38. Grimes, *Symbol and Conquest*, 62.

39. Ibid., 62.

40. Ibid.

41. Ibid., 67.

42. McKee, "Shouts, Shoves, Prayers," 3. *Cyber Arte* Collection, Museum of International Folk Art Archives.

43. Allen, "Our Lady of Eternal Conflict." *Cyber Arte* Collection, Museum of International Folk Art Archives.

44. Antonio López, "Our Lady Fleshing Out the 'Our,'" 74. *Cyber Arte* Collection, Museum of International Folk Art Archives.

45. Caster, "Staging Prisons," 114; emphasis in original.

46. Coggan, "Our Lady," 6. *Cyber Arte* Collection, Museum of International Folk Art Archives.

47. Phelan, *Unmarked*, 130; emphasis in original.

48. Ibid., 131.

49. Ibid., 132.

50. Ibid., 145; emphasis in original.

51. Caster, "Staging Prisons," 107.

52. Report to the MNM [Museum of New Mexico] Committee on Sensitive Materials. *Cyber Arte* Collection, Museum of International Folk Art Archives.

53. Grimes, *Symbol and Conquest*, 67.

54. The Tradition, Family, Property/America Needs Fatima (TFP/ANF) Group started an aggressive letter-writing campaign with worldwide outreach to have the offensive art piece removed from the exhibition. The campaign included a pread-dressed postcard of the traditional Guadalupe with some inflammatory text about the blasphemous "bikini" Virgin that just needed to be signed, stamped, and mailed to the museum in New Mexico. The *Cyber Arte* archives logged over 24,000 cards, some of them coming from as far as Belize and Brazil. The TFP/ANF group's website, however, states that their campaign brought 65,000 cards to the museum.

55. Horton, "Ritual and Return," 199.

56. Pawloski, "Church Gives 'Our Lady' Mock Burial," 1, 3. *Cyber Arte* Collection, Museum of International Folk Art Archives.

57. J.C., quoted in Gilot, "Idolaters Doth Protest Our Lady," 6.

58. The performance was "censored by the museum," said Sedeño in a press release. *Cyber Arte* Collection, Museum of International Folk Art Archives.

59. Sharpe, "Artist Calls for Backing of 'Our Lady,'" B4. *Cyber Arte* Collection, Museum of International Folk Art Archives.

60. Long live Mexico! Long live the Virgin of Guadalupe! Death to the Spaniards!

61. I was one of the first six faculty hired in 1994 with full-time appointments in the newly instituted César E. Chávez Center for Interdisciplinary Instruction in Chicana and Chicano Studies, which was the compromise reached after the Hunger Strike Agreement. In 2005, the Chávez Center became a department, of which I served as chair from 2007 to 2010.

62. Cultural nationalism is a form of identity politics that expresses allegiance to a culture instead of a nation. Regardless of where they located their birthplace, in the United States or in Mexico, Chicano cultural nationalists claimed Mexican culture, which included the Catholic faith and the Spanish language, as their nation. Now seen as an outdated form of Chicano identity politics, cultural nationalism continues to be seen as a tenet of the Chicano movement and a seminal aspect of the ideology of Chicanismo.

63. López, "The Artist of *Our Lady*," 14.

64. Gaspar de Alba, "There's No Place Like Aztlán: Homeland Myths and Embodied Aesthetics," Chapter 3 in this volume; emphasis in original.

65. Rebolledo, *Chronicles of Panchita Villa*, 179.

66. Paz, "Sons of La Malinche," 207–208.

67. See *Bikini Virgin on Trial*, directed by Cynthia Buzzard, Alma López private collection. Portions of Buzzard's video are included in *I Love Lupe* (2011), the 47-minute video that Alma López produced to accompany our book, *Our Lady of Controversy*.

68. Orsini, "The Lady Has Many Faces," 9. *Cyber Arte* Collection, Museum of International Folk Art Archives.

69. *La Herencia del Norte* (Spring 1999): 6. *Cyber Arte* Collection, Museum of International Folk Art Archives.

70. For more about the pedophilia scandals in the Catholic Church, with emphasis on the Santa Fe Archdiocese, see "Archbishop Asks for Forgiveness," The Associated Press State & Local Wire March 11, 2000; "Archbishop Says It Wasn't Easy to Put Priest on Leave," The Associated Press State & Local Wire, January 19, 2000; Benke, "Archbishop"; Constable, "Sheehan," A1; Frazier, "Catholic Church"; Logan, "Sheehan Wants Stricter Rules," A1; Logan, "Bishop's Denial," A1; Lumpkin, "Embattled Priest Says Goodbye," A1; Presley, "Lone Star Living"; Sanchez, "Archdiocese of Santa Fe," A1; Wade, "Sheehan Can Fix It," A4.

71. The archbishop called the settlement "Chernobyl on the Rio Grande." Quoted in Siemon-Netto, "Analysis."

72. See Calvo, "Art Comes for the Archbishop," 123.

73. Semiotics is the science of signs, or rather, the reading of cultural signs to unveil the dominant political ideologies inherent in them. Deconstruction refers to the practice of challenging the mythological constructs (as we see in the writing of cultural myths that have both historical and teleological functions) of these political ideologies. And again, meta-ideologizing is the revolutionary appropriation of cultural signs for the purpose of transforming their mythologized meanings and resignifying those meanings for the empowerment of the oppressed. For more about how Alma López engages the "methodology of the oppressed," see Román-Odio, "Queering the Sacred."

74. Montoya, "Un/braiding Stories," 9.

75. López, "The Artist of *Our Lady*," 14.

76. The Santuario Diocesano de Nuestra Señora de Guadalupe website no longer has information on how to become a member of the Guadalupe Family. To read more about how to donate to the shrine, see http://www.ologsf.com/aca.

77. Constable, "Parishioners Welcome Marian Statue."

78. The oldest shrine to the Virgin of Guadalupe in the New World is actually not the Santuario in Santa Fe. The first and oldest Guadalupe Church is located in Ciudad Juárez, across the border from El Paso, Texas, having been built over a hundred years earlier than the Santuario in Santa Fe. In fact, it was to this site that De Vargas and his missionaries, colonists, and fellow conquistadores repaired in 1680 when the Pueblo Indians revolted and drove the Spaniards out of New Mexico. With the territorial redistribution of 1848, when the Mexican North became the American West and Southwest, but only after 1912, when New Mexico was admitted as a state, the honor of being the first and oldest church to Our Lady of Guadalupe *in the United States* fell to the Guadalupe Church in Santa Fe.

79. Constable, "Journey of Devotion."

80. For more about La Conquistadora and the Fiestas of Santa Fe, respectively, see González, "Making Privates Public"; see also FitzCallaghan Jones, "The War of the Roses."

81. There are strict nativity and marital requirements for the man and woman who are selected as the King and Queen of the Fiesta. They must both be born in New Mexico, but while the man is expected to be a family man, that is, married with children, the young woman must be unmarried, in other words, a virgin, and remain that way through the end of the Fiesta.

82. For more information about the Santa Fe Fiestas, see www.santafefiesta.org.

83. Another big tourist attraction, the miraculous spiral staircase, is located in the Loretto Chapel, a few blocks away from the Cathedral Basilica. According to local legend, it was Saint Joseph himself, in the guise of a nameless humble carpenter looking for work, who paid a visit to the Sisters of Loretto, the first nuns of Santa Fe, and built the staircase that would connect the chapel's nave to the choir. What is "miraculous" is that the wood curves dramatically in 360-degree turns and is held together without nails.

84. New Mexico is the home of the penitent, the conquered, and the miraculous, but also of the explosive, the covert, and the alien. The atom bomb was invented in Los Alamos, New Mexico, and Roswell has long been associated with the sighting of Unidentified Flying Objects and the secret government laboratory known as Area 51 where supposed extra-terrestrial aliens are studied.

85. I added this section in 2012.

86. For more about the *Splendors of Faith/Scars of Conquest: Arts of the Missions of Northern New Spain, 1600–1821* exhibition, see www.museumca.org/exhibit /splendors-faithscars-conquest.

87. Personal e-mail sent to Alma López from Drew Johnson, October 25, 2010. Shared by the artist.

88. Drew Johnson, e-mail, November 1, 2010.

89. Ironically, the book's release date was exactly ten years after Jon Richards's cartoon lampooning Archbishop Sheehan and the Ayatollah Khomeini standing in front of *Our Lady* and planning a fatwa of the artist was published in Santa Fe's *Journal North*.

90. Accessed June 12, 2011, www.almalopez.com/ORnews3/20110611ANF.html.

91. Accessed June 17, 2011, www.almalopez.com/ORnews3/20110616ANF.html.

92. This quote is taken from the Network for Church Monitoring Blog, which reprinted and commented on a story about the Irish controversy printed in *The Guardian.* See churchandstate.org.uk/2011/06/irish-bishop-criticizes-our-lady-in -bikini-exhibit/.

93. See Ireland's Department of Justice and Equality webpage, www.inis.gov.ie /en/JELR/ (search for Defamation Act).

94. On a personal note, thank you, dear Nuala, for taking the heat for us and for *Our Lady.* Your solidarity and that of your students, colleagues, and staff will always be remembered.

95. All of this coverage on the Irish controversy may be viewed on Alma López's website at www.almalopez.com/ORnews/news.html.

96. Irish Defamation Act of 2009; accessed June 21, 2011, http://www.irish statutebook.ie/pdf/2009/en.act.2009.0031.pdf.

97. Irish Defamation Act of 2009.

98. English, Eoin, "I never intended to offend," *Irish Examiner.* López's state-ment was also published in the Cork Student News Blog. It may be accessed from her website at www.almalopez.com/ORnews3/20110706ifp.html.

Chapter Seven

1. Author's translation of Sor Juana's "Romance en reconocimiento a las inimi-tables plumas de Europa, que hicieron mayores sus obras con sus elogios: que no se halló acabado," or, "Romance in Recognition of the Inimitable Pens of Europe, who enlarged her work with their praise: found unfinished." For the full text of the poem, see Romance 51 in *Obras completas*, Vol. 1, *Lírica personal*, 158–161.

2. The English translations of all my citations from *Respuesta a Sor Filotea* are taken from Peden, *Poems, Protest, and a Dream.*

3. The bishop of Puebla at the time was Manuel Fernández de Santa Cruz, who, along with Sor Juana's father confessor, Padre Antonio Núñez de Miranda, and the archbishop of Mexico, Francisco Aguiar y Seijas, conspired to curtail Sor Juana's celebrity in both Spain and New Spain. Sor Juana's "Carta Atenagórica," or "Letter Worthy of Athena," published against Sor Juana's wishes and without her knowledge or consent, was the first step in ruining her reputation.

4. Peden, *A Woman of Genius*, 30.

5. Ibid., 74.

6. This is my translation of Sor Juana's "Philosophical Satire." To read the full poem, see Peden, *Poems, Protest, and a Dream*, 149–151.

7. I argue that her first love was Leonor Carreto, Marquesa de Mancera, whom Juana Inés served as a lady-in-waiting at the viceregal court (1664–1669), but it wasn't until her intimate friendship with María Luisa Manrique de Lara, Condesa de Paredes (1680–1688), that Sor Juana's lesbian desire was given free rein.

8. Peden, *A Woman of Genius*, 42. I read the word "inclination" as a referent for not only what Sor Juana calls her "natural impulse" for learning, which she admits to never being able to curtail or control, but also as a coded signifier of her lesbian

desire, something else she was born with and that motivated her choices, behaviors, and attitudes throughout her life.

9. In seventeenth-century New Spain, a *beata* was a woman who had offered her life and service to the convent in exchange for room and board. Usually, older women and widows who did not have the money for a dowry nor the inclination to profess joined the convent as *beatas*. Like slaves, they received no compensation for their work, but they occupied a higher social status than either slaves or servants only because of their race. They had absolutely no power within the political sphere of the convent.

10. De la Cruz, "Petición que en forma causídica presenta al Tribunal Divino la Madre Juana Inés de la Cruz, por impetrar perdón de sus culpas," in *Fama y obras póstumas*, 129–131. Author's translation: "the most undignified and ungrateful creature ever created by the Omnipotent . . . for all these years that I have lived in religion, not only without religion, but worse than a pagan." The full text of this book has been digitized by the University Library of Bielefeld, Germany. It may be accessed at www.ub.uni-bielefeld.de/diglib/delacruz/fama/. Accessed March 28, 2012.

11. See the convent's *Book of Professions*, titled *Libro de profesiones y elecciones de prioras y vicarias del Convento de San Gerónimo (1586–1713)*.

12. "Y en señal de cuanto deseo derramar la sangre en defensa de estas verdades, lo firmo con ella," she asserts at the end of "Protesta que rubricada con su sangre, hizo de su fe, y amor a Dios, la Madre Juana Inés de la Cruz, al tiempo de abandonar los estudios humanos, para proseguir, desembarazada de este afecto, en el camino de la perfección," *Fama y obras*, 124–126. My translation: "As a sign of how much I want to let blood in defense of these truths, I sign this with it."

13. Schons, "Sor Juana: A Chronicle."

14. See Sabat-Rivers, "Biografías."

15. See Schons, "The First Feminist in the New World," *Equal Rights*, October 31, 1925, 11–12.

16. Schons, "Sor Juana: A Chronicle," n.p.

17. This is Gloria Anzaldúa's term for self-knowledge, an epistemology of the self that Anzaldúa talked and wrote about extensively in interviews and later pieces, such as her "now let us shift . . . the path of *conocimiento* . . . inner work, public acts," in Anzaldúa and Keating, *This Bridge We Call Home*, 540–578.

18. Portillo Trambley, *Sor Juana*, in *Sor Juana and Other Plays*, 146.

19. Ibid., 184.

20. Ibid.

21. Rueda Esquibel, *With Her Machete*, 73.

22. Portillo Trambley, *Sor Juana*, 177.

23. Ibid., 178.

24. Rueda Esquibel, *With Her Machete*, 74.

25. Portillo Trambley, *Sor Juana*, 162.

26. Rueda Esquibel, *With Her Machete*, 77.

27. See Chapter 1 in this volume. I created my "interview" while doing doctoral work in 1991. Eight decades earlier, Amado Nervo had also authored a type of "interview" with La Décima Musa in which they discourse about similar subjects that Sor Juana and I discussed; the purpose of my interview was to reveal how Sor Juana preceded feminist and postmodern theory by three hundred years, neither of which was

Nervo's intention. See Amado Nervo, "Una conversación con Sor Juana," in Nervo and Méndez, *Juana de Asbaje*, 93–105.

28. Gaspar de Alba, *Sor Juana's Second Dream*. I had many vivid, lucid dreams of communicating with Sor Juana while working on the novel. Once, I dreamed I was talking on the phone with Sor Juana, asking her what kind of shoes she was wearing, while staring at my black wingtips. Was Sor Juana telling me she was a butch woman, or was I imagining her walking in my own butch shoes?

29. See Boswell, *Christianity, Social Tolerance, and Homosexuality*; see also his *Same-Sex Unions in Pre-Modern Europe*.

30. My theory builds on the Anzaldúan notion of *conocimiento* as the process of self-knowledge and consciousness-raising about the inner and outer expressions of the self. *Re-conocimiento* moves out of the self into a process of perceiving, naming, knowing, acknowledging, and accepting the Other at the same time that the self is mirrored in the Other, and therefore identifies with and recognizes the Other as the self.

31. Muñoz, *Disidentifications*, 11.

32. Quoted in ibid., 7.

33. Ibid.

34. Ibid., 12.

35. D. González, *Refusing the Favor*, 120.

36. For more about the process of Chicana identity construction, see also D. González, "Chicana Identity Matters."

37. See Hernández-Avila and Anzaldúa, "Quincentennial," 177.

38. To see how Anzaldúa has conceptualized the seven stages of *conocimiento*, see her "now let us shift . . . the path of *conocimiento*," in Anzaldúa and Keating, *This Bridge We Call Home*, 544–574.

39. Ibid., 542.

40. Ibid., 571.

41. Yarbro-Bejarano, *The Wounded Heart*, 151.

42. See Anzaldúa, *Borderlands/La Frontera*, 25–51.

43. The etymology of "crisis" is the Greek κρίσις, or *krisis*, which means the power to separate, to distinguish, to decide, to make a choice. See http://en.wiktionary.org /wiki/crisis. In its modern application, a crisis is seen as a traumatic, painful, or destabilizing experience, but it is also a turning point, a decisive moment in which change becomes necessary in order to grow and move forward.

44. de la tierra, *For the Hard Ones*, 49.

45. See Soto, *Reading Chican@ Like a Queer*, 1–3.

46. Definition of *anagnorisis* on MerriamWebster.com. www.merriam-webster .com/dictionary/anagnorisis.

47. Aristotle, *Poetics*, section XI. See the *Project Gutenberg EBook of Poetics* by Aristotle, translated by S. H. Butcher, http://www.gutenberg.org/files/1974/1974 -h/1974-h.htm. Accessed July 2, 2012.

48. Aristotle enumerates different kinds of literary recognition. See ibid., section XVI.

49. Sandoval, *Methodology of the Oppressed*, 141.

50. For many Latino/a and Latin Americanist scholars, Octavio Paz is the eminent "voice of Mexico," the Nobel prize–winning poet laureate and self-appointed guru of all things Mexican, but some of us who find his work racist, misogynistic, and

homophobic to the *extreme*—in the same way that he finds Pachucos, Mexican Americans of the 1940s and 1950s, "extreme" examples of Mexicans corrupted by the United States—give him a break because he was such a good poet, after all, or because he really did have some remarkably accurate things to say about expressions of Mexicanness such as fiestas and the Day of the Dead. Chicana lesbians, however, who are implicated not only as cultural cousins to those extremely degenerate Pachucos but also as tainted daughters of La Chingada—we tend not to be overly patient or generous with Octavio Paz. Paz is dangerous, particularly to those of us who fit all of the categories that he maligns: women, Mexican Americans, and lesbians. See his "The *Pachuco* and Other Extremes" and "The Sons of La Malinche" in *The Labyrinth of Solitude*.

51. Paz, *Sor Juana*, 217.

52. Ibid., 218.

53. Ludwig Pfandl referred to the sexual symbolism in Sor Juana's work as a consequence of her own castration complex caused by a forbidden desire. In Pfandl's words: "No significa más que el castigo de castración a causa de un deseo prohibido." See Arias de la Canal, *Intento de psicoanálisis*, 20. My translation: "Sor Juana's sexual symbolism signifies nothing more than the punishment of castration caused by a forbidden desire."

54. See Rich, "Compulsory Heterosexuality."

55. See De la Cruz, Poema 19, "Puro amor, que ausente y sin deseo de indecencias, puede sentir lo que el más profano," in *A Sor Juana Anthology*, 36–40. This is Poem 3 in English, its title translated as "A pure love, however, distant, eschewing all unseemliness, may feel whatever the most profane might feel"; the lines in question appear on page 38.

56. See Beauvoir, *The Second Sex*.

57. See "In Reply to a Gentleman from Peru, Who Sent Her Clay Vessels while Suggesting She Would Better Be a Man," in *Sor Juana Inés de la Cruz: Poems*, 21, 23.

58. De la Cruz, Poem 5 (Poem 91 in Spanish), "Excusing herself for silence, on being summoned to break it," in *A Sor Juana Anthology*, 43.

59. De la Cruz, Poem 113, "She Assures That She Will Hold a Secret in Confidence," in *Sor Juana Inés de la Cruz: Poems*, 45.

60. Here is an epigraph about Sappho that is completely applicable to Sor Juana: "She was considered one of their finest poets, an integral part of their cultural history. Her face was engraved on coinage, her statue erected, her portrait painted on vases. Many ancient commentators praised her literary genius, while Plato, among others, called her 'the tenth Muse.'" See Balmer's introduction to *Sappho: Poems and Fragments*.

61. Paz, *Sor Juana*, 217.

62. There's no proof she had "an excess of libido," either, or that she felt at some point "an impossible passion for a man," though these seem plausible enough explanations for Sor Juana's melancholia for the peaceful Paz.

63. Paz, *Sor Juana*, 111.

64. Ibid., 226.

65. See Zinn, *A People's History of the United States*. "My argument cannot be against [the historian's task of] selection, simplification, emphasis, which are inevitable for both cartographers and historians. But the mapmaker's distortion is a technical

necessity for a common purpose shared by all people who need maps. The historian's distortion is more than technical, it is ideological; it is released into a world of contending interests, where any chosen emphasis supports (whether the historian means to or not) some kind of interest, whether economic or political or racial or national or sexual. . . . The history of any country, presented as the history of a family, conceals fierce conflicts of interest (sometimes exploding, most often repressed) between conquerors and conquered, masters and slaves, capitalists and workers, dominators and dominated in race and sex. And in such a world of conflict, a world of victims and executioners, it is the job of thinking people, as Albert Camus suggested, not to be on the side of the executioners" (8–10).

66. See Pérez, *Decolonial Imaginary.*

67. Ibid., xv.

68. For more about what Emma Pérez calls "the Oedipal conquest triangle," see Chapter 2, "Malinche's Revenge," in this volume.

69. See Pérez, "Sexuality and Discourse."

70. Discussing why it took her a while to decide whether or not to join the convent, Sor Juana writes in *Respuesta* that her desires for solitude, for study, for writing were so strong they felt like "temptation," one which she knew she had to overcome if she entered life in community. However, she admits that "once dimmed and encumbered by the many activities common to Religion, that inclination exploded in me like gunpowder, proving how *privation is the source of appetite*" (emphasis in original). Peden, *A Woman of Genius*, 32.

71. Pérez, *Decolonial Imaginary*, 7.

72. Ibid., 6.

73. Pérez, "Irigaray's Female Symbolic."

74. Spivak, *The Post-Colonial Critic*, 109.

75. To see the full text of Sor Juana's "Romance en reconocimiento a las inimitables plumas de Europa, que hicieron mayores sus obras con sus elogios: que no se halló acabado," see *Fama y obras póstumas*, 157–162. The full text of this book has been digitized by the University Library of Bielefeld, Germany; accessed July 21, 2012, at www.ub.uni-bielefeld.de/diglib/delacruz/fama/. As explained at the end of the poem in an editorial comment, it was found "en borrador y sin mano última," in draft form and without a final hand, or copy.

76. For a summary of these endorsements, what Octavio Paz calls the seven vindications of Sor Juana, which were published in place of an introduction to Sor Juana's second volume of collected works, see Paz, *Sor Juana*, 431–433.

77. For an English translation of this letter, see "Admonishment: The Letter of Sor Philothea de la Cruz" in *A Sor Juana Anthology*, 199–203.

78. Pérez, *Decolonial Imaginary*, 7.

79. Spivak, *Post-Colonial Critic*, 109.

80. See "Inés, cuando te riñen por *bellaca*," or "Inés, When Someone Tells You You're a Bitch," in Larkin and Manrique, *Sor Juana's Love Poems/Poemas de Amor*, 56–59. See, for example, the queer phallic reading of the following lines: "*sabe mi amor muy bien lo que se peca* / The way I love you is a sin, I know it— / *y así con tu afición no se embabuca*, / but the way you fuck me is no trick. Your hard-on's real, / *aunque eres zancarrón y yo de Meca* / and I'm a field just waiting to be plowed.

81. Bebout, *Mythohistorical Interventions*, 174, 176.

82. Anderson, *Hunger's Brides*.

83. At the risk of sounding like "sour grapes," my point here is that when a random white man, whose only connection to Sor Juana is that he and his wife lived in Mexico for a while, publishes a novel on Sor Juana Inés de la Cruz, it becomes a media event, but when a Chicana lesbian with solid academic credentials publishes a book on the same historical figure five years earlier, it makes hardly a ripple in the publishing industry (and is all but summarily ignored by critics on both sides of the border and in both Spain and Mexico).

84. See www.hungersbrides.com. The website requires Flash.

85. Sor Juana's section became the abridged version, published separately two years later. See P. Anderson, *Sor Juana, or the Breath of Heaven*.

86. P. Anderson, *Hunger's Brides*, 76.

87. Ibid., 143.

88. If one can call a coerced marriage and a life of breeding children as a promising worldly existence.

89. See Isaiah 62:4. See also an online discussion of the covenant of marriage and the biblical reference to Beulah at www.reformedwitnesshour.org/1997/1997feb16.html.

90. P. Anderson, *Sor Juana, or the Breath of Heaven*, 387.

91. Gaspar de Alba, *Sor Juana's Second Dream*, 52–53.

92. See Erauso, *Lieutenant Nun*.

93. P. Anderson, *Hunger's Brides*, 365.

94. Gaspar de Alba, *Sor Juana's Second Dream*, 33.

95. Ibid., 37.

96. Ibid., 37, 38.

97. Ibid., 275–276.

98. The letter appears in the third edition of Octavio Paz's *Sor Juana Inés de la Cruz, o, Las trampas de la fe*. Another unknown letter of Sor Juana's was discovered in 1995 by a Jesuit priest in a library of ancient texts in Madrid, Spain. Titled "Carta de Serafina de Cristo," and dated February 1, 1691, exactly one month prior to *Respuesta*, the letter was studied for thirteen years by the Mexican historian Elías Trabulse, who, with the support and approval of a good number of contemporary Sorjuanista scholars, including Margo Glantz, Asunción Lavrin, Sara Poot Herrera, and Georgina Sabat de Rivers, declared the letter another authentic missive from Sor Juana Inés de la Cruz.

99. P. Anderson, *Hunger's Brides*, 389.

100. English translation: *Castalian Inundation of the Only Poetess, the Tenth Muse, Sor Juana Inés de la Cruz, Professed Nun of the Monastery of Saint Jerome in the Imperial City of Mexico, Which, in Various Meters, Languages, and Styles, Fertilizes Various Matters with Elegant, Subtle, Clear, Ingenious, and Useful Verses: For Teaching, Delight, and Admiration*. Dedicated to Her Excellency, Doña María Luisa Manrique de Lara, Condesa de Paredes, Marquesa de la Laguna, sending these papers Her Excellency asked for and which Sor Juana was able to collect from the many hands they were in, not so much divided as hiding like treasure, with others she did not have time to find or copy. Published in Madrid, Spain, 1689.

101. Gaspar de Alba, *Sor Juana's Second Dream*, 328.

102. P. Anderson, *Hunger's Brides*, 539.

103. Ibid., 535, 538, 539.

104. Ibid., 542.

105. Ibid., 513.

106. See www.hungersbrides.com/Inquisition.html. Accessed July 23, 2005.

107. Allatson, "A Shadowy Sequence," 24.

108. Rohrleitner, "Recovering Afro-Mestizaje," 48.

109. University of New Mexico Press found Liliana Wilson's image "too academic" and commissioned a different cover for the novel by Francisco Benítez with Sor Juana in the ecstatic pose of Santa Teresa levitating over what looks like the Rio Grande and the landscape of New Mexico.

110. P. Anderson, *Hunger's Brides*, 440.

111. Harss, *Sor Juana's Dream*, 24.

112. Ibid., 134.

113. De la Cruz, Poem 165, "Que contiene una fantasía contenta con amor decente" (Which recounts how fantasy contents itself with honorable love), *A Sor Juana Anthology*, 64.

114. Quoted in Nadia Tamez-Robledo, "Muralist Guest Speaker Highlights Cultural Understanding," Arts and Life page, *The Pan-American Online* (March 24, 2012), Blog of the University of Texas Pan-American, accessed April 29, 2013, www.panamericanonline.com/art-and-activism/.

115. From Poem 25 (Poem 56 in Spanish), titled "In which she expresses the effects of Divine Love and proposes to die loving, despite the risk," *A Sor Juana Anthology*, 89.

116. Gaspar de Alba, *Sor Juana's Second Dream*, 313.

BIBLIOGRAPHY

Archives

Cyber Arte: Tradition Meets Technology Collection. Museum of International Folk Art, Santa Fe, New Mexico, Archives Department.
Dorothy Schons Papers, 1586–1955. Nettie Lee Benson Latin American Collection, University of Texas Libraries, University of Texas at Austin. www.lib.utexas.edu /benson.

Motion Pictures and Documentaries

Bajo Juárez: A City Devouring Its Girls. Directed by Alejandra Sánchez Orozco and José Antonio Cordero. Los Angeles: Indymedia, 2006.
Border Echoes. Directed by Lorena Méndez. Los Angeles: Peace at the Border Films, 2006.
Bordertown. Directed by Gregory Nava. Los Angeles: El Norte Productions, Nuyorican Productions, 2006.
El Traspatio/Backyard. Directed by Carlos Carrera. Los Angeles: Paramount Pictures, 2009.
Las Muertas de Juárez. Directed by Enrique Murillo. Mexico City: Laguna Productions, 2002.
On the Edge: Femicide in Ciudad Juárez. Directed by Steev Hise. Bloomington, IN: Illegal Art, 2006.
Señorita Extraviada (Missing Young Woman). Directed by Lourdes Portillo. San Francisco: Xochitl Films, 2001.
The Virgin of Juárez. Directed by Kevin James Dobson. Los Angeles: Las Mujeres LLC, 2006.
Yo, La Peor de Todas. Directed by María Luisa Bemberg. Buenos Aires, Argentina: GEA Cinematográfica, 1990.

Primary and Secondary Sources

ABC News. "Natalee Holloway Is Dead, Judge Decides." Accessed April 25, 2013. http://abcnews.go.com/News/judge-pronounces-natalee-holloway-dead /story?id=15346993#.UX2EaoJAtQY.

Adler, Amy, et al. *The New Gatekeepers: Emerging Challenges to Free Expression in the Arts*. New York: Columbia University/National Arts Journalism Program, 2003.

Agosín, Marjorie. *Secrets in the Sand: The Young Women of Ciudad Juárez*. Translated by Celeste Kostopulos-Cooperman. New York: White Pine Press, 2006.

Aguirre, Mirta. *Del encausto a la sangre: Sor Juana Inés de la Cruz*. La Habana: Casa de las Américas, 1975.

Alarcón, Norma. "The Theoretical Subject(s) of *This Bridge Called My Back* and Anglo-American Feminism." In Saldívar and Calderón, *Criticism in the Borderlands*, 28–39.

Allatson, Paul. "A Shadowy Sequence: Chicana Textual/Sexual Reinventions of Sor Juana." *Chasqui: Revista de Literatura Latinoamericana* 33, no. 1 (2004): 3—27.

Allen, Steven Robert. "Our Lady of Eternal Conflict." Editorial. *Weekly Alibi* 10, no. 16 (April 19–25, 2001): 14. Accessed August 19, 2008. www.alibi.com.

Alma López Artist's Website. "*Our Lady* Controversy Continues." http://www .almalopez.com/ORindex.html.

Amigos de Las Mujeres de Juárez. www.amigosdemujeres.org. This site has been discontinued but may still be accessed at http://web.archive.org/web/20031207124 648/http://www.amigosdemujeres.org/.

Amnesty International Website. http://www.amnestyusa.org/news?id=engamr41012 2006.

Anderson, Benedict. *Imagined Communities*. 2nd edition. New York: Verso, 2006. Originally published in 1983.

Anderson, Paul. *Sor Juana, or the Breath of Heaven: The Essential Story from the Epic,* Hunger's Brides. New York: Carroll and Graf, 2006.

———. *Hunger's Brides*. New York: Carroll and Graf, 2005. Originally published in 2004 by New Specs in Canada.

Anzaldúa, Gloria E. "Border arte: Nepantla, el lugar de la frontera." In *La Frontera/ The Border: Art about the Mexico/United States Border Experience*, 107–123. San Diego, CA: Centro Cultural de la Raza: Museum of Contemporary Art, San Diego, 1993.

———. *Borderlands/La Frontera: The New Mestiza*. 1st ed. San Francisco: Aunt Lute Books, 1987.

———. "Entering into the Serpent." In Anzaldúa, *Borderlands/La Frontera*, 25–39.

———. "Haciendo caras/una entrada (an introduction)." In *Making Face, Making Soul/Haciendo Caras*, ed. Gloria Anzaldúa, xv–xxviii. San Francisco: Aunt Lute Foundation, 1990.

———. *Interviews/Entrevistas: Gloria E. Anzaldúa*. Edited by AnaLouise Keating. New York: Routledge, 2000.

———. "La herencia de Coatlicue/The Coatlicue State." In Anzaldúa, *Borderlands/ La Frontera*, 41–51.

———. "Speaking in Tongues: A Letter to 3rd World Women Writers." In Moraga and Anzaldúa, *This Bridge Called My Back*, 165–173.

———. "*Tlilli, Tlapalli*/The Path of the Red and Black Ink." In Anzaldúa, *Borderlands*/La Frontera, 65–75.

Anzaldúa, Gloria E., and AnaLouise Keating, eds. *This Bridge We Call Home: Radical Visions for Transformation.* New York: Routledge, 2002.

"Archbishop Asks for Forgiveness." The Associated Press State & Local Wire, March 11, 2000.

"Archbishop Says It Wasn't Easy to Put Priest on Leave." The Associated Press State & Local Wire, January 19, 2000.

Archuleta, Margaret, and Rennard Strickland, eds. *Shared Visions: Native American Painters and Sculptors in the Twentieth Century.* New York: The New Press, 1991. Exhibition catalog.

Arias de la Canal, Fredo. *Intento de psicoanálisis de "Juana Inés" y otros ensayos sorjuanistas.* Mexico City: Frente de Afirmación Hispanista, 1988. Spanish translation of Ludwig Pfandl's *Die Zehnte Muse von Mexico, Juana Inés de la Cruz: Ihr Leben, Ihre Dichtung, Ihre Psyche.* Munich: Hermann Rinn, 1946. Published under Military Government Information Control License Nr. US-E-161.

Arriola, Elvia. "Voices from the Barbed Wire of Despair: Women in the *Maquiladoras*, Latina Critical Legal Theory, and Gender at the U.S-Mexico Border." *DePaul Law Review* 729 (2000): 1–69.

Baerwaldt, Wayne, et al. *Memories of Overdevelopment: Philippine Diaspora in Contemporary Art.* Manitoba, Canada: Plug In Editions, 1997. Exhibition catalog.

Balmer, Josephine, trans. *Sappho: Poems and Fragments.* Secaucus, NJ: Lyle Stuart, 1988.

Bard, Patrick. *La Frontera: Una novela de denuncia sobre las muertas de Juárez.* Translated by José Antonio Soriano. Mexico City: Grijalbo, 2002.

Barkan, Elazar, and Marie-Denise Shelton, eds. *Borders, Exiles, Diasporas.* Stanford: Stanford University Press, 1998.

Baud, Michiel, and Rosanne Rutten. "Introduction." *International Review of Social History* 49, supplement 12 (2004): 1–18.

Baum, Frank L. *The Wonderful Wizard of Oz.* Reprint. New York: dilithium Press, 1994. Originally published 1900.

Beauvoir, Simone de. *The Second Sex.* Translated by H. M. Parshley. New York: Bantam Books, 1970.

Bebout, Lee. *Mythohistorical Interventions: The Chicano Movement and Its Legacies.* Minneapolis: University of Minnesota Press, 2011.

Benford, Robert D., and David A. Snow. "Framing Processes and Social Movements: An Overview and Assessment." *Annual Review of Sociology* 26 (2000): 611–639.

Benítez, Rohry, Adriana Candia, Patricia Cabrera, Guadalupe de la Mora, Josefina Martínez, Isabel Velásquez, and Ramona Ortiz. *El silencio que la voz de todas quiebra: Mujeres y víctimas de Ciudad Juárez.* Chihuahua: Ediciones del Azar, 1999.

Benke, Richard. "Archbishop: New Mexico Dealt with Its Own Sex Scandals." The Associated Press State & Local Wire, March 22, 2002.

———. "Bikini-Clad Virgin Mary 'a Tart': Archbishop." *Ottawa Citizen*, April 5, 2001, A12.

Bhabha, Homi K. "Beyond the Pale: Art in the Age of Multicultural Translation." In Sussman et al., *1993 Biennial Exhibition Catalog*, 62–73.

Blake, Debra J. *Chicana Sexuality and Gender: Cultural Refiguring in Literature, Oral History, and Art*. Durham, NC: Duke University Press, 2008.

Bolaño, Roberto. *2666*. Translated by Natasha Wimmer. New York: Farrar, Straus, and Giroux, 2008.

Border Lines Juárez Tourist Website. http://www.blines.com/page1.html. This site has been discontinued but may still be accessed at http://web.archive.org/web/20000 605023811/http://blines.com/page9.html.

Borunda, Daniel. "Woman's Body Found in Juárez; Homicide Toll Surpasses 700." *El Paso Times*, April 12, 2011. Accessed April 30, 2011. http://www.elpasotimes .com/juarez/ci_17821047.

Boswell, John. *Christianity, Social Tolerance, and Homosexuality: Gay People in Western Europe from the Beginning of the Christian Era to the Fourteenth Century*. Chicago: University of Chicago Press, 1980.

———. *Same-Sex Unions in Pre-Modern Europe*. New York: Vintage, 1995.

Bowden, Charles. *Juárez: The Laboratory of the Future*. New York: Aperture, 1998.

———. *Murder City: Ciudad Juárez and the Global Economy's New Killing Fields*. New York: Nation Books, 2010.

Braine, Theresa. "Argentine Experts Study Juárez Murder Remains." Women's eNews, April 16, 2006. http://womensenews.org/story/crime-policylegislation /060416/argentine-experts-study-juarez-murder-remains.

Broude, Norma, and Mary D. Garrard, eds. *The Power of Feminist Art: The American Movement of the 1970s, History and Impact*. New York: Harry Abrams, 1994. Exhibition catalog.

Brown, Judith. *Immodest Acts: The Life of a Lesbian Nun in Renaissance Italy*. New York: Oxford University Press, 1986.

Bustillos, Maria. "When PR Goes Wrong: The Mac-Rodarte Fiasco." *The Awl*. Accessed August 3, 2010. http://www.theawl.com/2010/08/when-pr-goes-wrong-the-mac -rodarte-fiasco.

Calvo, Luz. "Art Comes for the Archbishop: The Semiotics of Contemporary Chicana Feminism and the Work of Alma López." In Gaspar de Alba and López, *Our Lady of Controversy*, 96–120.

Canseco Rodal, Raúl, Daniel López Durán, Iván Martínez Reyes, and Manuel Trinidad Bacilio. *Espacio Escultórico de Ciudad Universitaria*. National Autonomous University of Mexico's Culture and Communication Program in the Engineering Department Blog, November 26, 2007. Accessed July 13, 2011. http://culturay comunicacionfi.blogspot.com/2007/11/espacio-escultrico-de-ciudad.html.

Caputi, Jane. "Afterword: Goddess Murder and Gynocide." In Gaspar de Alba with Guzmán, *Making a Killing*, 279–294.

———. *The Age of Sex Crime*. Bowling Green, OH: Bowling Green State University Popular Press, 1987.

———. "The Sexual Politics of Murder." *Gender and Society* 3, no. 4 (December 1989): 437–456.

Caputi, Jane, and Diana E. H. Russell. "Femicide: Sexist Terrorism against Women." *Feminista!* 2, nos. 3/4. Accessed October 16, 2002. http://www.feminista.com /v2n3/Russell.html. This site has been discontinued but may still be accessed at

http://web.archive.org/web/20030816145233/http://www.feminista.com/v2n3
/russell.html.

Caster, Peter. "Staging Prisons: Performance, Activism, and Social Bodies." *The Drama Review* 48, no. 3 (Fall 2004): 107–116.

Castillo, Ana, ed. *Goddess of the Americas: Writings on the Virgin of Guadalupe.* New York: Riverhead Books, 1996.

———. *Massacre of the Dreamers: Essays on Xicanisma.* New York: Plume Books, 1994.

Cawelti, John G. *Adventure, Mystery, and Romance.* Chicago: University of Chicago Press, 1976.

Chabot, Sean. "Framing, Transnational Diffusion, and African-American Intellectuals in the Land of Ghandi." *International Review of Social History* 49, no. 12 (2004): 19–40.

Chávez, John R. *The Lost Land: The Chicano Image of the Southwest.* Albuquerque: University of New Mexico Press, 1984.

Chavoya, C. Ondine, and Rita González, eds. *Asco: Elite of the Obscure: A Retrospective (1922–1987).* Los Angeles: Los Angeles Museum of Art, 2011. Exhibition catalog.

Chmaj, Betty. "A Decade of Déja Vu." *American Quarterly* 31, no. 3 (1979): 358–364.

City-Data.com. "Registered Sex Offenders in El Paso, Texas." Accessed on April 28, 2013. http://www.city-data.com/so/so-El-Paso-Texas.html.

"Ciudad Juárez: Gobierno de Chihuahua desacreditó informe de AI." *Mujereshoy* Program Website. Accessed August 15, 2003. http://foro.univision.com/t5/Asesi natos-de-Mujeres-en-Ju%C3%A1rez-close/Ciudad-Ju%C3%A1rez-Gobierno -de-Chihuahua-desacredit%C3%B3-informe-de-AI/td-p/167738247.

Coco Fusco's Virtual Laboratory Website. http://www.thing.net/~cocofusco/.

Coggan, Catherine. "Our Lady: From Light Switch Covers to Bikinis." *Crosswinds Quarterly*, April 5–12, 2001.

Collins, Patricia Hill. *Black Feminist Thought: Knowledge, Consciousness, and the Politics of Empowerment*, 2nd ed. New York: Routledge, 2000.

———. *On Intellectual Activism.* Philadelphia: Temple University Press, 2013.

ColorLines: News for Action. "MAC, Rodarte Say Sorry for Juárez-Inspired Makeup." Accessed August 4, 2010. http://colorlines.com/archives/2010/07/rodartes _unfortunate_line_of_juarez-inspired_cosmetics.html.

Constable, Anne. "Journey of Devotion." *Santa Fe New Mexican*, July 26, 2008. Accessed February 26, 2009. www.santafenewmexican.com.

———. "Parishioners Welcome Marian Statue after Safe Arrival from Mexico." *Santa Fe New Mexican*, July 23, 2008. Accessed February 16, 2009. www.santafenew mexican.com.

———. "Sheehan: I Never Reinstated Molesters." *The Santa Fe New Mexican*, June 18, 2002, A1.

Convent of San Jerónimo *Book of Professions. Libro de profesiones y elecciones de prioras y vicarias del Convento de San Gerónimo (1586–1713).* Dorothy Schons Papers, 1586–1955, Nettie Lee Benson Latin American Collection, University of Texas Libraries, University of Texas at Austin.

Cope, Douglas R. *The Limits of Racial Domination: Plebeian Society in Colonial Mexico City, 1660–1720.* Madison: University of Wisconsin Press, 1994.

Córdova, Teresa, ed. *Chicano Studies: Critical Connections Between Research and Community*. Albuquerque, NM: National Association for Chicano Studies (NACS), March 1992. The work can be accessed online at http://scholarworks .sjsu.edu/cgi/viewcontent.cgi?article=1056&context=naccs.

Cortez, Constance. "Imágenes e Historias: Meditations on a Donkey Cart." Paper presented at the annual American Anthropological Association meeting, Washington, DC, November 28–December 2, 2001.

Crenshaw, Kimberlé. "Mapping the Margins: Intersectionality, Identity Politics, and Violence against Women of Color." *Stanford Law Review* 43 (July 1991): 1241–1299.

Cruz, Laura. "101 on Sex Offender List Violated Rules, Police Say." *El Paso Times*, March 10, 2000.

Cypess, Sandra Messinger. *La Malinche in Mexican Literature: From History to Myth*. Austin: University of Texas Press, 1991.

Davies, Hugh M., et al. *La Frontera/The Border: Art about the Mexican/United States Border Experience*. San Diego: Centro Cultural de la Raza/Museum of Contemporary Art, 1993. Exhibition catalog.

Davis, Allen F. "The Politics of American Studies." *American Quarterly* 42, no. 3 (September 1990): 353–374.

de la Cruz, Juana Inés, Sor. *Fama y obras póstumas del Fénix de México, décima musa y poetisa americana, Sor Juana Inés de la Cruz*. Madrid: Ruiz de Murga, 1700.

———. *Inundación castálida de la única poetisa, musa décima, Soror Juana Inés de la Cruz, Religiosa profesa en el Monasterio de San Gerónimo de la Imperial Ciudad de México. Que en varios metros, idiomas y estilos fertiliza varios assumptos; con elegantes, sutiles, claros, ingeniosos, útiles versos: para enseñanza, recreo y admiración*. Madrid: Juan García Infanzón, 1689.

———. *Obras completas de Sor Juana Inés de la Cruz*. Vol. 1, *Lírica personal*. Edited, prologue, and notes by Alfonso Méndez Plancarte. Mexico City: Fondo de Cultura Ecónomica, 1988.

———. *Obras completas de Sor Juana Inés de la Cruz*. Vol. 2, *Villancicos y letras sacras*. Edited, introduction, and notes by Alberto G. Salceda. Mexico City: Fondo de Cultura Económica, 1976.

———. *Obras completas de Sor Juana Inés de la Cruz*. Vol. 3, *Autos y loas*. Edited, introduction, and notes by Alberto G. Salceda. Mexico City: Fondo de Cultura Económica, 1976.

———. *Obras completas de Sor Juana Inés de la Cruz*. Vol. 4, *Comedias, sainetes y prosa*. Edited, introduction, and notes by Alberto G. Salceda. Mexico City: Fondo de Cultura Económica, 1976.

de la tierra, tatiana. *For the Hard Ones: A Lesbian Phenomenology*. San Diego: Calaca Press; Buffalo, NY: Chibcha Press, 2002.

Del Castillo, Adelaida R., ed. *Between Borders: Essays on Mexicana/Chicana History*. Encino, CA: Floricanto Press, 1990.

Delgadillo, Victoria, and Rigo Maldonado. "Journey to the Land of the Dead: A Conversation with the Curators of the *Hijas de Juárez* Exhibition." *Aztlán: A Journal of Chicano Studies* 28, no. 2 (Fall 2003): 179–202.

Desert Blood: The Juárez Murders website by Alicia Gaspar de Alba. http://www .desertblood.net.

Dillon, Sam. "Sex Bias Is Reported by U.S. at Border Plants in Mexico." *New York Times*, January 13, 1998, A8.

Doss, Erika. "'I *Must* Paint': Women Artists of the Rocky Mountain Region." In Trenton, *Independent Spirits*, 209–242.

Driskell, David C., ed. *African American Visual Aesthetics: A Postmodernist View.* Washington, DC: Smithsonian Institution Press, 1995.

———. "Introduction: The Progenitors of a Postmodernist Review of African American Art." In Driskell, *African American Visual Aesthetics*, 1–16.

During, Simon, ed. *The Cultural Studies Reader.* New York: Routledge, 1993.

Duro, Paul, ed. *The Rhetoric of the Frame: Essays on the Boundaries of the Artwork.* Cambridge: Cambridge University Press, 1996.

"El Feminicidio." Casa Amiga/Esther Chávez Cano Website. Statistics on the Juárez femicides 1993–2003. http://www.casa-amiga.org.mx/index.php/Contenido/el-feminicidio.html.

English, Eoin. "I never intended to offend, says 'Our Lady' artist." *Irish Examiner*, June 24, 2011, News 7.

Ensler, Eve. *The Vagina Monologues.* New York: Villard, 2000.

Equiluz, Federico, Amaia Ibarrarán, M. Felisa López Liquete, and David Río. *Aztlán: Ensayos sobre literatura chicana.* Vitoria Gasteiz, Spain: Universidad del País Vasco, 2004.

Erauso, Catalina de. *Lieutenant Nun: Memoir of a Basque Transvestite in the New World.* Translated from the Spanish by Michele Stepto and Gabriel Stepto. Boston: Beacon Press, 1996.

Fanon, Frantz. *Black Skin, White Masks.* Translated by Richard Philcox. New York: Grove Press, 2008. Originally published in 1952 in French by Editions du Seuil.

Federici, Silvia. *Caliban and the Witch: Women, the Body and Primitive Accumulation.* Brooklyn, NY: Autonomedia, 2004.

Fields, Virginia M., and Victor Zamudio-Taylor, eds. *The Road to Aztlán: Art from a Mythic Homeland.* Los Angeles: Los Angeles County Museum of Art/University of New Mexico Press, 2001. Exhibition catalog.

FitzCallaghan Jones, Kathleen. "The War of the Roses: Guadalupe, Alma López, and Santa Fe." In Gaspar de Alba and López, *Our Lady of Controversy*, 43–68.

Flores, Paula. "The Government Has Tried to Divide Us." In Gaspar de Alba with Guzmán, *Making a Killing*, 263–267.

Foucault, Michel. *The History of Sexuality.* Vol. 1, *An Introduction.* Translated by Robert Hurley. New York: Vintage Books, 1990.

———. *The Order of Things: An Archaeology of the Human Sciences.* Reprint, New York: Vintage Books, 1994. Originally published 1970.

Franco, Jean. *Plotting Women: Gender and Representation in Mexico.* New York: Columbia University Press, 1989.

Frazier, Joseph B. "Catholic Church, Accusers Reach Deal." Associated Press Online, October 10, 2000.

Fregoso, Rosa-Linda. "Voices without Echo: The Global Gendered Apartheid." *Emergences* 10, no. 1 (2000): 137–155.

Fregoso, Rosa-Linda, and Cynthia Bejarano, eds. *Terrorizing Women: Feminicide in the Americas.* Durham, NC: Duke University Press, 2010.

Freire, Paulo. *Pedagogy of the Oppressed*. 30th anniversary edition. London: Continuum, 2000; 1993. Originally published in Portuguese in 1968.

Frontera NorteSur. "Mexico Is Accountable for Femicides: European Parliament." May 10, 2010. Accessed August 29, 2012. http://mexidata.info/id2659.html.

Frueh, Joanna. "The Body through Women's Eyes." In Broude and Garrard, *The Power of Feminist Art*, 190–207.

Fuentes, Carlos. *The Crystal Frontier: A Novel in Nine Stories*. Translated by Alfred MacAdam. New York: Farrar, Straus, and Giroux, 1997.

Gamson, William. *The Strategy of Social Protest*. 2nd ed. Belmont, CA: Wadsworth Publishing, 1990.

———. *Talking Politics*. New York: Cambridge University Press, 1992.

García, Alma M., ed. *Chicana Feminist Thought: The Basic Historical Writings*. New York: Routledge, 1997.

García, Ignacio. "Juncture in the Road: Chicano Studies since 'El Plan de Santa Barbara.'" In Maciel and Ortiz, *Chicanas/Chicanos at the Crossroads*, 181–203.

Garza, Carmen Lomas. *Directions: Carmen Lomas Garza*. Washington, DC: Smithsonian Institution, 1995. Pamphlet produced for an exhibition of her work held at the Hirshhorn Museum and Sculpture Garden.

Gaspar de Alba, Alicia. *Calligraphy of the Witch*. 1st ed.: New York: St. Martin's Press, 2007. 2nd ed.: Houston: Arte Público Press, 2012.

———. *Chicano Art Inside/Outside the Master's House: Cultural Politics and the CARA Exhibition*. Austin: University of Texas Press, 1998.

———. "Crop Circles in the Cornfield: Remembering Gloria Anzaldúa, 1942–2004." *American Quarterly* 56, no. 3 (2004): iv–vii.

———. *Desert Blood: The Juárez Murders*. Houston: Arte Público Press, 2005.

———. "Excerpts from the Sapphic Diary of Sor Juana Inés de la Cruz." *Frontiers: A Journal of Women Studies* 12, no. 3, 171–179. Reprinted in *Tasting Life Twice: Lesbian Literary Fiction by New American Writers*, edited by Ellen Levy. New York: Avon, 1995.

———. "How the CARA Exhibition Saved My Academic Career." *Aztlán: A Journal of Chicano Studies* 35, no. 1 (Spring 2010): 189–192.

———. "Juana Inés." In *New Chicana/Chicano Writing*, ed. Charles Tatum, 1–15. Tucson: University of Arizona Press, 1992. Reprinted in *Growing Up Chicana/o*, ed. Tiffany López. New York: William Morrow Books, 1993.

———. *La Llorona on the Longfellow Bridge: Poetry y otras movidas, 1985–2001*. Houston: Arte Público Press, 2003.

———. "Literary Wetback." In Gaspar de Alba, *La Llorona on the Longfellow Bridge*, 40–43.

———. "Malinche's Revenge." In Romero and Nolacea Harris, *Feminism, Nation and Myth*, 44–57.

———. "The *Maquiladora* Murders: 1993–2003." *Aztlán: A Journal of Chicano Studies* 28, no. 2 (Fall 2003): 1–17.

———. "The *Maquiladora* Murders, Or, Who Is Killing the Women of Juárez?" *Latino Policy and Issues Brief* 7 (August 2003): 1–4. Available online through the UCLA Chicano Studies Research Center. http://www.chicano.ucla.edu/publications/report-brief/maquiladora-murders-or-who-killing-women-juárez-mexico.

———. "Mi Casa [No] Es Su Casa: The Cultural Politics of the Chicano Art: Resistance and Affirmation Exhibit." PhD diss., University of New Mexico, 1994.

———. "The Price of Free Trade Is Dead Women." *UCLA Today*, September 23, 2003. http://www.today.ucla.edu/portal/ut/030923voices_freetrade1.aspx.

———. *Sor Juana's Second Dream*. Albuquerque: University of New Mexico Press, 1999.

———. "A Theoretical Introduction: Alter-Native Ethnography, *a lo rasquache.*" In Gaspar de Alba, *Chicano Art Inside/Outside*, 1–28.

———. "There's No Place Like Aztlán: Embodied Aesthetics in Chicana Art." *The New Centennial Review* 4, no. 2 (Fall 2004): 103–140.

———, ed. *Velvet Barrios: Popular Culture and Chicana/o Sexualities*. New York: Palgrave/Macmillan, 2003.

Gaspar de Alba, Alicia, and Alma López, eds. *Our Lady of Controversy: Alma López's "Irreverent Apparition."* Austin: University of Texas Press, 2011.

Gaspar de Alba, Alicia, with Georgina Guzmán, eds. *Making a Killing: Femicide, Free Trade, and La Frontera*. Austin: University of Texas, 2010.

Gilot, Louie. "Idolaters Doth Protest Our Lady." *Weekly Alibi* 10, no. 17 (2001): 6.

———. "Sex Offenders Trickle Out of El Paso." *El Paso Times*, June 19, 2002.

———. "Some Neighbors Wary of Sex Offenders." *El Paso Times*, December 26, 2000.

Gitlin, Todd. *The Whole World Is Watching: Mass Media in the Making and Unmaking of the New Left*. Berkeley: University of California Press, 1981.

———. *The Sixties: Years of Hope, Days of Rage*. New York: Bantam, 1993.

Goffman, Erving. *Frame Analysis: An Essay on the Organization of Experience*. New York: Northeastern, 1986.

Gómez, Laura E. *Manifest Destinies: The Making of the Mexican American Race*. New York: New York University Press, 2007.

Gómez-Cano, Grisel. *The Return to Coatlicue*. La Verne, CA: Xlibris, 2010.

Gómez Peña, Guillermo. *Warrior for Gringostroika*. Saint Paul, MN: Graywolf Press, 1993.

Gonzales, Phillip B., ed. *Expressing New Mexico: Nuevomexicano Creativity, Ritual, and Memory*. Tucson: University of Arizona Press, 2007.

Gonzales, Rodolfo "Corky." *I Am Joaquín*. Denver, CO: Crusade for Justice, 1967.

González, Deena J. "Chicana Identity Matters." *Aztlán: A Journal of Chicano Studies* 22, no. 2 (Fall 1997): 123–138.

———. "Encountering Columbus." In Córdova, *Chicano Studies*, 13–19.

———. "Making Privates Public: It's Not about La Virgen of the Conquest, but about the Conquest of La Virgen." In Gaspar de Alba and López, *Our Lady of Controversy*, 69–95.

———. *Refusing the Favor: The Spanish-Mexican Women of Santa Fe, 1820–1880*. New York: Oxford University Press, 1999.

González, María R. "El embrión nacionalista visto a través de la obra de Sor Juana Inés de la Cruz." In Del Castillo, *Between Borders*, 239–253.

González, Rita. "The Said and the Unsaid: Lourdes Portillo Tracks Down Ghosts in *Señorita Extraviada.*" *Aztlán: A Journal of Chicano Studies* 28, no. 2 (Fall 2003): 235–240.

González Rodríguez, Sergio. *Huesos en el desierto*. Barcelona, Spain: Editorial Anagrama, 2002.

Grimes, Ronald E. *Symbol and Conquest: Public Ritual and Drama in Santa Fe*. Albuquerque: University of New Mexico Press, 1976.

Hale, Charles R., and Craig Calhoun, eds. *Engaging Contradictions: Theory, Politics, and Methods of Activist Scholarship*. Berkeley: University of California Press, 2008.

Hall, Stuart. "Encoding/Decoding." In During, *The Cultural Studies Reader*, 507–517.

———. *Stuart Hall: Critical Dialogues in Cultural Studies*. New York: Routledge, 1996.

Harss, Luis, trans., introduction, and commentary. *Sor Juana's Dream*. New York: Lumen Books, 1986.

Hawken, Sam. *The Dead Women of Juárez*. London: Serpent's Tail, 2011.

Hernández-Avila, Inés, and Gloria Anzaldúa. "Quincentennial: From Victimhood to Active Resistance." In Keating, *Interviews/Entrevistas*, 177–194.

Hernández, Daniel. "Fashion, Make-up Lines Inspired by Ciudad Juárez Spark Apology." *Los Angeles Times* Blog. Accessed July 30, 2010. http://latimesblogs.latimes.com/laplaza/2010/07/juarez-fashion-label-rodarte-women.html.

Hing, Julianne. "The Beauty Bloggers Who Blew MAC and Rodarte's Juarez Cover." Accessed July 22, 2010. http://colorlines.com/archives/2010/07/rodarte_mac_juarez.html.

Holland, Jack. *Misogyny: The World's Oldest Prejudice*. Philadelphia, PA: Running Press Book Publishers, 2007.

Horton, Sarah. "Ritual and Return: Diasporic Hispanos and the Santa Fe Fiesta." In Gonzales, *Expressing New Mexico*, 187–206.

Human Rights Watch. "From the Household to the Factory: Sex Discrimination in the Guatemalan Labor Force." Accessed November 3, 2012. http://www.hrw.org/reports/2002/02/12/household-factory.

Hurtado, Aida. "Relating to Privilege: Seduction and Rejection in the Subordination of White Women and Women of Color." *Signs* (Autumn 1989): 833–855.

Iglesias Prieto, Norma. *La flor más bella de la maquiladora*. Tijuana, Mexico: Secretaría de Educación Pública, Centro de Estudios Fronterizos, El Colegio de la Frontera Norte, 1985.

"Insigne y Nacional Basílica de Santa María de Guadalupe." www.virgendeguadalupe.org.mx. Accessed September–December 2008.

Ireland Department of Justice and Equality. http://www.inis.gov.ie/en/JELR/.

"Irish Bishop Criticises 'Our Lady in Bikini' Exhibit." *The Guardian Online*, June 24, 2011. Accessed June 24, 2011. http://churchandstate.org.uk/2011/06/irish-bishop-criticizes-our-lady-in-bikini-exhibit/.

"Irish Defamation Act of 2009." Accessed June 21, 2011. http://www.oireachtas.ie/viewdoc.asp?fn=/documents/bills28/bills/2006/4306/b43c06s.pdf.

Johnston, Hank, and John A. Noakes, eds. *Frames of Protest: Social Movements and the Framing Perspective*. New York: Rowman and Littlefield, 2005.

Justicia para Nuestras Hijas. Blog. http://justiciaparanuestrashijas.blogspot.com/. Last updated February 6, 2013.

Kaminsky, Amy. *After Exile: Writing the Latin American Diaspora* Minneapolis: University of Minnesota Press, 1996.

Kendall, Diana. *Framing Class: Media Representations of Wealth and Poverty in America*. New York: Rowman and Littlefield, 2005.

Kennedy, Randy. "Generation Mex." *New York Times Style Magazine*, September 22, 2010, 86–91. http://www.nytimes.com/2010/09/26/t-magazine/26well-mexico-t .html?_r=0.

Kerber, Linda. "Diversity and the Transformation of American Studies." *American Quarterly* 41, no. 4 (1989): 415–431.

Kolenc, Vic. "El Paso's ASARCO Smokestacks Gone in 35 Seconds." *El Paso Times* online. Accessed April 15, 2013. http://www.elpasotimes.com/newupdated/ci_23 015235/el-pasos-asarco-smokestacks-demolished.

Kun, Josh. "The Personal Equator: Patssi Valdez at the Border." In Chavoya and González, *Asco*, 356–361.

Larkin, Joan, and Jaime Manrique, trans. *Sor Juana's Love Poems/Poemas de Amor*. New York: Painted Leaf Press, 1997.

Lavrin, Asunción. "Values and Meanings of Monastic Life for Nuns in Colonial Mexico." *Catholic Historical Review* 58, no. 3 (1972–1973): 367–387.

Leuthold, Steven. *Indigenous Aesthetics: Native Art, Media, and Identity*. Austin: University of Texas Press, 1998.

Limerick, Patricia. *The Legacy of Conquest: The Unbroken Past of the American West*. New York: W. W. Norton, 1988.

Lindsay, Arturo. *Santería Aesthetics in Contemporary Latin American Art*. Washington, DC: Smithsonian Institution Press, 1996. Exhibition catalog.

Linton, John R. "'Our Lady' Artwork Is an Offense." *Albuquerque Tribune*, April 5, 2001, C2.

Lippard, Lucy. *The Lure of the Local: Senses of Place in a Multicentered Society*. New York: The New Press, 1997.

Logan, Paul. "Bishop's Denial Brings Back Pain." *Albuquerque Journal*, April 21, 2002, A1.

———. "Sheehan Wants Stricter Rules." *Albuquerque Journal*, June 10, 2002, A1.

López, Alma. "The Artist of *Our Lady* (April 2, 2001)." In Gaspar de Alba and López, *Our Lady of Controversy*, 14–16.

———. "It's Not about the Santa in My Fe, but about the Santa Fe in My Santa." In Gaspar de Alba and López, *Our Lady of Controversy*, 249–292.

López, Antonio. "Our Lady Fleshing Out the 'Our.'" *Santa Fe Trend*, n.d. Cyber Arte Collection, Museum of International Folk Art Archives.

López-Portillo, Margarita. *Estampas de Sor Juana Inés de la Cruz*. Mexico City: Bruguera Mexicana de Ediciones, 1979.

López Pulido, Alberto. *The Sacred World of the Penitentes*. Washington, DC: Smithsonian Institution Press, 2000.

Lorde, Audre. *Sister/Outsider*. Freedom, CA: The Crossing Press, 1984.

Lubhéid, Eithne. *Entry Denied: Controlling Sexuality at the Border*. Minneapolis: University of Minnesota Press, 2002.

Luevano, Rafael. *Woman-Killing in Juárez: Theodicy at the Border*. Maryknoll, NY: Orbis Books, 2012.

Lumpkin, John J. "Embattled Priest Says Goodbye." *Albuquerque Journal*, January 17, 2000, A1.

Maciel, David R., and Isidro D. Ortiz, eds. *Chicanas/Chicanos at the Crossroads: Social, Economic, and Political Change.* Tucson: University of Arizona Press, 1996.

"The Maquiladora Murders, Or, Who Is Killing the Women of Juárez?/*Maquilando mujeres en Juárez, o ¿quiénes son los asesinos?*" Conference Website. http://www.sscnet.ucla.edu/maqui_murders/.

Marin, Louis. "The Frame of Representation and Some of Its Figures." In Duro, *Rhetoric of the Frame,* 79–95.

Márquez, María Theresa. "The Manuel Ramos Mile-High Murders: From Hardboiled to Huevos Rancheros." In *Literatura chicana: Reflexiones y ensayos críticos,* ed. Rosa Morillas Sánchez and Manuel Villar Raso, 219–225. Granada, Spain: Editorial Comares, 2000.

Martínez, Elizabeth. *De Colores Means All of Us: Latina Views for a Multi-Colored Century.* Boston: South End Press, 1998.

Marx, Leo. *The Machine in the Garden: Technology and the Pastoral Ideal in America.* New York: Oxford University Press, 1967.

Masters, Christopher. "Helen Escobedo, Obituary: Mexican Sculptor Who Strove to Integrate Her Art with Nature and the Environment." *The Guardian Online,* October 29, 2010. Accessed September 18, 2010. http://www.guardian.co.uk/artanddesign/2010/oct/29/helen-escobedo-obituary.

Mata, Irene. "Markings on the Walls: Writing in Opposition in Alicia Gaspar de Alba's *Desert Blood.*" In Román-Odio and Sierra, *Transnational Borderlands in Women's Global Networks,* 45–76.

Mays, Robert E. "Manifest Destiny." Accessed October 12, 2011. http://www.pbs.org/kera/usmexicanwar/prelude/md_manifest_destiny2.html.

McKee, Jennifer. "Shouts, Shoves, Prayers Filled Foyer Outside." *Albuquerque Journal North,* April 5, 2001, 3.

McVeigh, Rory, and David Sikkink. "God, Politics, and Religion: Religious Beliefs and the Legitimation of Contentious Tactics." *Social Forces* 79, no. 4 (2001): 1425–1458.

McWilliams, Carey. *North from Mexico: The Spanish-Speaking People of the United States.* Reprint, New York: Praeger, 1990. Originally published 1948.

Mechling, Jay. "If They Can Build a Square Tomato: Notes Toward a Holistic Approach to Regional Studies." *Prospects* 4 (1979): 59–77.

Memmi, Albert. *The Colonizer and the Colonized.* Translated by Howard Greenfield. Introduction by Jean-Paul Sartre. Boston: Beacon Press, 1965. Originally published in 1957 in French by Buchet/Chastel, Paris, France.

Mendez, Jennifer Bickham. "Globalizing Scholar Activism: Opportunities and Dilemmas through a Feminist Lens." In Hale and Calhoun, *Engaging Contradictions,* 136–163.

Merrim, Stephanie, ed. *Feminist Perspectives on Sor Juana Inés de la Cruz.* Detroit: Wayne State University Press, 1991.

Mieri, Magdalena. "Latino Representation at the Smithsonian: Still Willful Neglect?" Paper presented at the annual American Anthropological Association meeting, Washington, DC, November 28–December 2, 2001.

Milbrath, Susan. "Decapitated Lunar Goddess in Aztec Art, Myth and Ritual." *Ancient Mesoamerica* 8 (1997): 185–206.

Miller, Perry. *Errand into the Wilderness*. Cambridge: Belknap Press of Harvard University Press, 1956.

Mithlo, Nancy Marie. *Our Indian Princess: Subverting the Stereotype*. Santa Fe, NM: School for Advanced Research, 2009.

Mohanty, Chandra Talpade. *Feminism without Borders: Decolonizing Theory, Practicing Solidarity*. Durham, NC: Duke University Press, 2003.

Monárrez Fragoso, Julia Estela. "La cultura del feminicidio en Ciudad Juárez, 1993–1999." *Frontera Norte* (Revista del Colegio de la Frontera Norte de Tijuana, B.C.) 23, no. 12 (January–June 2000): 87–118.

———. "Serial Sexual Femicide in Ciudad Juárez, 1993–2001." *Aztlán: A Journal of Chicano Studies* 28, no. 2 (Fall 2003): 153–178.

———. *Trama de una injusticia: Feminicidio sexual sistemático en Ciudad Juárez*. Ciudad Juárez, Mexico: El Colegio de la Frontera Norte, 2009.

Monárrez Fragoso, Julia Estela, and María Socorro Tabuenca Córdoba, eds. *Bordeando la violencia contra las mujeres en la frontera norte de México*. Ciudad Juárez, Mexico: El Colegio de la Frontera Norte, 2007.

Montoya, Delilah. Talk delivered at the "Puro Corazón: Chicana Art Symposium," Pomona College, February 1995.

Montoya, Margaret. "Un/braiding Stories about Law, Sexuality, and Morality." *Chicano-Latino Law Review* 24 (2003): 1–11.

Moraga, Cherríe. *The Last Generation: Prose and Poetry*. Boston: South End Press, 1993.

———. *Loving in the War Years: Lo que nunca pasó por sus labios*. Expanded 2nd edition. Boston: South End Press, 2000.

———. "Queer Aztlán: The Re-Formation of Chicano Tribe." In Moraga, *The Last Generation*, 145–174.

Moraga, Cherríe, and Gloria Anzaldúa, eds. *This Bridge Called My Back: Writings by Radical Women of Color*. Boston: Kitchen Table Press, 1983.

Morillas Sánchez, Rosa, and Manuel Villar Raso, eds. *Literatura chicana: Reflexiones y ensayos críticos*. Granada, Spain: Editorial Comares, 2000.

Morris, Aldon D., and Caro McClurg Mueller, eds. *Frontiers in Social Movement Theory*. New Haven, CT: Yale University Press, 1992.

Morrison, Keith. "The Global Village of African American Art." In Driskell, *African American Visual Aesthetics*, 17–44.

Muñoz, José Esteban. *Disidentifications: Queers of Color and the Performance of Politics*. Minneapolis: University of Minnesota Press, 1999.

Nelson, Kate. "Our Lady of All This Fuss Can't Rock a Faith Built on More Than Scorn." *Albuquerque Tribune*, April 5, 2001, A3.

Nervo, Amado, and Aureliano Tapia Méndez. *Juana de Asbaje*. Reprint, Mexico City: Instituto Mexiquense de Cultura, 1955. Originally published in Madrid in 1910.

Nicholson, Henry B. "The New Tenochtitlan Templo Mayor Coyolxauhqui-Chantico Monument. In *Indiana: Gedenkschrift Gerdt Kutscher*, Vol. 10, Part 2, 77–98. Berlin, Germany: Ibero-Amerikanisches Institut, 1985.

Noakes, John A., and Hank Johnston. "Frames of Protest: A Road Map to a Perspective." In Johnston and Noakes, *Frames of Protest*, 1–29.

Norwood, Vera, and Janice Monk, eds. *The Desert Is No Lady: Southwestern Land-scapes in Women's Writing and Art*. 2nd edition. Tucson: University of Arizona Press, 1997.

Nuestras Hijas de Regreso a Casa. Blog. http://nuestrashijasderegresoacasa.blogspot .com/. Accessed December 31, 2013.

Oakland Museum of California. "*Splendors of Faith/Scars of Conquest: Arts of the Missions of Northern New Spain, 1600–1821* Exhibition." http://museumca.org /exhibit/splendors-faithscars-conquest.

Oliver, Pamela E., and Hank Johnston. "What a Good Idea! Ideologies and Frames in Social Movement Research." In Johnston and Noakes, *Frames of Protest*, 185–203.

Orsini, Jacqueline. "The Lady Has Many Faces." *La Herencia del Norte* 20 (Winter 1998): 9–13.

Ortega, Gregorio. *Las muertas de Ciudad Juárez: El caso de Elizabeth Castro García y Abdel Latif Sharif Sharif*. Mexico City: Fontamara, 1999.

Orwell, George. "Politics and the English Language." In *Shooting an Elephant and Other Essays*. London: Secker and Warburg, 1950.

O'Sullivan, John L. "Annexation." *The United States Magazine and Democratic Review* 17, no. 1 (July 1845): 5–10.

———. "The Great Nation of Futurity." *The United States Magazine and Demo-cratic Review* 6, no. 3: 426–430. Accessed October 12, 2011. www.mtholyoke .edu/acad/intrel/osulliva.htm.

Otero Calderón, Ángel, ed. *Homicidios de mujeres: Auditoría periodística: enero 1993–julio 2003*. Ciudad Juárez, Mexico: Instituto Chihuahense de la Mujer, 2003.

"Our Lady of Guadalupe: Patroness of the Americas" Website. www.sancta.org.

Padilla, Genaro. *My History, Not Yours: The Formation of Mexican American Auto-biography*. Madison: University of Wisconsin Press, 1993.

Pawloski, Jeremy. "Church Gives 'Our Lady' Mock Burial." *Albuquerque Journal North*, October 29, 2001, 1, 3.

Paz, Octavio. "Juana Ramírez." Translated by Diane Marting. *Signs* (Autumn 1979): 80–97.

———. *The Labyrinth of Solitude*. Translated by Lysander Kemp, Yara Milos, and Rachel Phillips Belash. Reprint, New York: Grove Press, 1985.

———. "The Sons of La Malinche." In Castillo, *Goddess of the Americas*, 197–208.

———. *Sor Juana: Or, the Traps of Faith*. Translated by Margaret Sayers Peden. Cam-bridge: Harvard University Press, 1988. Originally published in 1982 in Spanish as *Sor Juana Inés de la Cruz, o, Las trampas de la fe* by Editorial Seix Barrall, Barcelona, Spain.

Peden, Margaret Sayers, trans. *Poems, Protest, and a Dream: Selected Writings of Sor Juana Inés de la Cruz*. Introduction by Ilan Stavans. New York: Penguin Books, 1997.

———, trans. *Sor Juana Inés de la Cruz: Poems: A Bilingual Anthology*. Tempe, AZ: Bilingual Press, 1985.

———, trans., introduction, and ed. *A Woman of Genius: The Intellectual Auto-biography of Sor Juana Inés de la Cruz*. Salisbury, CT: Lime Rock Press, 1987. Translation of *Respuesta a Sor Filotea de la Cruz*.

Pérez, Emma. *The Decolonial Imaginary: Writing Chicanas into History*. Blooming-ton: Indiana University Press, 1999.

———. "Irigaray's Female Symbolic in the Making of Chicana Lesbian *Sitios y Len-guas* (Sites and Discourses)." In *Living Chicana Theory*, ed. Carla Trujillo, 87–101. Berkeley: Third Woman Press, 1998.

———. "Sexuality and Discourse: Notes from a Chicana Survivor." In *Chicana Les-bians: The Girls Our Mothers Warned Us About*, ed. Carla Trujillo, 159–184. Berkeley: Third Woman Press, 1991.

———. "So Far from God, So Close to the United States: A Call for Action by U.S. Au-thorities." *Aztlán: A Journal of Chicano Studies* 28, no. 2 (Fall 2003): 146–151.

"Petition to End Violence Against Women in Juárez and Chihuahua" Website. http://www.petitiononline.com/NiUnaMas/petition.

Phelan, Peggy. *Unmarked: The Politics of Performance*. New York: Routledge, 1993.

Piñeda-Madrid, Nancy. *Suffering and Salvation in Juárez*. Minneapolis: Fortress Press, 2011.

Pinkola Estes, Clara. *Untie the Strong Woman: Blessed Mother's Immaculate Love for the Wild Soul*. Boulder, CO: Sounds True, 2011.

Poot Herrera, Sara, ed. *Sor Juana y su mundo: Una mirada actual*. México, DF: Uni-versidad del Claustro de Sor Juana, 1995.

Pope Duarte, Stella. *If I Die in Juárez*. Tuscon: University of Arizona Press, 2007.

Portillo, Lourdes. "Filming *Señorita Extraviada*." *Aztlán: A Journal of Chicano Stud-ies* 28, no. 2 (Fall 2003): 229–234.

Portillo Trambley, Estela. *Sor Juana and Other Plays*. Ypsilanti: Eastern Michigan University, 1983.

Presley, Fran. "Lone Star Living: Sheehan Has Faith-Filled Desire to Bring Christ to the People." The Associated Press State & Local Wire, February 23, 2000.

Pulido, Laura. "FAQs: Frequently (Un)Asked Questions about Being a Scholar Activ-ist." In Hale and Calhoun, *Engaging Contradictions*, 341–366.

Quiñones, Sam. "The Maquiladora Murders." *Ms.* (May/June 1998): 11–16.

———. *True Tales from Another Mexico: The Lynch Mob, the Popsicle Kings, Chali-no, and the Bronx*. Albuquerque: University of New Mexico Press, 2001.

Radford, Jill, and Diana E. H. Russell. *Femicide: The Politics of Woman Killing*. New York: Twayne Publishers, 1992.

Ramírez, Christina. "Police Look to Track Sex Offenders." *El Paso Times*, May 9, 1999.

Rebolledo, Tey Diana. *The Chronicles of Panchita Villa and Other Guerrilleras*. Aus-tin: University of Texas Press, 2005.

Rendón, Armando B. *Chicano Manifesto: The History and Aspirations of the Second Largest Minority in America*. Berkeley: Ollin Books, 1996. Originally published in 1971 by Collier Books.

Rich, Adrienne. *Blood, Bread, and Poetry: Selected Prose, 1979–1985*. New York: Norton, 1986.

———. "Compulsory Heterosexuality and Lesbian Existence." *Signs* 5, no. 4 (Summer 1980): 631–660.

———. "Notes toward a Politics of Location." In Rich, *Blood, Bread, and Poetry*, 210–231.

Ridgeway, Cecilia L. *Framed by Gender: How Gender Inequality Persists*. New York: Oxford University Press, 2011.

Rodríguez, Ralph. *Brown Gumshoes: Detective Fiction and the Search for Chicana/o Identity*. Austin: University of Texas Press, 2005.

Rodríguez, Theresa, Diana Montoné, and Lisa Pulitzer. *The Daughters of Juárez: A True Story of Serial Murder South of the Border*. New York: Atria Books, 2007.

Rohrleitner, Marion. "Not in Our Mother's Image: Ekphrasis and Challenges to Recovering Afro-Mestizaje in Contemporary Latina/Chicana Historical Fiction." In Rohrleitner and Ryan, *Dialogues across Diasporas*, 37–55.

Rohrleitner, Marion, and Sarah E. Ryan, eds. *Dialogues across Diasporas: Women Writers, Scholars, and Activists of Africana and Latina Descent in Conversation*. Lanham, MD: Lexington Books, 2013.

Román-Odio, Clara. "Queering the Sacred: Love as Oppositional Consciousness in Alma López's Visual Art." In Gaspar de Alba and López, *Our Lady of Controversy*, 121–147.

Román-Odio, Clara, and Marta Sierra, eds. *Transnational Borderlands in Women's Global Networks: The Making of Cultural Resistance*. New York: Palgrave Macmillan, 2011.

Romero, Rolando, and Amanda Nolacea Harris, eds. *Feminism, Nation and Myth: La Malinche*. Houston: Arte Público Press, 2005.

Ronquillo, Víctor. *Las muertas de Juárez*. Mexico City: Booket, Editorial Planeta, 2004.

Rueda Esquibel, Catrióna. *With Her Machete in Her Hand: Reading Chicana Lesbians*. Austin: University of Texas Press, 2006.

Rushing, W. J. "Authenticity and Subjectivity in Post-War Painting: Concerning Herrera, Scholder, and Cannon." In Archuleta and Strickland, *Shared Visions*, 12–21.

Russell, Diana E. H. "Defining Femicide and Related Concepts." In Russell and Harmes, *Femicide in Global Perspective*, 12–28.

Russell, Diana E. H., and Roberta A. Harmes, eds. *Femicide in Global Perspective*. New York: Teachers College Press, 2001.

Rutten, Rosanne, and Michiel Baud. "Concluding Remarks: Framing Protest in Asia, Africa, and Latin America." *International Review of Social History* 49, supplement 12 (2004): 197–217.

Ryan, Charlotte, and William Gamson. "Are Frames Enough?" In *The Social Movements Reader: Cases and Concepts*, ed. Jeff Goodwin and James M. Jasper, 167–174. Malden, MA: Blackwell Publishing, 2009.

Sabat-Rivers, Georgina. "Biografías: Sor Juana vista por Dorothy Schons y Octavio Paz." *Revista Iberoamericana* 51, nos. 131–132 (July–December 1985): 927–937.

Sahagún, Bernardino de, Fray. *Florentine Codex: General History of the Things of New Spain*. Translated by Arthur Anderson and Charles Dibble. Santa Fe, NM: School of American Research, 1950. (This source is available online through the World Digital Library at http://www.wdl.org/en/item/10096/#languages=spa&item_type=manuscript.)

Saldívar, José David, and Héctor Calderón, eds. *Criticism in the Borderlands: Studies in Chicano Literature, Culture, and Ideology*. Durham, NC: Duke University Press, 1991.

Salzinger, Leslie. *Genders in Production: Making Workers in Mexico's Global Factories*. Berkeley: University of California Press, 2003.

Sanchez, Isabel. "Archdiocese of Santa Fe on Mend after Lawsuits." *Albuquerque Journal*, January 13, 2002, A1.

Sandoval, Chela. *Methodology of the Oppressed*. Minneapolis: University of Minnesota Press, 2000.

Santa Fe Fiestas, Inc. Website. www.santafefiesta.org.

Schons, Dorothy. "Sor Juana: A Chronicle of Old Mexico." Unpublished book manuscript. Dorothy Schons Papers, 1586–1955, Nettie Lee Benson Latin American Collection, University of Texas Libraries, University of Texas at Austin. www.lib.utexas.edu/benson.

Sharpe, Tom. "Artist Calls for Backing of 'Our Lady.'" *The Santa Fe New Mexican*, June 2, 2001, B1, B4.

Sheehan, Michael. Letter to the editor. *La Herencia del Norte* 21 (Spring 1999): 6.

Siemon-Netto, Uwe. "Analysis: Bishop's Trial in France." United Press International, June 15, 2001.

Smith, Henry Nash. *The Virgin Land: The American West as Symbol and Myth*. Cambridge: Harvard University Press, 1971.

Smith, Jeremy. "Outside and Against the Quincentenary: Modern Indigenous Representations at the Time of the Columbian Celebrations." *Atlantic Studies* 6, no. 1 (2009): 63–80.

Snow, David A., and Robert D. Benford. "Master Frames and Cycles of Protest." In Morris and Mueller, *Frontiers in Social Movement Theory*, 133–155.

Soto, Sandra K. *Reading Chican@ Like a Queer: The De-Mastery of Desire*. Austin: University of Texas Press, 2010.

Spivak, Gayatri Chakravorty, with Sarah Harasym. *The Post-Colonial Critic: Interviews, Strategies, Dialogues*. New York: Routledge, 1990.

Staudt, Kathleen A. *Violence and Activism at the Border: Gender, Fear, and Everyday Life in Ciudad Juárez*. Austin: University of Texas Press, 2008.

Staudt, Kathleen, and Irasema Coronado. *Fronteras No Más: Toward Social Justice at the U.S.-Mexico Border*. New York: Palgrave Macmillan, 2002.

Steinberg, Leo. *The Sexuality of Christ in Renaissance Art and in Modern Oblivion*. New York: Pantheon Books, 1983.

Stoller, Marianne L. "Peregrinas with Many Visions: Hispanic Women Artists of New Mexico, Southern Colorado, and Texas." In Norwood and Monk, *The Desert Is No Lady*, 125–145.

Sussman, Elisabeth, Thelma Golden, John G. Hanhardt, and Lisa Phillips. *1993 Biennial Exhibition Catalog*. New York: Whitney Museum of American Art in association with Harry N. Abrams Publishers, 1993. Exhibition catalog.

Tabuenca Córdoba, María Socorro. "Ghost Dance in Ciudad Juarez at the End/Beginning of the Millennium." In Gaspar de Alba with Guzmán, *Making a Killing*, 95–120.

Tadiar, Neferti X. M., and Angela Y. Davis, eds. *Beyond the Frame: Women of Color and Visual Representation*. New York: Palgrave Macmillan, 2005.

Tani, Stefano. *The Doomed Detective: The Contribution of the Detective Novel to Postmodern American and Italian Fiction*. Carbondale: Southern Illinois University Press, 1984.

Treat, Jonathan. "Casa Amiga: Leading the Fight to Protect Women in Ciudad Juárez," *Americas Program*. December 3, 2002. http://www.cipamericas.org /archives/1274.

Trenton, Patricia, ed. *Independent Spirits: Women Painters of the American West, 1890–1945*. Los Angeles: Autry Museum of Western Heritage, 1995. Exhibition catalog.

Trueblood, Alan S., trans., ed., introduction. *A Sor Juana Anthology*. Foreword by Octavio Paz. Cambridge: Harvard University Press, 1988.

Trujillo, Carla, ed. *Chicana Lesbians: The Girls Our Mothers Warned Us About*. Berkeley, CA: Third Woman Press, 1991.

———, ed. *Living Chicana Theory*. Berkeley: Third Woman Press, 1998.

Turner, Frederick Jackson. *The Frontier in American History*. 1920. Reprint, New York: Dover Publications, 1996.

Ulrich, Laurel Thatcher. *Well-Behaved Women Seldom Make History*. New York: Vintage Books, 2007.

Vasconcelos, José. *La raza cósmica/The Cosmic Race: A Bilingual Edition*. Translated by Didier T. Jaén. Baltimore: Johns Hopkins University Press, 1997.

Viera, Ricardo, and Randall Morris. "Juan Boza: Travails of an Artist-Priest." In Lindsay, *Santería Aesthetics in Contemporary Latin American Art*, 171–187.

Viramontes, Helena María. *The Moths and Other Stories*. Houston: Arte Público Press, 1995.

Volk, Steven S., and Marian E. Schlotterbeck. "Gender, Order and Femicide: Reading the Popular Culture of Murder in Ciudad Juárez." In Gaspar de Alba with Guzmán, *Making a Killing*, 121–153.

Wade, Meredith. "Sheehan Can Fix It, Local Clergy Say." *Albuquerque Tribune*, June 18, 2003, A4.

Walker, Hollis. "Whose Lady? Laying Claim to the Virgin Mary." In Adler et al., *The New Gatekeepers*, 42–44.

Washington Valdez, Diana. *Cosecha de mujeres: Safari en el desierto mexicano*. Mexico City: Editorial Océano, 2005.

———. "Death Stalks the Border: List of Victims." Special insert, *El Paso Times*, January 31, 2008. http://www.elpasotimes.com/ci_8129511.

———. "Officials Say State Dumps Sex Offenders in El Paso." *El Paso Times*, December 8, 2001.

Washington Valdez, Diana, and Aileen B. Flores. "Court Blasts Mexico for Women's Murders." Accessed August 29, 2012. http://www.elpasotimes.com/news/ci _13981319.

Weedon, Chris. *Feminist Practice and Poststructuralist Theory*. Oxford: Basil Blackwell, 1987.

Whitechapel, Simon. *Crossing to Kill: The True Story of the Serial-Killer Playground*. 3rd ed. London: Virgin Publishing, 2002.

Wilson Gilmore, Ruth. "Public Enemies and Private Intellectuals: Apartheid USA." *Race and Class* 35, no. 1 (1993): 69–78.

Wittig, Monique. "One Is Not Born a Woman." *Feminist Issues* 1, no. 2 (Winter 1981): 47–54.

Wright, Melissa. "The Dialectics of Still Life: Murder, Women, and the *Maquiladoras*." *Public Culture* 11, no. 3 (1999): 453–474.

———. *Disposable Women and Other Myths of Global Capitalism*. New York: Routledge, 2006.

———. "A Manifesto against Femicide." *Antipode* 33, no. 3 (July 2001): 550–566.

Yarbro-Bejarano, Yvonne. "Laying It Bare: The Queer/Colored Body in Photography by Laura Aguilar." In Trujillo, *Living Chicana Theory*, 277–305.

———. *The Wounded Heart: Writings on Cherríe Moraga*. Austin: University of Texas Press, 2001.

Zilles, Klaus. "Microstructure and Macrostructure in Rolando Hinojosa-Smith's Klail City Death Trip Series: The Case of the Rafe Buenrostro Mysteries." In *Aztlán: Ensayos sobre literatura chicana*, ed. Federico Equiluz et al., 257–267. Vitoria-Gasteiz, Spain: Universidad del Pais Vasco, 2004.

———. "Postmodernism and Discourses of Gender, Language, and Ethnicity in Recent Works of Rolando Hinojosa." In *Literatura chicana: Reflexiones y ensayos críticos*, ed. Rosa Morillas Sánchez and Manuel Villar Raso, 333–344. Granada, Spain: Editorial Comares, 2000.

Zinn, Howard. *A People's History of the United States, 1492–Present*. Revised and updated edition, New York: Harper Perennial, 1995. Originally published 1980.

originally in *Our Lady of Controversy: Alma López's "Irreverent Apparition,"* ed. Alicia Gaspar de Alba and Alma López (Austin: University of Texas Press, 2011), 212–248. Reprinted with permission of University of Texas Press.

INDEX

Chicano Studies Research Center,
(UCLA), xviii, 140–141
Chichimecs, 107
Chingada, La (the fucked one), 8,
19, 66, 159: and Chingona, 77;
hijos de la (children of the), 69; in
Our Lady protests, 225–226; and
repudiation of *el chingón*, 65, 76.
See also Martínez: chingón politics;
Paz: on La Malinche/Chingada;
Tres Marías Syndrome
Chmaj, Betty, x
cholas, 186
cholos, 145, 310n51
"chosen children of God," 15, 101
Cíbola, Legend of, 109
Cihuacoatl, 27, 291, 296n48
cimarron(a) (refugee slave), 274
Clinton, Hillary, 166
Coatepec, 131, 193, 195–198, 200
Coatlicue: Aztec goddess, 27–28, 131,
191–200, 292, 296n45; State, x,
34, 48–49, 260, 299n20. *See also*
Coyolxauhqui
colonial imaginary, 65, 67, 69,
107, 205, 261, 266, 285–286;
decolonial imaginary, 266; and
Paz's interpretation of Malinche,
225, 267; sexing the, 118. *See also*
Pérez, Emma
colonialism. *See* colonial imaginary;
feminism: colonial; López, Alma:
colonial "conquest triangle"
Comanches, 107
compulsory heterosexuality, 47, 262
conocimiento, 38, 192, 252, 286,
321n17; and *re-conocimiento,* 38,
257, 259–260, 322n30; and Sor
Juana, 252, 288. *See also* Anzaldúa,
Gloria
conquests of Mexico: Anglo, 95, 99,
102, 107–108, 111–113; Spanish,
65, 76, 102, 107–109, 113, 115,
216–217, 241, 252, 303n28
conquistadores, 103–105, 107–108,
232, 319n78

consciousness: border, xiv-xv,
xviii; Chicano, 94, 303n31;
Coyolxauhqui, 192–193;
differential, 257–258, 316n13;
feminist, 19; mestiza, x, 27–28, 33,
49, 297n50; nationalist, 47–48;
oppositional, 34, 212, 214, 287
contradictions, xi, 106, 120, 297n50
convent of Saint Paula of the Order
of Saint Jerome, 16, 43, 248–250,
282
Cope, Douglas R., 68. *See also* caste
system
Corpi, Lucha, 175
Cortés, Hernán, 65–66, 76–77,
107–108, 225
Cortéz, Constance, 126
Coyolxauhqui: legend, 7, 18–19, 25,
131–132, 190–193, 200–201, 203,
286–287; modern-day, 172; revised
legend, 193–201; stone of, 201,
226, 296n45, 315n35. *See also*
Centzon Huitznahua; Coatlicue;
consciousness: Coyolxauhqui;
Huitzilopochtli
Crenshaw, Kimberlé, 24, 167–168
criolla: colonial social position, 50,
287; Sor Juana's rights as, 43, 48,
52, 248, 256
criollos, 50, 68–69, 91, 109, 298n5. *See
also* caste system
crisis: etymology, 322n43
Cuahuitlicac, 191–192, 196–200. *See
also* Coyolxauhqui
cultural myths. *See* Aztlán; *Four quadrants of Aztlán*; Manifest Destiny;
myths of origin
cultural nationalism, 70, 94, 117, 222,
303n31, 318n62
cultural schizophrenia, xi, xviii, 6, 66
Cultural Studies, xvi
cunt, 85, 116, 292
Cyber Arte exhibition, 203, 206–207,
215, 218, 220–222, 240
Cypess, Sandra Messinger, 76

Kaminsky, Amy, 113
Kant, Immanuel, 30, 32
Keating, AnaLouise, 294n18
Kendall, Diana, 23–24
Kerber, Linda, xii
Khomeini, Ayatollah, 204, 319n89

Lactans, Maria, 242
Lavrín, Asunción, 52
law of the father/penis, 35, 71–73, 115.
    See also patriarchy
lenguas de fuego (tongues of fire). See
    under Anzaldúa, Gloria
Leuthold, Steven, 90–91
Lilith, 8, 25. See also Biblical figures;
    Montoya, Delilah: La Llorona in
    Lilith's Garden
linguistic terrorism, xi, 2, 7, 123
Lion King, 72
Lippard, Lucy, 100
Little Mermaid, 72
Liveline (Irish radio show), 237
Llorona: folktale, 123; legend, 7, 25,
    116, 291, 297n48; song, xix
Lomas Garza, Carmen, 93, 118,
    122–124
López, Alma, xxiv, xxv, 17, 35, 172,
    201, 287, 316n29; The colonial
    "conquest triangle," 67; Coyolx-
    auhqui's Tree of Life, 140–141;
    Desert Blood, 174; The four
    quadrants of Aztlán, 106; History
    in Our Hands, 178; Lady/Virgen,
    202; La Llorona Desperately Seek-
    ing Coyolxauhqui, 130, 172; Our
    Lady, 1, 34, 205; La peor de todas,
    246; Our Lady controversy, 37,
    203–216, 218–226, 229–245. See
    also censorship; irreverent appari-
    tion
López, Yolanda, 116
López-Portillo, Margarita, 42
Lorde, Audre, 77, 259
lost land, 82, 94, 109, 111, 113,
    303n31; See also Aztlán; Chávez,
    John

love: as decolonizing movida, 261; her-
    meneutic of, 34, 316n13; platonic
    love-friendship between Sor Juana
    and La Condesa, 44, 264, 280;
    as political awareness, 34–35; as
    punctum in decolonization praxis,
    34. See also Sandoval, Chela
loyalists to patriarchy. See antifeminists
lucha (political struggle): Chicana femi-
    nist, xi; and the Chicano Move-
    ment, 70; for self-determination,
    xiv. See also Causa Chicana
lunar eclipse, 131, 277

Macbeth, 203, 282
Magdalene, Mary. See Biblical figures
Malcolm X, 2
MALCS (Mujeres Activas en Letras y
    Cambio Social), 134
Malinche, La, 35, 159, 292; and
    "bad woman" frame, 25, 33; in
    Chicana iconography, 65, 69–70,
    73–74, 77, 115; Chicana resistance
    symbol, 78, 116–117; as Chingona,
    77; as maternal figure, 113;
    Nahuatl for "outsider," 76–77;
    Octavio Paz on, 65–66, 225; as
    pejorative for Chicana lesbian,
    74–76; and racial hierarchy,
    68; and sexuality, 161. See also
    Chingada; Malintzín Tenepal;
    Oedipal-conquest triangle; Paz,
    Octavio; Pérez, Emma; Tres Marías
    Syndrome
Malinchismo, xviii, 78, 116
Malinchista, 65, 78, 116
Malintzín Tenepal, 76–77, 258, 278
Manifest Destiny, 71, 86, 95, 105–106;
    and Aztlán myth, 100–101, 112;
    and frontier myth, 97–98, 112. See
    also The four quadrants of Aztlán;
    myths of origin
Manrique, Jaime, 270
Manrique de Lara y Gonzaga, María
    Luisa, Countess (a.k.a. la Condesa),
    44, 255–256, 279, 320n7, 325n100